THE FAILURE OF THE "NEW ECONOMICS"

THE FAILURE OF THE "NEW ECONOMICS"

An Analysis of the Keynesian Fallacies

HENRY HAZLITT

Cover design is: "Cropped version of NPG 5587, John Maynard Keynes, Baron Keynes; Lydia Lopokova (Lady Keynes) by William Roberts, © National Portrait Gallery, London."

Ludwig von Mises Institute, 518 West Magnolia Avenue, Auburn, Ala. 36832; www.mises.org

ISBN 10 digit: 1-933550-11-2
ISBN 13 digit: 978-1-933550-11-4

ACKNOWLEDGMENTS

I am indebted to Harcourt, Grace & Co., the American publishers of Keynes's *General Theory*, for their generous permission to reprint so many passages from that book. This extensive quotation rather than mere paraphrase seemed to me almost unavoidable in the present critical work because of the many existing and possible interpretations and disputes concerning what Keynes actually said.

I wish to thank *The New York Times* for permission to reprint, as an appendix, my article on Keynes's *Economic Consequences of the Peace* in its issue of March 22, 1945. I also wish to thank *Newsweek* for permission to use tables, charts, and excerpts from some of my articles that originally appeared in its pages.

My indebtedness to other publishers for permission to quote from authors or books published by them is, I hope, sufficiently indicated in the text or in footnotes.

I am grateful to Ludwig von Mises for reading the galleys and offering some invaluable suggestions. For the opinions expressed and any errors made, I alone, of course, must be held responsible.

My wife, as usual, has helped me in scores of details.

HENRY HAZLITT

January, 1959

CONTENTS

FOREWORD

Murray N. Rothbard

For most people, economics has ever been the "dismal science," to be passed over quickly for more amusing sport. And yet, a glance at the world today will show that we pass over economics at our peril. The influence of economic ideas on human history, especially political history, has been momentous; how different would be the lives of all of us if Karl Marx had never lived and spun his fatal vision! In the twentieth century, the most influential economist has been John Maynard Keynes, who swept the world of economics like an avalanche in 1936 with his *General Theory of Employment, Interest, and Money*, his teachings quickly becoming a new, entrenched economic orthodoxy.

Henry Hazlitt, in this vitally important and desperately needed book throws down the challenge in a detailed, thoroughgoing refutation of the *General Theory*. Anyone tempted to scoff at this debate as simply a tempest in an abstract academic teapot, unrelated to the current practical world, might ponder such statements as these, which can be found, unquestioned and unchallenged, in almost any news magazine or newspaper column: "we need no longer worry about a depression, because now government knows how to cure it—with deficit spending and built-in stabilizers"; "the government's X billion dollars of military spending is a useful prop to the economy"; "business will improve in the next quarter because government intends to grant more contracts and run a larger

This book review was written by Murray N. Rothbard and appeared in *National Review* (August 15, 1959): 279–80.

deficit"; "to check the threat to inflation, the government should impose high taxation to sop up excess purchasing power"; "the government's main economic duty is to stabilize the economy and insure full employment"; "in contrast to the capitalism of the nineteenth century, which emphasized thrift and production, our modern capitalism depends for its prosperity on consumer demand."

These are the common coin of the land, to such an extent that they are now virtually "noncontroversial," accepted by both political parties. And yet, they are not primeval truths, but mischievous fallacies, every one of them introduced into the modern world by Lord Keynes and his disciples.

How was the Keynesian Revolution accomplished? How was this mare's nest of discredited Mercantilist fallacies put over? In the first place, by intellectual intimidation. The old fallacies were dressed up by Keynes in such a wilderness of unclear writing and pretentious jargon, in such a bewildering morass of strange concepts, that the Keynesian disciples claimed to be the only ones able to understand the Master. And they trumpeted Youth on their side. The older economists were cowed by newer lights who arrogantly proclaimed that no one over thirty-five was competent to understand the New Economics. Paul A. Samuelson has written of his joy at being under thirty-five when this New Revelation was announced to the world. And as their Master they had an eminent, aristocratic Englishman, witty, charming, and thoroughly irresponsible.

In their conquest, the Keynesians were aided by two other factors. For one thing, the world, inclined ever more toward statism, was looking for an economic theory which would at last make government spending and inflation respectable, while making private thrift and laissez-faire capitalism anathema in their ancient home—among economists. Second, the "neoclassical" economic theory taught at Cambridge (Keynes's home) and also in America, did have important gaps: in failing to integrate monetary theory and general economics, in lacking an adequate theory of the business cycle. For these reasons, the conquest was absurdly easy.

But the real *trahison des clercs* came, not so much from Keynes and the Keynesians, nor from the older neoclassical economists, as from those economists who knew better, and who capitulated, for one reason or another, to the new orthodoxy. These were the economists trained in the "Austrian School," headed in this century by Ludwig von Mises who had brilliantly filled in the gaps of the older tradition and had shown that the causes and the remedies of the business cycle and unemployment were almost exactly the opposite of what Keynes was to preach.

This Misesian theory, which revealed the depression to be the inevitable burden imposed on the economy by the preceding inflationary boom, and unemployment to be caused by excessive union-imposed and government-imposed wage rates, was beginning to get a hearing in Britain and even in America just before the *General Theory* was published. But when the Keynesian sweep occurred, the bulk of the economists in Britain and the United States, who had been trained in the Austrian tradition, surrendered to the newly reigning fashion without a fight. It was not simply the shock of the Great Depression, by the way, that drowned out the Austrian theory, for that theory had been gaining acceptance precisely as an explanation for the Depression.

This, then, was the critical betrayal of the intellectuals: that Henry Hazlitt's magnificent *The Failure of the "New Economics"* was not written twenty years ago by one of those "Austrian" economists—by a Lionel Robbins or a Gottfried von Haberler. If this had been done, the whole history of our time would have been different. But there is no use in crying over spilt milk. This is a great book, the best and most thorough exercise in economic demolition since Böhm-Bawerk (himself one of the founders of the "Austrian School") exploded Marx's labor theory of value.

Keynes's *General Theory* is here riddled chapter by chapter, line by line, with due account taken of the latest theoretical developments. The complete refutation of a vast network of fallacy can only be accomplished by someone thoroughly grounded in a sound positive theory. Henry Hazlitt has that groundwork. An "Austrian" follower of Ludwig von Mises, he is uniquely qualified for this task, and performs it surpassingly well. It is no exaggeration to say that this is by far the best book on economics published since Mises's great *Human Action* in 1949. Mises's work set forth the completed structure of the modern "Austrian" theory. Hazlitt's fine critique of Keynes, based on these principles, is a worthy complement to *Human Action*.

Henry Hazlitt, a renowned economic journalist, is a better economist than a whole host of sterile academicians, and, in contrast to many of them, he is distinguished by courage: the courage to remain an "Austrian" in the teeth of the Keynesian holocaust, alongside Mises and F.A. Hayek. On its merits, this book should conquer the economics profession as rapidly as did Keynes. But whether the currently fashionable economists read and digest this book or not is, in the long run, immaterial; it will be read, and it will destroy the Keynesian System. At the very least, there is now a new generation under thirty-five, to bring this message to fruition.

Chapter I

INTRODUCTION

1. *Canonization*

The most famous economist of the twentieth century is John Maynard Keynes; and the most influential economic book of the present era, both on theory and on economic policy, is his *General Theory of Employment, Interest, and Money,* published in 1936.

The fact is recognized not only by his admirers and disciples, but even by his sharpest critics. Open any issue of almost any of the scholarly economic journals, and you will find his name and the phrases that he coined or popularized sprinkled generously through its pages. Open the newspaper, and you will find interpretations of current economic events, or proposals for economic and monetary policies, that owe at least their ubiquity, if not their origin, to his writings.

To illustrate the unique place that Keynes's reputation occupies, I select a few quotations almost at random.

On his death the London *Times* [1] called him "a very great Englishman . . . a man of genius, who as a political economist had a world-wide influence on the thinking both of specialists and of the general public. . . . To find an economist of comparable influence one would have to go back to Adam Smith."

G. D. H. Cole, the Socialist economist, calls the *General Theory:*

[1] April 22, 1946. Reprinted in *The New Economics,* ed. by Seymour E. Harris, (New York, Alfred Knopf, 1952).

> The most important theoretical economic writing since Marx's "Capital," or, if only classical economics is to be considered as comparable, since Ricardo's "Principles." . . . What he has done, triumphantly and conclusively, is to demonstrate the falsity, even from a capitalist standpoint, of the most cherished practical "morals" of the orthodox economists and to construct an alternative theory of the working of capitalist enterprise so clearly nearer to the facts that it will be impossible for it to be ignored or set aside.

Professor Alvin H. Hansen of Harvard, usually regarded as Keynes's leading American disciple, writes of the *General Theory:*

> There are few who would deny, as of now, seventeen years later, that the book has had a greater impact on economic analysis and policy even in this short time than any book since Ricardo's *Political Economy*. It may be a little too early to claim that, along with Darwin's *Origin of Species* and Karl Marx's *Das Capital,* the *General Theory* is one of the most significant books which have appeared in the last hundred years. . . . But . . . it continues to gain in importance.[2]

In the starry eyes of some admirers, even the book's faults seem somehow to add to its greatness. Professor Paul A. Samuelson, of the Massachusetts Institute of Technology, author of the most widely used college textbook in economics at the present time, writes of the *General Theory:*

> It is a badly written book, poorly organized; any layman who, beguiled by the author's previous reputation, bought the book was cheated of his 5 shillings. It is not well suited for classroom use. It is arrogant, bad-tempered, polemical, and not overly generous in its acknowledgments. It abounds in mares' nests and confusions. . . . In short, it is a work of genius.[3]

Even stranger is Samuelson's implication that the very obscurity of the book is an embarrassment, not to the disci-

[2] *A Guide to Keynes,* (New York, McGraw-Hill, 1953).

[3] *The Development of Economic Thought,* ed. by Henry William Spiegel (New York: Wiley, 1952), p. 767.

ples of Keynes, but chiefly to his critics: "It bears repeating that the *General Theory* is an obscure book so that would-be anti-Keynesians must assume their position largely on credit." [4]

It is of course not surprising to find an extravagant judgment by R. F. Harrod, Keynes's biographer:

> To put the matter quite bluntly, I believe that the future historian of economic thought will regard the assistance rendered by Keynes on the road of progress as far more important than that of his revered master, Alfred Marshall. He seems, to my judgment, to stand rather in the same class as Adam Smith and Ricardo. In logical penetration he was much superior to Adam Smith, in lucidity of writing to Ricardo.[5]

Professor Dudley Dillard of the University of Maryland, in his book *The Economics of John Maynard Keynes* writes:

> By any test, Keynes ranks as one of the great economists of all time and as the most influential economic thinker the twentieth century has so far produced. . . .
>
> Within the first dozen years following its publication, John Maynard Keynes' *The General Theory of Employment, Interest, and Money* (1936) has had more influence upon the thinking of professional economists and public policy makers than any other book in the whole history of economic thought in a comparable number of years. Like Adam Smith's *Wealth of Nations* in the eighteenth century and Karl Marx's *Capital* in the nineteenth century, Keynes' *General Theory* has been the center of controversy among both professional and non-professional writers. Smith's book is a ringing challenge to mercantilism, Marx's book is a searching criticism of capitalism, Keynes' book is a repudiation of the foundations of laissez-faire. Many economists acknowledge a heavy debt to the stimulating thought of Lord Keynes.
>
> If the influence of Lord Keynes were limited to the field of technical economic doctrine, it would be of little interest to

[4] *Ibid.*, p. 768.

[5] *The Life of John Maynard Keynes,* (New York, Harcourt Brace, 1951), p. 466.

the world at large. However, practical economic policy bears even more deeply than economic theory the imprint of Keynes' thought.[6]

Quotations like this could be continued indefinitely, but they already grow repetitive. Even the most hostile critics of Keynes's theories do not question the extent of his influence. I cite but one: "[Keynes's] influence in the Roosevelt Administration was very great. His influence upon most of the economists in the employ of the Government is incredibly great. There has arisen a volume of theoretical literature regarding Keynes almost equal to that which has arisen around Karl Marx." [7]

2. *Uses of Refutation*

Yet about the *General Theory* there is a strange paradox. The Keynesian literature has perhaps grown to hundreds of books and thousands of articles. There are books wholly devoted to expounding the *General Theory* in simpler and more intelligible terms. But on the critical side there is a great dearth. The non-Keynesians and anti-Keynesians have contented themselves either with short articles, a few parenthetic pages, or a curt dismissal on the theory that his work will crumble from its own contradictions and will soon be forgotten. I know of no single work that devotes itself to a critical chapter-by-chapter or theorem-by-theorem analysis of the book. It is this task that I am undertaking here.

In view of the quotations I have just made, such an undertaking should require no apology. But there are two possible objections that I should like to consider. The first is the claim that Keynes's theories have been rapidly losing their influence in recent years, that they have been refuted by the actual course of events, and require no further answer. The second is the contention that we need only present true the-

6 (New York, Prentice-Hall, 1948), pp. vii and 1-2.

7 Benjamin M. Anderson, *Economics and the Public Welfare,* (New York, Van Nostrand, 1949), p. 391.

ories in a positive form; that it is of little value to analyze error because the possibilities of error are infinite and the mere statement of the truth is itself a refutation of error.

Concerning the first of these possible objections, I may reply that though there has been some diminution of Keynes's influence, and though several of his theories have been given a decent burial, his influence both on academic thought and on practical policy is still tremendous. It would in any case be a poor service to clear thinking simply to allow his theories to be forgotten, even if we assume that this is what may occur. "One of the peculiarities of recent speculation, especially in America," once wrote Santayana, "is that ideas are abandoned in virtue of a mere change of feeling, without any new evidence or new arguments. We do not nowadays refute our predecessors, we pleasantly bid them good-bye." [8]

Simply to bid our predecessors good-bye does not further clarity or progress of thought. Unless we know not only that some past doctrine was wrong, but precisely why it was wrong, we have not learned all the lessons that the error has to teach us, and there is real danger that it may make its appearance in another form.

In the history of thought great new contributions have often been made as a sort of by-product of what were originally intended to be merely refutations. Adam Smith's *Wealth of Nations* grew in large part out of a refutation of the errors of the mercantilists. Malthus's famous *Essay on Population* grew out of an attempt to refute the optimistic doctrines of Godwin. Kant's *Critique of Pure Reason* began as an effort to refute the theories of Hume. John Stuart Mill's *Examination of Sir William Hamilton's Philosophy* became more famous than any of the writings of the philosopher he attacked.

I hope I shall not be regarded as presumptuous enough

[8] George Santayana, *Character and Opinion in the United States,* (New York, Scribner's, 1920), p. 9.

to be comparing the present modest work with any of the great books just mentioned. I cite them merely to show that refutation of error is far from a futile occupation. It is an important method, not only of defending, expounding, and clarifying known truths, but of advancing to new truths and greater insight. As logic and mathematics sufficiently prove, the more we understand the implications of any theorem, the better we understand the theorem itself.

Nor, in examining the views put forward by a single man (or his disciples), do we necessarily confine ourselves to those views. Their analysis becomes a way of gaining a clearer and wider grasp of the problems with which that writer dealt. In the first chapter of his *Examination of Sir William Hamilton's Philosophy* (1865), Mill wrote: "My subject, therefore, is not Sir W. Hamilton, but the questions which Sir W. Hamilton discussed. It is, however, impossible to write on those questions in our own country and in our own time, without incessant reference, express or tacit, to his treatment of them."

The subject of this book, likewise, is not John Maynard Keynes but the problems he discussed. And we cannot discuss these problems at the present day without discussing his treatment of them.

3. *A Path-Breaking Pioneer?*

Now though I have analyzed Keynes's *General Theory* in the following pages theorem by theorem, chapter by chapter, and sometimes even sentence by sentence, to what to some readers may appear a tedious length, I have been unable to find in it a single important doctrine that is both true and original. What is original in the book is not true; and what is true is not original. In fact, as we shall find, even much that is fallacious in the book is not original, but can be found in a score of previous writers.

Frankly, when I began this task I did not think I would arrive at so sweeping a conclusion. My first thought was that I might do a short work, analyzing Keynes's chief doctrines so that the reader who wished a critical analysis would be able to find one in a brief and readable form. But when I actually embarked upon a line-by-line analysis, my experience was strangely like the one John Stuart Mill describes in his *Autobiography* regarding his analysis of Sir William Hamilton: "As I advanced in my task, the damage to Sir W. Hamilton's reputation became greater than I at first expected, through the almost incredible multitude of inconsistencies which showed themselves on comparing different passages with one another." [9] So I have found in Keynes's *General Theory* an incredible number of fallacies, inconsistencies, vaguenesses, shifting definitions and usages of words, and plain errors of fact. My desire for thoroughness in pointing these out has carried the length of this book much beyond what I originally intended.

There has, however, I venture to think, been a certain compensation for the length of this analysis. The results are not merely negative. They do not merely prove that Keynes's main contentions were wrong. For in dealing with the Keynesian fallacies we are obliged not only to scrutinize very closely his own arguments, but the "classical" or "orthodox" doctrines that he was denying. And in doing this, we shall often find that some of these "orthodox" doctrines have been only dimly understood, even by many of their proponents. In other cases we shall find errors or gaps in the usual statement of some of the "orthodox" doctrines themselves.

One other possible objection to the present volume remains to be considered. This is that it is directed against an author no longer in a position to reply. But any advantage that I might gain from this will certainly be more than outbalanced by the number and controversial ardor of Keynes's disciples. For the same reason, I make no apology

9 (Oxford, World's Classics edition), p. 234.

for the outspokenness of my criticism,[10] or for the fact that I write of Keynes in the present tense and often discuss his work as if the author were still living. This is, after all, only a way of confessing that Keynes's doctrines are still very much alive in the influence they exert.

In one respect the range of the present book is narrower than I had originally intended. There is no effort to cope with all the errors in the immense body of Keynesian literature. Such an effort would have been hopeless, as I realized when I was once well launched on my task. The reader will find only a few passing references to works of the Keynesians or "post-Keynesians." Even my references to Keynes himself are confined almost entirely to the *General Theory,* other of his works being cited only when I am calling attention to some inconsistency or to some statement of the same doctrine in another form. The examination of the fallacies of Keynes himself, in the *General Theory* alone, has carried me to as great a length as I felt my task could justify.

Once we have thoroughly examined the fallacies in the master, we can economize time by not troubling to dissect them again, usually in an even more vulnerable form, in the disciples.

In the preface to the *General Theory,* Keynes tries to anticipate some general criticisms. He apologizes for the "highly abstract argument" that is to follow, by declaring that his book "is chiefly addressed to my fellow-economists" (p. v), and that "at this stage of the argument the general public, though welcome at the debate, are only eavesdroppers" (p. vi).

I do not think we can excuse the bad writing in most of the *General Theory* on this ground. For Keynes succeeds,

10 Keynes's own attitude is thus described by his biographer: "There is no doubt that Keynes . . . thought that all was fair in argument, and that a man should not have a grievance if he was refuted without mercy. . . . If sensitiveness was not in place in a game, still less was it so in the discussion of public affairs or economic problems." R. F. Harrod, *The Life of John Maynard Keynes,* (New York: Harcourt Brace, 1951), pp. 329-330.

as we shall see, in being involved and technical without being precise. One of the most striking characteristics of the book is the looseness of many of the leading terms, and the constantly shifting senses in which they are used.

Attempting to anticipate another criticism, Keynes remarks: "Those, who are strongly wedded to what I shall call 'the classical theory,' will fluctuate, I expect, between a belief that I am quite wrong and a belief that I am saying nothing new" (p. v). This insinuates an *argumentum ad hominum.* It attempts to discredit critics in advance for not being converted to the new revelation. Actually, as we shall find, it is not necessary to "fluctuate" between these two beliefs. Keynes's main "contributions" are demonstrably wrong, and in those cases in which he is saying something that is true he is indeed saying nothing new.[11]

Finally, Keynes presents himself to the reader, not very modestly, as a great intellectual pioneer "treading along unfamiliar paths" (p. vii). What is strange about this, however, is that toward the end of his book, in Chapter 23, he cites as confirmation of the truth of these new path-breaking ideas the fact that most of them were held by the mercantilists of the seventeenth century!

4. *The "General" Theory*

After some hesitation, I have decided that the best way to analyze the *General Theory* is to do so chapter by chapter.

[11] I may supplement this by a footnote in a review of the *General Theory* by Professor Frank H. Knight, in *The Canadian Journal of Economics and Political Science* of February, 1937, p. 122: "This, of course, is one of two 'arguments' regularly hurled by revolutionary thinkers at those who do not immediately join up, the other being that the refusal is based on a vested interest. . . . Since it has become quite the fashion to account for differences in intellectual position by psychoanalysing, or somehow 'explaining,' one's opponent (and the example of following the fashion having in this case been set by Mr. Keynes), it may be permissible to note that our civilization of today, being essentially romantic, loves and extols heretics quite as much as its direct antecedent a few centuries back hated and feared them. The demand for heresy is always in excess of the supply and its production always a prosperous business. Where once it was necessary in writing to pose as merely restating and interpreting doctrine handed down from the Fathers, the surest way to public interest and acclaim now lies through pulling down and overturning everything established or accepted."

Keynes's book is not well organized. Therefore my criticism, like the book itself, will not follow the most logical order and will be sometimes repetitive. To compensate for these shortcomings, I have given my own chapters for the most part the same numbers as the corresponding chapters that they discuss in the *General Theory*. This will make it easier for readers who may wish to confirm or amplify any quotation I have made from the *General Theory*, or to follow Keynes's argument in its original form if they should question my own interpretation.

Fortunately Keynes's Chapter 1, "The General Theory," is only a single paragraph long. But that paragraph raises three points that call for comment.

> I have called this book *The General Theory of Employment, Interest and Money*, placing the emphasis on the prefix *general*. The object of such a title is to contrast the character of my arguments and conclusions with those of the *classical* theory of the subject, upon which I was brought up and which dominates the economic thought, both practical and theoretical, of the governing and academic classes of this generation, as it has for a hundred years past (p. 3).
>
> I shall argue [Keynes continues] that the postulates of the classical theory are applicable to a special case only and not to the general case, the situation which it assumes being a limiting point of the possible positions of equilibrium (p. 3).

Good economics prior to 1936, however, like good economics since then, did not depend on postulates that fitted special cases only. It dealt with the business cycle, with periods of prosperity and depression, as well as with simplified "static" theory. It is Keynes's economics, as we shall find, that applies to a special case only; and it does not give a correct analysis of that special case.

> The characteristics of the special case assumed by the classical theory [Keynes goes on] happen not to be those of the economic society in which we actually live, with the result that its teaching is misleading and disastrous if we attempt to apply it to the facts of experience (p. 3).

This is not argument but mere assertion. For the present I shall content myself with the counter-assertion that sound "orthodox" economics was always flexible enough to analyze actual conditions, and that it is Keynes's assumptions that "happen not to be those of the economic society in which we actually live."

My criticisms of Chapter 1 must apply to every sentence in it. They must apply, also, to his curious use of the term "classical," which he defends in a footnote. There he points out that "the classical economists" was a name invented by Marx to cover Ricardo and James Mill and their predecessors. "I have become accustomed," he writes, "perhaps perpetrating a solecism, to include in 'the classical school' the *followers* of Ricardo, those, that is to say, who adopted and perfected the theory of the Ricardian economics, including (for example) J. S. Mill, Marshall, Edgeworth, and Prof. Pigou" (p. 3).

This extended use of the term "classical" is merely confusing. It gives the reader a quite false picture. He is being asked, in effect, to consider practically all economics prior to the appearance of the *General Theory* in 1936, no matter by whom written, as both a *uniform* theory and an *agreed upon* theory. But there was enormous diversity in the views of particular writers, and many controversies between the so-called "classical" economists. There were also points which some of them did not pretend to have settled. Keynes writes as if all the economists before him had dozed off into a sort of dogmatic slumber, thoughtlessly incanting after each other some unexamined clichés of thought.

His references to the "classical" school are misleading in more than one respect. He includes among the classical economists the pioneers and continuers of the subjective-value or marginal-utility theories that represent a break with the "classical" economics. And when he writes about orthodox economics he seems to confine himself most of the time to Marshall and Pigou. He writes as if he were unaware of the great advances beyond these writers that were made, particularly in capital and interest theory, by Böhm-Bawerk, John Bates Clark, Knut Wicksell, Irving Fisher, Ludwig von Mises, and F. A. Hayek.

Keynes's frame of reference is strangely provincial. He seems to assume that whatever was not discovered by either Marshall or Pigou, or discussed in his little circle at Cambridge, was never thought of at all.

Chapter II

POSTULATES OF KEYNESIAN ECONOMICS

1. *What Is the Classical Theory of Employment?*

Chapter 2 of the *General Theory* is called "The Postulates of the Classical Economics."

> Most treatises on the theory of Value and Production [Keynes begins] are primarily concerned with the distribution of a *given* volume of employed resources between different uses and with the conditions which . . . determine their relative rewards. . . . But the pure theory of what determines the *actual employment* of the available resources has seldom been examined in great detail (p. 4).

I doubt whether this factual statement can be supported. Many treatises before 1936 had explained in great detail how labor and other resources may come to be idle, and how goods already produced may long remain unsold, because of the rigidity or "stickiness" of some wages or prices, i.e., because of the refusal of unions or other sellers to accept the lowered market or "equilibrium" wage or price for the services or goods that they have to offer.

"The classical theory of employment—supposedly simple and obvious—has been based," Keynes thinks, "on two fundamental postulates, though practically without discussion" (p. 5). The first of these is "I. *The wage is equal to the marginal product of labor.*" (His italics, p. 5.)

This postulate is correctly and clearly stated. It is not, of course, part of the *classical* theory of employment. That adjective should be reserved, in accordance with custom and in the interests of precision, for theory prior to the subjective-value or "marginalist" revolution of Jevons and Menger. But the postulate has become part of "orthodox" theory since its formulation by the "Austrian" school and, particularly in America, by John Bates Clark.

Having written this simple postulate, Keynes adds eight lines of "explanation" which are amazingly awkward and involved and do more to obfuscate than to clarify.

He then proceeds to state the second alleged "fundamental postulate" of "the classical theory of employment," to wit: "II. *The utility of the wage when a given volume of labor is employed is equal to the marginal disutility of that amount of employment.*" (His italics, p. 5.) He adds, as part of his explanation: "Disutility must be here understood to cover every kind of reason which might lead a man, or a body of men, to withhold their labor rather than accept a wage which had to them a utility below a certain minimum" (p. 6).

"Disutility" is here so broadly defined as to be almost meaningless. It may be seriously doubted, in fact, whether this whole second "fundamental postulate," as Keynes frames and explains it, is or ever was a necessary part of the "classical" or traditional theory of employment. Keynes does name and (later) quote A. C. Pigou as one whose theories rested on it. Yet it may be seriously questioned whether this "second postulate" is representative of any substantial body of thought, particularly in the complicated form that Keynes states it.

The "orthodox" marginal theory of wages and employment is simple. It is that wage-rates are determined by the marginal productivity of workers; that when employment is "full" wage-rates are equal to the marginal productivity of all those seeking work and able to work; but that there will be unemployment whenever wage-rates exceed this marginal productivity. Wage-rates may exceed this marginal productivity either through an increase in union demands or through a drop in this marginal productivity. (The latter may be caused either by less efficient work, or by a drop in the price of, or demand for, the products that workers are helping to produce.)

That is all there is to the theory in its broadest outlines. The "second postulate," in the form stated by Keynes, is unnecessary and unilluminating.

Subject to certain qualifications, Keynes contends, "the volume of employed resources is duly determined, according to the classical theory, by the two postulates [which Keynes has named]. The first gives us the demand schedule for employment; the second gives us the supply schedule; and the amount of employment is fixed at the point where the utility of the marginal product balances the disutility of the marginal employment" (p. 6).

Is this indeed the "classical" theory of employment? The first postulate—that "the wage is equal to the marginal product of labor"—does not merely give us the "demand schedule" for labor; it tells us *the point of intersection* of both the "demand schedule" *and* the "supply schedule." The demand schedule for workers is the wage-rate that employers are willing to offer for workers. The "supply schedule" of workers is fixed by the wage-rate that workers are willing to take. This is not determined, for the individual worker, by the "disutility" of the employment—at least not if "disutility" is used in its common-sense meaning. Many an individual unemployed worker would be more than willing to take a job at a rate below a given union scale if the union members would let him, or if the union leader would consent to reduce the scale.

But we can return to this subject later. After all, Keynes is not here stating his own theory; he is merely giving a garbled version of the orthodox theory.

Further, according to Keynes, "classical" theory allows only for two possibilities—"frictional" unemployment and "voluntary" unemployment. "The classical postulates do not admit of the possibility of the third category, which I shall define below as 'involuntary' unemployment" (p. 6).

Here is a classification that would trouble any logician.

Unemployment must be either voluntary or involuntary. Surely these two categories exhaust the possibilities. There is no room for a third category. "Frictional" unemployment must be either voluntary or involuntary. In practice it is likely to be made up of a little of each. "Frictional" unemployment may be involuntary through illness, disability, failure of a firm, unexpected cessation of seasonal work, or discharge. "Frictional" unemployment may be voluntary because a family has moved to a new place, because a man has relinquished an old job in the hope of getting a better one, because he thinks he can get more pay than he is offered, or because he is taking a vacation between jobs. Such unemployment is the result of a *decision,* good or bad, on the part of the man who is unemployed. "Friction," though a traditional term, is perhaps not the most fortunate metaphor to describe it.

One reason Keynes's thought is so often difficult to follow, above all in the *General Theory,* is that he writes so badly (notwithstanding the dithyrambic admiration of the "lucidity," "charm," and "brilliance" of his style).[1] And one reason he writes so badly (at least in the *General Theory*) is that he is constantly introducing technical terms that are not only unnecessary but inappropriate and misleading. Most of his worst terms are of his own coinage, but if someone else's term is sufficiently bad he embraces it. Thus at this point he introduces the term "wage-goods industries," describing it as "Professor Pigou's convenient term for goods upon the price of which the utility of the money-wage depends" (p. 7). He then contrasts "wage-goods" with "non-wage-goods."

This introduces a terminology that seems as needless as it

[1] There are only a few oases of lucidity and eloquence in a vast Sahara of obscurity. This bad writing has been commented upon both by admirers like Paul A. Samuelson (already cited) and by less sympathetic critics like Jacob Viner and Frank H. Knight. Knight refers several times to "the hard labor involved" in reading the book. "Familiar terms and modes of expression seem to be shunned on principle." "My difficulty (and no little annoyance) has been that of choosing between interpretations, one apparently nonsensical and the other more or less commonplace." *The Canadian Journal of Economics and Political Science,* February, 1937, pp. 123, 108, and 122.

is confusing. Do "wage-goods" mean anything essentially different from consumer goods? Do "non-wage-goods" mean anything essentially different from capital goods? No doubt "wage-goods" would not include mink coats or villas on the Riviera, but the common sense of the reader might be trusted not to introduce these items into an imaginary index of consumers' goods prices. It hardly seems necessary to invent a special term to keep them out. This bad term is unfortunately continued throughout the *General Theory*. The reader is forced to translate it back each time into the familiar "consumers' goods," and to remind himself that it does *not* mean "goods the production of which requires the payment of wages."

2. *Wage-Rates and Unemployment*

Section II of Chapter 2 is notable as the first attempt by Keynes in the *General Theory* to disprove a fundamental proposition of traditional economics—that the most frequent cause of unemployment is excessive wage-rates. This, of course, for "classical" economics, is merely the parallel of the proposition that the most frequent cause for an unsold surplus of a commodity is the refusal of sellers to accept a price that will clear the market. If the proposition is not true with regard to labor, it is not true with regard to commodities either. Both propositions rest upon the same line of reasoning. Both are special cases of a wider proposition covering both commodities and services.

It is instructive to notice that Keynes never challenges this proposition head-on, or by any coherent and clear-cut argument. He attacks it rather by a series of oblique sallies, in which the argument is usually involved and obscure and often clearly fallacious.

He begins by contending that "labor" is usually more interested in its "money-wage" than in its "real wage":

> Ordinary experience tells us, beyond doubt, that a situation where labor stipulates (within limits) for a money-wage rather

> than a real wage, so far from being a mere possibility, is the normal case. Whilst workers will usually resist a reduction of money-wages, it is not their practice to withdraw their labor whenever there is a rise in the price of wage-goods (p. 9).

So far as the United States is concerned (and, I suspect, so far as nearly every industrially advanced country is concerned), this contention is already obsolete. The big American unions all have their "economists" and "directors of research," who are acutely aware of the monthly changes in the official Consumer Price Index. As of January, 1958, more than 4 million workers, moreover, mainly in the heavy industries—steel, automobiles, railroads—had insisted on, and secured, contracts providing for automatic wage increases with increases in the cost of living.[2] So while it is true that unions will resist a fall in money wage-rates, even if it is less than the fall in consumer prices, it is not true that unions will acquiesce in stationary wage-rates when consumer prices are rising.

Even if Keynes's contention, moreover, had been factually true, it would still have been irrelevant to the "classical" contention. The classical contention is that if wage-rates (whether considered in terms of money wage-rates or real wage-rates) are above the level of the marginal productivity of labor, there will be unemployment.

Why is Keynes so concerned to make this point about "labor's" attitude toward money wage-rates and real wage-rates respectively? The collectivist word "labor" implies that we need not think in terms of what individual workers would wish or do, but only in terms of what union monopolists wish or do. He is concerned because he will be later eager to prove that while it is "impossible" to persuade unions to accept a cut in money wage-rates, it will be easy to deceive them into accepting a cut in real wage-rates by the simple process of monetary inflation—erosion of the purchasing power of the monetary unit. It will be noticed

[2] Monthly Labor Review, U. S. Department of Labor, Dec., 1957.

that even this argument, however, tacitly accepts the "classical" contention that the chief reason for unemployment is the existence of wage-rates above the point of labor's marginal productivity.

> Moreover, [Keynes goes on to maintain] the contention that the unemployment which characterizes a depression is due to a refusal by labor to accept a reduction of money-wages is not clearly supported by the facts. It is not very plausible to assert that unemployment in the United States in 1932 was due either to labor obstinately refusing to accept a reduction of money-wages or to its obstinately demanding a real wage beyond what the productivity of the economic machine was capable of furnishing (p. 9).

The reader will notice that there is no argument here, merely assertion. "It is not very plausible." That is, it is not very plausible to *Keynes,* which proves nothing. Most of us require something more than *ex cathedra* pronouncements.

A trick that Keynes uses here and elsewhere is the attempt to discredit a doctrine by overstating it. The causes of the 1929 crisis, and of the depression from 1930 to 1940, were complex. I shall not try to go into all of them here. But I do not know of any serious economist who maintained or maintains that the *initiating* cause of the 1929 crisis was excessive wage-rates. What responsible economists did and do assert is that once the crisis had developed, and demand and prices had collapsed, it was necessary for wage-rates to adjust themselves to the reduced level of demand and of prices if mass unemployment was to be averted. It was the failure of this wage adjustment to occur that led to prolonged mass unemployment for ten years.

The insistence of unions on excessive [2] wage-rates, it is

[2] Whenever I speak of "excessive" wage-rates I refer, of course, merely to wage-rates that exceed the marginal productivity of labor. The term "excessive" must not be taken to imply moral disapprobation of such wage-rates. But it does imply that, whenever such wage-rates exist, there will be unemployment and a failure of the whole body of workers to receive the maximum total wage-income that conditions otherwise make possible.

true, may not always be a *full* explanation of total unemployment at any given time. But it is always *part* of the explanation. Though it is not always a *sufficient* cause, it cannot be dismissed also (as Keynes dismisses it) as a *necessary* cause. Rigidity or stickiness of contractual interest rates and rents, or unusual uncertainty or fear among buyers and consumers, may also be causes. But they are likely to be *temporary* causes. The longer mass unemployment is prolonged, the more warranted we are in assigning excessive wage-rates as the dominant cause of it.

Even Keynes feels the need of offering reasons why he finds the attribution of unemployment to excessive wage-rates "not very plausible." But the reasons he offers are either fallacious or contrary to established fact. In explanation of the passage I have just quoted, he goes on:

> Wide variations are experienced in the volume of employment without any apparent change either in the minimum real demands of labor or in its productivity. Labor is not more truculent in the depression than in the boom—far from it. Nor is its physical productivity less. These facts from experience are a *prima facie* ground for questioning the adequacy of the classical analysis (p. 9).

Are they? Keynes has here tumbled into a glaring fallacy. The absence of change in *physical* productivity is completely irrelevant to *money* wage-rates. What counts in economics is only *value* productivity—and value productivity stated in this case, of course, in *monetary* terms. If the marginal productivity of a worker is a given unit of a commodity that previously sold for $10, and the price of that unit has now fallen to $5, then the marginal value productivity of that worker, even though he is turning out the same number of units, has fallen by half. If we assume that this fall in prices has been general, and that this represents the average fall, then the worker who insists on retaining his old money wage-rate is in effect insisting on a 100 per cent increase in his real wage-rate.

Whether the worker is "truculent" or not is entirely beside the point. If prices fall by 50 per cent, and unions will accept a wage cut, but of no more than 25 per cent, then the unions are in effect demanding an increase in real wage-rates of 50 per cent. The only way they can get it, and retain full employment, is by an *increase* of 50 per cent in their physical (or "real" value) marginal productivity to make up for the drop in the price of the individual unit of the commodity they help to produce.

The passage I have just quoted is in itself *prima facie* ground for questioning the adequacy of the whole Keynesian analysis.

"It would be interesting to see the results of a statistical enquiry," writes Keynes, "into the actual relationship between changes in money-wages and changes in real wages" (pp. 9-10). But without waiting for the results, he proceeds to tell the reader what they would be: "When money-wages are rising . . . it will be found that real wages are falling; and when money-wages are falling, real wages are rising" (p. 10). The second half of this statement is historically correct. The first half, in the modern world, is demonstrably not correct. The statistical results which Keynes expressed such an interest in seeing already existed, but he did not bother to look them up. Let us cite a few.

In the eighteen-year period between 1939 and 1957, weekly wages in manufacturing in the United States, according to the figures of the Department of Labor, rose from $23.86 in 1939 to $82.39 in 1957, an increase of 245 per cent. This compared with an increase in the official Consumer Price Index for the same period of only 102 per cent, making an increase in real weekly wages in the period of 71 per cent. The comparison is not very different if we take hourly wage-rates as the base of comparison instead of weekly wages. These rose from 63 cents an hour in 1939 to $2.07 in 1957, an increase of 229 per cent. In other words, when money-wages were rising in this period, real wages were also rising. Whatever historic foundation there may be for the traditional belief that in an inflation prices rise first and wages lag behind, the proposition has not been true for the United States, or for many other countries, in the last twenty years.

The second half of Keynes's proposition, that "when money-wages are falling, real wages are rising" is, however, generally true. It is not easy to find in American statistical history extensive periods when money-wages were falling, but two such periods do exist in recent times—between 1920 and 1922, and between 1929 and 1933. I append a comparison for a selected series of years taken from a table published by the government [3] comparing average hourly earnings of workers in manufacturing industries in "current prices," *i.e.*, in terms of the actual money wage-rates paid, and in "1954 prices," *i.e.*, in terms of "real" wage-rates, or money wage-rates expressed in terms of a dollar of assumed constant purchasing power:

Year	*Current Prices*	*1954 Prices*
1920	$0.555	$0.743
1921	.515	.773
1922	.487	.780
1923	.522	.822
1924	.547	.859
1929	.566	.886
1930	.552	.887
1931	.515	.910
1932	.446	.876
1933	.442	.917
1934	.532	1.068

Let us look first at the period from 1920 to 1924. Between 1920 and 1922 there was a substantial drop in money wage-rates; yet they did not drop as much as consumer prices, and therefore real wage-rates, or wage-rates in "con-

[3] *1955 Historical and Descriptive Supplement to Economic Indicators.* Prepared for the Joint Committee on the Economic Report by the Committee Staff and the Office of Statistical Standards, Bureau of the Budget, p. 29.

stant dollars," actually increased between 1920 and 1922. Beginning in 1923, money wage-rates started up again; but real wages also rose, once more refuting Keynes's proposition that "when money-wages are rising . . . it will be found that real wages are falling."

Take, now, the period between 1929 and 1934. From 1929 to 1933 money wage-rates fell; but real wage-rates rose. There was a sole exception between the years 1931 and 1932; but it did not change the comparative trend over the whole period. Between 1933 and 1934, however, there was a dramatic jump both in money wage-rates and in real wage-rates, once more contradicting Keynes's "law."

It is only fair to point out that this jump in both money and real wage-rates in 1934 was the direct result of governmental intervention—the National Recovery Administration codes put into effect under government pressure in the first years of the New Deal. But it is precisely this jump in both money and real wage-rates that helps to explain the continuance of mass unemployment throughout the Thirties. This again is a statistical disproof of Keynes's central thesis that unemployment has nothing to do with the height of wage-rates—or even that unemployment is rather owing to wage-rates being too *low* than to their being too *high*. From 1931 through 1939 both money wage-rates and real wage-rates rose. Money wage-rates rose from 51 cents an hour in 1931 to 63 cents in 1939. In constant (1954) prices, real wage-rates rose from 91 in 1931 to 122 in 1939. What was the result? In that ten-year period there was an average annual unemployment of 10 million men and women.

Before we proceed further with a direct consideration of Keynes's argument on this point, it may be more profitable to digress a moment to consider the kind of argument, and particularly the set of assumptions, with which we have to deal. It is pertinent here to make three observations:

1. When Keynes writes about "classical theory" or "traditional theory," it almost invariably turns out that what

he is discussing is neither of these, strictly speaking, but some caricature, or the specific theories of the "Cambridge school" (consisting mainly of Marshall, Edgeworth, and Pigou) in which he was brought up.

2. This school never quite rid itself of a cost-of-production theory of prices, and neither did Keynes.

3. Keynes is even inferior to the Cambridge economists he criticizes in his addiction to lump thinking, in-block thinking.

Once we recognize the existence of these assumptions in Keynes's thinking we can economize our detailed criticism. We can ignore many of his criticisms of the theories of Marshall and Pigou, for example, because those theories had already been superseded by the best economic thought long prior to the appearance of the *General Theory*. And we need not waste too much time over Keynes's criticisms when we find that these themselves rest on crude lump thinking. Keynes writes on page 11, for example: "The traditional theory maintains, in short, *that the wage bargains between the entrepreneurs and the workers determine the real wage.*" (His italics.) Now there is no such thing as *"the"* real wage. Neither is there any such thing as "the general level of money-wages" (pp. 10, 12, 13, etc.). "The" wage, real or money, is a figment of the bad economist's imagination. It is a violent oversimplification that assumes away the thousands of differences in individual wages and salaries that make up reality.

In the same way, "the general *level* of wages," like "the general *level* of prices" (both of which concepts are central to Keynes's thought), has no existence in reality. It is a statistician's construct, a mathematical average which has a limited value in simplifying certain problems. But it simplifies away some of the chief dynamic problems in economics. The same relationship between an *average* of prices and an *average* of wages in two different periods may conceal gross changes in the relationship of specific prices to specific wages. It is precisely the latter that may be relevant to equilibrium or the lack of it, to the health of specific industries, to full employment or to substantial unemployment.

The word "level" can give rise to an additional false assumption—that prices and wages rise or fall evenly or *uniformly*. It is precisely their failure to do so that creates most of the problems of inflation or deflation. It is also the failure of specific prices or wages to rise or fall as much as the average that permits the continuous structural changes in production and in the labor force necessary for continuous economic efficiency and progress.

Keynes writes on page 13:

> There may be *no* method available to labor as a whole whereby it can bring the wage-goods equivalent of the general level of money-wages into conformity with the marginal disutility of the current volume of employment. There may exist no expedient by which labor as a whole can reduce its *real* wage to a given figure by making revised *money* bargains with the entrepreneurs. This will be our contention.

I shall not attempt here to analyze thoroughly this highly implausible contention. It is enough to point out, for the moment, that "labor" does not act or do anything else "as a whole," any more than "business" does. "Labor" certainly doesn't set "its" wage-rate. There are thousands of different wage-rates being set every working day, sometimes industry by industry, more often company by company, or union by union, and most often individual by individual. Even an industry-wide union sets, not a single uniform rate, but a complicated *scale* of rates, fixed by "classifications."

The whole dilemma that Keynes presents, as we shall later see, exists not in the real world of economics, but in his own confused method of thinking.

3. *No "General Level" of Wage-rates*

Section III of Keynes's Chapter 2 is less than a page and a half in length, and yet it is so packed with fallacies and misstatements of fact, and these fallacies and misstatements are so crucial to Keynes's whole theory, that it requires more than a page and a half of analysis.

Keynes's argument in this section rests on three major confusions:

1. The word "wages" is sometimes used in the sense of wage-*rates* and sometimes in the sense of wage *income* or total *payrolls*. There is no warning to the reader as to when the meaning shifts, and Keynes himself is apparently unaware of it. This confusion runs through the *General Theory*, and gives birth to a host of sub-confusions and sub-fallacies.

2. "Labor" is treated in a Marxian manner as a lumped total, with a lumped interest opposed to an equally lumped interest of entrepreneurs. This kind of treatment overlooks both the frequent conflict of interest between different groups of workers and the frequent identity of interest between workers and entrepreneurs in the same industry or firm.

3. Keynes is constantly confusing the real interest of workers with their illusions regarding their interests.

Take this strange sentence from page 14: "Any individual or group of individuals, who consent to a reduction of money-wages relatively to others, will suffer a *relative* reduction in real wages, which is a sufficient justification for them to resist it." (His italics.)

To see how bad this argument is, let us try to apply it to commodities. We would then have to say, for instance, that if wheat fell in price relatively to corn, the wheat farmers would be "justified" in combining to refuse to accept the lower price. If they did so, of course, they would simply leave part of their wheat unsold on the market. The result of this would be to hurt both wheat farmers and wheat consumers.

In a free, fluid, workable economy *relative* changes in prices are taking place every day. There are as many "gainers" as "losers" by the process. If the "losers" refused to accept the situation, and kept their prices frozen (or raised them as much as "the general level" had risen), the result would merely be to freeze the economy, restrict consumption, and lower production, particularly of the goods that otherwise have fallen relatively in price. This is precisely what happens in the labor field when the members of a single union refuse to accept a "relative" reduction of real wage-rates. By refusing to accept it they do not, in fact, improve their position. They merely bring about unemployment, particularly in their own ranks, and hurt their own interests as well as those of the entrepreneurs who employ them.

Keynes remained blind to the most glaring fact in real economic life—that prices and wages *never* (except perhaps in a totalitarian state) change *uniformly* or as a *unit,* but *always* "relatively." It is individual prices and individual wages that go up or down, and adjust to each other in accordance with hourly changes in relative supply and relative demand.

After a given calendar year or month has closed, along comes a statistician and figures out a new average. If he is a bad statistician, he tells us that there has been such-and-such a change in the average "level" of prices or wages. Then bad economists build false theories on this misleading terminology. They reify this alleged "level." Their next step is to announce that if the wages or prices in a free economy do *not* act in this completely uniform or lump way, there must be outrageous injustice going on, and that there is "sufficient justification" for any group of workers to resist a relative reduction in real wage-rates, even though, by resisting it, they merely create unemployment in their own ranks. This is adding pseudo-ethics to pseudo-economics. It is like telling a man that he is justified in cutting off his nose to spite his face.

"It would be impracticable," Keynes continues, for any group of workers "to resist every reduction of real wages, due to a change in the purchasing power of money which affects all workers alike; and in fact reductions of real wages arising in this way are not, as a rule, resisted unless they proceed to an extreme degree" (p. 14). The second part of this statement, as we have already seen, is contrary to the facts of the modern world. Unions now insist on escalator contracts or wage boosts to offset changes as small as 1 per cent in the cost-of-living index.

Nor is it ever true that "a change in the purchasing power of money . . . affects all workers alike." Such a change in purchasing power is always accompanied, and partly caused by, increases in some wage-rates. Keynes's fallacy here arises once more from the crude supposition that "the price level" as a whole goes up in an inflation while "the wage level" as a whole stays where it is. Statistical averages may sometimes make this *seem* to happen, but this is precisely because mere averages hide the real diversity and dispersions of the economic process.

Keynes is constantly falling into this fallacy of averages or aggregates. His "aggregate" or "macro-economics" is not a step in advance; it is a retrograde step which conceals real relationships and real causation and leads him to erect an elaborate structure of fictitious relationships and fictitious causation.

> The effect of combination on the part of a group of workers [Keynes goes on] is to protect their *relative* real wage. The *general* level of real wages depends on the other forces of the economic system.
>
> Thus it is fortunate that the workers, though unconsciously, are instinctively more reasonable economists than the classical school, inasmuch as they resist reductions of money-wages, which are seldom or never of an all-around character . . . whereas they do not resist reductions of real wages. . . . (His italics, p. 14.)

Notice, first of all, the semantics of the word "protect." The purpose and effect of unions, of course, is to *increase* the *relative* wage-rates of the union members as compared with other workers. The "general level" of real wages is merely the composite average of individual wage-rates. It does not depend "on the other forces of the economic system." It depends on the calculations of statisticians. Of course any debasement of the monetary unit through inflation causes a rise in the average of wages and prices. But this occurs, in actuality, through a different (though sometimes only slightly different) percentage rise in the price of each individual commodity or each individual wage-rate. The exchange ratio of wheat and corn is determined by the value both of a bushel of wheat and of a bushel of corn, and never merely by the value of one of them. A monetary price or wage-rate is determined both by the exchange value of the monetary unit and the exchange value of a unit of a commodity or service, and not merely by the value of the monetary unit alone.

Finally, the ironical remark about workers being "more reasonable economists than the classical school" is based on a misconception both of how wages change and how "classical" economists think. *No* reductions of wages, except those that might be imposed by an authoritarian government, are *ever* "of an all-round character." If the economy is free, individual wage-rates vary as much as individual prices, and there is great dispersion both when they go up and when they go down. (See charts on pp. 284 and 285.)

4. *"Non-Euclidean" Economics*

Sections IV and V of Keynes's Chapter 2 are outstanding even in the *General Theory* for the involution and obscurity of their style, and for Keynes's remarkable propensity for stating everything backwards. He begins by telling us that "classical theory" does not admit even the possibility of "involuntary" employment in the strict sense. Whether this is true or not depends upon the definition we give to "involuntary," and also upon whether we interpret the word in relation to the plight of an individual worker or in relation to unions that insist on a given scale of wage-rates and see to it by their methods of intimidation not only that none of their own members, but nobody else, accepts employment below that wage-rate.

But here is Keynes's own definition of "involuntary unemployment":

> *Men are involuntarily unemployed if, in the event of a small rise in the price of wage-goods relatively to the money-wage, both the aggregate supply of labor willing to work for the current money-wage and the aggregate demand for it at that wage would be greater than the existing volume of employment.* (His italics, p. 15.)

It would be hard to imagine a definition more wordy, involved or obfusc. I have read it an indefinite number of times, and as nearly as I can make out it means simply this: *Men are involuntarily unemployed if an increase in prices relatively to wage-rates would lead to more employment.*

As soon as we translate Keynes's statement into plainer English, its falsity becomes evident. Keynes's statement overlooks the fact that such an increase of employment could have been brought about equally well by a *lowering* of money wage-rates, with commodity prices remaining the same. To recognize this possibility, however, would have been to recognize that the unemployment was not in fact involuntary. Keynes tries to dismiss the possibility by pretending, on quite unconvincing grounds, that there would have to be a uniform and simultaneous reduction of wages throughout the entire economic system to make this result possible. But as I have already pointed out, wages never do go up or down uniformly or simultaneously. (See again the charts on pp. 284 and 285.)

We shall not now spend further time over Sections IV and V, though they are full of further involved and implausible propositions. Keynes advises us that: "The Theory of Wages in relation to employment, to which we are here leading up, cannot be full elucidated, however, until Chapter 19 and its appendix have been reached" (p. 18). We, too, can wait for that chapter before we make any further analysis of Keynes's theory on this point.

Before leaving these sections, however, it is worth taking note of an extravagantly pretentious claim that has apparently taken in some of Keynes's more fervent disciples.

> The classical theorists [he writes] resemble Euclidean geometers in a non-Euclidean world who, discovering that in experience straight lines apparently parallel often meet, rebuke the lines for not keeping straight. . . . Yet, in truth, there is no remedy except to throw over the axiom of parallels and to work out a non-Euclidean geometry. Something similar is required today in economics (p. 16).

If we are to talk in these pretentious terms, I should like to suggest that the real economic world in which we live is, after all, pretty "Euclidean," and that we had better stick to sound "Euclidean" economics in describing it. It is precisely Keynes, as we shall find, who starts rebuking the real economic world for not acting according to his theories—as when he contends, for example, against all experience under free economies, that wage-rates "ought" to go up or down or adjust themselves to "the price level" uniformly and simultaneously or not at all.

Chapter III

KEYNES vs. SAY'S LAW

1. *Keynes's "Greatest Achievement"*

We come now to Keynes's famous "refutation" of Say's Law of Markets. All that it is necessary to say about this "refutation" has already been said by Benjamin M. Anderson, Jr.,[1] and Ludwig von Mises.[2] Keynes himself takes the matter so cavalierly that all he requires to "refute" Say's Law to his own satisfaction is less than four pages.

Yet some of his admirers regard this as alone securing his title to fame:

> Historians fifty years from now may record that Keynes' greatest achievement was the liberation of Anglo-American economics from a tyrannical dogma, and they may even conclude that this was essentially a work of negation unmatched by comparable positive achievements. Even, however, if Keynes were to receive credit for nothing else . . . his title to fame would be secure . . . [Yet] the Keynesian attacks, though they appear to be directed against a variety of specific theories, all fall to the ground if the validity of Say's Law is assumed.[3]

I think I am justified, therefore, in devoting a special chapter to the subject.

It is important to realize, to begin with, as Mises [4] has pointed out, that what is called Say's Law was not originally

[1] *Economics and the Public Welfare,* (New York: Van Nostrand, 1949), pp. 390-393.

[2] *Planning for Freedom.* (South Holland, Ill.: Libertarian Press, 1952), pp. 64-71.

[3] Paul M. Sweezy in *The New Economics,* ed. by Seymour E. Harris, (New York: Alfred Knopf, 1947), p. 105.

[4] *Op. cit.,* pp. 64-65.

designed as an integral part of classical economics but as a preliminary—as a refutation of a fallacy that long preceded the development of economics as a recognized special branch of knowledge. Whenever business was bad, the average merchant had two explanations at hand: the evil was caused by a scarcity of money and by general overproduction. Adam Smith, in a famous passage in *The Wealth of Nations,*[5] exploded the first of these myths. Say devoted himself to a refutation of the second.

For a modern statement of Say's Law, I turn to B. M. Anderson:

> The central theoretical issue involved in the problem of postwar economic adjustment, and in the problem of full employment in the postwar period, is the issue between the equilibrium doctrine and the purchasing power doctrine.
>
> Those who advocate vast governmental expenditures and deficit financing after the war as the only means of getting full employment, separate production and purchasing power sharply. Purchasing power must be kept above production if production is to expand, in their view. If purchasing power falls off, production will fall off.
>
> The prevailing view among economists, on the other hand, has long been that purchasing power grows out of production. The great producing countries are the great consuming countries. The twentieth-century world consumes vastly more than the eighteenth-century world because it produces vastly more. Supply of wheat gives rise to demand for automobiles, silks, shoes, cotton goods, and other things that the wheat producer wants. Supply of shoes gives rise to demand for wheat, for silks, for automobiles, and for other things that the shoe producer wants. Supply and demand in the aggregate are thus not merely equal, but they are identical, since every commodity may be looked upon either as supply of its own kind or as demand for other things. But this doctrine is subject to the great qualification that the proportions must be right; that there must be equilibrium.[6]

[5] Vol. I, Book IV, Chap. I, (Edwin Cannon edition, 1904), p. 404 ff.
[6] *Economics and the Public Welfare*, p. 390.

Keynes's "refutation" of Say's Law consists in simply ignoring this qualification.

He takes as his first target a passage from John Stuart Mill:

> What constitutes the means of payment for commodities is simply commodities. Each person's means of paying for the production of other people consist of those which he himself possesses. All sellers are inevitably, and by the meaning of the word, buyers. Could we suddenly double the productive powers of the country, we should double the supply of commodities in every market; but we should, by the same stroke, double the purchasing power. Everybody would bring a double demand as well as supply; everybody would be able to buy twice as much, because every one would have twice as much to offer in exchange.[7]

By itself, this passage from Mill, as B. M. Anderson [8] has pointed out, does not present the essentials of the modern version of Say's Law:

> If we doubled the productive power of the country, we should not double the supply of commodities in every market, and if we did, we should not clear the markets of the double supply in every market. If we doubled the supply in the salt market, for example, we should have an appalling glut of salt. The great increases would come in the items where demand is elastic. We should change very radically the proportions in which we produced commodities.

But as Anderson goes on to point out, it is unfair to Mill to take this brief passage out of its context and present it as if it were the heart of Say's Law. If Keynes had quoted only the three sentences immediately following, he would have introduced us to the conception of balance and proportion and equilibrium which is the heart of the doctrine—a conception which Keynes nowhere considers in his *General Theory*.

[7] *Principles of Political Economy,* Book III, Chap. xiv. Sect. 2.
[8] *Op. cit.,* p. 392.

Mill's next few lines, immediately following the passage torn from its context, quoted above, are as follows:

> It is probable, indeed, that there would now be a superfluity of certain things. Although the community would willingly double its aggregate consumption, it may already have as much as it desires of some commodities, and it may prefer to do more than double its consumption of others, or to exercise its increased purchasing power on some new thing. If so, the supply will adapt itself accordingly, and the values of things will continue to conform to their cost of production.

The doctrine that supply creates its own demand, in other words, is based on the assumption that a proper equilibrium exists among the different kinds of production, and among prices of different products and services. And it of course assumes proper relationships between prices and costs, between prices and wage-rates. It assumes the existence of competition and free and fluid markets by which these proportions, price relations, and other equilibria will be brought about.

No important economist, to my knowledge, ever made the absurd assumption (of which Keynes by implication accuses the whole classical school) that thanks to Say's Law depressions and unemployment were impossible, and that everything produced would automatically find a ready market at a profitable price. Say's Law, to repeat, was, contrary to the assertions of the Keynesians, *not* the cornerstone on which the great edifice of the positive doctrines of the classical economists was based. It was itself merely a refutation of an absurd belief prevailing prior to its formulation.

To resume the quotation from Mill:

> At any rate, it is a sheer absurdity that all things should fall in value, and that all producers should, in consequence, be insufficiently remunerated. If values remain the same, what becomes of prices is immaterial, since the remuneration of producers does not depend on how much money, but on how

much of consumable articles, they obtain for their goods. Besides, money is a commodity; and if all commodities are supposed to be doubled in quantity, we must suppose money to be doubled too, and then prices would no more fall than values would.

In sum, Say's Law was merely the denial of the possibility of a *general* overproduction of all goods and services.

If you had presented the classical economists with "the Keynesian case"—if you had asked them, in other words, what they thought would happen in the event of a fall in the price of commodities, if money wage-rates, as a result of union monopoly protected and insured by law, remained rigid or rising—they would have undoubtedly replied that sufficient markets could not be found for goods produced at such economically unjustified costs of production and that great and prolonged unemployment would result. Certainly this is what any modern subjective-value theorist would reply.

2. *Ricardo's Statement*

We might rest the case here. But such a hullabaloo has been raised about Keynes's alleged "refutation" of Say's Law that it seems desirable to pursue the subject further. One writer [9] has distinguished "the four essential meanings of Say's Law, as developed by Say and, more fully, by [James] Mill and Ricardo." It may be profitable to take her formulation as a basis of discussion. The four meanings as she phrases them are:

(1) Supply creates its own demand; hence, aggregate overproduction or a "general glut" is impossible.

(2) Since goods exchange against goods, money is but a "veil" and plays no independent role.

(3) In the case of partial overproduction, which necessarily implies a balancing underproduction elsewhere, equilibrium

9 Bernice Shoul, "Karl Marx and Say's Law," *The Quarterly Journal of Economics,* Nov., 1957, p. 615.

is restored by competition, that is, by the price mechanism and the mobility of capital.

(4) Because aggregate demand and supply are necessarily equal, and because of the equilibrating mechanism, output can be increased indefinitely and the accumulation of capital proceed without limit.

I shall contend that of these four versions, 1, 3 and 4 are correct, properly interpreted and understood; that only version 2 is false as stated, and that even this is capable of being stated in a form that is correct.

Now Ricardo clearly stated the doctrine in versions 1, 3, and 4; and though he implied it also in version 2, his statement even of this can be interpreted in a sense that would be correct:

> M. Say has . . . most satisfactorily shown that there is no amount of capital which may not be employed in a country, because a demand is only limited by production. No man produces but with a view to consume or sell, and he never sells but with an intention to purchase some other commodity, which may be immediately useful to him, or which may contribute to future production. By producing, then, he necessarily becomes either the consumer of his own goods, or the purchaser and consumer of the goods of some other person. It is not to be supposed that he should, *for any length of time,* be ill-informed of the commodities which he can most advantageously produce, to attain the object which he has in view, namely, the possession of other goods; and, therefore, it is not probable that he will *continually* produce a commodity for which there is no demand.
>
> There cannot, then, be accumulated in a country any amount of capital which cannot be employed productively until wages rise so high in consequence of the rise of necessaries, and so little consequently remains for the profits of stock, that the motive for accumulation ceases. While the profits of stock are high, men will have a motive to accumulate. Whilst a man has any wished-for gratification unsupplied, he will have a demand for more commodities; and it

will be an *effectual demand* while he has any new value to offer in exchange for them. . . .

Productions are always bought by productions, or by services; money is only the medium by which the exchange is effected. Too much of a particular commodity may be produced, of which there may be such a glut in the market as not to repay the capital expended on it; but this cannot be the case with respect to all commodities.[10]

The italics above are my own, intended to bring out the fact that Ricardo by no means denied the possibility of gluts, but merely of their indefinite prolongation.[11] In his *Notes on Malthus,* in fact, Ricardo wrote: "Mistakes may be made, and commodities not suited to the demand may be produced—of these there may be a glut; they may not sell at their usual price; but then this is owing to the mistake, and not to the want of demand for productions." [12]

The whole of Ricardo's comment on this phase of Malthus's thought will repay study. "I have been thus particular in examining this question [Say's Law]," wrote Ricardo, "as it forms by far the most important topic of discussion in Mr. Malthus' work." [13]—*i.e.,* Malthus's *Principles of Political Economy.*

It was Malthus who, in 1820, more than a century before Keynes, set himself to "refuting" Say's Law. Ricardo's answer (most of which was not discovered or available until recent years) is devastating. If it had been earlier available in full, it would have buried Malthus's fallacious "refuta-

[10] David Ricardo, *The Principles of Political Economy and Taxation,* (Everyman ed., New York), pp. 193-194.

[11] The phrase "effectual demand," however, was italicized merely to bring out here the fact that Keynes did not invent this phrase. Ricardo even uses the phrase "effective demand" in his *Notes on Malthus* (Sraffa edition, Cambridge University Press, p. 234). The term "effectual demand" was actually introduced by Adam Smith in *The Wealth of Nations* (Book I, Chap. 7). John Stuart Mill explains. "Writers have . . . defined [demand as] the wish to possess, *combined with the power of purchasing.* To distinguish demand in this technical sense, from the demand which is synonymous with desire, they call the former *effectual* demand." *Principles of Political Economy,* 1848, Book III, Chap. II, § 3.

[12] Sraffa edition, Cambridge University Press, p. 305.

[13] *Op. cit.,* pp. 306-307.

tion" forever. Even as it was, it prevented its exhumation until Keynes's time.

Ricardo's answer was, it is true, weak or incomplete at certain points. Thus he did not address himself to the problem of what happens in a crisis of confidence, when for a time even the commodities that are relatively underproduced may not sell at existing price levels, because consumers, even though they have the purchasing power and the desire to buy those commodities, do not trust existing prices and expect them to go still lower. But the basic truth of Say's Law (and Say's Law was only intended as a basic or *ultimate* truth) is not invalidated but merely concealed by a temporary abnormal situation of this kind. This situation is possible only in those periods when a substantial number of consumers and businessmen remain unconvinced that "bottom" has been reached in wages and prices, or feel that their job or solvency may still be in danger. And this is likely to happen precisely when wage-rates are artificially forced or held above the equilibrium level of marginal labor productivity.

Again, it is true that Ricardo declares at one point (already quoted) that "Money is only the medium by which the exchange is effected." If this is interpreted to mean, as Bernice Shoul interprets it, that money "plays no independent role," then of course it is not true. But if it is interpreted to mean: "If we, for the moment, *abstract from* money, we can see that *in the ultimate analysis* goods exchange against goods," then it is both true and methodologically valid.

Having recognized this truth, of course, we must in the solution of any dynamic problem *put money back* into our equation or "model" and recognize that in the modern world the exchange of goods is practically always through the medium of money, and that the interrelationship of goods and money-prices must be right for Say's Law to be valid. But this is merely to return to the qualification of correct price relationships and equilibrium that has always been implicit in the statement of Say's Law by the leading classical economists.

3. *The Answer of Haberler*

Before leaving this subject it may be important to address ourselves to some of the confusions about it, not of Keynes himself, but of the "post-Keynesians." Prof. Gottfried Haberler has been by no means uncritical of Keynes,[14] but his discussion of Keynes's discussion of Say's Law is peculiar. He presents part of the quotation I have already presented from Ricardo (on pp. 37-38) but does so in truncated form, and ends with the sentence: "Money is only the medium by which the exchange is effected." He then declares: "The meaning of this original formulation of this law seems to me quite clear: It states that income received is always spent on consumption or investment; in other words, money is never hoarded. . . ." [15]

Now the meaning of Ricardo's formulation of Say's Law is already quite clear, particularly when it is given in full. It does not require any exegesis by Haberler or anyone else, and certainly no paraphrase that quite changes its meaning. Not only did Ricardo never explicitly assert the proposition that Haberler attributes to him; there is every reason to suppose that he would have repudiated it. At several points he actually describes what we today might call money hoarding and its effects. At many points in his *Notes on Malthus* he writes, regarding some view that Malthus attributes to him: "Where did I ever say this?" [16] We may be confident that he would have written the same regarding this Haberler "interpretation."

> Our conclusion, thus [Haberler goes on] is that there is no place and no need for Say's Law in modern economic theory

[14] Haberler's comments on the *General Theory* in Chap. 8 of the third edition of his *Prosperity and Depression* (Geneva: League of Nations, 1941) contain many penetrating observations.

[15] *The New Economics*, ed. by Seymour E. Harris, p. 174.

[16] See, e.g., Sraffa edition, p. 424.

> and that it has been completely abandoned by neo-classical economists in their actual theoretical and practical work on money and the business cycle. . . . Summing up, we may say that there was no need for Keynes to rid neo-classical economics of Say's Law in the original, straightforward sense, for it had been completely abandoned long ago.[17]

The short answer to this is that there is still need and place to assert Say's Law whenever anybody is foolish enough to deny it. It is itself, to repeat, essentially a negative rather than a positive proposition. It is essentially a rejection of a fallacy. It states that a *general* overproduction of *all* commodities is not possible. And that is all, basically, that it is intended to assert.

Haberler is right insofar as he denies the belief of Keynes (and such disciples as Sweezy) that Say's Law "still underlies the whole classical theory, which would collapse without it" (*General Theory,* p. 19). It is true that Say's Law is not *explicitly* needed in the solution of specific economic problems *if its truth is tacitly taken for granted.* Mathematicians seldom stop to assert that two and two do not make five. They do not explicitly build elaborate solutions of complicated problems upon this negative truth. But when someone asserts that two and two make five, or that an existing depression is the result of a general overproduction of everything, it is necessary to remind him of the error.

There is still another line of attack on Say's Law, which Haberler among others seems to adopt, and this is to assert that in the sense in which Say's Law is true it is "mere tautology." If it is tautological, it is so in the same sense in which basic logical and mathematical propositions are tautological: "Things that are equal to the same thing are equal to each other." One does not need to say this as long as one does not forget it.

To sum up, Keynes's "refutation" of Say's Law, even if it had been successful, would not have been original: it does not go an inch beyond Malthus's attempted refutation

17 *Op. cit.,* pp. 175-176.

more than a century before him. Keynes "refuted" Say's Law only in a sense in which no important economist ever held it.

4. *To Save Is to Spend*

Risking the accusation of beating a dead horse, I should like to address myself to one more effort by Keynes to disprove Say's Law, or what he calls "a corollary of the same doctrine" (p. 19). "It has been supposed," he writes, "that any individual act of abstaining from consumption necessarily leads to, and amounts to the same thing as, causing the labor and commodities thus released from supplying consumption to be invested in the production of capital wealth" (p. 19). And he quotes the following passage from Alfred Marshall's *Pure Theory of Domestic Values* (p. 34) in illustration:

> The whole of a man's income is expended in the purchase of services and of commodities. It is indeed commonly said that a man spends some portion of his income and saves another. But it is a familiar economic axiom that a man purchases labor and commodities with that portion of his income which he saves just as much as he does with that he is said to spend. He is said to spend when he seeks to obtain present enjoyment from the services and commodities which he purchases. He is said to save when he causes the labor and the commodities which he purchases to be devoted to the production of wealth from which he expects to derive the means of enjoyment in the future.

This doctrine, of course, goes much further back than Marshall. Keynes could have quoted his *bête noir,* Ricardo, to the same effect. "Mr. Malthus," wrote Ricardo, "never appears to remember that to save is to spend, as surely as what he exclusively calls spending." [18] Ricardo went much further than this, and in answering Malthus answered one of Keynes's chief contentions in advance: "I deny that the

[18] David Ricardo, *Notes on Malthus* (Sraffa edition), p. 449.

wants of consumers generally are diminished by parsimony —they are transferred with the power to consume to another set of consumers." [19]

And on still another occasion Ricardo wrote directly to Malthus: "We agree too that effectual demand consists of two elements, the *power* and the *will* to purchase; but I think the will is very seldom wanting where the power exists, for the desire of accumulation [*i.e.*, saving] will occasion demand just as effectually as a desire to consume; it will only change the objects on which the demand will exercise itself." [20]

For the present, however, it may be sufficient merely to note Keynes's contention on this point rather than to try to analyze it in full. There will be plenty of opportunity for that later. As we shall see, Keynes himself alternates constantly between two mutually contradictory contentions: (1) that saving and investment are "necessarily equal," and "merely different aspects of the same thing" (p. 74), and (2) that saving and investment are "two essentially different activities" without even a "nexus" (p. 21), so that saving not only *can* exceed investment but *chronically* tends to do so. The second is the view which he chooses to support at this point. We shall have occasion to analyze both views later. For the present it is sufficient merely to note the presence of this deep-seated contradiction in Keynes's thought.[21]

19 *Ibid.*, p. 309.

20 *Letters of Ricardo to Malthus*, ed. by Bonar (1887). Letter of Sept. 16, 1814, p. 43.

21 Supplementing the present chapter, the reader is referred to the remarkable statement and defense of Say's Law by John Stuart Mill, quoted at length on pp. 364-371.

Chapter IV

OVERTURE

1. *"Effective Demand"*

Chapter 3 of the *General Theory* bears the impressive title, "The Principle of Effective Demand," but the title gives a wrong impression of its contents. Its function in Keynes's book is rather like that of an overture to a light opera, in which the composer weaves together and writes variations on the principal themes that are to follow.

The chapter consists of three sections. The first two are technical and "scientific," the third gay and satiric. As the whole chapter merely foreshadows what is to be unfolded in detail in the following pages, we need not make a lengthy analysis of it here. But as the first two sections purport to present "the essence of the General Theory of Employment," some general comments seem called for.

The whole of the *General Theory* might be described as an exercise in obfuscation, and the obfuscation begins at an early point. L. Albert Hahn has compared the reading of Keynes to watching "a sort of trick film. Everything happens in a manner that is exactly the opposite of what [the non-Keynesian] is used to." [1]

The comparison is apt. Keynes is constantly reversing cause and effect, putting the cart before the horse. "Entrepreneurs," he tells us, "will endeavor to fix the amount of employment at the level which they expect to maximize the excess of the proceeds over the factor cost" (pp. 24-25).

Now this statement is not flatly untrue; but it is certainly a misleading way of describing what happens. Entrepre-

[1] *Common Sense Economics,* (New York: Abelard-Schuman, 1956), p. ix.

neurs do not "endeavor to fix the amount of employment" at any preconceived "level." Each entrepreneur is trying to make a profit by producing and selling a certain product. The product having been decided upon, he then decides what sort of factory to put up, what sort of equipment to install, what raw materials to order, and what particular kinds of labor to employ. His decision regarding his total output will depend in part upon the amount of capital he can raise and upon his estimate of comparative gross receipts and costs. In determining the relative amounts of equipment he will buy or labor he will hire, he will be guided by the prices of the first and the wage-rates of the second; his proportions may vary depending upon this price-wage relationship. As a result of this complex of decisions, a certain number of workers of different kinds will be hired. But this is simply *one* of the consequences of the *total complex* of decisions. Entrepreneurs are certainly not "endeavoring to fix," in advance, any given "level" of employment. The amount of employment is not their object; it is merely incidental to their object.

If the foregoing sentence from Keynes had existed in isolation, it would not be worth all this discussion. But Keynes repeatedly and chronically describes the matter in this way. His mathematical equations implicitly take for granted that entrepreneurs think in this way and decide the amount of employment they will provide. His equations also often seem to imply that all entrepreneurs are organized as a monopoly. This way of thinking and of stating the case, in fact, seems to be essential to his theory.

And Keynes launches early upon a great deal of quite unnecessary and merely confusing algebra, which he makes still more confusing by the use of symbols which have no simple and natural connection with the thing they symbolize. In fact, it may be doubted whether this algebra is either appropriate or valid as applied to the loose abstractions with which Keynes deals.

The first equations in his book occur on page 25:

> Let Z be the aggregate supply price of the output from employing N men, the relationship between Z and N being written $Z = \phi(N)$, which can be called the *Aggregate Supply Function*. Similarly, let D be the proceeds which entrepreneurs expect to receive from the employment of N men, the relationship between D and N being $D = f(N)$, which can be called the *Aggregate Demand Function*.

As "aggregate supply price" in this context merely means aggregate cost or marginal cost, this paragraph could have been simply written, without any mathematical ostentation, about as follows: "The total cost of producing a given output will vary with the number of men employed, and the proceeds that entrepreneurs expect to receive from the sale of that output will also vary with the number of men employed."

Roughly speaking, this may often be true. But Keynes, by putting his statements into the form of mathematical equations, affects to be speaking *precisely*. To assert, in a mathematical equation, that one quantity is a function of another, is to assert that, at least within a specified range of values, there is *always a precise, determinate, and predictable* relationship between the two quantities. I choose a definition from the nearest algebra text on my shelves: "If a variable y is related to a variable x in such a way that each assignment of a value to x *definitely determines* one or more values of y, then y is called a FUNCTION of x." [2] (My italics.)

As soon as we apply rigorous standards, Keynes's equations simply fade away. Is there a constant, precise, determinate, and predictable relationship between the number of men a manufacturer employs and either his costs or his gross receipts? Obviously not. Both his costs and his receipts will depend, not merely upon the *number* of men he employs, but upon the quality of the individual

[2] Gerald E. Moore, *Algebra*, (New York: Barnes & Noble, 1956 edition), p. 50.

men and the nature of their skills. His costs will depend not only upon the individual and total wage-*rates* he pays, but upon his plant, the equipment he installs, the raw materials he buys, his transport costs, and the changing prices of all of these. His receipts will depend upon the changing prices he gets for his output. The price he pays for raw materials may change in relation to the price he gets for his finished product, and the prices he pays or gets will constantly change in relation to the wage-rates he has to pay. Changes in relative costs, or technical progress, may constantly alter the relationship of the number of men employed to the total product. In short, any relationship between payrolls and total costs on the one hand, and payrolls and expected gross receipts on the other, will exist only for an instant of time. There is no assurance whatever that any change in the number of men employed—*i.e.,* any change in N—will mean any precise or predeterminable change in either Z or D.

Many other things are wrong with Keynes's formulation, besides its mere invalidity. No manufacturer says to himself: "I shall hire N number of men, and this will give me total cash costs of Z and total cash receipts of D." He begins the other way round. He begins by deciding either how much money he can afford to lay out, say Z, or how much of a product he could make or sell, getting receipts of D. And *then* he decides how many men he will need or can afford. So if a functional relationship could be posited at all, it ought to be the converse of the one posited by Keynes, and N would be, say, a function of D or a function of Z.

There are further difficulties with the formulation. Z is apparently defined as a real sum, and N is certainly defined as a real sum, but D is defined merely as an *expectation.* "Let D be the proceeds which entrepreneurs *expect* to receive from the employment of N men." No doubt expectations concerning the future, if reasonable, can bear a rough relationship to present realities. But can we posit a *constant, determinate, or precise* relationship of expectations to realities? Can we put expectations into a meaningful mathematical equation?

If Keynes, here or elsewhere, used the word "function" as a mere *figure of speech,* we might let it pass. But to put these alleged relationships solemnly into the form of an equation, without attempting to support this equation with any rigorous deductive argument, or any appeal to statistical confirmation, or anything but a bald dogmatic *ipse dixit,* is another matter.

Moreover, Keynes continues: "The value of D at the point of the aggregate demand function, where it is intersected by the aggregate supply function, will be called *the effective demand."* (His italics, p. 25.) But as D has been defined as "the proceeds which entrepreneurs *expect* to receive," surely this should be called only the *expected* effective demand. If it is merely expected, it can hardly be called "effective."

The whole term "effective demand" is today either nonsensical or confusing anyway. Modern economists do not need the adjective "effective" in front of "demand." Demand is effective by definition. If it is not effective, it is not called demand but need, desire, wish, or longing. The word "demand" implies the requisite desire along with the requisite purchasing power. If Keynes meant *aggregate* demand, then that is the adjective he should have used and stuck to. If he meant aggregate *monetary* demand or aggregate monetary purchasing power, then these are the terms he ought to have used when this was what he meant.

The confusions in his terminology merely compound the confusions in his thought. Immediately after the equation and the definition I have just quoted, Keynes tells us: "This is the substance of the General Theory of Employment" (p. 25). And on the baseless fabric of this vision are all his cloud-capp'd towers built!

This invalid equation is part of Keynes's "disproof" of Say's Law.

> The classical theory assumes [he writes] that the aggregate demand price (or proceeds) always accommodates itself to the aggregate supply price. . . . Thus Say's law, that the aggregate demand price of output as a whole is equal to its aggregate supply price for all volumes of output, is equivalent to the proposition that there is no obstacle to full employment (p. 26).

This passage misstates both "classical theory" and the substance of Say's Law. Classical theory [3] does *not* assume that demand price (aggregate or otherwise) "always" accommodates itself to (aggregate) supply price. Neo-classical theory asserts that *under conditions of equilibrium,* such-and-such consequences or corollaries follow. But it does *not* assert that conditions will necessarily be in equilibrium. It does assert that under conditions of free competition, with flexible and fluid prices and wages, there will always be a *tendency* toward equilibrium. Say's Law, of course, does not declare, either actually or by implication, that "there is no obstacle to full employment." It does declare that the only obstacle to full employment is lack of equilibrium somewhere.

2. *The Propensity to Consume*

The second section of Chapter 3 gives us our first introduction to "the propensity to consume." This is the proposition that: "The psychology of the community is such that when aggregrate real income is increased aggregate consumption is increased, but not by so much as income" (p. 27).

[3] It is often difficult to know precisely how to treat Keynes's terminology. When he speaks of "classical" theory he usually means what it would be more accurate to call neo-classical theory or, still more specifically, Marshallian or Pigovian theory. He seldom means modern subjective-value theory, the existence of which he most often prefers to ignore. Still less does he consider the actual divergence of theories among economists. Is it in order to be considered original that he tries to lump all other views than his own under the common epithet "classical" or "orthodox"? It would be tedious, however, to pick him up each time on his misuse of terms. I shall try to economize the reader's time by accepting some of his terms, after filing the requisite caveat on their first appearance, in order to get on with the analysis.

There will be plenty of time later for full analysis of this curious proposition, about which there has been so much ado, but one or two observations may be made here. By speaking of the "psychology" of the community, and by using the slightly contemptuous term "propensity," Keynes manages to insinuate the notion that the way people spend their incomes is essentially non-rational or irrational.

It will also be noticed that his proposition is vague, and open to several different interpretations. If the community, as it grows richer, spends *the same proportion* of its income on consumption, then of course consumption will not increase by *the same absolute amount* as income; but the difference will presumably be made up by the same proportional increase in investment. If the community, as it grows richer, spends *a smaller proportion* of its income on consumption, then of course it must spend a larger proportion on investment. But Keynes never tells us unequivocally which, or what, he means. In drawing inferences from his "psychological law," he goes on to declare: "Thus, to justify any given amount of employment there must be an amount of current investment sufficient to absorb the excess of total output over what the community chooses to consume when employment is at the given level" (p. 27).

Here is a truism introduced under the guise of a great discovery. Naturally if we divide all spending under a full-employment equilibrium into two kinds—"consumption" and "investment" spending—there must be sufficient "investment" spending to make up the difference between "consumption" spending and total spending if we are to have full employment. But this portentous discovery could be applied not only to "investment" but to anything whatever. If we divide the amount of spending necessary for full employment into spending on everything else but beer, plus the spending on beer, then full employment depends on the amount spent on beer. Or, putting it into the same Keynesian phraseology as that quoted above: "To justify any given amount of employment there must be an amount of beer consumed sufficient to absorb the excess of total output over what the community chooses to spend on everything else but beer when employment is at the given level." And you can also put all this into an impressive set of mathematical equations.

(I may anticipate later discussion here by pointing out that the difference between "consumption" and "investment" is at least to some extent arbitrary, and not at all as clear-cut as Keynes sometimes makes it out to be. Is the purchase of a house a consumption expenditure or an investment? If you buy it as a home it is considered a consumption good; but if you buy it to rent to somebody else it is an investment. This would apply as well to an automobile or a power mower. "Consumption" and "investment" goods are not necessarily different *kinds* of goods: they change their nature with their state of processing, whose hands they are in, or the changing purposes of their owners.)

Having made his great division between "consumption" and "investment" goods, Keynes proceeds to build the whole of Keynesian economics upon it. He sums this up in the following paragraph (on p. 28) and in a series of eight propositions on the next page. These two pages might be called the heart of Keynesian economics. As I have already stated, the propositions will be analyzed at length in the following pages; but as this is our first acquaintance with them, we may make some preliminary remarks.

"Given the propensity to consume," he begins, "and the rate of new investment, there will be only one level of employment consistent with equilibrium" (p. 28). The independent clause in this sentence would be completely true, especially without the dependent phrases. *There is only one level of employment consistent with full equilibrium, and that is full employment.* This is true *by definition.* If there is unemployment, there must be disequilibrium somewhere. When Keynes writes: "The effective demand associated with full employment is a special case, only realized when the propensity to consume and the inducement to invest stand in a particular relationship to one another" (p. 28), he is either resorting to inexcusable mystification or he is writing nonsense. With equilibrium there is always full employment.

We could, of course, write the foregoing sentence from Keynes like this: "Full employment is a special case, only realized when there is full equilibrium, which in turn is only realized when consumption and investment are together sufficient to provide full employment." This would be true, but it would all be true by the very definition of our terms. We would only put the statement in that form as a sort of joke, as if one were to say: "A week is a special case, only realized when it contains just seven days, no more and no less, in succession."

Equilibrium, in short, exists only when the conditions of equilibrium are fulfilled. One of those conditions is full employment. And full employment *always* exists when there is equilibrium.

When Keynes speaks, therefore, as he does here and elsewhere, of "equilibrium" with underemployment, he is talking nonsense. This is a contradiction in terms, like talking of an orderly chaos or a triangular circle. When Keynes speaks, in short, of an "equilibrium" with unemployment, *he is not really speaking of a position of equilibrium at all,* but of something quite different. He is speaking of a *frozen* situation, a frozen *dis*equilibrium, a situation in which some price, interest rate, or wage-rate, or many prices, interest rates, and wage-rates, are prevented, either by contract, labor-union resistance, or government intervention, from adjusting to an equilibrium level.

This flagrant misuse of terms is one of the central fallacies of the whole Keynesian system. When this misuse is recognized, his whole system collapses.[4]

[4] Sir William Beveridge, writing in 1931, stated the "classical" position as it was clearly understood before the Keynesian obfuscation: "Demand and supply in the long run are adjusted and production is directed only by movements of prices; if what should be flexible in the economic system is made rigid, there comes disequilibrium and a breaking strain. Is not that what is happening with

All this is not to argue—as Keynes sometimes likes to pretend the neo-classical economists do argue—that unemployment or disequilibrium is impossible, or even that full employment or full equilibrium is the usual state of affairs. On the contrary, the best neo-classical economists have always recognized that *completely* full employment or *perfect* equilibrium is *never* a fact, any more than perfection in any human condition.

The concept of "equilibrium" is primarily an economist's methodological *tool of thought*. Nor because perfect equilibrium is never realized in practice can this be dismissed as a useless tool of thought. An engineer speaks of a frictionless engine or one of 100 per cent efficiency, realizing quite well that no engine is frictionless and no machine 100 per cent efficient. But he needs these concepts as bench marks, standards, tools of thought. A mathematician deals conceptually with points without dimensions and lines without thickness, though the points and lines in his textbook do have dimensions and thickness or they could not be seen. The mathematician finds it highly valuable, and even indispensable, to use concepts of "irrational" numbers and "imaginary" numbers—such as the square root of minus one —the reality or rationality of which he may find it embarrassing to explain.

The economist too finds logical difficulties when he tries to think through the concept of perfect equilibrium. But such difficulties are encountered with nearly all the leading concepts of economics: "perfect competition," "full employment," "a stationary economy," "supply curves," "demand curves," etc. It is not my purpose here to discuss the merits of any particular concept. But most of those just named are useful and necessary tools of thought. The concept of equilibrium is indispensable, either for so-called "static" or so-called "dynamic" theory. The error comes

labor and its prices in Britain today—a rigidity of money wages out of accord with economic conditions, leading to incurable disequilibrium?" *Tariffs: The Case Examined* (London: Longmans, 1931), p. 240.

either when "equilibrium" is thought of as an existing fact, or ridiculed merely because it is not an existing fact. What is real is an ever present *tendency* toward equilibrium. Equilibrium tends to be more and more closely and quickly approached in proportion as competition, prices, and wages are fluid and free.

Keynes's error lies in using the word equilibrium in two quite different senses, one of which is entirely invalid. This is the confusion of "equilibrium" with a situation that for one reason or another is merely *frozen,* such as prolonged mass unemployment because of a prolonged maladjustment between prices of different commodities, or between individual wage-rates, or most often between prices and wage-rates. All of Keynes's propositions and deductions on pages 28-31 are the result of a misconception or misstatement of neo-classical theory.

We need not, therefore, try here to disentangle the errors in detail. But one general comment should be made. Keynes absurdly talked as if no classical economist had ever heard of panics, depressions, or unemployment. Of course the assumptions of static equilibrium, or the assumptions of a "stationary economy," are not in themselves sufficient to deal with business cycles. But they are necessary methodological pre-conditions for the understanding of business cycles. Unless we understand "static" assumptions, we cannot understand "dynamic" assumptions.

3. *Derision of Thrift*

In Section III of Chapter 3 Keynes really lets himself go for two and a half pages (32-34). There is, strictly speaking, no argument here—merely derision of the classical economists and of whatever they happened to think was an economic virtue. I quote some of his sentences seriatim, in separate paragraphs, followed by my own counterstatement.

"Ricardo conquered England as completely as the Holy Inquisition conquered Spain." The Inquisition conquered

Spain by force and torture; the only force Ricardo used was the force of logic. If we bring Keynes's comparison up to date, we shall have to say that Keynes has conquered the present Anglo-American academic world, and the present Western political world, almost as completely as Marx has conquered Russia and China.

"Not only was [Ricardo's] theory accepted by . . . statesmen and by the academic world. But controversy ceased; the other point of view completely disappeared; it ceased to be discussed." This has almost been the fate today, alas, at least in the universities, of non-Keynesian economics.

"The great puzzle of Effective Demand with which Malthus had wrestled vanished from economic literature. You will not find it mentioned even once in the whole works of Marshall, Edgeworth and Professor Pigou, from whose hands the classical theory has received its most mature embodiment." It was provincial of Keynes to treat his Cambridge teachers as representing the highest point reached by economics prior to his own emergence. After all, among his predecessors, there were Menger and Böhm-Bawerk in Austria, Walras in Switzerland, Wicksell in Sweden, John Bates Clark and Irving Fisher in America, and Jevons and Wicksteed in his own country. And among Keynes's contemporaries such figures as Mises, Hayek, Anderson, Knight and Röpke were carrying the logical rigor and unity of economics much beyond the point where Marshall had left it.

"It [the great puzzle of Effective Demand] could only live on furtively, below the surface, in the underworlds of Karl Marx, Silvio Gesell or Major Douglas." "Economic underworld" is a felicitous description of this literature. But Keynes seemed to imagine that his avowed association with it would suddenly make it respectable.

"The completeness of the Ricardian victory is something of a curiosity and a mystery." Far less of a mystery than the completeness of the Keynesian victory. The Ricardian system, at least, had an elegant self-consistency; it was logical within its assumptions, within its limited frame of reference; and it did not hopelessly confuse, as the Keynesian system does, short-term effects with long-term effects, or "static" theory with "dynamic" theory.

"It [the completeness of the Ricardian victory] must have been due to a complex of suitabilities in the doctrine to the environment into which it was projected." As the Keynesian victory must have been due to the political environment of 1936?

"That it reached conclusions quite different from what the ordinary uninstructed person would expect, added, I suppose, to its intellectual prestige." Keynes certainly reached conclusions quite different from what the ordinary uninstructed person would expect—for instance, that saving is a sin and squandering a virtue. And perhaps this had added to its current intellectual prestige.

"That its teaching, translated into practice, was austere and often unpalatable, lent it virtue." The "virtue" of Keynes's teaching is that it praised thriftlessness, reckless spending, and unbalanced budgets and was therefore extremely palatable to the politicians in power.

"That it was adapted to carry a vast and consistent logical superstructure, gave it beauty." This is true. As much, unfortunately, cannot be said for Keynesian economics, which is jerry-built and inconsistent, without economy or elegance.

"That it could explain much social injustice and apparent cruelty as an inevitable incident in the scheme of progress, and the attempt to change such things as likely on the whole to do more harm than good, commended it to authority." As Keynes's doctrine of government spending, artificially low interest rates, and printing-press money commends it to present-day political authorities?

"That it afforded a measure of justification to the free activities of the individual capitalist, attracted to it the support of the dominant social force behind authority." This is pure Marxian demagogy, which attributes beliefs to discreditable motives rather than to disinterested logic. A reply in kind might be that the popularity of Keynes's theory in academic circles reflects the poorly paid academician's envy of the successful businessman.

"But although the [Ricardian] doctrine itself has remained unquestioned by orthodox economists up to a late date, its signal failure for purposes of scientific prediction has greatly impaired, in the course of time, the prestige of its practitioners." The implied claim that Keynesian economics can make possible "scientific prediction" of future business fluctuations is pure claptrap. No system of economics can do this. The most that any economic reasoning can do is to say that such-and-such conditions, if they existed in isolation, would tend to have such-and-such results.[5] The Ricardian system, for all its shortcomings, did this much better than the Keynesian system. Forecasts based on Keynesian theory have had a pathetically bad record.

"For professional economists, after Malthus, were apparently unmoved by the lack of correspondence between the results of their theory and the facts of observation." This "lack of correspondence" existed mainly in Keynes's mind. Keynes never troubled to compare his own theory with "the facts of observation." As we shall see later, he was fond of making sweeping statements, not only without any attempt at statistical proof, but even where statistical proof already existed of their "lack of correspondence" with "the facts of observation."

> The celebrated *optimism* of traditional economic theory, which has led to economists being looked upon as Candides, who, having left this world for the cultivation of their gardens, teach that all is for the best in the best of all possible worlds provided we will let well alone, is also to be traced, I think, to their having neglected to take account of the drag on prosperity which can be exercised by an insufficiency of effective demand.

[5] For the reasons why economic forecasting cannot be "scientific" see Ludwig von Mises, *Human Action,* 1949, pp. 649, 866-868.

Keynes here allows his own rhetoric to carry him so far away from reality that it is hard to know where to begin in dissecting the passage. First of all, traditional economic theory was not celebrated in the popular mind for optimism but for pessimism. Carlyle's famous epithet, "the dismal science," sums up the popular nineteenth-century judgment of the economic theory of the day. Malthus's "laws of population" were thought to condemn the world to eternal existence at the merest subsistence level for the masses of the people. Ricardo's so-called "iron law of wages" (never his own description) was thought to make improvement in real wages impossible, at least without a slow increase in the "wages fund." Still again, it was not Candide who was the incurable optimist of Voltaire's blistering novel, but Pangloss; and Candide did not decide to cultivate his own garden until *after* his optimistic illusions had been completely shattered. Finally, the neo-classical economists never assumed prosperity and full employment except on the assumption of equilibrium. They did not assume that there was always equilibrium, but they did assume that there was a constant *tendency* back to equilibrium, however much disturbed, as long as competition and free prices and wages prevailed.

> For there would obviously be a natural tendency towards the optimum employment of resources in a Society which was functioning after the manner of the classical postulates. It may well be that the classical theory represents the way in which we should like our Economy to behave. But to assume that it actually does is to assume our difficulties away.

This passage merely shows that Keynes did not understand what the neo-classical postulates really were. It is because the labor unions and the politicians intervened to prevent the self-adjustments that would otherwise have taken place in the economy that prolonged mass unemployment and underemployment of resources occurred. Keynes blamed on the "classical postulates" the very stagnation caused by policies based on the Keynesian postulates.

For the Keynesian postulates and the Keynesian policies existed years before Keynes approved and tried to systematize them in the *General Theory*. They were, as we shall see, simply the old, old postulates and policies of inflationism (building up to an inevitable crash), government restrictionism, government "price-stabilization" policies, and wage-rates inflexible in the downward direction. The flexibility of wages, prices, and markets postulated by the neo-classical economists was prevented; and then the consequences were blamed on the neo-classical economics.

Chapter V

"LABOR UNITS" AND "WAGE UNITS"

We come now to a short chapter of Keynes's called "The Choice of Units." It is less than nine pages long; but it repays close analysis because it strikingly illustrates the inconsistencies in his thinking, as well as the loose, shifting, and sometimes self-contradictory concepts that he considered basic.

He begins by pointing out that the units in terms of which economists commonly work are unsatisfactory. He illustrates this by "the concepts of the National Dividend, the stock of real capital and the general price-level" (p. 37). The national dividend, for example, as defined by Alfred Marshall and A. C. Pigou, measures "the volume of current output or real income and not the value of output or money-income" (p. 38). On this basis, Keynes goes on, an attempt is made to erect "a quantitative science." But it is "a grave objection to this definition for such a purpose that the community's output of goods and services is a non-homogeneous complex which cannot be measured, strictly speaking, except in certain special cases, as for example when all the items of one output are included in the same proportion in another output."

This objection to the attempt to measure the national dividend (or, as Americans would call it, the national income) in "real" terms is perfectly valid as far as it goes. So, too, are Keynes's further objections to the way Pigou attempts to deal with the factor of obsolescence. As Keynes points out, when Pigou deducts for obsolescence, where there has been no change in the physical quantity of the factories or equipment under consideration, he "is covertly introducing changes in *value*" (p. 39). (Keynes's italics.) Keynes goes on to make the further objection that Pigou is unable, in real terms, "to evaluate new equipment against old when, owing to changes in technique, the two are not identical." And Keynes concludes that though Pigou is aiming at "the right and appropriate concept for economic analysis . . . until a satisfactory system of units has been adopted, its precise definition is an impossible task." He adds that the attempt to compare "real" outputs of non-homogeneous commodities or equipment presents "conundrums which permit, one can confidently say, of no solution."

These criticisms of the "quantitative indeterminacy" (p. 39) of such concepts as "the national income" and "the general price-level" must be accepted as correct. Keynes adds that such concepts properly belong only in "the field of historical and statistical description . . . for which perfect precision . . . is neither usual nor necessary":

> To say that net output today is greater, but the price-level lower, than ten years ago or one year ago, is a proposition of a similar character to the statement that Queen Victoria was a better queen but not a happier woman than Queen Elizabeth —a proposition not without meaning and not without interest, but unsuitable as material for the differential calculus. Our precision will be a mock precision if we try to use such partly vague and non-quantitative concepts as the basis of a quantitative analysis (p. 40).

Having made all these perfectly valid criticisms, Keynes does an astonishing thing. After pointing out that we cannot add non-homogeneous commodities or non-homogeneous capital equipment together to get any meaningful total in "real" terms (but only in terms of monetary value) he blandly assumes that we can add non-homogeneous labor together to get a meaningful total of "real" "labor-units."

Surely it ought to be clear that the labor of different individual workers is not only as non-homogeneous as commodities or capital equipment, but infinitely more so. True, it is not possible to add a ton of sand to a ton of gold watches and get a total that is meaningful in any other sense than as a weight, which is of no *economic* significance. But it is quite legitimate to add together millions of bushels of wheat of the same commercial grade, or millions of pounds of cotton of the same grade, to get a total that is significant economically.

When we try to add "labor-units" together in "real" terms, however, we are completely without any common standard of measurement. How can we add an hour's labor of a great surgeon to an hour's labor of a shoe clerk? How can we add an hour's work of a Yehudi Menuhin to an hour's work of a bricklayer? From a strictly scientific standpoint, even an hour's labor by a file clerk is never strictly equal in "real" terms to that of another file clerk. Differences in speed, accuracy, and intelligence must be taken into account. There may even be significant differences, in "real" terms, between the first hour's work of the same file clerk in the morning and his last hour's work in the afternoon.

None of these problems seems to give Keynes the slightest concern. Oblivious of all he has written a few pages back about the "mock precision" of attempts to add commodities in real terms, he writes:

> In dealing with the theory of employment I propose, therefore, to make use of only two fundamental units of quantity, namely, quantities of money-value and quantities of employment. The first of these is strictly homogeneous, and the second can be made so. For, insofar as different grades and kinds of labor and salaried assistance enjoy a more or less fixed relative remuneration, the quantity of employment can be sufficiently defined for our purpose by taking an hour's employment of ordinary labor as our unit *and weighting an hour's employment of special labor in proportion to its remunera-*

tion; i.e., an hour of special labor remunerated at double ordinary rates will count as two units. (My italics, p. 41.)

That an eminent economist should be capable of using such a concept and writing such a paragraph in 1936 seems incredible. This is precisely the concept that Karl Marx used in his attempt to establish his famous labor theory of value in "Das Kapital" in 1867. This concept was demolished unanswerably by Böhm-Bawerk in 1896.

Marx attributed all the value of commodities to the labor that went into them. When asked what he meant by this labor, and how he measured it, he called it "simple average labor":

> Skilled labor [he wrote] counts only as intensified, or rather multiplied, simple labor, so that a smaller quantity of skilled labor is equal to a larger quantity of simple labor. Experience shows that skilled labor can always be reduced in this way to the terms of simple labor. No matter that a commodity may be the product of the most highly skilled labor, its value can be equated with that of the product of simple labor, so that it represents merely a definite amount of simple labor.[1]

Böhm-Bawerk travestied this in a passage in his *Karl Marx and the Close of His System,* (English ed., 1898, p. 162):

> With the very same reasoning one could affirm and argue the proposition that the quantity of material contained in commodities constitutes the principle and measure of exchange value—that commodities exchange in proportion to the *quantity of material incorporated in them.* Ten pounds of material in one kind of commodity exchange against ten pounds of material in another kind of commodity. If the natural objection were raised that this statement was obviously false because ten pounds of gold do not exchange against ten pounds of iron but against 40,000 pounds, or against a still greater number of pounds of coal, we may reply after the

[1] Karl Marx, *Capital* (Everyman's edition), I, 13-14.

> manner of Marx, that it is the amount of *common average material* that affects the formation of value, that acts as unit of measurement. Skillfully wrought, costly material of special quality *counts* only as compound or rather multiplied common material, so that a small quantity of material fashioned with skill is equal to a larger quantity of common material. *That this reduction is constantly made experience shows.* A commodity may be of the most exquisite material; its *value* makes it equal to commodities formed of common material, and *therefore represents only a particular quantity of common material.*

Keynes's "quantity of employment" in terms of "labor-units" is as incapable of physical or "real" measurement as is Marx's quantity of labor.

"It is my belief," writes Keynes, "that much unnecessary complexity can be avoided if we limit ourselves strictly to the two units, money and labor, when we are dealing with the behavior of the economic system as a whole" (p. 43). Yet these supposedly independent units of quantity, namely, "quantities of money value" and "quantities of employment," *are both merely quantities of money value.* If ten laborers each working for $8 a day are dismissed and two specialists each working for $40 a day are taken on, there is no change in the volume of employment, according to Keynes's method of reckoning in the quotation on page 62. Keynes's "quantity of employment" is not a quantity of employment. It is the quantity of money received by laborers who are employed.[2]

This interpretation is not shaken, but proved, by the very arguments that Keynes puts forward to defend his so-called "labor-unit." He writes:

> This assumption of homogeneity in the supply of labor is not upset by the obvious fact of great differences in the spe-

[2] Cf. Benjamin M. Anderson, *Economics and the Public Welfare,* p. 393. Also Frank H. Knight, *The Canadian Journal of Economics and Political Science,* February, 1937, p. 115: "What *can* anyone think he means by a physical unit of labor? Yet from beginning to end Mr. Keynes treats labor as a homogeneous fluid with a uniform price per unit."

> cialized skill of individual workers and in their suitability for different occupations. For, if the *remuneration* of the workers is proportional to their efficiency, the differences are dealt with by our having regarded individuals as contributing to the supply of labor in proportion to their remuneration. (My italics, pp. 41-42.)

If this remarkable assumption were valid, we should be equally justified in assuming homogeneity in the physical supply of goods and services. For if the market price of every article or service is proportional to its value, then "the differences are dealt with" by regarding each commodity or service as contributing to the total physical supply in proportion to its price!

We could follow Keynes through the still further logical legerdemain by which he seeks to defend his "labor-unit" concept. But this would be superfluous and tedious. The plain truth is that Keynes's "labor-unit" concept is open not only to every objection that he himself makes to the quantitative measurement of commodities, of the national income, or of the level of prices, but to objections of an even more serious and fundamental nature. He leaps out of the frying pan into the fire. He rejects concepts with a limited usefulness in order to embrace a concept that is worthless for any purpose. After having explained to us that such things as "net real output and the general level of prices" are "unsuitable as material for the differential calculus," he blandly proceeds to apply algebraic symbols and the differential calculus to his invalid concept of quantity of employment.

The chapter ends with some pretentious mathematical formulas and equations attempting to show that one of his nebulous and ill-defined "quantities" is a "function" of the other. It is a perfect example of "mock precision," of an inappropriate and worthless application of mathematics to economic analysis.

Chapter VI

THE ROLE OF EXPECTATIONS

Chapter 5 of the *General Theory,* "Expectation as Determining Output and Employment," is in the main both sensible and realistic.

Keynes begins by pointing out what ought to be obvious:

> All production is for the purpose of ultimately satisfying a consumer. Time usually elapses, however—and sometimes much time—between the incurring of costs by the producer (with the consumer in view) and the purchase of the output by the ultimate consumer. Meanwhile the entrepreneur . . . has to form the best expectations he can . . . and he has no choice but to be guided by these expectations, if he is to produce at all by the processes which occupy time (p. 46).

Keynes then goes on to distinguish "short-term" expectations, concerned with current production, from "long-term" expectations, concerned with additions to capital equipment. After introducing many needless elaborations and complications, he concludes:

> An uninterrupted process of transition . . . to a new long-period position can be complicated in detail. But the actual course of events is more complicated still. For the state of expectation is liable to constant change, a new expectation being superimposed long before the previous change has fully worked itself out. . . . (p. 50).

There would be little need to devote much attention to this chapter if Keynes's admirers and disciples had not made so much ado about it. "Expectations," writes Alvin H. Hansen (commonly regarded as Keynes's leading American disciple), "play a role in all Keynes's basic functional relations." [1] The British economist, J. R. Hicks, hails this

[1] *A Guide to Keynes,* (New York: McGraw-Hill, 1953), p. 53.

as a new and vitally significant element: "Once the missing element—anticipation—is added, equilibrium analysis can be used, not only in the remote stationary conditions to which many economists have found themselves driven back, but even in the real world, even in the real world in 'dis-equilibrium.' "[2]

Such a statement makes a reader rub his eyes in incredulity. It may be true that it has only recently become fashionable for academic economists to lay a great deal of emphasis on "expectations"—under that specific name. But most economists since Adam Smith's day have taken them into account, if only by implication. No one could ever have written about the fluctuations in the stock market, or in the price of wheat or corn or cotton, without doing so, at least implicitly, in terms of the expectations of speculators, investors, and the business community. And most writers on the business cycle have recognized the role that changes of expectations play in booms, panics, and depressions.

It was the practice of the older writers to introduce this element under the names of "optimism" and "pessimism," or "confidence" and "lack of confidence." Thus, to cite only a single example, Wesley C. Mitchell, as early as 1913, wrote:

> Virtually all business problems involve elements that are not precisely known, but must be approximately estimated even for the present, and forecast still more roughly for the future. Probabilities take the place of certainties, both among the data upon which reasoning proceeds and among the conclusions at which it arrives. This fact gives hopeful or despondent moods a large share in shaping business decisions.[3]

Even if academic economists had entirely neglected the role of expectations in economic changes, every speculator, investor, and businessman must from time immemorial

[2] "Mr. Keynes' Theory of Unemployment," *Economic Journal,* June, 1936, p. 240.

[3] *Business Cycles and Their Causes,* (University of California Press, 1941 edition), p. 5.

have been aware of the central role that expectations play. Every sophisticated speculator knows that the level of prices on the stock market reflects the composite expectations of the speculative, investment, and business communities. His own purchases or short sales are in effect a wager that his own expectations about future security prices are better than the composite current expectations against which he bets. Every investor and businessman is inescapably in part a speculator. The businessman not only has to calculate what consumers will be willing to pay for his product when it is ready for the market; he also has to guess correctly whether they are going to want that product at all.

The chief criticism to be made of Keynes's treatment of expectations (in Chapter 5) is not that it gives them too much emphasis, but too little. For that chapter is concerned with the effect of expectations merely on output and employment. Keynes should have recognized also that expectations are embodied and reflected in every price—including the price of the raw materials that the individual businessman has to buy, and the wage-rates that he has to pay.

One further observation, however, must be made on Chapter 5 of the *General Theory*. Throughout it Keynes makes the tacit (but never explicit) assumption that there is nearly *always* substantial unemployment. He assumes that when new workers are demanded in the capital equipment industries, for example, they are always *added* to the total volume of employment. They are apparently drawn out of some unspecified army of unemployed. Keynes never considers the possibility that the new capital-goods workers might have to be recruited from existing consumer-goods workers. He never considers what the effect of this competion for workers might be on raising wage-rates rather than merely increasing the volume of employment. Wage-rates are tacitly assumed to remain unchanged.

The limitations and nature of Keynes's assumptions, in short, make his theory of employment at best a *special* theory, not a *general* theory, as his title boasts.

Chapter VII

"STATICS" vs. "DYNAMICS"

The admirers of Keynes's *General Theory* never tire of contending that it is "dynamic." "It has helped to make us think of economics in dynamic rather than in static terms" writes Hansen.[1] And again: "The *General Theory* is something more than just static theory. Over and over again Keynes is thinking in highly dynamic terms."

Particularly since the appearance of the *General Theory,* there has grown up a whole pedantic literature about "period analysis," "rates-of-change analysis," and "comparative-statics analysis." This last is supposed to investigate "the response of a system to changes in given parameters."

Perhaps a word or two would not be out of place at this point about this obsession with methodology.

Most of the writers who compare "static" with "dynamic" economic analysis use the word "static" in a derogatory and the word "dynamic" in a laudatory sense. This disparagement of the "static" and love of the "dynamic" long precedes the appearance of the *General Theory* in 1936. It has existed in many fields besides economics. It seems to have had its origin in the popular association of "static" with stick-in-the-mud, and of "dynamic" with the idea of progress. Much of the current approbation of the "dynamic" and dislike of the "static" can be traced back, in fact, to the fashionable philosophies of Henri Bergson and John Dewey, as developed in the early part of the present century.

In economics, at all events, the great emphasis on the contrast between the two methods rests in large part on a mis-

1 Alvin H. Hansen, *A Guide to Keynes,* p. 47 and 51.

understanding. Economic analysis, even among the early classical economists, was to some extent dynamic. It is hard to think, in fact, of an important example of strictly "static" analysis. Such an analysis would merely portray economic relationships at a given instant of time. It would resemble a single snapshot. Even the analysis of the early classical economists was much closer to a motion picture. It devoted itself to explaining how and why changes took place.

This applies even to the famous concept of "the stationary state," notwithstanding the many confusions in that concept as held by Mill [2] and his predecessors. The concept of the stationary state did not profess to give a picture of the economy at a frozen instant of time. It was not like John Keats's Grecian Urn, with its "still unravish'd bride of quietness," and its

> Bold Lover, never, never canst thou kiss,
> Though winning near the goal—yet, do not grieve;
> She cannot fade, though thou hast not thy bliss,
> For ever wilt thou love, and she be fair!

The modern concept of the stationary economy, at all events, is a concept that envisages change, but change within certain constants. The stationary economy is one which does not grow and does not shrink; which does not on net balance either accumulate or consume capital; which is not subject to booms or depressions; in which prices and wages and the relative size of industries do not change; but in which, nonetheless, manufacturers constantly buy new raw materials as they sell finished products, and in which production, employment, buying, and consumption go steadily on.

Ludwig von Mises has more appropriately called this the *"evenly rotating economy."* [3] In the evenly rotating econ-

[2] See John Stuart Mill, *Principles of Political Economy,* Book IV, Chap. VI.

[3] See *Human Action,* (Yale University Press, 1949), esp. pp. 245-252. Mises, in fact, makes a distinction between the "evenly rotating economy" and "the stationary economy." Both are valid but refer to slightly different imaginary constructions.

omy the daily round and the seasonal or annual round of production and consumption and capital replacements are endlessly repeated. We might even call this, borrowing a phrase from Nietzsche, an "eternal recurrence" economy. Or we might think of it simply as an *"even-flow"* economy.

In any case, no good modern economist ever mistakes such concepts for descriptions of any actual economy. Some of the classical economists, it is true, thought of the stationary economy as a condition which would some day be achieved. Or they thought of it as an ideal condition. This was sheer confusion of thought, as is also the notion, still often met with today, that a state of economic "equilibrium" is necessarily more desirable than a state of "disequilibrium."

The "stationary" or "evenly rotating" economy is not, in short, a description of any actual state of affairs, or even of any achievable state of affairs. It is a *concept,* a *tool of thought,* a *postulate,* an *imaginary construction*—or (to use a word which is becoming increasingly fashionable) a model. It is necessary to frame such postulates, such imaginary constructions, in order to study their implications and deduce their hypothetical consequences. If we wish to study the effects of certain changes in the economy, we must understand first of all what the consequences would be if there were no such changes. We cannot know the meaning of motion unless we know the meaning of rest. We cannot understand a complex dynamic economy unless we first of all understand a simplified static economy. This method of setting up postulates, imaginary constructions, simplified models, and studying their implications and hypothetical consequences, is the main tool of modern economic analysis.[4]

We begin, say, by setting up a model of a stationary or evenly rotating economy, and drawing the deductions and consequences that follow from this simplified model. Next,

[4] Cf. Mises, *Human Action,* p. 237.

say, we set up a model of a changing economy—a shrinking or an expanding one, or one in which the relative size of individual firms or industries is changing. Next, perhaps, we study an economy in inflation and deflation. And finally, perhaps, we study the business cycle.[5]

In other words, we make a series of postulates or imaginary constructions beginning with the most simplified and moving on to the more complex and the more "realistic." Despite the enormous recent literature which implies, or explicitly states, the contrary, there is no difference *in kind* between the methods of "static analysis" and the methods of "dynamic analysis." There is merely a difference *in the specific hypotheses* made. "Static" analysis is a necessary first step to "dynamic" analysis. In static analysis we assume that only one thing (or one set of things) changes and everything else remains the same. We then study the necessary implications or consequences of this hypothesis. In "dynamic" analysis we successively assume that two things, then three things, then four things, then *n* things change. The more complicated "dynamic" hypotheses are not necessarily superior to the simpler "static" ones. The appropriateness or utility of the hypothesis we use depends mainly on the particular problem we are trying to solve. As we complicate our hypotheses we never, of course, do reach the nearly infinite complications of the real economic world, but we approach them as a limit.

Many modern economists, in a hurry, despise all the more simple or "static" assumptions and imagine that they can analyze full dynamic reality in a single leap by a sufficiently complicated set of simultaneous algebraic equations. This is self-deception. No doubt there are enough symbols in the Latin and Greek alphabets to go around, but there is likely to be considerable question about the quantitative determinateness of the concepts for which the symbols stand. Even after the algebraic solution of these complicated hy-

[5] For an excellent example of this procedure, see L. Albert Hahn, *Common Sense Economics* (New York: Abelard-Schuman, 1956).

potheses is arrived at, it will be very doubtful whether real (rather than merely hypothetical) numerical values can be attached either to the symbols or the results.

But the more modest method of beginning with simple hypotheses and advancing step by step to increasingly complicated ones has been increasingly refined and clarified, and used with increasing awareness, care, and precision, by a long line of great economists since the time of Ricardo. The method was developed to deal precisely with the problems of a "dynamic" economy, to deal precisely with the characteristics of "the economic society in which we actually live." It is a mistake to believe that we can skip over all "static" assumptions for the superficial reason that such assumptions are "unreal." This would be as foolish as it would be for a ballistic-missile designer to skip over all preliminary calculations of the probable flight or parabola of his missile through a frictionless medium, on the ground that no actual medium is every really frictionless.

In order to understand the consequences of dynamic assumptions we must first of all understand the consequences of static assumptions. The method of science is that of experimental or (when that is impossible) "hypothetical isolation." [6] It is the method of "successive approximations." [7] It is to study one change, force, or tendency at a time, whenever that is possible, even when it usually, or perhaps always, acts in combination with other forces, and then to study later the combinations, interrelations, and mutual influences of all the main changes, forces, or tendencies at work.

The belief that we can skip over all these tedious preliminaries, and surprise the secrets of the actual economy in one great leap by the use of simultaneous differential equations, is a double delusion. It disdains a method that is

[6] See Philip H. Wicksteed, *The Common Sense of Political Economy,* 1910. (London: George Routledge, 1946), I, 201-205.

[7] See Frank H. Knight, *Risk, Uncertainty and Profit,* (Boston: Houghton Mifflin, 1921), p. 8.

indispensable in order to embrace a method that is inappropriate and illegitimate.

But to the fallacies of "mathematical economics" we shall return later.

Before we leave this topic for the time being, it may be pointed out that even the concept of "equilibrium" (of a single price, a set of prices, or the whole economy), which is commonly cited as pre-eminently a "static" concept, is in large part dynamic.[8] It is a mental tool for enabling us to study, not merely a frozen state or a state of stable rest, but the forces and tendencies that are constantly at work (even when thwarted by institutional forces) to bring a state of disequilibrium back toward a state of equilibrium.

The very terms *equilibrium* and *disequilibrium, statics* and *dynamics,* are derived from physical and mechanical analogies. The most frequent examples chosen to illustrate the meaning of "static equilibrium" in economics are water tending toward its level, a swinging pendulum tending toward a state of rest, or marbles coming to rest against each other at the bottom of a basin. But when we examine any specific problem (or even these analogies), we find that we are chiefly concerned with equilibrium in economics not as a state of rest, but as a *process of moving* toward rest. We are concerned not with the abstract conditions of achieved equilibrium (the "balance" or mutual "cancellation" of opposing forces), but with the forces which bring a *tendency toward* equilibrium. But when we are considering the *process* by which an equilibrium is established, we are not in the field of statics but of dynamics.

What most economists really mean when they accuse other economists of using merely "static" analysis is that these other economists consider some important factor or factors as given or fixed, rather than as unknown or variable. In particular cases such criticisms may be quite valid. But if we try to solve any economic problem by assuming *noth-*

[8] Cf. Frank H. Knight, *The Ethics of Competition,* (London: Allen & Unwin, 1935), p. 141. Cf. also pp. 161-185.

ing as given and *everything* as variable, the world becomes simply a chaos—"a big, blooming, buzzing confusion." Fortunately, the economist is commonly able to do in thought what the physicist is often able to do in fact—to change *a, b, c, d,* etc., one at a time, then perhaps two at a time, then three at a time, to discover the separate effect of each, as well as their interrelations.

Appendix on "User Cost"

Chapter 6 of the *General Theory* begins with a few paragraphs about Keynes's concept of "user cost." It goes on to discuss the general concept of *income,* a discussion which is again interrupted by an eight-page "Appendix on User Cost."

This appendix on "user cost" is technical, needlessly obscure, and a digression. Few Keynesians give it much analysis. Alvin H. Hansen, indeed, tells us that the whole section on income (*G. T.* pp. 52-61, 66-73) "is of no great importance for an understanding of the *General Theory* and might quite well be omitted if the student so wishes." [9] However, not merely the section on Income, but the "Appendix on User Cost," deserve discussion for the light they throw on Keynes's thinking and writing in general.

The discussion of user cost, in fact, is an outstanding example of the incredibly awkward exposition that marks the *General Theory* through most of its length. Keynes begins (pp. 52-54) by throwing at the reader a complicated set of arbitrary algebraic symbols, with a slapdash and inadequate explanation of what they stand for, and almost no explanation of why they are necessary at all. It is not until the second half of this appendix that he tells us: "We have defined the user cost as the reduction in the value of the equipment due to using it as compared with not using it" (p. 70). This definition (which has not in fact been put in this simple and direct form until this point) should have been at

[9] *A Guide to Keynes,* (New York: McGraw-Hill, 1953), p. 54.

the very beginning of the exposition. Dudley Dillard has paraphrased it still more simply and compactly: "The loss of value resulting from using equipment rather than not using it is called the *user cost.*" [10]

The importance of this concept for Keynes's theory is that the entrepreneur is supposed to have to take this factor into consideration when he decides how many men to employ. No doubt he does. But this "user cost" is usually so small in comparison with total depreciation and maintenance costs which must be incurred in any event, that it is doubtful whether it plays a role of any real importance in determining the volume of production and employment at any given time.

The role played by it, in fact, is probably so small that it may be questioned whether a special name is needed to identify it. But if such a special name *is* needed, a more natural term such as "*using* cost" would perform the function better. Alfred Marshall, indeed, has put this cost under the simple heading of "extra wear-and-tear of plant." [11] Marshall is right, despite Keynes's protests, when he does little more than mention this in a discussion of prime and supplementary costs. A. C. Pigou is also right when he assumes that: "The differences in the quantity of wear-and-tear suffered by equipment and in the costs of non-manual labor employed, that are associated with differences in output, [can be] ignored, as being, in general, of secondary importance." [12]

Keynes tries to make his concept of "user cost" seem important by *including* in it the cost of raw materials (say, pounds of copper) that are "used up" in the process of manufacturing. The costs of such raw materials can, of course, be decisively important. But it is only confusing, not clarifying, to lump such costs with the cost of using

10 *The Economics of John Maynard Keynes,* (New York: Prentice-Hall, 1948), p. 68.

11 *Principles of Economics,* (New York: Macmillan, Eighth Edition), p. 360.

12 *The Theory of Unemployment,* (New York: Macmillan, 1933), p. 42.

fixed equipment that is depreciating or growing obsolete anyway. Where the raw material is of an unspecialized nature, as it most often is, the individual manufacturer commonly has the choice of deciding to resell it in the open market rather than use it to make some specialized finished article for which demand may have fallen.

The traditional analysis, in short, here corresponds much more closely with the facts of economic life and the decisions of entrepreneurs than does the more academic classification of Keynes. If Keynesians wish to call the cost of using-up *raw materials* the "using-up cost" (which would suggest the facts better than "user cost") they are entitled to do so. But in that case it would avoid confusion and be more appropriate to call the cost of using *equipment* rather than not using it "the wear-and-tear cost."

All this may be making much ado about a matter of very minor importance. But Keynes makes much ado about it in this appendix—though the matter plays no discoverable rôle whatever in the rest of his volume.

Chapter VIII

INCOME, SAVING, AND INVESTMENT

1. *Confusing Definitions*

Chapter 6, "The Definition of Income, Saving, and Investment," and Chapter 7, "The Meaning of Saving and Investment Further Considered" are among the most confused that even Keynes ever wrote. And upon their confusions are built some of the major fallacies in the *General Theory*.

Let us start with a sentence on page 55: "Furthermore, the *effective demand* [Keynes's italics] is simply the aggregate income (or proceeds) which the entrepreneurs expect to receive. . . ." This is loose writing, loose thinking, or both. Surely the "effective demand" cannot be what the entrepreneurs *expect* to receive, but what they do in fact receive. What they *expect* to receive must be merely what they *expect* the "effective demand" to be.

This confusion between expectations and realities, as we shall see, runs throughout the *General Theory*. Yet many Keynesians single out his treatment of expectations as Keynes's great "contribution" to, or even "revolution" in, economics. "This process of bringing anticipations out from between the lines," writes Albert G. Hart,[1] "is nowhere more dramatically illustrated than in the work of Keynes." Keynes himself confesses that in his *Treatise on Money* he "did not . . . distinguish clearly between expected and realized results." (*G. T.*, p. 77.) He repeatedly fails to do so also in his *General Theory*.

[1] In *The New Economics*, ed. by Seymour E. Harris, (New York: Alfred Knopf), p. 415.

> The aggregate demand function relates various hypothetical quantities of employment to the proceeds which their outputs are expected to yield; and the effective demand is the point on the aggregate demand function which becomes effective because, taken in conjunction with the conditions of supply, it corresponds to the level of employment which maximizes the entrepreneur's expectation of profit (p. 55).

Particularly as he has not bothered up to this point to explain some of the leading terms employed, this is as choice a specimen of involution and technical gobbledygook as one is likely to find anywhere. But the *General Theory* is rich in such jewels, and we shall have occasion to examine the multiple facets of many of them before we are through. (I spare the reader footnote 2, p. 55, which weaves mathematical equations into already intricate verbal crochet work; but the curious may wish to consult it.)

We are now ready to proceed to Keynes's definitions, respectively, of *Income, Saving,* and *Investment,* and of his reasons for finding saving and investment always equal.

But before we do this I must call attention to Keynes's apology for the "considerable confusion" (p. 61) he caused in his *Treatise on Money* by his use of the terms there, and to his confession (p. 78) that "the exposition in my *Treatise on Money* is, of course, very confusing and incomplete." It remains now to examine which is the more confusing—Keynes's exposition and use of the terms in his *Treatise on Money,* or his exposition and use of the terms in the *General Theory.*

If Keynes gives any simple definition of national income in Chapters 6 and 7, I cannot find it. As we shall see, his concept of income seems to be subject to change without notice. I am willing to accept Professor Hansen's word for it that: "Income in the current period is defined by Keynes as equal to current investment plus current consumption expenditures. Saving in the current period is, moreover, defined as equal to current income minus current consumption." [2]

Each of these key words, it will be noticed, is here defined in terms of the others. Such definitions are merely circular, and not in themselves enlightening. If we are told that X equals Y plus Z, then of course we know that Y equals X minus Z, and that Z equals X minus Y. Furthermore, if we know that X equals Y plus Z and that X also equals Y plus W, we know that W equals Z. But none of these transpositions or deductions can advance us very much until we have further knowledge of W, X, Y, or Z.

There are two chief questions to be asked concerning the use of terms and their definitions: (1) Is a given term and its definition *clear* and *consistent?* (2) Is a given set of terms or definitions more *useful* or enlightening than a more traditional set, or than possible alternatives? Let us now apply these two tests.

"Amidst the welter of divergent usages of terms," writes Keynes (p. 61), "it is agreeable to discover one fixed point. So far as I know everyone has agreed that *saving* means the excess of income over expenditure on consumption."

This definition, while at first sight apparently both simple and clear, ignores the vagueness in both the terms "saving" and "income." Either of these may be conceived in terms of *commodities,* or purely in terms of *money,* or in terms of a mixture of commodities and money. If an automobile dealer, for example, takes 100 cars from a manufacturer in a given year, and sells only 75 of them, the 25 cars that he has been unable to get rid of may be regarded by some economists as part of his "income" during that year and part of his "savings" during that year. He himself, however, may measure his income and savings purely in terms of his cash position, and regard his unsold cars as a mere misfortune. They will probably be carried on his books at cost or at some other arbitrary valuation; but the

2 Alvin H. Hansen, *A Guide to Keynes,* p. 58.

dealer will only measure his "income" and "savings" in accordance with the money-price at which his surplus cars are ultimately unloaded. We shall return to some of these points later.

2. *Why "Savings" Equals "Investment"*

> Our definition of income [continues Keynes] also leads us at once to the definition of *current investment*. For we must mean by this the current addition to the value of the capital equipment which has resulted from the productive activity of the period. This is, clearly, equal to what we have just defined as saving. For it is that part of the income of the period which has not passed into consumption (p. 62).

Now it is to be noticed here that Keynes has not only defined "investment" so that it is necessarily equal to "saving," but he has also so defined it that "investment" and "saving" must be *identical*. He does not admit this clearly, however, until twelve pages later, at the beginning of Chapter 7: "In the previous chapter *Saving* and *Investment* have been so defined that they are necessarily equal in amount, being, for the community as a whole, merely different aspects of the same thing" (p. 74). But before he gets to this admission of identity, he has already made and expanded upon his contention of equality:

> Whilst, therefore, the amount of saving is an outcome of the collective behavior of individual consumers and the amount of investment of the collective behavior of individual entrepreneurs, these two amounts are necessarily equal, since each of them is equal to the excess of income over consumption. . . . Provided it is agreed that income is equal to the value of current output, that current investment is equal to the value of that part of current output which is not consumed, and that saving is equal to the excess of income over consumption . . . the equality of saving and investment necessarily follows. In short—
>
> Income = value of output = consumption + investment.
> Saving = income − consumption.
> Therefore saving = investment (p. 63).

Now if, following the symbols used by the Keynesians, we let income be called Y, consumption C, investment I, and saving S, we arrive at the famous formulas:

$$Y = I + C.$$
$$S = Y - C.$$

Therefore:

$$I = S.$$

All this is undeniable—provided we define these terms and symbols as Keynes *in this chapter* defines them. We cannot say that this use of these terms, or that these definitions, are *wrong*. If Keynes, in fact, had *explicitly* defined *both* "saving" and "investment" as meaning simply *unconsumed output* (which he never did do) then not only the equality but the identity of "saving" and "investment" would have been obvious.

But while, to repeat, no usage or definition of words can be arbitrarily dismissed as "wrong," we may properly ask some questions of it. Is it in accordance with common usage? Or does it depart so much from common usage as to cause confusion—in the mind of the reader, or of the user himself? Does it help, or hinder, study of the problems involved? Is it precise, or vague? And finally, is it used or applied consistently?

We shall find, in fact, that Keynes's definitions of "saving" and "investment" which make them necessarily equal (and, indeed, "merely different aspects of the same thing," p. 74), have created great embarrassments for the Keynesians, and confusions and contradictions in the master. The embarrassments to the Keynesians come not only from the fact that Keynes had previously so defined "saving" and "investment" as to make them usually *un*equal (or occasionally equal only by a sort of happy accident), but from the fact that these *General Theory* definitions create many difficulties in subsequent Keynesian doctrines. In fact, Keynes abandons these definitions, without notice to the reader, in the latter part of the *General Theory,* and returns to his older concepts.

I have already referred to the apologies of one or two lines that Keynes makes (pp. 74 and 78) in the *General Theory* for the "very confusing and incomplete" definitions and exposition in his *Treatise on Money.* What he fails to point out, however, is that his whole concept of the terms is different, and that his whole theory of the relation of saving and investment has been radically changed. We do not have to do here with any mere differences in "definition" or in "exposition"; we have to do with the abandonment and repudiation of one of the major theories presented in the *Treatise on Money.* For in that treatise Keynes explains the whole Credit Cycle in terms of *differences* between "saving" and "investment."

"We shall mean by Savings," he writes, "the sum of the differences between the money-incomes of individuals and their money-expenditure on current consumption.[3]

It is to be noticed here that he defines "savings" specifically in terms of *money* incomes and expenditures. In his *General Theory* definitions, however, money is not explicitly mentioned either in defining savings or in defining investment. Keynes does declare, in defining investment in the *General Theory*: "Investment, thus defined, includes, therefore, the increment of capital equipment, whether it consists of fixed capital, working capital or liquid capital" (p. 75). He then adds: "The significant differences of definition . . . are due to the exclusion from investment of one or more of these categories" (p. 75).

Keynes's definition of investment quoted in the *General Theory,* therefore, includes "liquid capital," by which he apparently means both money and securities. But it surely merely adds confusion to call cash, for example, a part of "capital equipment." This confuses Keynes himself as he proceeds.

[3] *A Treatise on Money,* (New York: Harcourt-Brace, 1931), I, 126.

Let us return to his use of the terms *saving* and *investment,* and the theory he builds around this use, in his *Treatise on Money.* Keynes there explains the whole Credit Cycle in terms of "Saving running ahead of investment or vice versa" (I, 178). "On my theory," he writes, "it is a large volume of saving which does *not* lead to a correspondingly large volume of investment (not one which *does*) which is the root of the trouble." [4]

A hundred pages later on he is even more explicit: "It is not surprising that Saving and Investment should often fail to keep step. In the first place—as we have mentioned already—decisions which determine Saving and Investment respectively are taken by two different sets of people influenced by different sets of motives, each not paying very much attention to the other." [5] And he adds, in the same paragraph: "There is, indeed, no possibility of intelligent foresight designed to equate savings and investment unless it is exercised by the banking system." And at the end of the chapter he gives the reader to understand that this difference in effect describes "the genesis and life-history of the Credit Cycle." [6]

The distinction between "saving" and "investment" is, if anything, even more sharply drawn in Chapter 12 of the *Treatise on Money*:

> This "saving" relates to units of money and is the sum of the differences between the money-incomes of individuals and their money-expenditure in current consumption; and "investment" relates to units of goods. The object of this chapter is to illustrate further the significance of the distinction between these two things.
>
> Saving is the act of the individual consumer and consists in the negative act of refraining from spending the whole of his current income on consumption.
>
> Investment, on the other hand, is the act of the entre-

[4] *Ibid.,* I, 179.
[5] *Ibid.,* I, 279.
[6] *Ibid.,* I, 291.

> preneur whose function it is to make the decisions which determine the amount of the non-available output, and consists in the positive act of starting or maintaining some process of production or of withholding liquid goods. It is measured by the net addition to wealth whether in the form of fixed capital, working capital or liquid capital (I, 172).

It is significant that though Keynes here defines "saving" explicitly in terms of "units of money" and "investment" explicitly in terms of "units of goods," he then surreptitiously (or absentmindedly) introduces the element of money in "investment" under the term "liquid capital." Small wonder that he himself later found the whole thing "very confusing!" It may be pointed out here that in the *General Theory* Keynes constantly uses a word like "income" without specifying or distinguishing between real income and money income. This leads to constant confusion. And as we shall see, when we do distinguish constantly and clearly between real income and money income, such plausibility as the Keynesian theories may have begins to wear off. His "system" needs this ambiguity and confusion.

3. *Saving as the Villain*

It will be noticed, also, that in the very terms of his definitions in the *Treatise on Money,* Keynes manages to disparage saving while commending investment. The truth is that saving has always been the villain in the Keynesian melodrama. As far back as *The Economic Consequences of the Peace,* (1920), the book that first brought Keynes into world notice, we find passages like this:

> The railways of the world which [the nineteenth century] built as a monument to posterity, were, not less than the Pyramids of Egypt, the work of labor which was not free to consume in immediate enjoyment the full equivalent of its efforts.
>
> Thus this remarkable system depended for its growth on a double bluff or deception. On the one hand the laboring

> classes accepted from ignorance or powerlessness, or were compelled, persuaded, or cajoled by custom, convention, authority and the well-established order of Society into accepting, a situation in which they could call their own very little of the cake that they and Nature and the capitalists were co-operating to produce. And on the other hand the capitalist classes were allowed to call the best part of the cake theirs and were theoretically free to consume it, on the tacit underlying condition that they consumed very little of it in practice. The duty of 'saving' became nine-tenths of virtue and the growth of the cake the object of true religion. There grew round the non-consumption of the cake all those instincts of puritanism which in other ages has withdrawn itself from the world and has neglected the arts of production as well as those of enjoyment. And so the cake increased; but to what end was not clearly contemplated. Individuals would be exhorted not so much to abstain as to defer, and to cultivate the pleasures of security and anticipation. Saving was for old age or for your children; but this was only in theory,—the virtue of the cake was that it was never to be consumed, neither by you nor by your children after you (pp. 19-20).

This is a typical example of the satire and prose style of the Bloomsbury School (of which Keynes was a prominent member along with Lytton Strachey), but it cannot be taken seriously as economics. Its main purpose is obviously *pour épater le bourgeois;* it illustrates the frivolity and irresponsibility which are recurrent in Keynes's work. It is obviously absurd, for example, to say that labor "was not free to consume in immediate enjoyment the full equivalent of its efforts." It was the *capitalists* who were doing the saving; the workers saved only to the extent that their incomes permitted and their own voluntary prudence prescribed. Labor then, as now, was getting the full amount of its marginal contribution to the value of the product. There was no "bluff" and no "deception." As a result of this saving, the size of the "cake," it is true, was growing practically every year. But more "cake" was also being *consumed* practically every year.

I have tried to illustrate what was happening in my *Economics In One Lesson.*[7] As a result of annual saving and investment, total annual production increased each year. Ignoring the irregularities caused by short-term fluctuations, and assuming for the sake of mathematical simplicity an annual increase in production of 2½ percentage points, the picture that we would get for an eleven-year period, say, would run something like this in terms of index numbers:

Year	*Total Production*	*Consumers' Goods Produced*	*Capital Goods Produced*
First	100	80	20*
Second	102.5	82	20.5
Third	105	84	21
Fourth	107.5	86	21.5
Fifth	110	88	22
Sixth	112.5	90	22.5
Seventh	115	92	23
Eighth	117.5	94	23.5
Ninth	120	96	24
Tenth	122.5	98	24.5
Eleventh	125	100	25

* This of course assumed the process of saving and investment to have been already under way at the same rate.

What I tried to illustrate by this table is that total production increased each year *because of the saving,* and would not have increased without it. The saving was used year after year to increase the quantity or improve the quality of existing machinery and other capital equipment, and so to increase the output of goods. There was a larger and larger "cake" each year. Each year, it is true, not all of the currently produced "cake" was consumed. But there was no irrational or cumulative consumer constraint. For each year a larger and larger cake was in fact consumed; until, at the end of the eleventh year in our illustration, the

[7] (New York: Harper, 1946), p. 198.

annual consumers' cake alone was equal to the combined consumers' and producers' cakes of the first year. Moreover, the capital equipment, the ability to produce goods, was itself 25 per cent greater than in the first year. (My illustration of course assumed the long-run equality and identity of saving and investment.)

Now it is a notorious fact that in the nineteenth century, which Keynes is here deriding, there was not only continuous saving, and a tremendous increase in capital equipment, but a huge increase in population and a constant increase in the living standards of that population. Keynes himself, in fact, in the succeeding paragraph of the *Economic Consequences,* took the whole thing back. He was just having his little joke. But the problem is to know, even in his *Treatise on Money* and in his *General Theory,* when he is just having his little joke and when he is really in earnest. I suspect that he himself was sometimes a little confused on this point.

Benjamin M. Anderson, indeed, has suggested that Keynes's confusion on the whole concept of savings and investment in the *General Theory* could be interpreted as due to an effort

> to carry out a puckish joke on the Keynesians. He had got them excited in his earlier writings about the relation between savings and investment. Then, in his *General Theory,* he propounds the doctrine that savings are always equal to investment. This makes the theology harder for the devout follower to understand, and calls, moreover, for a miracle by which the disturbing factor of bank credit may be abolished.[8]

Keynes has certainly given his followers a great deal of embarrassment and trouble. Alvin H. Hansen, in his *Guide to Keynes,* tries manfully to save Keynes from himself:

[8] *Economics and the Public Welfare,* (New York: Van Nostrand, 1949), pp. 398-399. Frank H. Knight at the time expressed even wider doubts concerning Keynes's earnestness in the *General Theory:* "I for one simply cannot take this new and revolutionary equilibrium theory seriously, and doubt whether Mr. Keynes himself really does so." *The Canadian Journal of Economics and Political Science,* February, 1937, p. 121.

"One source of confusion arose from the failure of his critics to realize that while investment and saving are always *equal,* they are not always in *equilibrium.* All this could have been avoided had Keynes made it clear from the outset that the *equality* of saving and investment does not mean that they are necessarily in equilibrium" (p. 59).

They can be equal but not in equilibrium, Hansen goes on to suggest, if there is a "lag" or "lagged adjustment" of some kind. I confess myself unable to follow this argument. It seems to me a self-contradiction; for it seems to assume that because of a "lag" in "adjustment" savings and investment are not *always* equal.

Paul A. Samuelson tries to save Keynes from himself by suggesting that "The *attempt* to save may lower income and actually *realized* saving." On the other hand, "A net autonomous increase in investment, foreign bonds, government expenditure, consumption, will result in increased income *greater* than itself," etc., etc.[9]

I do not know how far it is intentional and how far unintentional humor when Samuelson suggests that the obscurities and contradictions of the *General Theory* are an embarrassment for the *anti-Keynesians* rather than for the Keynesians. But he actually writes, as I have previously quoted: "It bears repeating that the *General Theory* is an obscure book so that would-be anti-Keynesians must assume their position largely on credit unless they are willing to put in a great deal of work and run the risk of seduction in the process."

4. *Keynesian Paradoxes*

As we shall now see, however, Samuelson's suggested escape from the Keynesian saving-investment dilemma corresponds closely with the exit that Keynes himself tries to take. But this only lands Keynes into more confusions and contradictions. There are so many of these, in fact, that it

[9] Seymour E. Harris (ed.), *The New Economics,* p. 159.

would be tedious and unprofitable to attempt to point out more than a few.

Keynes argues at times, as we have seen, that saving and investment are not only always equal but "merely different aspects of the same thing." Yet he still keeps to his old habit of deploring saving while approving investment. So he must argue that saving *reduces* income and investment *increases* income—though "they are necessarily equal in amount," and "merely different aspects of the same thing" (p. 74)!

From here on I find it impossible to follow his distinctions, oscillations, reverses, and contradictions. In a long section (pp. 81-85) we are told: "The prevalence of the idea that saving and investment, taken in their straightforward sense, can differ from one another, is to be explained, I think, by an optical illusion . . ." (p. 81). There follows a long explanation of the "two-sided" nature of an individual depositor's relation to his bank. Then "the new-fangled view that there can be saving without investment or investment without 'genuine' saving" (p. 83) is described as erroneous: "The error lies in proceeding to the plausible inference that, when an individual saves, he will increase aggregate investment by an equal amount. It is true, that, when an individual saves he increases his own wealth. But the conclusion that he also increases aggregate wealth fails to allow for the possibility that an act of individual saving may react on someone else's savings and hence on someone else's wealth" (pp. 83-84). From this it somehow follows that it is "impossible for all individuals simultaneously to save any given sums. Every such attempt to save more by reducing consumption will so affect incomes that the attempt necessarily defeats itself" (p. 84).

In sum, we are apparently to understand that while saving and investment are "necessarily equal" and "merely different aspects of the same thing," yet saving *reduces* employment and incomes and investment *increases* employment and incomes!

There is still another Keynesian paradox of savings (though they are "necessarily equal" to investment and "merely different aspects of the same thing"):

> Though an individual whose transactions are small in relation to the market can safely neglect the fact that demand is not a one-sided transaction, it makes nonsense to neglect it when we come to aggregate demand. This is the vital difference between the theory of the economic behavior of the aggregate and the theory of the behavior of the individual unit, in which we assume that changes in the individual's own demand do not affect his income (p. 85).

The only way in which we can make any sense whatever of this whole otherwise baffling passage is to assume that when Keynes uses the word "saving" he is thinking merely of the negative act of not buying consumption goods; but when he uses the word "investment" he is thinking merely of the positive act of buying capital goods. And he falls into this primary error because he forgets his own previous insistence that "saving" and "investment" are "necessarily equal" and "merely different aspects of the same thing." He is, in fact, thinking in each case of only one side of the transaction: "Saving" equals merely the negative act of not buying consumption goods; "investment" equals merely the positive act of buying or making capital goods. Yet these two acts are both parts of the same act! The first is necessary for the second. An analagous thing happens in the realm of consumption goods alone. A man's tastes change, and he switches from chicken to lamb. We don't scold him at one moment for hurting the poultry raisers and praise him at the next for aiding the sheep raisers. We recognize that his purchasing power has gone in one direction rather than another, and that if he had not given up the chicken he would not have had the money to buy the lamb. Unless a man refrains from spending all his money on consumption goods (*i.e.,* unless he saves), he will not have the funds to buy investment goods, or to lend to others to buy investment goods.

If I may anticipate here my own later argument and conclusions, there cannot be a given amount of real net investment in a community without an equal amount of real net saving. When we are talking in "real" terms, (net) saving and (net) investment are not only *equal,* but saving *is* investment. When we are talking in monetary terms, however, the problem is more complicated. In monetary terms today's saving is not necessarily tomorrow's investment, and today's investment is not necessarily yesterday's saving; but this is because the money supply may have contracted or expanded in the meanwhile.

To return to Keynes's reasoning. Keynes has himself become entangled in the sort of naive and one-sided interpretation of the two terms, saving and investment, that so often trips up the man in the street when he talks of economic problems. We get some confirmation of this when Keynes writes:

> In the aggregate the excess of income over consumption, which we call saving, cannot differ from the addition to capital equipment which we call investment. . . . Saving, in fact, is a mere residual. *The decisions to consume and the decisions to invest between them determine incomes.* (My italics, p. 64.)

Why savings should be a "mere residual" (whatever that may mean) I cannot say. But the sentence I have put in italics reveals the undercurrent of Keynes's thinking. It is not *production* that determines incomes; it is not *work* that determines incomes; it is "the decisions to consume and the decisions to invest"!

It may be hard to imagine Robinson Crusoe as a Keynesian, but if he had been, when he returned to England, and the reporters had interviewed him at the pier, the results might have run something like this:

"How do you account for your big income when on the island?" the reporters might have asked.

"Very simple," Crusoe would have replied. "I decided to

consume an awful lot, and what I didn't consume I decided to invest; and as a result, of course, my income grew and grew."

"Wasn't your income determined by what you produced?" one puzzled reporter might have asked.

"Produced? Worked?" Robinson Crusoe Keynes would have replied, "What nonsense! We have changed all that!"

What we have in this sentence ("The decisions to consume and the decisions to invest between them determine income") is, in fact, a typical example of Keynes's inveterate habit of describing causation not only from an arbitrary point, but rear-end foremost. It is true, of course, that in economic life cause and effect are continuous and endlessly recurrent, as in the chain of life. This is the truth expressed paradoxically in Samuel Butler's definition: "A hen is only an egg's way of making another egg." Now this statement is not untrue, philosophically speaking, but it is confusing to common sense. For practical purposes (say for a poultry raiser or someone in the egg business) it is more useful to look at the subject from the hen's point of view. So while Keynes's method of treating consumption as a "cause" of production and income cannot be called entirely erroneous, it is certainly misleading, and in fact disastrous as the major premise for public policy. The orthodox and perhaps stodgy view that work and production are the primary cause of incomes, and make consumption possible, will be found far more useful in the long run, and far less likely to lead to the intoxicating assumption that prosperity and full employment can be made perpetual through government spending and the printing press.

5. *Can Savings be Printed?*

Before leaving this subject, it may be useful to explore a little further the possible sources of Keynes's confusions. He has told us that "saving" and "investment" are "necessarily equal in amount, being, for the community as a whole, merely different aspects of the same thing" (p. 74). Eleven pages later he tells us that certain propositions "follow merely from the fact that there cannot be a buyer without a seller or a seller without a buyer" (p. 85).

This is a truism. Yet Keynes does well to state it explicitly; for it is astonishing how often it is forgotten by economists, by journalists, and by "practical" men. On a day when the stock market has had an unusual rise, one will see such headlines as "2,000,000 shares bought." When it has had an unusual fall, the headlines are likely to read, instead, "3,000,000 shares sold." Yet in the first case 2,000,000 shares must have been sold, and in the second case 3,000,000 shares must have been bought. In the first case public attention was fixed by the *rise* on the *buying,* whereas in the second case public attention was fixed by the *fall* on the *selling.* The difference is not, as journalists often carelessly or foolishly imply or state, that in the first case there was "more buying than selling," or in the second "more selling than buying." In both cases buying and selling *had to be equal.* No doubt there was a difference in the relative *urgency* of the buying and selling. To put the matter in another and more generalized form, there was a change in the *valuation* that *both* buyers and sellers put on shares. A rising market, in other words, is a sign not only that buyers are willing to bid more than on the day before, but that sellers insist on getting more. The converse is true as regards a falling market.

If we assume that, in the *General Theory,* Keynes is trying to apply the analogy of selling and buying to saving and investment (the "saver" being the one who puts aside the cash, and the "investor" the one who borrows it or uses it to buy raw materials or capital equipment), we encounter certain difficulties. In the first place, the "saver" and the "investor," on these definitions, *may often be the same person.* This is not true (except perhaps occasionally for certain technical bookkeeping purposes) of the "buyer" and "seller." It may often be difficult even for an individual entrepreneur, when he uses part of his net income to buy additional raw materials or capital equipment, to *distinguish* between his "saving" and his "investment." They are both part of the same act. They *are* the same act. For he cannot buy the raw materials unless he has the money to buy them; and if he does buy them he does not have that money to buy goods for his own consumption.

But we get very little help from Keynes, even in the *Treatise on Money,* in learning precisely where to draw the line between "savings" and "investment." If the reader will turn back, for example, to page 84, and to the quotation there from Chapter 12 of the *Treatise on Money,* he will find that the respective definitions are at once nebulous and biassed. Saving, we are told, "is the act of the individual consumer," whereas investment "is the act of the entrepreneur."

Now the definition of an act, onc would supposc, would be expressed solely in terms of the act itself, without the irrelevant introduction of *who does it.* When an "individual consumer" saves, we are apparently to understand, he merely "negatively" refrains from spending. Yet it should be obvious that he also, necessarily, invests in *cash or bank deposits.* When an entrepreneur "invests" he is, according to Keynes, doing something "positive," even if it is only adding to his "liquid capital"—*i.e.,* doing precisely the same thing as the naughty consumer who is merely refraining from spending all his income!

It is impossible to make sense of the Keynesian definitions. But let us, in spite of Keynes's own confusions, persist with his apparently intended analogy of the relationship of saving and investment to that of selling and buying. If buying and selling are merely two sides of the same act, then it is obviously silly to treat buying as virtuous and selling as wicked. It is no less silly to treat investing as virtuous and saving as sinful; or to argue, as Keynes does, that "saving" *reduces* income and employment while "investing" *increases* them.

If everybody *tried* to sell something and nobody bought it, there would simply be no sales. If there were suddenly greater *urgency* to sell than to buy, the practical result would be either an *unreduced* volume of sales *at lower prices,* or a somewhat reduced volume of sales at lower prices —depending on the relative willingness to buy and on other factors.

Similarly with saving and investment. When there is greater relative *urgency* to "save" than to "invest," then the volume of saving and investment may be lower than formerly. In any case *interest rates* will tend to fall. But it does not follow that the decline of the urgency to invest (in anything other than cash or short-term securities) is wicked, or itself the basic cause of unemployment and depression. It is much more profitable to ask *what it is that has caused* the decreased urgency to invest.

But we are getting ahead of our present point, which has to do chiefly with the conception and definition, respectively, of "saving" and "investment." What *are* the most useful definitions of saving and investment respectively?

The answer will depend largely on the particular problem which we are trying to clarify or to solve. In certain contexts there will be no need for distinguishing between them: we may treat them as interchangeable terms, meaning the same thing. (This is what Keynes *really* does in parts of the *General Theory.* "Saving" and "investment" are equal there not by some sort of continuous miracle; they are equal because they are so defined as to mean precisely the same thing!) In other contexts it may be useful to treat savings as referring merely to cash, and investment as referring to goods. And in still other contexts, more important than the distinction between "savings" and "investment" will be the distinction between money savings and real savings, money investment and real investment. [9]

[9] And more important than any of these, perhaps, because it reveals the escape from the Keynesian confusions and contradictions on this point, is the distinction between *prior* savings and *subsequent* investment. But this discussion will be deferred to Chapter XVI.

Keynes, as we shall see, only seldom and haphazardly makes these latter distinctions. On the contrary, he often works very hard to argue them away. The "savings" which result merely from increased bank credit (or, for that matter, from the mere printing of more fiat money), he argues, "are just as genuine as any other savings" (p. 83).

Of course if this were so, the problem of a community's acquiring sufficient savings would never exist. It could simply *print* them!

It is not hard to understand *why* Keynes disapproves of "the new-fangled view that there can be . . . investment without 'genuine' saving" (p. 83). For this "new-fangled" view (properly interpreted) exposes the whole set of Keynesian "full employment" card tricks.

I have said that we may legitimately use "saving" and "investment" with different meanings in different contexts. We must be careful, however, of course, that our meanings are always unequivocal and our definitions explicit. Above all we must not shift meanings or definitions without explicit notice in the course of dealing with a particular problem.

Chapter IX

"THE PROPENSITY TO CONSUME": I

1. *Digression on Mathematical Economics*

When we come in the *General Theory* to the two chapters on "The Propensity to Consume," we meet all our previous difficulties magnified: (1) a specialized and self-coined technical vocabulary to cover complex concepts (which, however, are never consistently adhered to); (2) loose, unverified, unverifiable, or meaningless statements; (3) a constant confusion or scrambling of cause and effect; and (4) the same aversion to, and derision of, anything resembling individual thrift, prudence, or forethought that was evident sixteen years previously in *The Economic Consequences of the Peace*.

In the *General Theory,* in brief, Keynes did not suddenly discover that the traditional economic virtues were really vices, and *vice versa;* he had practically always thought so. All that he hit upon was a new rationalization for his old bias.

> The ultimate object of our analysis [he begins] is to discover what determines the volume of employment. So far we have established the preliminary conclusion that the volume of employment is determined by the point of intersection of the aggregate supply function with the aggregate demand function (p. 89).

Here we meet two special Keynesian technical terms, so we look back to remind ourselves what they mean. And on page 25 we find the so-called definition:

> Let Z be the aggregate supply price of the output from employing N men, the relationship between Z and N being written $Z = \phi(N)$, which can be called the *Aggregate Supply Function*. Similarly, let D be the proceeds which entrepreneurs expect to receive from the employment of N men, the relationship between D and N being written $D = f(N)$, which can be called the *Aggregate Demand Function*.

Here we have not so much two definitions as two mathematical equations, each of which expresses a complex relationship. If the volume of employment is determined by the *point of intersection* of the "aggregate supply function" with the "aggregate demand function," then the volume of employment depends upon the relationship between two complex relationships. This ought to be difficult enough to keep in mind; but our troubles have only begun. For if we go back again to Keynes's "definitions" on page 25, we find that while the Aggregate Supply Function depends upon the relationship between two *actualities* (supply price and number of men employed), the Aggregate Demand Function depends upon the relationship between an *expectation* (of proceeds), and an actuality (number of men employed). Most logicians or mathematicians would doubtless agree that some actualities could be equated with other actualities, and some expectations with other expectations. But I doubt whether many would agree that expectations could be mixed up with actualities in the same mathematical goulash, or that the resulting equations could have any precise value or meaning.

And if a mathematical equation is not precise, it is worse than worthless; it is a fraud. It gives our results a merely spurious precision. It gives an illusion of knowledge in place of the candid confession of ignorance, vagueness, or uncertainty which is the beginning of wisdom.

A short digression seems desirable at this point not merely on Keynes's mathematical economics but on mathematical economics in general. It is said in defense of mathematical economics (by, for example, Keynes's father, John Neville

Keynes, in *The Scope and Method of Political Economy*) that "exact numerical premises . . . are not always essential to the employment of mathematical methods" (p. 257). Mathematical methods, in other words, can still be useful in economics even when they do not deal with known or even determinable quantities, but are a means of clarifying merely hypothetical relationships.

Francis Edgeworth, for example, in his *Mathematical Psychics* (1881), writes:

> It is necessary to realize that mathematical reasoning is not, as commonly supposed, limited to subjects where numerical data are attainable. Where there are data which though not *numerical* are *quantitative*—for example, that a quantity is *greater* or *less* than another, *increases* or *decreases*, is *positive* or *negative*, a *maximum* or a *minimum*—there mathematical reasoning is possible and may be indispensable. To take a trivial instance: *a* is greater than *b*, and *b* is greater than *c*, therefore, *a* is greater than *c*. Here is mathematical reasoning applicable to quantities which may not be susceptible of numerical evaluation.[1]

All this is doubtless true. But the mathematical economists who make such points then tend to forget that out of a merely hypothetical equation or set of equations they can never pull anything better than a merely hypothetical conclusion. As Whitehead remarks: "The conclusion of no argument can be more certain than the assumptions from which it starts." [2] If mathematicians cannot in some way or other determine the numerical values of their *x*'s and *y*'s, their equations are useless for applied or applicable economics. And Keynes's *General Theory* professes to be a theory applicable to real situations; he does, in fact, constantly profess to apply it to real situations.

But we may go much further in our criticism. Even a merely hypothetical equation may be worse than worthless

[1] See pp. 1-9, and 83-93.

[2] A. N. Whitehead, *An Introduction to Mathematics*, (New York: Henry Holt, 1911), p. 27.

if there is not only no initial evidence that the posited relationship is true, but no way in fact of determining whether it is true. A mathematical statement, to be scientifically useful, must, like a verbal statement, at least be *verifiable,* even when it is not verified. If I say, for example (and am not merely joking), that John's love of Alice varies in an exact and determinable relationship with Mary's love of John, I ought to be able to prove that this is so. I do not prove my statement—in fact, I do not make it a whit more plausible or "scientific"—if I write, solemnly, let X equal Mary's love of John, and Y equal John's love of Alice, then

$$Y = f(X)$$

—and go on triumphantly from there.

Yet this is the kind of assertion constantly being made by mathematical economists, and especially by Keynes. The model was set by Augustin Cournot, in his *Récherches sur les principes mathématiques de la théorie des richesses,* published more than a century ago, in 1838. "Let us admit therefore that the sales or the annual demand *D* is, for each article, a particular function *F(p)* of the price *p* of such article." And he went on to explain how "a curve can be made to represent the function in question." It is from this that the famous "Marshallian" supply and demand curves later developed, and today's immense and bewildering body of mathematical economics.

Yet there is no proof whatever that even the most elementary of these functional economic equations represents a fact of the real world. There is no proof that demand *is* "a particular function" of the price of a particular article. We can, of course, *assume* such a relationship. We can draw a *hypothetical* "demand curve," and derive from it a *hypothetical* "functional relationship" between demand and price. We can then point out that according to our hypothetical curve and hypothetical table, when the hypothetical price of our hypothetical commodity is x, the amount demanded will be y; when the price is x_1, the amount demanded will be y_1; when the price is x_2, the amount demanded will be y_2, etc. We can, in short, assert that a general hypothetical relationship implies specific hypothetical relationships.

But of what practical *use* will all these deductions be? Is there any way in which we can apply them to the real world?

When we ask this, we find that our mathematical equations are of very little use indeed. For whether our hypothetical demand curve corresponds to any *real* "demand curve" we can never know. Our equation is useful only on the completely unreal assumption that we can in fact know what the relationship between the amount demanded and the price will be at every point along our curve. More unreal still, our equation is valid only for *one* "state of demand," which cannot be assumed to exist for more than an instant of time. We can never tell whether a real change of price (between, say, today's closing price of wheat and yesterday's closing price of wheat) is the result of a change, or supposed change, in supply or the result of a change in the state of demand (or "demand curve").

In short, we can draw all the beautiful supply and demand curves we like and cross them at the points that please us most. We can thus help to clarify ideas for college freshmen and even for ourselves. But we constantly run the danger of deceiving ourselves by our own diagrams; of giving ourselves the illusion that we know what we in fact do not know. For these supply and demand curves are merely *analogies, metaphors, visual aids to thought,* which should never be confused with realities.

We never in fact do know what the present "demand curve" or "demand schedule" is for anything; we can only guess. Historical research or past statistics (and all statistics describe events in the *past*) may help entrepreneurs to do this guessing, and reduce their range of error. But such statistics can never enable entrepreneurs to *know* any future relationship of price to demand, or enable economists to predict it with confidence. Supply and demand curves, and functional equations, assume that an infinite number or an indefinitely large range of *simultaneous* relationships can be known, and even *known in advance.* But, as the physicists would say, this is not an operational concept. All that we can know is that, say, in 1956 the average price of wheat was P and the supply was S, whereas in 1957 the average price of wheat was $P - p_1$ and the supply was $S + s_1$. But were the supply curves and the demand curves *exactly the same* in 1956 and 1957? Were the differences caused merely by the supply curves crossing the same demand curve at different points? This we can never know, and the obtainable market data will never tell us.

Nor do we improve the situation, from a theoretical or mathematical standpoint, when instead of average annual prices we take average monthly or weekly or daily prices, or prices from hour to hour or minute to minute. As a matter of fact, on the organized speculative markets, we do *not* find that when the price of a commodity or a share goes *up,* the amount sold invariably *falls,* or that when the price goes *down,* the amount sold invariably *increases.* Often the price and the amount sold will *both* increase, or the price and the amount sold will *both* decline. A typical supply-and-demand-curve exposition tacitly assumes, say, that a demand curve remains fixed while a supply curve moves up and down and crosses it at different points, which constitute the changing prices. But the truth is that the level and shape of the supply curve, and more particularly of the demand curve, are themselves constantly changing *from hour to hour.* If they could really be discovered, and put on a motion-picture film, we might find them writhing, vibrating, and jumping in a way to discourage even the cockiest mathematical economist.

The stationary supply and demand curves of the textbooks, or the few alternatives shown, are grossly simplified static assumptions, and should never be taken for more than that. The attempt to put demand and price into a functional equation—and, worse than this, the belief that in real life we could discover a set of actual numerical values to which such an equation would apply—is chimerical. A little mathematical economics here and there, to repeat, or occasional diagrams, may be useful for clarifying or generalizing some economic concepts, for making them more precise, or for protecting us against some errors that otherwise might not be recognized. But the great bulk of mathematical economics today is a manipulation of hypothetical abstractions that have no useful application to the real world.[3]

Keynes does not advance in the slightest beyond Cournot in setting up his own "functions" and his own formulas. In fact, as we shall see, he goes backward. His equations are not merely unverified and unverifiable; they are invalid or inadmissible in other ways.

Let us begin, as an example, with the Aggregate Demand Function. "Let D," writes Keynes, "be the proceeds which

[3] Alfred Marshall, who was perhaps more influential in popularizing mathematical economics than any other writer, wisely confined his own mathematics and even diagrams mainly to footnotes and appendices, and preferred to present his conclusions in verbal form.

In reviewing Edgeworth's *Mathematical Physics* in 1881, he wrote a sentence that has proved to be prophetic of present-day developments: "It will be interesting, in particular, to see how far he succeeds in preventing his mathematics from running away with him, and carrying him out of sight of the actual facts of economics."

In the preface to the first edition (1890) of his *Principles of Economics,* Marshall wrote: "The chief use of pure mathematics in economic questions seems to be in helping a person to write down quickly, shortly and exactly, some of his thoughts for his own use . . . But when a great many symbols have to be used, they become very laborious. . . . It seems doubtful whether any one spends his time well in reading lengthy translations of economic doctrines into mathematics, that have not been made by himself."

Keynes himself, in his biographical essay on Marshall and even more in his essay on Edgeworth (*Essays in Biography,* 1933) expressed the gravest doubts about the utility of pure mathematics in economics. But he seems to have completely lost these doubts in the confident equations scattered through the *General Theory.*

The most uncompromising "classical" attack on mathematical economics is to be found in J. E. Cairnes, *The Character and Logical Method of Political Economy,* preface to the second edition, 1875. The most uncompromising modern attack on the mathematical method in economics is to be found in Ludwig von Mises, *Human Action,* 1949, (pp. 347-354, and elsewhere). There is an acute and instructive discussion of the limits of "The Mathematical Method in Economics" by George J. Stigler, *Five Lectures on Economic Problems,* 1949.

entrepreneurs expect to receive from the employment of N men, the relationship between D and N being written $D = f(N)$, which can be called the *Aggregate Demand Function*" (p. 25).

The first thing that troubles one about this (as I have pointed out previously) is that entrepreneurs practically never think or act in the way Keynes implies. The entrepreneur usually begins by trying to determine what his *net* income will be from producing a certain quantity of a certain *product* and selling it at a certain *price*. Only when he has made *this* estimate does he decide how many men will be needed to turn out this product. How many men he hires or keeps, moreover, will also be determined heavily by the *wage-rates* he is obliged to pay. Instead of thinking what his gross proceeds will be from hiring so-and-so-many men, he decides how many men he will have to hire (or how many he can *afford* to hire at a given wage-rate) to acquire a certain net income. (His decision will also be governed, of course, by how much capital he has or can borrow.)

But a Keynesian is never allowed to look at the matter the way an entrepreneur looks at it. Under threat of excommunication, he is not even permitted to hint that the amount of employment will have anything to do with wage-rates. That unemployment might be primarily the result of excessive wage-rates in relation to prices or the demand for products is the very doctrine that Keynes started out to disprove and to ridicule.

Thus there is no reason to suppose (and there is the most serious reason to doubt) that the causal relationship is the one tacitly assumed by Keynes in the equation $D = f(N)$. Nor is there any reason to suppose that the equation expresses a truth. There are too many factors, tangible and intangible, which entrepreneurs and consumers must take into account in their plans, which do not get into the equation. And there is no way of showing or knowing, even when an infinite number of other factors are assumed to remain unchanged or equal, that the functional relationship expressed in the equation actually exists.

How could this functional relationship be *proved?* We have already seen that this was impossible even in the simpler and more "orthodox" functional relationship postulated by Cournot. The Keynesian functional relationship cannot in fact be proved; it can only be arbitrarily and dogmatically *asserted.* And this is typical of practically all the Keynesian equations.

2. *The "Fundamental Psychological Law"*

Because of the foregoing digression on mathematical economics, it has seemed to take unconscionable space to analyze even a few Keynesian paragraphs. But we have really made far more progress than the distance so far covered in Keynes's first chapter on "the propensity to consume" may imply. For once we have recognized the slipperiness, vagueness, and changeability of most of Keynes's basic terms and concepts, and his habit of begging the question by unproved mathematical equations and sheer assertion, we can begin to economize in our analysis.

Still on the first page of the first "Propensity to Consume" chapter, we come to the assertion that "the factors which govern" two quantities—"the sum which will be spent on consumption when employment is at a given level, and the sum which will be devoted to investment"—"are largely distinct." Therefore, we are told, these "two quantities" will be discussed not only in separate chapters but in separate "books" of the *General Theory* (pp. 89-90).

But if we go back to Keynes's own equation that income = consumption + investment, or if we turn merely to common sense, we might conclude that every dollar of income spent on consumption goods must leave a dollar less to be spent on investment goods, while every dollar spent on investment must leave a dollar less to be spent on immediate consumption. How the factors governing two quantities related to each other as subtrahend and remainder could be "largely distinct" is puzzling. But we shall postpone consideration of this paradox to a later stage.

We come at last to the famous Keynesian concept of "the propensity to consume": "We will therefore define what we shall call *the propensity to consume* as the functional relationship between Y_w, a given level of income in terms of wage-units, and C_w the expenditure on consumption out of that level of income" (p. 90).

Keynes creates several difficulties here, as usual. He is trying to define the relationship of consumption to income in *real* rather than in monetary terms, and therefore he talks in terms of "wage-units." But we have seen (p. 64) that Keynes so defines the wage-unit as to make it in fact a concept that can only be conceived in *monetary* terms, since "wage-units" are added together exactly in proportion to *monetary* wages, because "an hour of special labor remunerated at double ordinary rates will count as two units" (p. 41). We must forget "wage-units," therefore, in order to substitute what Keynes *thought* he was comparing, which is *real* consumption with *real* income.

Another difficulty to be dealt with is the misleading nature of the term itself—"propensity to consume." Keynes's definition shows that he is not in fact dealing with a "propensity" in the dictionary sense—a "natural or habitual inclination or tendency"; he is dealing with a *mathematical relationship.* He is dealing with the *fraction* or *percentage* of its income that the community *in fact* spends *on consumption goods* at different levels of income, regardless of what its propensities or inclinations may be. If the community spends 90 per cent, or nine-tenths, of its income on "consumption," then its "propensity to consume" is nine-tenths, or $\frac{9}{10}$.

But the term, it can now be seen, is doubly misleading. The "propensity" part of it is not a propensity, but a "function" or a fraction. And we are not even talking about the fraction of income that is *spent,* but only of the fraction that is *spent on consumption goods.* If a man buys a capital good, this is not counted in his "propensity to consume," because this purchase is called an "investment." If a doctor, however, buys a house, and this house is both his residence and his office, how is this item entered on the Keynesian ledger—as part of the doctor's "propensity to consume," or as an "investment"? If you buy a power mower strictly to use on your own lawn, it is doubtless part of your "propensity to consume." If you buy it to rent out to others, it is an "investment." But what is it if you use it partly for your own lawn and partly to rent out to others?

Such questions are enough to show that the line between "consumption goods" and "capital goods," between "consumption" and "investment," is not as clear and sharp as Keynes's elaborate theoretical division implies. But they indicate also that from a practical standpoint it is irrelevant to the immediate total volume of employment whether a given amount of money is spent on "consumption" or on "capital" goods, whether it is to be included under "the propensity to consume" or under "investment."

In fact, they raise the further question whether, from the standpoint of the immediate effect on the volume of employment, there is any difference between the dollars that go into "consumption" and the dollars that go into "investment"—and therefore whether there is any good reason for dealing with each by two separate sets of equations; or, for that matter, whether there is any good reason for the whole elaborate structure of Keynesian theory.

Of course, it makes a great deal of difference to the *direction* or *allocation* of employment whether money is spent on consumption or on capital goods; but it also makes a good deal of difference to the direction or allocation of employment whether money is spent on one consumption good rather than another—say on houses rather than on automobiles, or on beef rather than on television machines.

At this point Keynes digresses to discuss the rate of interest. But it will help the exposition here if we do not follow him in this digression but reserve criticism of his interest-rate theories until we come to his Chapters 13 and 14, wholly devoted to the rate of interest.

The next point for us to pass on to, therefore, is Keynes's "fundamental law" upon which his confidence in the alleged propensity-to-consume "function" is based:

> The fundamental psychological law, upon which we are entitled to depend with great confidence both *a priori* from our knowledge of human nature and from the detailed facts of experience, is that men are disposed, as a rule and on the average, to increase their consumption as their income increases, but not by as much as the increase in their income. That is to say, if C_w is the amount of consumption and Y_w is income (both measured in wage-units) ΔC_w has the same sign as ΔY_w but is smaller in amount, *i.e.* $\frac{dC_w}{dY_w}$ is positive and less than unity (p. 96).

Before starting to analyze this, it is important to emphasize the central role that this alleged "consumption function" plays in Keynesian economics, and the huge importance his admirers and disciples attach to it. "Keynes's most notable contribution," writes Alvin H. Hansen, "was his consumption function . . . the behavior patterns of the community are such that a gap exists (which gap widens *absolutely* as real income increases) between the amount the community wishes to consume and the output the community is capable of producing." [4]

But let us allow Keynes to explain a little further exactly what he means. This "fundamental psychological law" is both a *secular* law and a *cyclical* law, and is apparently considered even more important as an explanation of business cycles than as a secular law. Continuing without gap from the quotation from Keynes above:

[4] *A Guide to Keynes,* p. 27.

> This is especially the case where we have short periods in view, as in the case of the so-called cyclical fluctuations of employment. . . . Thus a rising income will often be accompanied by increased saving, and a falling income by decreased saving . . .
>
> But, apart from short-period *changes* in the level of income, it is also obvious that a higher absolute level of income will tend, as a rule, to widen the gap between income and consumption. . . . These reasons will lead, as a rule, to a greater *proportion* of income being saved as real income increases. But whether or not a greater proportion is saved, we take it as a fundamental psychological rule of any modern community that, when its real income is increased, it will not increase its consumption by an equal *absolute* amount, so that a greater absolute amount must be saved . . . (p. 97).

Now how does Keynes try to establish this great discovery, this "fundamental psychological law"?

On his mere say-so.

Had he put this forward merely as a loose common-sense observation, with no mathematical equations based on it, and no startling or revolutionary conclusions drawn from it, it might be allowed to pass without challenge, or even accepted almost as a truism. Of course the "consumption function" is normally "less than unity" (p. 96). This is merely a pretentious way of saying that a community cannot as a whole consume more than it produces, and that any community that has advanced beyond the most primitive and miserable state will save against contingencies at least part of what it produces, and "invest" something in land improvement and tools to increase its future production. It is also true that richer people will, as a rule, save a greater proportion of their incomes than poorer people, for the simple reason that they have more above their present bare minimum consumption requirements to save; and some saving is the course dictated by common prudence.

But such truths, in this loose general form, have been

known from time immemorial. They were imbedded in proverbs long before the birth of Adam Smith, and no one has hitherto called them a great economic discovery. But let us listen again for a moment to Hansen:

> Even a little reflection on the course of economic history is enough to disclose the unmistakable fact that consumption has risen, broadly conceived, *more or less* in proportion to the spectacular growth in productivity which the last 150 years have witnessed. [Whoever supposed otherwise?] To this general knowledge, long and widely held, Keynes indeed added something very important, namely the precise formulation of the consumption-income schedule, together with the concept of the marginal propensity to consume. And more significant still, he developed a *theory* in which this and other functions, relevant to the determination of Aggregate Demand, are integrated.[5]

In brief, Keynes took a loose truism that everybody knew, and turned it into a double error: first, by attributing a precision to it that it simply does not have; and secondly, by making it the basis of a false theory.

I have said that Keynes tried to establish his "fundamental psychological law" by mere assertion, by an *ipse dixit.* There are two major ways in which an economic law, or any scientific law, might be established—deductively or inductively. In the deductive hypothetical method a truth is established because it is a demonstrable implication of another truth already known or postulated. This is the kind of truth embodied in the ordinary laws of supply and demand. If, the supply of an article remaining unchanged, the demand for it increases, the price will rise. If, with no increase in the demand for an article, the price is raised, less of it will be bought, etc. The conclusion follows inevitably from the premises, and from the very *meaning* of

[5] Alvin H. Hansen, *A Guide to Keynes,* p. 78.

such terms as *supply, demand,* and *price* (or, if one wishes to be more precise and technical, of such terms as the curve of price-and-amount demanded, the curve of price-and-amount offered, etc.).

In economics, induction consists usually either of common observation or of statistics. (Economic truths, like truths in almost all fields, are never established by pure induction or pure deduction but by a combination of both methods. From hypothetical premises only hypothetical conclusions can be drawn. For a conclusion to be true and to have practical application, the premises must be known, from common observation or otherwise, to be true.) In *confirming* a conclusion, statistics at best present nothing more than *presumptive* evidence, for they can never be complete. But though statistics can never fully *verify* an economic theory, they can *refute* it, by showing at least one instance or some instances in which it is false.[6]

Now though Keynes declares that his "fundamental psychological law" of the relation of consumption to income can be arrived at not only *"a priori"* but "from the detailed facts of experience," he never deigns to offer the slightest statistical confirmation. We can only assume that this is because he has none to offer. When we do look at available statistics, we find in fact a prima facie *refutation* of his "fundamental psychological law."

Here is a table, taken from official statistics, showing the disposable personal income in the United States for the twelve years 1944 through 1955, inclusive; the amount of personal savings in the same twelve years, and saving as a percentage of disposable income:

6 At least in the form originally stated. Statistical results may of course suggest qualifications in a theory which would make it fit the available statistics. But statistics in the field of economics, *i.e.,* in the field of human action, necessarily always refer to *complex phenomena* of the past and can neither prove nor falsify any proposition in the way in which such proof or falsification is ascribed to, say, experiments in physics.

Year	*Income (billions)*	*Savings (billions)*	*Savings as % of income*
1944	$146.8	$36.9	25.2
1945	150.4	28.7	19.1
1946	159.2	12.6	7.9
1947	169.0	4.0	2.4
1948	187.6	10.0	5.3
1949	188.2	7.6	4.0
1950	206.1	12.1	5.9
1951	226.1	17.7	7.8
1952	236.7	18.4	7.8
1953	250.4	19.8	7.9
1954	254.8	18.3	7.2
1955	269.4	17.1	6.3

Now let us see what these figures do to Keynes's alleged "psychological law." The events of 1955 were in themselves an emphatic contradiction. Disposable personal income *increased* by $14.6 billion, but savings *fell* by $1.2 billion. The total percentage of saving to disposable income fell from 7.2 to 6.3. The same thing happened between 1953 and 1954. Disposable income went *up* $4.4 billion, savings *down* $1.5 billion.

How many times Keynes's "law" was falsified in this twelve-year period depends on how the law is interpreted. Total income went up each year as compared with the preceding year. If we take the amount of saving in 1944 as our base figure, therefore, the "law" was falsified in every one of the succeeding eleven years, for income was higher in each than in 1944, but savings were lower. If we interpret Keynes's law, or "consumption function," as he calls it, to mean merely that savings must rise *in absolute amount* when income rises (but only as compared with the preceding year), then Keynes's "consumption function" was falsified in six years and worked only in five. If we interpret the "consumption function" to mean that savings will rise as a *percentage* of income with every rise in income, then

Keynes's law was falsified in seven of the eleven years and followed only in four.

I may be accused of unfairness for including the enormous savings in 1944 and showing their decline in 1945, 1946, and 1947 in spite of substantial rises in disposable income in each year. It will be said that savings were heavy in 1944 and 1945 because these were war years and consumer goods were not available. This is indeed part of the answer. But this only underlines the fact that Keynes's "law" is no law, and that the relationship of spending and saving does not depend solely on total income changes but on innumerable factors. Savings may depend less on what people earn today than on what they expect to earn tomorrow. Their spending this year may depend to a large extent on whether they expect the prices of the things they want to buy to be higher or lower next year. People may buy on impulse. They may refrain from buying through loss of confidence, either in the general business future or in their own. These reasons for spending or not spending will be discussed more at length later. It is sufficient to note here that experience and statistics fail to support the "consumption function," which Alvin H. Hansen regards as Keynes's most notable contribution.[7]

[7] *Cf.* Hansen's contribution to *The New Economics* (edited by Seymour E. Harris, Alfred Knopf, 1952): "It has been my conviction for many years that the great contribution of Keynes' *General Theory* was the clear and specific formulation of the consumption function. This is an epoch-making contribution to the tools of economic analysis" (p. 135).

In support of the argument in my text, however, see Milton Friedman, *A Theory of the Consumption Function,* (New York: National Bureau of Economic Research, 1957). Here are excerpts from the National Bureau's own summary of Friedman's thesis: "Friedman's explanation of change in consumption runs primarily in terms of consumers' expectations concerning income. . . . Naturally, expectations are influenced by developments in the past. Generally speaking, therefore, current consumption is correlated with the income experience of recent years. . . . But Friedman's analysis leads us to look ahead, not backward. . . . Further, the analysis embraces the idea that consumers take into account not only income expectations but also expectations with respect to the prices and availability of consumption of goods, when deciding what portion of income to spend. . . . It is evident that Friedman abandons the conception of the consumer as a mechanical link between current income and consumption, a notion that Keynes set forth in 1936. . . . Friedman returns to the older theory of consumer

There are, I suppose, various ways of refusing to accept the kind of statistical refutation I have just presented. One can say that Keynes was not talking about the relation of *money* income to *money* savings, but of *real* incomes to *real* savings. Changing the foregoing income figures to figures in terms of constant dollars (e.g. 1956 prices), however, does not change the result much: only in two years, 1946 and 1947, did the rise in money income cover a fall in "real" income.

One can argue, also, as Hansen apparently does (somewhat obscurely),[8] that when the "consumption function" fails to work out statistically it is because it has *shifted;* it still exists, and it is "a major landmark in the history of economic doctrines." But if the consumption function is always shifting or can be "upset completely" by economic "upheavals," then its existence can neither be proved nor disproved statistically (or in any other way), and it is worthless for cyclical or even secular prediction.

3. *Ambiguity of the "Consumption Function"*

Before we leave the "consumption function," it may be as well to call attention to the uselessness and illegitimacy of the concept in other ways. The concept is highly ambiguous in what it tells us about the relationship of consumption and income.

On page 116 I present a diagram to illustrate *five* main "functional" relationships that saving can bear to total income. Keynes could easily have clarified this point for himself and his readers by using a similar simple diagram; but though he peppers the *General Theory* with functional and differential equations, he seems to have despised any simple clarifying device, and uses only one diagram in the entire book.

---

behavior, in which consumers' plans and decisions are influenced by the future as well as the present and the past, and his explanation is consistent with much that economists have learned about consumer behavior over the past century or more."

[8] See Alvin H. Hansen, *A Guide to Keynes,* pp. 67-85.

For reasons which I shall explain more fully later, it seems to me much more profitable to discuss the relation of *savings* to total income than the relation of *consumption* to total income. Therefore I have labelled the lines in the diagram S_1, S_2, etc. rather than, as Keynes would, C_1, C_2, etc. This line, however, merely represents the dividing point between consumption and savings. The section below the line represents consumption and the section above the line represents savings. The line YY′ represents the line of total income. The vertical line OY represents total income in

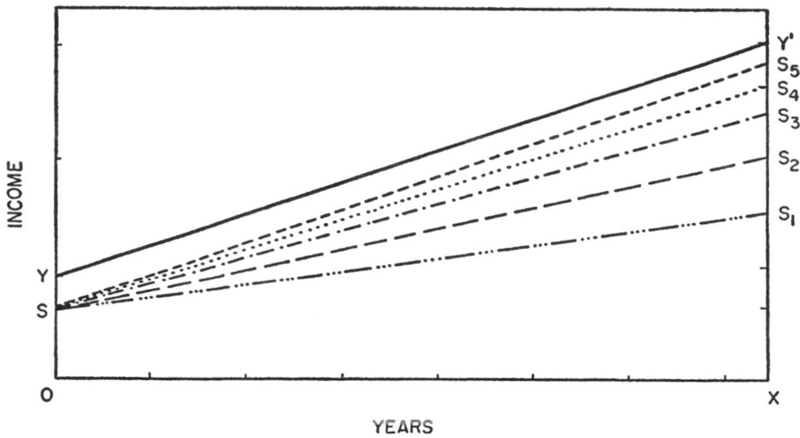

the year of origin; the vertical line XY′ total income in the final year in the diagram; the horizontal line OX the length of time in years over which the rise of income takes place. The various S lines, representing the dividing lines between savings and consumption, all begin at the two-thirds point of the origin year income line OY. This assumes that in the initial year under consideration saving is equal to one-half of consumption. This is, of course, a highly unrealistic assumption, because savings normally run, as we shall see, in the neighborhood of about one-tenth of total income. But the two-thirds point is taken in the origin year simply to make it easier for the eye to follow the various savings lines and not to crowd them into too narrow a space. For the same reason the unrealistic assumption is made that the national income in the terminal year of the diagram is three times as great as in the origin year.

Now the line SS_1 represents what Keynes *appears* to be saying in his "psychological law"—namely, that as total income increases, the *proportion* of saving to spending increases. *In the long run, and in the absence of innumerable other "disturbing" factors,* this is indeed what tends to happen. (It is also, as I shall later show, what both the saving individual *desires* to happen and what is most beneficial for the community.) If this were what Keynes was saying in his "consumption function," and if it were *all* that he was saying, it would have been true, but it would also have been a truth generally recognized, not only prior to 1936, but prior to the birth of Hume and Adam Smith. Those who have more income than they *must* spend for their immediate necessities can afford to save something out of the rest. The more income they have above their immediate necessities, the greater proportion of it they can afford to, and the greater proportion they do in fact tend to save.

The same broad relation of savings to income applies both to individuals and to a whole community. But it applies as a loose, rule-of-thumb generalization, and to the extent that it is true it must remain one. The moment it is put into a mathematical equation, as Keynes attempts to put it, it becomes false. The mathematical precision is spurious. It is useless for practical application or short-run analysis because the rise of income is only one among many factors, most of them intangible, that determine short-run changes in the volume of saving. And it is in any case astonishing, as I shall show, to regard the tendency toward increasing proportional saving when income increases as an ominous development that threatens to create secular unemployment and poverty.

The line SS_2 represents what *could* be meant by Keynes's "psychological law." It represents approximately what does happen in reality over a series of years when the increase in income is not substantial. People tend to save about the same *proportion* of their income from year to year. This situation is illustrated by the diagram on page 119 which covers the years (divided into quarters) from 1951 to 1957 in the United States. The diagram is reproduced exactly, without change of proportions, from an official diagram published by the President's Council of Economic Advisers in the April, 1958, issue of *Economic Indicators*.[9] The chart shows that savings, while they fluctuated mildly over this period, showed no consistent tendency either to increase or decrease, but in general remained at the same proportion of total income—an average of about 7 per cent.

This is in line with what previous attempts to measure savings statistically have shown, though the proportion of savings to income depends on the particular ways in which savings and income are defined and measured. Thus a study by Kuznets published in 1940 tended to show, in the words of Alvin H. Hansen, that "the *per cent* of income saved (and invested) over the long run has been more or less constant at, say, around 12 per cent." [10]

This would look on the surface like a stable situation, and a healthy and progressive one. This saving and investment constantly increases the total amount of consumption and capital goods produced. The producers both of consumption and of capital goods could count, by and large, in such a situation, on a reasonably stable market for their products. But Hansen goes on to insist, first, that even if the *percentage* of income saved does not increase, the result still conforms to Keynes's "psychological law"; and secondly, that this is a dangerous situation: "The *proportion* of income saved remained substantially constant. But at higher *absolute* levels of income a greater *absolute* amount was saved." [11]

9 U. S. Government Printing Office.
10 *A Guide to Keynes,* p. 75.
11 *Ibid.,* p. 75.

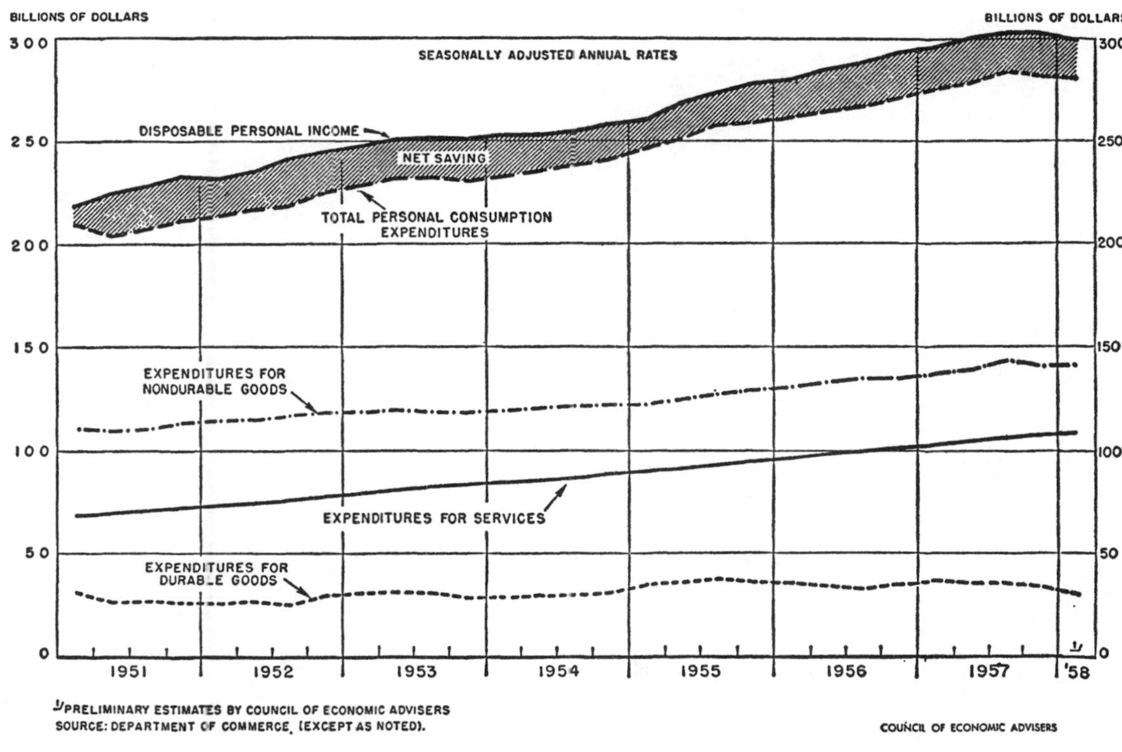

Disposition of Personal Income

This is mathematically indubitable. Hansen goes on to draw his horrendous conclusion: "If the gap, in *absolute* terms, between consumption and income widens as income increases, then Aggregate Demand will not be adequate to cover the Aggregate Supply price unless that gap is filled by an increase in investment." [12]

We shall later inquire whether or not Keynes and Hansen were unduly terrified by the prospect that saving might rise proportionately with income. On the same reasoning, Hansen should still be worried even if savings should be represented by the relation SS_3. For though, as income increased, a *smaller percentage* of income would be saved, it could still be greater in *absolute* amount than when income was lower! Only if the relationship were represented by the line SS_4 might the souls of the Keynesians be at peace; only then might the private enterprise system be allowed to take care of itself, without the solicitous forced spending of the Keynesian bureaucrats, "to fill the gap."

In fact, the Keynesians might be even more at peace if the relationship were represented by the line SS_5, in which savings would grow smaller and smaller even in *absolute* amount as income increased.

4. *The Meaning of "Saving"*

But now a tiny doubt, at first no bigger than a man's hand, begins to grow and grow. If we accept Keynes's concept of "saving" (which is quite unrelated to his formal *definition* of saving in the *General Theory*), can the Keynesian soul remain at peace *as long as there is any saving at all?* Or, to put it more accurately, as long as there is *any* "saving," of *any* amount, that is not compensated or offset by an equal amount of "investment"? For though Keynes tells us in his formal definitional chapters that he rejects "the new-fangled view that there can be saving without investment or investment without 'genuine' saving" (p. 83), and

[12] *A Guide to Keynes*, p. 85.

though he himself insists in these chapters on "the *identity* between saving and investment" (my italics, p. 84), the whole Keynesian theory of unemployment rests on the abandonment of these definitions and concepts and a return precisely to the (now tacit) definitions and concepts that he used in his *Treatise on Money,* and that he formally abandons in his definitional chapters of the *General Theory* "with much regret for the confusion they have caused" (p. 61).

The *real* (unstated) definition and concept that Keynes uses in his unemployment theory is that "saving" is the merely negative act of *failing or refusing to spend money on either consumption or capital goods, directly or indirectly.* To the extent that a community as a whole can have *any* such one-sided saving, or pure hoarding, or to the extent that it is even attempted, whether it can be universally achieved or not, then it must (other things unchanged) bring about unemployment. So Keynes did not even need his dubious "fundamental psychological law," or his pretentious consumption "function" equations, to prove that "saving," in the one-sided sense in which he thought of it, could cause unemployment.

This brings us to still another puzzle. If Keynes had in the back of his mind this purely negative concept of Saving, side-by-side with a positive concept of Investment, why did he talk about a pure "Consumption Function" at all? Unemployment, even on his theory, is not caused by the amount that Consumption falls short of Income, but only by the amount that Consumption and Investment *combined* fall short of income. Suppose we were to choose definitions according to which Saving and Investment would equal each other in a position of equilibrium or in the long-run, but in which for short transitional periods savings could exceed new investment or investment could exceed real savings. If Keynes had held such a concept (and this concept is strongly implied, in spite of explicit denials, in much of what he wrote in the *General Theory*), then it should have occurred to him that the relevant equations for his purposes did not concern the amount by which Consumption alone fell short of Income, but the amount by which Consumption and Investment *together* fell short of Income. He would not have worried about the gap between Consumption and Income but only about the far narrower gap between Consumption-plus-Investment and Income. It was merely *uninvested* savings that disturbed him, not all savings. If he had built his functional equations on such concepts, his exposition might have been much clearer—and also, of course, his fallacies.

Keynes's "fundamental psychological law," as we have seen, is contradicted by experience. But even if the "law" were found to exist it would prove very little about the future of over-all employment. It would merely mean that there would be a tendency (and, as I shall later show, a wholly desirable tendency) for a smaller percentage of the working force to be employed in turning out consumption goods and a larger percentage in turning out capital goods.

In fact, the so-called "general theory" rests on an arbitrary division and on a verbal trick. "Employment can only increase *pari passu,*" Keynes concludes (on p. 98), "with an increase in investment; unless, indeed, there is a change in the propensity to consume." But this is like saying that our combined supply of ham and eggs can only increase with an increase in our supply of ham; unless, indeed, there is also an increase in our supply of eggs. If, in fact, instead of dividing commodities into the two groups, "consumption goods" and "investment goods," we were to divide them, whether consumption goods or investment goods, into two different groups—those whose names begin with the letters from A to M, and those whose names begin with the letters from N to Z (which we shall call the AM commodities and the NZ commodities respectively)—then we could arrive at the following Keynesian conclusion: Employment can only increase *pari passu* with an increase in the purchase of the AM commodities; unless, indeed, there is also an increase in the purchase of the NZ commodities "to fill the gap." Brilliant, revolutionary discovery! The new economics!

But we shall elaborate upon this when we come to Keynes's own elaboration of this basic point in his *General Theory*.

5. *The Sinking-Fund Bogey*

The next thing Keynes begins to worry about is sinking funds. (Keynes, in fact, worries about practically everything that happens or can happen in a free enterprise system. His touching faith in the judgment and disinterestedness of government controllers is merely the other side of his distrust of the private businessman.)

> Take a house which continues to be habitable until it is demolished or abandoned. If a certain sum is written off its value out of the annual rent paid by the tenants, which the landlord neither spends on upkeep nor regards as net income available for consumption, this provision . . . constitutes a drag on employment all through the life of the house, suddenly made good in a lump when the house has to be rebuilt (p. 99).
>
> Thus sinking funds, etc. are apt to withdraw spending power from the consumer long before the demand for expenditure on replacements (which such provisions are anticipating) comes into play; *i.e.* they diminish the current effective demand and only increase it in the year in which the replacement is actually made. If the effect of this is aggravated by 'financial prudence,' *i.e.* by its being thought advisable to 'write off' the initial cost *more* rapidly than the equipment actually wears out, the cumulative result may be very serious indeed (p. 100).

There are so many things wrong with the foregoing passage that it is difficult to know where to begin an analysis. Keynes lumps everything together, and does not distinguish between a depreciation allowance or depreciation reserve, on the one hand, and an actual sinking fund on the other. A depreciation allowance (or "reserve") is merely a *bookkeeping technique,* a convenient accounting fiction. Its primary purpose is to give an entrepreneur a clearer idea of whether he is making a net profit or not, and if so, how much. A depreciation allowance has no necessary substance. An actual sinking fund is a fiscal technique, and does have substance, but even that almost never exists in the form of unused *cash.* It may be invested in long-term bonds of other corporations, or at the very least in short-term government securities. All but a modest percentage of it will exist, in short, in the form of *investments.* Or it may have been used to retire outstanding indebtedness.

When a corporation decides whether or not to abandon an old factory, to sell its equipment as scrap, or to erect an entirely new plant, its decision will probably be based solely on considerations of profitability. If continuing to work the old plant or old equipment results in a loss, or in a smaller net profit than a new plant would yield, or if a new plant, regardless of whether or not the old plant were scrapped, would promise to yield a profit, then old equipment will be scrapped or new equipment ordered (if the funds exist or are raisable) regardless of the technical state of the books as regards depreciation allowances.

Keynes's illustration of a landlord who writes off "a certain sum" from the value of his house out of the annual rent, but "neither spends [that sum] on upkeep nor regards [it] as net income available for consumption," but then suddenly rebuilds (and apparently exactly duplicates) the house "in a lump when the house *has* to be rebuilt," is so completely unrealistic that it hardly deserves serious discussion. No landlord with a grain of sense leaves his depreciation write-off as idle cash during the life of the house. The depreciation allowance, in the first place, may not even *exist* as a tangible sum. Depreciation allowances do not come into existence as tangible sums simply because they are deducted on the books. After deduction for depreciation, the landlord of a house (or the owner of any other business) may show a *loss.* If the loss is as great as the depreciation reserve, then there is no tangible reserve left to be either spent, invested, or hoarded. If the loss is greater than the depreciation reserve . . .

But if, for the sake of argument, the depreciation allowance does exist as a tangible fund, then the landlord may either spend it on his own consumption (he is under no legal *compulsion* to maintain the value of his investment or savings unimpaired), or invest it in *something else besides the house*—say corporate or government securities. In any case, he will not leave the money idle, not drawing interest.

But putting aside all these previous objections to Keynes's theories about "sinking funds," what an individual landlord or individual corporation does is not important for the state of employment or industrial activity of the community as a whole. What is important is only what the actions of landlords and corporations add up to *collectively.* And the spectacle of landlords and corporations collectively not putting up any new houses or factories for twenty or fifty years (say not from 1910 to 1959) and then suddenly putting them all up in one year (say 1960) is so absurd that one wonders how it could be seriously held for five consecutive minutes of thought.

What happens is that each year a certain number of houses, office buildings, factories, machines, bridges, and roads, are being built or replaced. They are being put up or installed regardless of the state of "sinking funds," and regardful mainly of the prospects of future profit. But even *if* the year in which a given structure were replaced were strictly dependent upon the year in which it was built, the replacement year would nevertheless differ with each plant or house, depending on when it was built. The individual "sinking fund" periods, collectively considered, overlap. This year, say, Corporation A is lending out its depreciation reserve to help build the new factory of Corporation B. Next year Corporation B will be lending out its depreciation reserve money to build the new factory of Corporation C, or even of Corporation A. And so around the circle.

But Keynes takes his whole preposterous theory so seriously that he virtually attributes the 1929 depression to it:

> In the United States, for example, by 1929 the rapid capital expansion of the previous five years had led cumulatively to the setting up of sinking funds and depreciation allowances, in respect of plant which did not need replacement, on so huge a scale that an enormous volume of entirely new investment was required merely to absorb these financial provisions; and it became almost hopeless to find still more new investment on a sufficient scale to provide for such new saving as a wealthy community in full employment would be disposed to set aside. *This factor alone was probably sufficient to cause a slump.* (My italics, p. 100.)

There have been some pretty silly "explanations" of the 1929 collapse, but it remained for Keynes to attribute it to the way in which corporations kept their books! Their new investment or lack of it, their actual amount of physical replacement in any given year, had in fact nothing to do with these accounting technicalities. It was determined by the actual physical need for replacement—or rather, more accurately, by the outlook (as it seemed to the corporation officers or directors) for *profits* from the replacement or new investment. A depreciation allowance may prove in practice to be either too great or too small. But entrepreneurs are not guided in their present decisions by their past expectations but by their present expectations. The drop in new investment was chiefly the *consequence* of the 1929 slump, not the cause.[13]

But this strange theory about sinking funds enables Keynes to indulge himself once more in his favorite sport

[13] An analysis of the causes of the 1929 slump would require a book in itself. The reader who is interested might consult: B. M. Anderson, *Economics and the Public Welfare,* (New York: Van Nostrand, 1946); Lionel Robbins, *The Great Depression,* (New York: Macmillan, 1934); Charles Rist, *Défense de l'Or* (Paris: Recueil Sirey, 1953), Philip Cortney, *The Economic Munich,* "The 1929 Lesson," (New York: Philosophical Library, 1949).

of ridiculing " 'financial prudence' " and " 'sound' finance." These, it turns out, are the great enemies of employment:

> Financial prudence will be liable to diminish aggregate demand and thus impair well-being. . . . The greater, moreover, the consumption for which we have provided in advance, the more difficult it is to find something further to provide for in advance, and the greater our dependence on present consumption as a source of demand. Yet the larger our incomes, the greater, unfortunately, is the margin between our incomes and our consumption. So, failing some novel expedient, there is, as we shall see, no answer to the riddle, except that there must be sufficient unemployment to keep us so poor that our consumption falls short of our income by no more than the equivalent of the physical provision for future consumption which it pays to produce today (p. 105).

6. *In a Nutshell*

Here is the General Theory in a nutshell, with its transvaluation of all values. The great virtue is Consumption, extravagance, improvidence. The great vice is Saving, thrift, "financial prudence." We shall reserve to a later point an exposition of why Keynes's "riddle" is a riddle of his own imagination, not of the free enterprise economic system. But we may anticipate one of our chief criticisms here by calling attention to Keynes's crude and naive conceptions of "consumption" and "investment" purely in *quantitative* terms, whereas every civilized human being in his actual consumption and use of capital equipment conceives them just as much in qualitative terms. There are definite limits, of course, to the quantitative use or consumption of food, clothing, housing, and capital equipment. But there are no assignable limits to possible improvements in the *quality* of capital equipment and in the products and services that it can help to produce.

Chapter X

"THE PROPENSITY TO CONSUME": II

1. *Reasons for Not Spending*

After a first chapter of eighteen pages on "The Propensity to Consume: I. The Objective Factors," Keynes has a chapter of only five pages on "The Propensity to Consume: II. The Subjective Factors." He begins by declaring that:

"There are, in general, eight main motives or objects of a subjective character which lead individuals to refrain from spending out of their incomes" (p. 107). It is worth quoting these practically in full:

> (i) To build up a reserve against unforeseen contingencies;
>
> (ii) To provide for an anticipated future relation between the income and the needs of the individual or his family different from that which exists in the present, as, for example, in relation to old age, family education, or the maintenance of dependents;
>
> (iii) To enjoy interest and appreciation, *i.e.*, because a larger real consumption at a later date is preferred to a smaller immediate consumption;
>
> (iv) To enjoy a gradually increasing expenditure, since it gratifies a common instinct to look forward to a gradually improving standard of life rather than the contrary, even though the capacity for enjoyment may be diminishing;
>
> (v) To enjoy a sense of independence and the power to do things, though without a clear idea or definite intention of specific action;
>
> (vi) To secure a *masse de manœuvre* to carry out speculative or business projects;
>
> (vii) To bequeath a fortune;

(viii) To satisfy pure miserliness, *i.e.* unreasonable but insistent inhibitions against acts of expenditure as such (pp. 107-108).

Now even if there were nothing seriously invalid about this particular classification of the motives to personal saving, there is certainly nothing uniquely illuminating or inevitable about it. One can list eight motives or objects of saving; or, if one wishes to be as specific as Keynes is in some instances, one can list twenty-eight.

It is striking that the most important reason (in relation to the light it throws on business cycles) why individuals sometimes refrain from spending is not specifically contained in Keynes's list. This is simply the expectation that prices are going to fall, or to fall further; and that if the buyer waits long enough he can get what he wants cheaper.

It could be argued that this might find a place under Keynes's sixth reason. But, for that matter, it could be argued that all of the more specific motives for personal saving could be summed up under a single broad motive—to build up a reserve against future requirements or contingencies, whether these are definite, probable, or merely possible.

The motive, in other words, is to provide both for the certainties and the uncertainties of the future—from buying tomorrow's dinner or paying next month's rent to taking advantage of a speculative opportunity or leaving one's family comfortably off in the event of one's death. Such things as pure miserliness, emphasized by Keynes, can safely be left out of account for practical analysis—first, because relatively few people are addicted to it (in a modern industrial society), and secondly, because the relative amount of it probably remains unchanged from year to year, if not from generation to generation.

If we are talking of all the motives to saving, there is a serious omission from Keynes's elaborate list of eight. People save to make roundabout methods of production possible, so that their productive capacity may be increased and their future incomes (whether thought of in terms of money or of the flow of goods and services) may be correspondingly enlarged. True, they do this usually in their capacity as entrepreneurs or corporation managers, in their role as "producers" rather than "consumers"; and Keynes listed merely the motives which lead "individuals" (presumably thought of as consumers only) "to refrain from spending out of their incomes."

But by omitting this productive motive he omits the very consequence that makes saving so essential for total economic growth, and so beneficent for society as a whole. If we wished to reduce our classification of the main motives to saving to just two, we should have to say that they were (1) to provide for future needs or contingencies out of part of present income (plain saving); and (2) to make roundabout methods of production possible (capitalistic saving) so as to increase future income. It is Keynes's almost total blindness to this second motive—and result—that accounts for his strange lifelong bias against thrift.

For Keynes had a definite bias against thrift, of at least twenty years standing (see my quotation on pp. 85-86 from *Economic Consequences of the Peace*). This is revealed again, in spite of Keynes's effort to seem impartial, in the paragraph immediately following the eight motives to saving quoted above:

> These eight motives might be called the motives of Precaution, Foresight, Calculation, Improvement, Independence, Enterprise, Pride, and Avarice; and we could also draw up a corresponding list of motives to consumption such as Enjoyment, Shortsightedness, Generosity, Miscalculation, Ostentation, and Extravagance (p. 108).

It may seem carping to notice it, but whereas Keynes lists eight motives, including Pride and Avarice, for saving, he lists only six motives for spending. He might easily have rounded out the latter list by adding Recklessness and Improvidence. It is true that these might overlap on some of the motives he does list, but the overlapping could hardly be greater than that of Precaution, Foresight, and Calculation.

Keynes does supplement his list of motives for individual saving with a list of four motives for institutional saving (by governments and business corporations). These four motives are listed under the heads of Enterprise, Liquidity, Improvement, and Financial Prudence. But Keynes treats these motives curtly and disparagingly, and hints that the last is almost certain to be excessive.

2. *The Fear of Thrift*

In the second section of his chapter on the subjective factors in the propensity to consume, Keynes explains more in detail the reasons for his hatred and fear of thrift. But let us begin with his conclusion rather than with his reasons:

> The more virtuous we are, the more determinedly thrifty, the more obstinately orthodox in our national and personal finance, the more our incomes will have to fall when interest rises relatively to the marginal efficiency of capital. Obstinacy can bring only a penalty and no reward. For the result is inevitable (p. 111).

As Keynes here anticipates some of his later arguments, we can also defer a closer analysis of them until later. But as the argument that he puts forward concerning interest rates is of central importance to his theory and to his recommendations concerning economic policy, some brief comment seems desirable.

> The influence of changes in the rate of interest on the amount actually saved is of paramount importance, but is *in the opposite direction* to that usually supposed. For even if the attraction of the larger future income to be earned from a higher rate of interest has the effect of diminishing the propensity to consume, nevertheless we can be certain that a rise in the rate of interest will have the effect of reducing the

> amount actually saved. For aggregate saving is governed by aggregate investment; a rise in the rate of interest (unless it is offset by a corresponding change in the demand-schedule for investment) will diminish investment; hence a rise in the rate of interest must have the effect of reducing incomes to a level at which saving is decreased in the same measure as investment (p. 110). [And Keynes goes on to conclude further that therefore] saving and spending will *both* decrease (p. 111).

It is amazing how many fallacies and inversions Keynes can pack into a small space, and especially how many fallacies, like a set of Chinese boxes, he can pack inside other fallacies.

A rise in the rate of interest, Keynes here argues, will not normally encourage an *increase* in the amount of savings but a *decrease*. Why? Because while a higher rate of interest might encourage more saving it would discourage borrowing. True. But the same sort of thing could be said not only about the price of loanable funds, but about the price of anything else. A higher price for any commodity will reduce the amount demanded unless the demand schedule is also higher. But it may be precisely because the demand for that commodity has increased that the price has been bid up in the first place. Therefore the higher price will not cause a reduction in the amount demanded for the simple reason that it is the increase in demand that has forced up the price.

The same reasoning applies to the interest rate, which is another name for the price of loanable funds. An arbitrary *uncaused* rise in the rate of interest would, other things remaining equal, lead to a reduction of borrowing, a reduction in the amount of loanable funds demanded. But a rise or fall of every sensitive competitive price is *caused* by something. If the rise in interest rates has been *itself* caused by a rise in the "demand schedule for investment" (as Keynes parenthetically and left-handedly admits to be possible) then the rise in interest rates is merely an adjustment to the rise in the "demand schedule for investment," and will not necessarily cause less loanable funds to be demanded than before. Indeed, if the rise in interest rates is not sufficient to offset the rise in the demand schedule for investment, *more* capital will be demanded at the higher interest rate than at the previous lower one. And as a rise in interest rates may encourage saving and lending, this rise in interest rates may be precisely what is needed to bring forth more loanable funds to meet the increased demand.

What Keynes illustrates in the paragraph quoted above is his persistent fallacy (upon which the whole structure of his General Theory rests) of considering the effects of interest rates only on borrowers and not on lenders, the effect of wage-rates only on workers' incomes and never on entrepreneurs' costs. It is this wilful blindness to the two-sidedness of every transaction—this concentration on the incentives to borrowing and obliviousness of those to lending, on the incentives of the buyer and not of the seller, of the Consumer and not of the Producer, this terrific to-do about the propensity to consume while the propensity to work is taken for granted or forgotten—it is this one-eyed vision that constitutes the Keynesian "revolution."

The natural consequences of the Keynesian economic philosophy were vividly portrayed by Patrick Barrington (two years before the particular rationalization that appeared in the *General Theory*) in his poem in *Punch:* [1]

I Want to be a Consumer

"And what do you mean to be?"
The kind old Bishop said
As he took the boy on his ample knee
And patted his curly head.
"We should all of us choose a calling
To help Society's plan;
Then what do you mean to be, my boy,
When you grow to be a man?"

"I want to be a Consumer,"
The bright-haired lad replied

[1] Issue of April 25, 1934. Reprinted by permission of *Punch,* London.

As he gazed up into the Bishop's face
  In innocence open-eyed.
"I've never had aims of a selfish sort,
  For that, as I know, is wrong.
I want to be a Consumer, Sir,
  And help the world along.

"I want to be a Consumer
  And work both night and day,
For that is the thing that's needed most,
  I've heard Economists say,
I won't just be a Producer,
  Like Bobby and James and John;
I want to be a Consumer, Sir,
  And help the nation on."

"But what do you want to be?"
  The Bishop said again,
"For we all of us have to work," said he,
  "As must, I think, be plain.
Are you thinking of studying medicine
  Or taking a Bar exam?"
"Why, no!" the bright-haired lad replied
  As he helped himself to jam.

"I want to be a Consumer
  And live in a useful way;
For that is the thing that's needed most,
  I've heard Economists say.
There are too many people working
  And too many things are made.
I want to be a Consumer, Sir,
  And help to further Trade.

"I want to be a Consumer
  And do my duty well;
For that is the thing that's needed most,
  I've heard Economists tell.
I've made up my mind," the lad was heard,
  As he lit a cigar, to say;
"I want to be a Consumer, Sir,
  And I want to begin today."

Chapter XI

"THE MULTIPLIER"

1. *The Magic of It*

We now come to the strange concept of "the multiplier," about which some Keynesians make more fuss than about anything else in the Keynesian system. Indeed, a whole literature has developed around this concept alone.

Let us try to see what Keynes means by the term.

> In given circumstances a definite ratio, to be called the *Multiplier,* can be established between income and investment and, subject to certain simplifications, between the total employment and the employment directly employed on investment. . . . This further step is an integral part of our theory of employment, since it establishes a precise relationship, given the propensity to consume, between aggregate employment and income and the rate of investment (p. 113).

Keynes gives credit to R. F. Kahn for first introducing the concept of the multiplier into economy theory in 1931. But Kahn's was an *"employment multiplier"* whereas Keynes's is an *"investment multiplier"* (p. 115).

Now the average propensity to consume, the reader will recall, is "the functional relationship . . . between . . . a given level of income in terms of wage-units, and . . . the expenditure on consumption out of that level of income" (p. 90). So, "if C_w is the amount of consumption and Y_w is income (both measured in wage-units) ΔC_w has the same sign as ΔY_w but is smaller in amount, *i.e.* $\frac{d\,C_w}{d\,Y_w}$ is positive and less than unity" (p. 96).

What this means, in simple and numerical terms, is that if out of three units of income, two are spent on consumption, the "propensity to consume" will be $\frac{2}{3}$.

Now in Chapter 10, and on page 115, Keynes advances to the concept of "the *marginal* propensity to consume." He defines this, however, by precisely the same mathematical expression and notation as he has previously used to express what he now calls "the *average* propensity to consume," viz. $\frac{d\,C_w}{d\,Y_w}$ (p. 115). The *marginal* propensity to consume is the relation of the *increase* in consumption to the *increase* in "real income" when the income of the community increases.

The reader might not be inclined to imagine, at first glance, that either the average propensity to consume or the marginal propensity to consume was a matter of much importance so far as the *business cycle* or the *extent of employment* was concerned. Keynes simply tells us that out of a given amount of income, or of increase of income, some, but not all of it, will be spent on consumption, and some, but not all of it, will be saved.

Now economists have long pointed out that the greater the percentage of the national income that is saved and invested, the more rapid, other things being equal, will be the growth in production and the more rapidly, therefore, will the real level of income in the community rise. But just how any significant discovery concerning fluctuations in business and employment could follow from the truism that people will spend something and save something out of their incomes it is difficult to see.

Yet Keynes does think he gets a magical result from this truism. The marginal propensity to consume "is of considerable importance, because it tells us how the next increment of output will *have to be* [sic! my italics] divided between consumption and investment" (p. 115). And from this Keynes derives the magic "investment Multiplier," *k*. "It tells us that, when there is an increment of aggregate investment, income will increase by an amount which is *k* times the increment of investment" (p. 115).

Let us try to find in plainer language what it is that Keynes is saying here. He explains on the next page: "It follows, therefore, that, if the consumption psychology of the community is such that they will choose to consume, e.g. nine-tenths of an increment of income, then the multiplier *k* is 10; and the total employment caused by (e.g.) increased public works will be ten times the primary employment provided by the public works themselves" (pp. 116-117).

What Keynes is saying, among other things, is that the more a community *spends* of its income, and the *less* it saves, the faster will its real income grow! Nor do the implications of its own logic frighten him. If a community spends none of its additional income (from, say, the increased public works), but saves all of it, then the public works will give only the additional employment that they themselves provide, and that will be the end of it. But if a community spends *all* of the additional income provided by the public works, then the multiplier is *infinity*.[1] This would mean that a small expenditure on public works would increase income without limit, provided only that the community was not poisoned by the presence of savers.

Keynes does not hesitate to accept this deduction, but he accepts it in a peculiar form. "If, on the other hand, they [the community] seek to consume the whole of any increment of income, there will be no point of stability and *prices will rise without limit*" (my italics, p. 117). But just how did prices get into it? The "propensity to consume," and "the multiplier," we have been assured up to this point, are expressed in terms of "wage-units," which, Keynes assures us, means "real" terms and not money terms. Why didn't we hear anything about the effect on prices until we got to an infinite multiplier? This leads us to still another

[1] See Alvin H. Hansen, *A Guide to Keynes*, p. 95, for a confirmation of this interpretation.

peculiarity of Keynesian economics (which we shall examine at a later point), which is the assumption that increased activity and employment have no significant effect on prices and wages until "full employment" is reached—and then everything happens at once. Only then does "true inflation" set in.

It is true, however, that the implications of their logic do frighten Keynes and the Keynesians just a little bit. Their multiplier is too good to be true. Moreover, when their schemes are tried, and their multiplier does not miraculously do its multiplying, they badly need an alibi. This is supplied by the doctrine of "leakages."

> Among the most important of these leakages are the following: (1) a part of the increment of income is used to pay off debts; (2) a part is saved in the form of idle bank deposits; (3) a part is invested in securities purchased from others, who in turn fail to spend the proceeds; (4) a part is spent on imports, which does not help home employment; (5) a part of the purchases is supplied from excess stocks of consumers' goods, which may not be replaced. By reason of leakages of this sort, the employment process peters out after awhile.[2]

2. *Not Fixed or Predictable*

I have said that a whole literature has developed around this concept of "the multiplier." [3] There are many different concepts, in fact: the "logical" theory of the multiplier, which assumes no time lag; the "period-analysis" concept, which assumes time lags; the "comparative-statics" analysis, and so on. Immense ingenuity has gone into the mathematical development of these theories. But if the reader wishes to economize his time before he plows through the monographs of the multiplier addicts he will ask a few simple questions: What reason is there to suppose that there *is* any such thing as "the multiplier"? Or that it is deter-

[2] Alvin H. Hansen, *A Guide to Keynes,* pp. 89-90.

[3] An analysis and a wealth of references will be found in Gottfried Haberler, *Prosperity and Depression,* (Geneva: League of Nations, 1941), pp. 455-479.

mined by the "propensity to consume"? Or that the whole concept is not just a worthless toy, the kind of thing made depressingly familiar by monetary cranks?

There are, in fact, so many things wrong with the "multiplier" concept that it is hard to know where to begin in dealing with them.

Let us try to look at one probable origin of the concept. If a community's income, *by definition,* is equal to what it consumes plus what it invests, and if that community spends nine-tenths of its income on consumption and invests one-tenth, then its income must be ten times as great as its investment. If it spends nineteen-twentieths on consumption and invests one-twentieth, then its income must be twenty times as great as its investment. If it spends ninety-nine-hundredths of its income on consumption and invests the remaining one-hundredth, then its income must be a hundred times its investment. And so *ad infinitum.* These things are true simply because they are different ways of saying the same thing. The ordinary man in the street would understand this. But suppose you have a subtle man, trained in mathematics. He will then see that, given the fraction of the community's income that goes into investment, the income itself can mathematically be called a "function" of that fraction. If investment is one-tenth of income, income will be ten times investment, etc. Then, by some wild leap, this "functional" and purely formal or terminological relationship is confused with a *causal* relationship. Next, the *causal* relationship is stood on its head and the amazing conclusion emerges that the greater the proportion of income spent, and the smaller the fraction that represents investment, the more this investment must "multiply" itself to create the total income!

I admit that all this sounds pretty fantastic; but I am at a loss otherwise how to explain how Keynes came to think that such an amazing *causal* mathematical relationship should exist. Let us, however, look at other observations and notions that might give rise to the hypothesis that there is such a thing as a multiplier.

When, after a depression, a business recovery sets in, then increased expenditure in any direction, whether for investment or consumption, seems to multiply itself many times over. Wesley C. Mitchell, in a book first published in 1913, described this process:

> The conspicuous agent in rousing business from its partial lethargy has often been some propitious event. . . . But . . . these propitious events did no more than accelerate a process of business recuperation already begun. . . . Among the ultimate effects of a period of hard times, then, are: a reduction in the prime and supplementary costs of manufacturing commodities, and in the stocks of goods held by wholesale and retail merchants, a liquidation of business debts, low rates of interest, a banking position that favors an increase in loans, and an increasing demand among investors for corporate securities. . . .
>
> Once started, a revival of activity spreads rapidly over a large part, if not all, of the field of business. For, even when the first impulse toward expansion is sharply confined to a single industry or a single locality, its effects in the restricted field stimulate activity elsewhere.
>
> In part this diffusion of activity proceeds along the lines of interconnection among business enterprises. . . . One line leads back from the industries first stimulated to the industries that provide raw materials and supplementary supplies. Another line leads forward to the chain of enterprises that handle the increased output of commodities. . . .
>
> The diffusion of activity is not confined to these definite lines of interconnection among business enterprises. It proceeds also by engendering an optimistic bias in the calculations of all persons concerned with the active direction of business enterprises and with providing loans. . . .
>
> Most men find their spirits raised by being in optimistic company. Therefore, when the first beneficiaries of a trade revival develop a cheerful frame of mind about the business

outlook, they become centers of infection, and start an epidemic of optimism. . . .

As it spreads, the epidemic of optimism helps to produce conditions that both justify and intensify it. . . .[4]

Those who have a long-term acquaintance with the worlds of business and finance will recognize this as an excellent realistic description of what actually happens in a period of recovery. But it is clear that this is *not a purely mechanical* process, determined by some fixed "fundamental psychological law" from which we cannot escape, or by some rigid and pre-determined "multiplier."

It is true that some consumers begin to spend more because they have more from somebody else (which they may have received in wages, say, from re-employment after idleness). This spending of newly acquired money does of course tend to *accelerate* a recovery. But in any case, in the days before "compensatory" governmental spending, the recovery was usually *initiated* (and certainly in large part continued) by people who had finally ceased to be pessimistic about the business future, and had become convinced that prices were "scraping rock bottom" and might even be due for an upturn.

Some of these people who initiate the upturn are entrepreneurs who have decided to re-stock on raw materials and re-employ some workers. They either borrow from the banks for this purpose, or simply reactivate balances that they have long allowed to remain comparatively idle. Some of the people who initiate the upturn are consumers—and not necessarily solely those who have just got new or increased incomes, but also those who have decided that their jobs are after all safe, or that they will not get a car or a house any cheaper by waiting any longer, and may even have to pay more if they wait. Optimism begets new in-

[4] Though this originally appeared in *Business Cycles,* published in 1913, Part III was separately republished in 1941 with the title *Business Cycles and Their Causes* (Los Angeles: University of California Press). The above excerpts are from pp. 1-5.

come, which by being spent begets still more income, and so on.

Optimism, income, consumption, and investment all *interact,* all mutually increase each other. *But there is never any precise, predictable, mathematical relationship; there is never any fixed, or purely mechanical relationship among these elements.*

"Income," "consumption," and "investment" may be measurable quantities (at least in monetary, though not in "real" terms); but the state of business sentiment, the individual and composite expectations of Messrs. A, B, C . . . N, is *not* a measurable quantity, and can never be put into a meaningful mathematical equation. If optimism is already present, a small "new" expenditure may touch off, or seem to touch off, a wave of expenditure and re-employment. But if the outlook of the community is still basically pessimistic, if some prices or wages or interest rates are still generally regarded, for example, as being unrealistically or unworkably high, the "new" expenditure may be completely wasted so far as any stimulating effect is concerned. In this whole process the concept of a fixed or predictable or predeterminable "multiplier" is *never* of any use.[5]

3. *"Saving" and "Investment" Again*

Keynes consistently fails to provide convincing deductive reasons for any of his leading propositions, or "laws." Nor does he compensate for this by offering any statistical proof of them, or even providing any prima facie statistical presumption in their favor. Instead, he gives us something like this: "It should not be difficult to compile a chart of the marginal propensity to consume at each stage of a trade cycle from the statistics (*if they were available*) of aggregate

[5] Cf. Benjamin M. Anderson, *Economics and the Public Welfare,* p. 397: "The soldiers' bonus payments by the Government under Mr. Hoover made no difference in the business picture. On the other hand, the soldiers' bonus payments under Mr. Roosevelt in 1936, at a time when the business curve was upward sharply, appear to have intensified the movement."

income and aggregate investment at successive dates. At present, however, our statistics are not accurate enough." (My italics, p. 127.)

One would suppose that he would wait until the statistics were compiled before telling us what we would find. It appears that some figures had been compiled, however, by Simon Kuznets; and though they are "very precarious," Keynes is surprised by what they show. "If single years are taken in isolation, the results look rather wild. But if they are grouped in pairs, the multiplier seems to have been less than 3 and probably fairly stable in the neighborhood of 2.5" (p. 128).

One would suppose that Keynes would show the reader how these figures were obtained, what years they covered, etc., but he does nothing of the kind. On the contrary, he says that the marginal propensity to consume shown by these figures—60 to 70 per cent—though "quite plausible for the boom" are "surprisingly, and, in my judgment, improbably low for the slump." In other words, if the statistics do not fit in with Keynes's preconceptions, it is the statistics, not the preconceptions, that are to be suspected or thrown out. If the facts do not substantiate the a priori theory, so much the worse for the facts. Time and again Keynes tries to carry his point by sheer ex cathedra pronouncement. His evident success in carrying it off can only be attributed to the docility of academic opinion.

The whole multiplier concept rests on the assumption of *already existing unemployment*. This of course is a deliberate, even when tacit, assumption on Keynes's part; for it is his contention that substantial unemployment is the "general" situation, and that "full employment" (even when defined to allow for "frictional" unemployment) is only a "special" situation. But this contention is never established.[6] It rests in turn on the assumption that there can be

[6] "In historical fact, as far as I know, unemployment on the scale of a serious social problem is not a typical state of affairs, and in every known case such a situation has followed at no long remove a period of relatively full employment

such a thing, and even that there normally is such a thing, as "an equilibrium with unemployment." This, as we have seen, and will see more fully later, is a contradiction in terms. For while Keynes's "multiplier" and other concepts *assume* unemployment, Keynes never correctly tells us the *reasons* for this unemployment. Those reasons always involve some disequilibrium, some maladjustment in the interrelationships of prices, wage-rates, interest rates, or other costs.

No "multiplier" can be calculated or even discussed except in relation to these maladjustments. If some wage-rates are excessively high in relation to some prices, and no specific voluntary adjustments are made, then a small amount of government spending will be completely ineffective in restoring employment in the specific industries involved. The government spending may have to be so big (and financed in such an inflationary manner) that it raises the nation's whole "price level" sufficiently to increase employment in the affected industries. But even so, the employment could much more easily be brought about by price-and-wage adjustment than by further government spending.

In fact, if unemployment is being caused by specific wage-rates that are too high, and the new government spending merely encourages the unions with excessive wage-rates to demand still higher wage-rates, the new spending may not result in any net increase in employment, and could even be followed by a decrease.

Another difficulty with Keynes's "multiplier" concept is that it does not clearly and consistently distinguish between "real" income (or income measured in constant dollars) and *money* income. True, he expresses his "multiplier"

. . . and, similarly, periods of serious unemployment have in due course come to an end. But the question of how unemployment comes to pass is excluded from this work [the *General Theory*] by the predetermination to make it a 'normal' phenomenon, characteristic of an enterprise economy in stable equilibrium." Frank H. Knight, *Canadian Journal of Economics and Political Science,* February, 1937, p. 106.

most of the time in terms of "wage-units." But we have already seen (p. 64) that he so defines "wage-units" as to make them in fact not a quantity of employment but a quantity of money received by workers who are employed. His "wage-units" are, in brief, not "real" units but monetary units.

And Keynes's "multiplier" jumps without notice from "real" terms to monetary terms. This jump becomes flagrant on pages 116 and 117. There we are told that if the propensity to consume is $\frac{9}{10}$:

> then the multiplier *k* is 10; and the total *employment* caused by (e.g.) increased public works will be ten times the primary *employment* provided by the public works themselves. . . . Only in the event of the community maintaining their consumption unchanged in spite of the increase in *employment and hence in real income,* will the increase of *employment* be restricted to the primary *employment* provided by the public works. [My italics.]

But this passage is immediately followed by this sentence: "If, on the other hand, they seek to consume the whole of any increment of income, there will be no point of stability *and prices will rise without limit.*" (My italics.)

To repeat our question (on p. 137), How did prices get into this? Just where did we jump from "real income" to prices rising without limit? This brings us to another peculiar Keynesian theory (for each fallacy depends for its support upon other fallacies). This is the theory that when there has been unemployment, and demand increases for any reason, the effect is *wholly* to increase employment and/or volume of goods sold—and *never* to increase wage-rates or prices—until the point of "full employment" is reached! Then (as by assumption there can be no more employment) "prices will rise without limit." Neither economic theory, general experience nor available statistics support this Keynesian notion. But we shall postpone further analysis of it until a later point.

One fallacy in the "multiplier" that is alone sufficient to discredit it completely is the assumption that the entire fraction of a community's income that is not "consumed" is *hoarded;* that *no part* of this unconsumed income is invested.

The "propensity to consume," in brief, determines the "multiplier" only on the assumption that *what is not spent on consumption is not spent on anything at all!* If the propensity to consume is 7/10, or 8/10, or 9/10, *or anything less than* 10/10, the economic machine will run down unless "investment" rushes in to fill the "gap" left by "saving." This "investment" can only be supplied by a *deus ex machina,* and this god turns out to be the government with "loan expenditure." All these assumptions are not only false in fact, but a contradiction of Keynes's own formal definitions in the *General Theory* of "saving" and "investment."

For Keynes himself has assured us that in Chapter *6: "Saving* and *Investment* have been so defined that they are necessarily equal in amount, being, for the community as a whole, merely different aspects of the same thing" (p. 74). He has also told us that "the prevalence of the idea that saving and investment, taken in their straightforward sense, can differ from one another, is to be explained, I think, by an optical illusion" (p. 81). Further, he has ridiculed "the new-fangled view that there can be saving without investment or investment without 'genuine' saving" (p. 83).

Yet the notion of a "multiplier" depending on a "propensity to consume" rests on precisely this "optical illusion" and this "new-fangled view." It rests on the assumption that there *can* be "saving" without "investment."

What is involved here is partly a question of fact and partly a question of definition. If we define "saving" as including both money and goods, and "investment" as including both money and goods (the goods in both cases being measured in current money prices) then "saving" and "investment" are at all times necessarily equal and, in fact, merely two names for the same thing. On these definitions the terms "saving" and "investment" could be freely interchanged in any context without change of meaning. Or a common term, such as "unconsumed output," could be substituted for either or both.

But if we define "savings" exclusively in terms of *money* or even of *goods plus money,* and if we define "investment" exclusively in terms of (capital) *goods* (either in "real" terms or at given prices), then there can frequently be discrepancies between "saving" and "investment."

Here is where the "new-fangled view" has its importance. For when investment (by these definitions) exceeds "genuine" saving, there must be inflation; and when "saving" exceeds "investment" (by these definitions) there must be deflation. In fact, only on the assumption that "investment without saving" means that new money-and-credit has been *created,* and "saving without investment" means that some former money-and-credit has been retired or *destroyed,* is the discrepancy between saving and investment possible. With a constant money-and-credit supply, and constant prices, saving and investment even on these second definitions must be equal. (And they must be equal at every moment under *all* conditions, of course, if saving money is defined and treated as "investing" in money.)

But Keynes's "propensity to consume" concept and "multiplier" concept would be meaningless unless he used the terms "saving" and "investment," not as he has defined them in the *General Theory,* but rather as he defined them in his repudiated definitions in *The Treatise on Money.* He assumes that there can in fact be saving without investment and investment without saving.

And he makes this assumption in an extreme degree, to which nothing in the real world corresponds. For his "propensity to save" depends, for its alleged deflationary effects, on the tacit assumption that *no* part of savings is invested. His magically rejuvenating "multiplier," to work out perfectly, assumes that this new investment comes into being without savings. In fact, the mathematics of the multiplier are upset if the recipients of the new income which the new investment is supposed to create do anything but spend the whole of the new income on consumption. If they "save" part of it, the multiplier is decreased. If they themselves "invest" part of it, the multiplier is increased. Yet this multiplier is supposed to be predeterminable by a mathematical formula, and used as a basis of policy and prediction!

4. *"Investment" Means Government Spending*

Close scrutiny reveals still another peculiarity of the "multiplier." "Investment" is supposed to "multiply" employment and income. And yet the amount of investment, *as such,* appears to be entirely irrelevant to the mathematics of the multiplier or the reasoning on which it rests.

For in connection with the multiplier (and indeed most of the time) what Keynes is referring to as "investment" really means *any addition to spending for any purpose.* Keynes shows not the slightest interest in real purpose of real investment, which is to increase productivity, both in quantitative and in qualitative terms, and to reduce costs. All he is interested in is *additional spending,* for any purpose, to produce his multiplier effects. By "investment," when he speaks of the multiplier, he means *government spending,* on no matter what, as long as it creates additional money.

This last idea is never *explicitly* introduced, but is constantly implied. "Loan expenditure," he declares (p. 128), even if "wasteful," "may nevertheless enrich the community on balance." And then he explains in a footnote: "It is often convenient to use the term 'loan expenditure' to include both public investment financed by borrowing from individuals *and also any other current public expenditure which is so financed. . . .* Thus 'loan expenditure' is a convenient expression for the net *borrowings* of public authorities *on all accounts,* whether on capital account *or to meet a budgetary deficit."* (My italics.)

What is really necessary to get the "multiplier" effect, in short, when we start calling things by their right names, is not "investment" but inflation.

"Investment" is irrelevant to the multiplier. If, to take another illustration, we find that the community is spending only eleven-twelfths of its income on goods whose names begin with the letters A to W, inclusive, then we get everything to come out right by having the community spend the other twelfth of its income on the goods beginning with the letters X, Y, Z. And it is of no importance whatever, for this effect, whether the A-W goods or XYZ goods consist wholly or partly of consumer goods or capital goods. The word "investment" is merely being used in a Pickwickian, or Keynesian, sense. And the great advantage of "loan expenditure" is not that it involves investment out of past income, but that it involves *the printing of more money.*

We shall have enough to do in this volume dissecting the errors of Keynes himself, without going into the supplementary or derivative errors introduced by some of the Keynesians. For that reason I shall make no effort here to analyze the "foreign-trade multiplier," which contains, in addition to all the fallacies in the "multiplier" concept itself, additional fallacies based on crude mercantilistic concepts of the effects of imports and exports respectively.

But two criticisms of the "multiplier" remain to be made, and both are basic. In the first place, even granting all of Keynes's other peculiar assumptions, it is difficult to understand just why the multiplier (except by sheer assertion) should necessarily be the reciprocal of the marginal propensity to save. If the marginal propensity to consume is $\frac{9}{10}$, we are told, the multiplier is 10. Why? How?

We have already tried to guess (p. 139) how Keynes might have arrived at this astonishing notion. But let us take an imaginary illustration. Ruritania is a Keynesian country that has a national income of $10 billion and consumes only $9 billion. Therefore it has a propensity to consume of $\frac{9}{10}$. But as in some way it manages to "save" 10 per cent of its income without "investing" the 10 per cent in anything at all, it has unemployment of 10 per cent. Then the Keynesian government comes to the rescue by spending, not $1 billion, but only $100 million on "investment." For as the "multiplier" is 10 (because Keynes has written out a mathematical formula which *makes* it 10 when the marginal propensity to consume is $\frac{9}{10}$), this $100 million dollars worth of direct new employment somehow multiplies itself to $1 billion of total new employment to "fill the gap," and lo! "full employment" is achieved.

(Expressing this in terms of employment, we might say: When the propensity to consume of Ruritania is $\frac{9}{10}$, then, unless something is done about it, only 9 million of Ruritania's working force of 10 million are employed. It is then simply necessary to spend enough to employ *directly* 100,000 more persons, and *their* spending, in turn, will ensure a total additional employment of 1 million.)

The question I am raising here is simply *why* such a relationship between the marginal propensity to consume and the multiplier is supposed to hold. Is it some inevitable mathematical deduction? If so, its causal inevitability somehow escapes me. Is it an empirical generalization from actual experience? Then why doesn't Keynes condescend to offer even the slightest statistical verification?

We have already seen that *investment,* strictly speaking, is irrelevant to the "multiplier"—that any extra spending on anything will do. We have already illustrated this by dividing commodities into those beginning with the letters from A to W, and those beginning with the letters X, Y, and Z. But a still further *reductio ad absurdum* is possible. Here is a far more potent multiplier, and on Keynesian grounds there can be no objection to it. Let Y equal the income of the whole community. Let R equal *your* (the reader's) income. Let V equal the income of everybody else. Then we find that V is a completely stable function of Y; whereas your income is the active, volatile, uncertain element in the social income. Let us say the equation arrived at is:

$$V = .99999\,Y$$

Then, $Y = .99999\,Y + R$

$$.00001\,Y = R$$

$$Y = 100{,}000\,R$$

Thus we see that your own personal multiplier is far more powerful than the investment multiplier. To increase social income and thereby cure depression and unemployment, it is only necessary for the government to print a certain number of dollars and give them to *you*. Your spending will prime the pump for an increase in the national income 100,000 times as great as the amount of your spending itself.[6]

The final criticism of the multiplier that must be made is so basic that it almost makes all the others unnecessary. This is that the multiplier, and the whole unemployment that it is supposed to cure, is based on the tacit assumption of inflexible prices and inflexible wages. Once we assume flexibility in prices and wages, and full responsiveness to the forces of the market, the whole Keynesian system dissolves into thin air. For even if we make the other thoroughly unrealistic assumptions that Keynes makes (even if we assume, for example, that people "save" a third of their incomes by simply sticking the money under the mattress, and not investing it in anything) completely responsive wages and prices would simply mean that wages and prices would fall enough for the former volume of sales to be made at lower prices and for "full employment" to continue at lower wage-rates. When the money was taken out from under the mattress again, it would simply be

[6] I am indebted for this illustration to a forthcoming book by Murray N. Rothbard.

equivalent to an added money supply and would raise prices and wages again.

I am not arguing here that prices and wages are *in fact* perfectly fluid. But neither, as Keynes assumes, are wage-rates completely rigid under conditions of less than full employment. And to the extent that they *are* rigid, they are so either through the anti-social policy of those who insist on employment only at above-equilibrium wage-rates, or through the very economic ignorance and confusion in business and political circles to which Keynes's theories themselves make so great a contribution.

But this is a subject that we shall develop more at length later.

5. *Paradox and Pyramids*

In Section VI of Chapter 10 on the multiplier, Keynes lets himself go in one of the irresponsible little essays in satire and sarcasm that run through the *General Theory* as they run through all his work. As these essays rest on obviously false assumptions, and as Keynes writes them with his tongue more or less in his cheek, it might seem to be as lacking in humor to "refute" them seriously as to "refute" a paradox of G. K. Chesterton or a epigram of Oscar Wilde. But these little essays are the most readable and the most easily understood part of Keynes's work. They are quoted by many laymen with chuckles of approval and delight. So we had better give them a certain amount of serious attention.

Keynes begins Section VI by assuming "involuntary unemployment" without explaining how it comes about. At the same time he assumes that the only way to cure it is by "loan expenditure"—no matter how wasteful. "Pyramid-building, earthquakes, even wars may serve to increase wealth, if the education of our statesmen on the principles of the classical economics stands in the way of anything better" (p. 129). (If our statesmen were *really* educated in the principles of classical economics, they would understand that unemployment is usually the result of union insistence on excessive wage-rates, or some similar price-cost maladjustment.)

One of the most revealing paragraphs in this section is the footnote on page 128, which I have already quoted (p. 148) and which I quote again with different italics: "It is often convenient to use the term 'loan-expenditure' to include both *public* investment financed by borrowing from individuals and also any other current *public* expenditure which is so financed. . . . Thus 'loan-expenditure' is a convenient expression for the net *borrowings* of *public* authorities on all accounts, whether on capital account or *to meet a budgetary deficit.*" This explains what Keynes really means by "investment" in his multiplier equations. It is not investment in the traditional or the dictionary sense. It means any *government* spending, provided the money is borrowed, *i.e.,* provided the spending is financed by inflation.

Keynes then goes on to write what he evidently considers a perfectly devastating satire on gold and gold-mining. "Gold-mining," he tells us, "which not only adds nothing whatever to the real wealth of the world but involves the disutility of labor, is the most acceptable" to the orthodox of all methods of creating employment. "If the Treasury were to fill old bottles with banknotes, bury them at suitable depths in disused coal mines which are then filled up to the surface with town rubbish, and leave it to private enterprise on well-tried principles of *laissez-faire* to dig the notes up again . . . there need be no more unemployment" (p. 129).

This sentence tells us a great deal more about the prejudices and confusions of Keynes than it does either about gold, gold-mining, the principles of private enterprise, or the purposes of employment. There would of course be no need for private enterprise to dig up the "banknotes." The Treasury could simply run off more on its printing presses for no more than it cost for the ink and paper. But there is a slight difference between digging up gold and digging up paper money which Keynes neglects to mention. This is that gold has kept its high value over the centuries, not only when it was the international monetary standard but even since it was "dethroned," whereas paper currencies, by an almost inexorable law, have sunk into worthlessness.

(A compilation by Franz Pick in 1957 of the depreciation of *fifty-six* different paper currencies showed that in the nine-year period from January 1948 to December 1956, for example, the American dollar, to which so many other currencies were ostensibly tied, itself lost 15 per cent of its purchasing power, while the British pound sterling lost 34 per cent, the French franc 52 per cent, and the paper currencies of Chile, Paraguay, Bolivia, and Korea, from 93 to 99 per cent.)

The reason for this difference is that the quantity of gold that could profitably (*i.e.*, with a surplus of proceeds over costs) be dug up and refined depends on natural factors largely beyond human control, whereas the amount of paper dollars that are printed, or that would be buried and then dug up under Keynes's scheme, would depend solely on the caprice of the politicians or "monetary authorities" in power.

Keynes proceeds to patronize gold mines further. He tells us that they "are of the greatest value and importance to civilization" because "gold-mining is the only pretext for digging holes in the ground which has recommended itself to bankers as sound finance" (p. 130). Only? One can think also of oil wells, water wells, canals, subways, railway tunnels, house foundations, quarries, coal mines, zinc, lead, silver and copper mines. . . . But it seems a pity to spoil the noble lord's rhetoric.

It is one of Keynes's fixed convictions, as it was of the churchmen and philosophers of the Middle Ages, that gold is absolutely worthless and "sterile." "Ancient Egypt was doubly fortunate, and doubtless owed to this its fabled wealth," he writes, "in that it possessed *two* activities, namely, pyramid-building as well as the search for the precious metals, the fruits of which, since they could not serve the needs of man by being consumed, did not stale with abundance" (p. 131).

Keynes did not think that gold had value because *he* could not understand the source of its value. The fact that nearly all men through the ages have valued gold only indicated, in Keynes's eyes, that they were incurably stupid. But perhaps the stupidity is with the critics of gold. It is true, as those critics are always insisting, that you cannot eat it or wear it; but it is more satisfactory than custard pies or overcoats as a medium of exchange. And it is enormously more satisfactory as a medium of exchange and a store of value, as we shall see, than paper money issued in accordance with political pressures or bureaucratic whim.

Chapter XII

"THE MARGINAL EFFICIENCY OF CAPITAL"

1. *Slippery Terms*

We have had frequent occasion to note the ambiguities, inconsistencies, and contradictions that run through the *General Theory;* but in Chapter 11, "The Marginal Efficiency of Capital," they reach an even higher level than in the chapters preceding.

We shall see, as we go on, that Keynes uses the phrase, "marginal efficiency of capital," in so many different senses that it becomes at last impossible to keep track of them. Let us begin with his first formal definition:

> The relation between the prospective yield of a capital asset and its supply price or replacement cost, *i.e.* the relation between the prospective yield of one more unit of that type of capital and the cost of producing that unit, furnishes us with the *marginal efficiency of capital* of that type. More precisely, *I define the marginal efficiency of capital as being equal to that rate of discount which would make the present value of the series of annuities given by the returns expected from the capital-asset during its life just equal to its supply price.* [My italics in this sentence.] This gives us the marginal efficiencies of particular types of capital-assets. The greatest of these marginal efficiencies can then be regarded as the marginal efficiency of capital in general.
>
> The reader should note that the marginal efficiency of capital is here defined in terms of the *expectation* of yield and of the *current* supply price of the capital-asset. It depends on the rate of return expected to be obtainable on money if it were invested in a *newly* produced asset . . . (pp. 135-136).

Keynes then goes on to tell us that we can build up a "schedule" of the marginal efficiency of capital which we can call alternatively the investment demand-schedule, and that "the rate of investment will be pushed to the point on the investment demand-schedule where the marginal efficiency of capital in general is equal to the market rate of interest" (p. 136-137).

Keynes next asks how his own definition of capital is related to common usage. "The *Marginal Productivity* or *Yield* or *Efficiency* or *Utility* of Capital are familiar terms which we have all frequently used" (p. 137). (Just why does he adopt the vaguest of them?)

"It is not easy by searching the literature of economics," Keynes goes on, "to find a clear statement of what economists have usually intended by these terms. There are at least three ambiguities to clear up" (pp. 137-138). It is amusing to find Keynes, that father of so many ambiguities, so persistently worried about the alleged ambiguities of others.

> There is, to begin with, the ambiguity whether we are concerned with the increment of physical product per unit of time due to the employment of one more physical unit of capital, or with the increment of value due to the employment of one more value unit of capital. The former involves difficulties as to the definition of the physical unit of capital, which I believe to be both insoluble and unnecessary. It is, of course, possible to say that ten laborers will raise more wheat from a given area when they are in a position to make use of certain additional machines; but I know of no means of reducing this to an intelligible arithmetical ratio which does not bring in values (p. 138).

All this is entirely true. But it is strange coming from the coiner and adopter of "wage-units." On Keynes's own definition, as we have seen, these are measured in proportion to remuneration; they are therefore not "real" units or "employment" units, but units of money value. If, in offering the above illustration, Keynes had remembered that it is also possible to say that five skilled or efficient laborers will raise as much wheat from a given area as ten unskilled or inefficient laborers, he would also have seen that there is no intelligible way of measuring "wage-units" which does not bring in values. Why was Keynes so much more acute in detecting the ambiguities of other writers than in detecting his own?

2. *Interest Rates Embody Expectations*

We next come to what Keynes seems to consider his special contribution:

> Finally, there is the distinction, the neglect of which has been the main cause of confusion and misunderstanding, between the increment of value obtainable by using an additional quantity of capital in the *existing* situation, and the series of increments which it is expected to obtain *over the whole life* of the additional capital asset. . . . This involves the whole question of the place of expectation in economic theory (p. 138).
>
> [And again:] The most important confusion concerning the meaning and significance of the marginal efficiency of capital has ensued on the failure to see that it depends on the *prospective* yield of capital, and not merely on its current yield (p. 141).

All this is true. And yet one of Keynes's own principal errors in his discussion of the relation of the marginal efficiency of capital [1] to interest rates is his failure or refusal to recognize that current *interest rates* are *also* determined in large part by expectations regarding the future. The comparison is analogous to that between the valuation of a share of stock and the valuation of a bond. When the long-term interest rate is 4 per cent, a high grade bond yielding

[1] It is difficult to analyze Keynes's theories without *beginning* with his own terminology and concepts. Some economists contend that there is no such thing as the "marginal efficiency (or productivity) of capital." They admit that capital *goods* have marginal value but argue that capital *value* is derived from income value rather than the other way round. But this question will be postponed to later consideration.

$4 a year will sell at $100. At the same time a good stock currently paying a dividend of $5 a year may also sell at $100. It does not sell at more because the continuation of the dividend is less certain than the continuation of the interest on the bond, and more liable to fluctuation from year to year. But a stock currently paying a dividend of only $3 a year may sell at $100 because market opinion believes it highly probable that the stock will soon be paying more. The current price of *both* dividend-paying (or non-dividend-paying) stocks and interest-paying bonds is determined by expectations regarding the future. When the interest rate is 4 per cent, some bonds paying $4 a year will be selling much below $100, and yielding, say 5 or 5½ per cent interest on their capital value, because they embody greater risk than gilt-edge bonds.

(In the preceding paragraph I have used the phrase "the interest rate." This is in accordance with the practice of Keynes and many other economists, who sometimes write of "the" interest rate and sometimes of "the complex [or constellation] of interest rates." "The interest rate" is usually a simpler and more convenient phrase and concept provided it is not misused—that is, provided its arbitrary and over-simplified nature is constantly kept in mind. When I use the term, I shall be taken to mean something like "the current average annual percentage yield on AAA bonds maturing in twenty years or longer." Even so, it is safer most of the time at least to make explicit whether one is talking of "the long-term interest rate" or "the short-term interest rate"—even though each of these phrases also refers to a whole complex of interest rates, and even though the line dividing "short-term" from "long-term" is an arbitrary one—"short-term" sometimes meaning, say, five years or less to maturity, sometimes one year or less to maturity.)

Because Keynes (usually) refuses to recognize that the interest rate as well as "the marginal efficiency of capital" is governed by expectations, he makes unjustified criticisms of other writers and builds up a false theory of his own. "The expectation of a fall in the value of money stimulates investment," he declares, "and hence employment generally, because it raises the schedule of the marginal efficiency of capital, *i.e.* the investment demand-schedule; and the expectation of a rise in the value of money is depressing, because it lowers the schedule of the marginal efficiency of capital" (pp. 141-142). This is the equivalent of saying that inflation, and even more, the threat of further inflation, is good because it stimulates investment and employment.

And it is because it interferes with the foregoing theory that Keynes criticizes Irving Fisher's "distinction between the money rate of interest and the real rate of interest where the latter is equal to the former after correction for changes in the value of money" (p. 142).

> It is difficult to make sense of this theory as stated, [declares Keynes] because it is not clear whether the change in the value of money is or is not assumed to be foreseen. There is no escape from the dilemma that, if it is not foreseen, there will be no effect on current affairs; whilst, if it is foreseen, the prices of existing goods will be forthwith so adjusted that the advantages of holding money and of holding goods are again equalized, and it will be too late for holders of money to gain or to suffer a change in the rate of interest which will offset the prospective change during the period of the loan in the value of the money lent (p. 142).

It is inexcusable, in the first place, for Keynes to write of Fisher's statement of his theory that "it is not clear whether the change in the value of money is or is not assumed to be foreseen." Irving Fisher wrote clearly, for example, in *The Theory of Interest* (1930, p. 37): "The influence of such changes in the purchasing power of money on the money rate of interest will be different according to whether or not that change is *foreseen*." The italics here are not mine but Fisher's own. And the sentence is followed by paragraphs of further unequivocal explanation.

It is, moreover, not too difficult to escape from Keynes's

"dilemma." The easiest way is to point to an undeniable and repeated fact of experience—that in the later stages of a hyper-inflation, when further inflation is generally expected, interest rates do begin to soar. This happened, for example, in the great inflation in Germany in 1923:

> In the first phases of the inflation the rate of interest tended to rise in Germany, as always happens at a time of monetary depreciation. But for a long time the rise in interest rates was appreciably less than the rate of currency depreciation. Subsequently the rate of interest became more sensitive to the influence of the currency depreciation. As the depreciation became more rapid, the premium for the creditor's risk was bound to increase, and consequently in the final phase of inflation the rate of interest was extremely high. At the beginning of November 1923 the rates for 'call money' rose as high as 30 per cent per day! [2]

This situation will practically always be found in the later stages of a serious inflation. For example, as I write this, there is a serious inflation in Chile, and the commercial bank rate [according to *International Financial Statistics* (June, 1957), published by the International Monetary Fund] rose from 7.84 per cent in 1937 to 13.95 per cent in 1956.[3]

As I write this, also, the same phenomenon has occurred in England itself, and in large part, ironically, because of the cheap money policy that Keynes took such leadership in advocating. In June of 1957 the British Treasury 2½ per cent bonds, which had been issued in 1946, during the last phases of the cheap-money policy, could be bought at 50, or half the original purchase price. But while prime bonds in

2 Constantino Bresciani-Turroni, *The Economics of Inflation* (London: Allen & Unwin, 1937), p. 360. (Italian edition, 1931.)

3 Unfortunately, as I have found, statistics giving the real lending rates of commercial banks are not easily available, and often require on-the-spot investigation in the country concerned. Official discount rates have become fictions or artifacts designed rather to conceal than to reveal the actual situation. Perhaps the comparative inaccessibility of the actual interest rates charged accounts for Keyne's otherwise astonishing ignorance on this point.

Britain were going begging in June of 1957 at heavy discounts, prices of corporate shares were being bid up to levels where, despite the risks they involved, their return to the investor was in many cases substantially lower than those available on gilt-edge bonds. As one leading London investment house explained:

> Clearly, the main cause of the trouble lies in the barely checked progress of the creeping inflation. . . . The argument is, indeed, put forward that, since the pound has been depreciating in the past decade at an average rate of $4\frac{3}{4}$ per cent per annum, any investment likely to show a total net return on income and capital accounts over a given period of less than this amount is giving a negative yield and should be discarded.[4]

A similar development took place in the United States in July, 1957, and again in the summer and fall of 1958.

3. *Effects of Expected Inflation*

Now let us look at the theoretical explanation of this. It is true that in a period of inflation, and when further inflation is widely foreseen, prices of existing goods rise in anticipation. *But prices of different goods rise in different degrees, determined by the nature of the commodity and the nature of its market.* This year's perishable foodstuffs, for example, reflect this year's monetary inflation in their price; but they cannot reflect next year's *expected* inflation because they cannot be *held* till next year; they must be consumed *now.* The same reasoning applies to current *services* of all kinds. A durable good with a two-year life can reflect less expected further inflation in its present price than a durable good with a five-year life, and that in turn can reflect less than a durable good with a still longer life. I do not mean to suggest that the reflection of further expected inflation in present prices is directly proportional

[4] Quoted by the First National City Bank of New York, in its monthly letter of August, 1957.

to the life span of particular goods; this is only one of the factors involved. It is sufficient to note that expected further inflation is reflected in different degrees in the current price response of different goods.

Now when other conditions are such that they would bring about both a real and a money rate of interest of, say, 4 per cent, but when lenders generally believe that next year's average price level (including both perishable and durable goods, in the proportions in which they are expected to be consumed) will be 3 per cent higher than this year's price level (for the same goods "mix"), they will charge 7 per cent in order to get the real return of 4 per cent. And borrowers will pay this 7 per cent *if* they expect to use the borrowed funds *for acquiring durable goods or investments that they believe will rise even more than 3 per cent in the year*. (Or at more than that rate over a series of years corresponding to the period of the loan.)

Keynes constantly goes wrong, as we shall see, because he chronically thinks in terms of averages and aggregates that conceal the very causal relations he is trying to study. This aggregate, in-block, or lump thinking is the exact opposite of economic analysis. Its recent prevalence, largely under Keynes's influence, represents a serious retrogression in economic thought.

Keynes even argues that the rate of interest *cannot* rise under the conditions he assumes, because if it did it would spoil his theory about the "stimulating" effect of the expectation of further inflation:

> The stimulating effect of the expectation of higher prices is due, not to its raising the rate of interest (that would be a paradoxical way of stimulating output—insofar as the rate of interest rises, the stimulating effect is to that extent offset), but to its raising the marginal efficiency of a given stock of capital. *If* the rate of interest were to rise *pari passu* with the marginal efficiency of capital, here would be *no* stimulating effect from the expectation of rising prices. For the stimulus to output depends on the marginal efficiency of a given stock

of capital rising *relatively* to the rate of interest. (His italics, p. 143.)

Keynes's admissions here are quite correct. "*If* the rate of interest were to rise *pari passu* with the marginal efficiency of capital, there would be *no* stimulating effect from the expectation of rising prices." But what is Keynes's reason for supposing that the rate of interest will *not* rise with the marginal efficiency of capital? It lies in his assumption that "the marginal efficiency of capital" embodies expectations and that the rate of interest does not. The marginal efficiency of capital, by Keynes's order, has entered the realm of "dynamic" economics, but the rate of interest, also by Keynes's order, has been kept in the realm of "static" economics.

There is no warrant for his assumption. It does not correspond with the facts of economic life. If the marginal efficiency of capital embodies expectations, so do interest rates. To assume otherwise is to assume that entrepreneurs are influenced by their expectations but that lenders are not. Or it is to assume that entrepreneurs as a body can be expecting prices to rise while lenders as a body do not expect prices to rise. Or it is to assume that lenders are too stupid to know what borrowers know. If the borrowers wish to borrow more because they expect higher commodity prices, this means, in other words, that they expect to pay the lenders back in depreciated dollars. And, according to Keynes, the lenders will be perfectly agreeable to this. They will not demand a higher interest rate as an insurance premium against the depreciated dollars in which they expect to be repaid. They will not even ask a higher interest rate because the demand for their loanable funds has increased. In brief, the Keynesian assumption that the marginal efficiency of capital is influenced by expectations regarding the future, but that the rate of interest is not, rests on inconsistent premises.

The sad truth is that Keynes has no consistent assumptions regarding any of his major concepts or theses. The assumption of one sentence is as likely as not to be contradicted in the next. Thus on the very page from which the foregoing quotation is taken Keynes tells us that "the *expectations,* which are held concerning the complex of rates of interest for various terms which will rule in the future, will be *partially* reflected in the complex of rates of interest which rule today." (My italics, p. 143.) Here is an admission that an expected rise in future interest rates *will* be reflected in present interest rates, but only "partially." Yet as Keynes promises us that in his Chapter 22, "we shall show that the succession of Boom and Slump can be described and analyzed in terms of the fluctuations of the marginal efficiency of capital relatively to the rate of interest" (p. 144), we shall wait till then to pursue our own analysis of this relationship.

4. *Does Lending Double the Risk?*

In Section IV of Chapter 11 Keynes finds it "important to distinguish" between "two types of risk" affecting the volume of investment "which have not commonly been distinguished.... The first is the entrepreneur's or borrower's risk and arises out of doubts in his own mind as to the probability of his actually earning the prospective yield for which he hopes" (p. 144). (I may point out in passing that to the extent to which the risk is real, it arises out of the objective situation, and not out of the doubts in the entrepreneur's own mind. These doubts may overestimate or underestimate the real risk involved, but do not determine it.)

> But where a system of borrowing and lending exists [Keynes continues], by which I mean the granting of loans with a margin of real or personal security, a second type of risk is relevant which we may call the lender's risk. This may be due either to moral hazard, *i.e.* voluntary default or . . . involuntary default due to the disappointment of expectation (p. 144).

> A third source of risk might be added, namely, a *possible* adverse change in the value of the monetary standard which renders a money-loan to this extent less secure than a real asset; though all *or most* of this should be already reflected, and therefore absorbed, in the price of durable real assets. (My italics, p. 144.)

This sentence is significant because it admits, in the grudging phrase "or most," that not *all* the risk to the lender of a *possible* rise in prices will necessarily be *already* reflected in the price of "durable real assets." But this admission contradicts the inescapable "dilemma" that Keynes had presented only two pages previously to prove that the present money rate of interest could not be raised by lenders to protect themselves against an expected further inflation. Let us continue, however, with Keynes's "two types of risk":

> Now the first type of risk is, in a sense, a real social cost . . . The second, however, is *a pure addition to the cost of investment* which would not exist if the borrower and lender were the same person. [My italics.] Moreover, it involves in part a duplication of a proportion of the entrepreneur's risk, which is added *twice* to the pure rate of interest to give the minimum prospective yield which will induce the investment (pp. 144-145).

This is pure nonsense. The risk is not "duplicated"; it is not "added twice"; it is simply shared. To the extent that the entrepreneur assumes the risk the lender is relieved of it; the lender assumes a risk only to the extent that the entrepreneur fails to assume it. Suppose entrepreneur E borrows $10,000 from lender L to start a small business. Suppose the entrepreneur loses the whole $10,000. Then a total of $10,000 is lost, not $20,000. If the entrepreneur makes the whole loss good out of his own pocket, none of it falls on the lender. If the entrepreneur goes bankrupt, or leaves town, without repaying the lender a cent, then the lender takes a loss of $10,000. But the borrower E has lost nothing of his own; he has simply thrown away L's $10,000. If the borrower is able to make good $6,000 of the loss out of his own resources, but is compelled to default on the rest, then $4,000 of the loss falls on the lender—not more. Would Keynes argue that fewer houses are built with the mortgage system than would be built without it, because mortgages "double the risk," or constitute "a pure addition to the cost of investment"? It is the mortgage, on the contrary, that enables the builder or owner to build or own the house. The mortgagor, on his part, assumes that the market value of the house above the amount of the mortgage gives him *additional* security (beyond the good faith of the mortgagee, the other resources of the mortgagee, and the mortgagor's legal recourse against the mortgagee) which removes or minimizes his own risk.

But if the objective "social" risk is clearly not increased "where a system of borrowing and lending exists," perhaps, it may be said, Keynes was arguing that the *subjective* risk, the *feeling* of risk, is doubled or "added twice." This too is an incredible and self-contradictory assumption. For the lender contents himself with a fixed rate of interest, and with the eventual return merely of the original amount (in dollar terms) of his capital investment, on the assumption that he is leaving the risk of loss as well as the prospect of gain to the borrower. Corporations have found that they can raise the maximum amount of capital by issuing a judicious mixture of common stock, preferred stock, debenture bonds, first mortgage bonds, etc., partly depending on market (and tax) conditions at the time of issue, but depending, also, on the diverse temperaments and purposes of the different investors to whom they are appealing. Those who are willing to assume the entrepreneurial risks in exchange for the entrepreneurial prospects of profit and capital gain become common stockholders. Those who wish to minimize their risks, and are content with a low but presumably dependable and regular interest rate, and the mere return of their dollar capital investment, will buy what they regard as "gilt-edge" bonds. They become technically the creditors of the stockholders in the same corporation.

To argue that such an arrangement *increases* or "duplicates" either the objective risk or the subjective sense of risk is as absurd as it would be to argue that the institution of fire insurance increases the risk, or sense of risk, of fire. It is precisely because the institution of insurance *shares* and *diffuses* risks that risks are more freely taken; that more houses are built and more investments made. And it is precisely "where a system of borrowing and lending exists" that investment increases enormously compared with what it would be where such a system did not exist.

I regret having taken so much space to point out this elementary error. I have done so only because it illustrates once more, and so clearly, the kind of perverse logic typical of the *General Theory*.

5. *Confusions About "Statics" and "Dynamics"*

Section V of Chapter 11 is less than a page in length, but none the less reveals the extraordinary arbitrariness of Keynes's reasoning:

> The schedule of the marginal efficiency of capital is of fundamental importance because it is mainly through this factor (much more than through the rate of interest) that the expectation of the future influences the present. The mistake of regarding the marginal efficiency of capital primarily in terms of the *current* yield of capital equipment, which would be correct only in the static state where there is no changing future to influence the present, has had the result of breaking the theoretical link between today and tomorrow. Even the rate of interest is, virtually, a *current* phenomenon; and if we reduce the marginal efficiency of capital to the same status, we cut ourselves off from taking any direct account of the influence of the future in our analysis of the existing equilibrium.
>
> The fact that the assumptions of the static state often un-

derlie present-day economic theory, imports into it a large element of unreality (pp. 145-146).

Few passages even of Keynes are more arbitrary or confused. Boom and Slump, we were told on page 144, are to be "described and analyzed in terms of the fluctuations of the marginal efficiency of capital relatively to the rate of interest." But now we are to understand that whereas the marginal efficiency of capital is to be treated as a "dynamic" concept, the rate of interest is to be treated as a "static" concept. The rate of interest is a "current" phenomenon, but apparently the marginal efficiency of capital is not. The marginal efficiency of capital reflects expectations regarding the future, but the rate of interest "virtually" does not. And then even this contrast is partly repudiated. For in the passage just quoted, Keynes puts a footnote mark after the word "virtually," and the footnote says: "Not completely; for its [the rate-of-interest's] value partly reflects the *uncertainty* of the future. Moreover, the relations between rates of interest for different terms depends on expectations" (p. 145).

But this footnote gives away the point of the passage to which it refers. The truth is that both "static" and "dynamic" analysis are necessary in economics; that "static" analysis is a necessary preliminary to "dynamic" analysis; but that the one unforgivable sin is to confuse them in the same analysis.

One of the chief defects in Keynes's analysis, not only in the passage quoted above but throughout the *General Theory,* is his failure to adhere to any fixed meanings for his terms. He plays particularly fast and loose, as we have seen already and shall see later, with his term "the marginal efficiency of capital." The ambiguities and bad reasoning that he falls into could have been avoided by dropping this vague term completely, and substituting for it any one of half a dozen different terms, depending upon which was really appropriate to his meaning in a given context. A simpler and less vague term than "efficiency" in connection with capital is "yield." (Keynes himself uses it as a synonym even in the passage quoted above.) Substituting this for greater clarity, we would then have several terms depending upon what we wished to say in a given context:

1. The *current* yield of a specific capital instrument.
2. The *expected future* yield of a specific capital instrument.
3. The *current* marginal yield of a *type* of capital equipment (like lathes).
4. The *expected future* marginal yield (over its life span, say) of a *type* of capital equipment.
5. The *current* marginal yield of capital (in general).
6. The *expected future* marginal yield of capital (in general).

If Keynes had consistently maintained even the distinction between terms and concepts 5 and 6 he would have avoided a host of errors. He could have done this, modifying his chosen vocabulary in only a slight degree, if instead of confusing both concepts under the common term "marginal efficiency of capital," he had at least distinguished at all times between the *current* marginal efficiency of capital and the *anticipated* marginal efficiency of capital.

But if Keynes had been constantly careful to make such distinctions, he might not have written the *General Theory* at all; for the theory could not have been born without the confusions that gave rise to it.

Chapter XIII

EXPECTATION AND SPECULATION

1. *The State of Confidence*

Keynes's Chapter 12, "The State of Long-Term Expectation," is crowded with confusions. It is one of those chapters in which Keynes revels in pure satire and ends by believing his own paradoxes. All this is in the tradition of Bernard Mandeville, Bernard Shaw, and Lytton Strachey rather than of serious economics. But as passages from this chapter are often quoted with delighted approval by those who wish to rationalize their antipathy to the system of free enterprise and free markets, it is worth examining them in some detail.

First we must notice that here the definition of "the marginal efficiency of capital" undergoes what B. M. Anderson called one of its many "metamorphoses," and that causes and effects are arbitrarily selected:

> The *state of confidence,* as they term it, is a matter to which practical men always pay the closest and most anxious attention. But economists have not analyzed it carefully and have been content, as a rule, to discuss it in general terms. In particular it has not been made clear that its relevance to economic problems comes in through its important influence on the schedule of the marginal efficiency of capital. There are not two separate factors affecting the rate of investment, namely, the schedule of the marginal efficiency of capital and the state of confidence. The state of confidence is relevant because it is one of the major factors determining the former, which is the same thing as the investment demand-schedule (pp. 148-149).

We saw that, in his original definition of the marginal efficiency of capital (pp. 135-136), Keynes tied it up with the yield of specific capital instruments or assets, and particularly with the expected yield of *newly produced* assets. But here it is broadened out to mean business profits generally, or rather, *expectations* concerning business profits generally.

It is hard to see why the "relevance to economic problems" of "the state of confidence" should come in only "through its important influence on the schedule of the marginal efficiency of capital"—particularly if the latter phrase refers merely to the specific yield of new capital assets. For the "state of confidence" refers to *all* future expectations—including the future prices of consumption as well as capital goods, the future of wage-rates, of foreign trade, of the likelihood of war or peace, of a change of political administration, of a Supreme Court decision, etc. Why should "the marginal efficiency of capital" be singled out as the sole factor which makes the state of confidence "relevant" to "economic problems"? It is true, of course, that if "the schedule of the marginal efficiency of capital" is *identified* with "the investment demand-schedule," it becomes very important. But employment may increase without a rise in new investment, or disproportionately to new investment, as a result of a rise in the state of confidence or a (relative) fall of wage-rates.

2. *Fictions About the Stock Market*

But Chapter 12 is chiefly an essay in satire. And in order to patronize the behavior of enterpreneurs and to ridicule the behavior of speculators Keynes finds it necessary to patronize and ridicule the human race in general:

> If we speak frankly, we have to admit that our basis of knowledge for estimating the yield ten years hence of a railway, a copper mine, a textile factory, the goodwill of a patent medicine, an Atlantic liner, a building in the City of London amounts to little *and sometimes to nothing.* (My italics, pp. 149-150.)

It is true, of course (and this seems to be mainly what Keynes is saying) that with regard to the future we can never act on the basis of *certainty*. We are not *certain* that an earthquake will not destroy our house next week. We are not even *certain* that the sun will rise tomorrow. We are forced to act on the basis of *probabilities*. But to admit that our knowledge of the future of an investment necessarily contains elements of *uncertainty* is far different from saying that it amounts to little or "nothing."

Keynes's trick in this chapter is to mix plausible statements with implausible statements, hoping that the latter will seem to follow from the former. "It is probable," he declares, "that the actual average results of investments, even during periods of progress and prosperity, have disappointed the hopes which prompted them" (p. 150). It is probable. "If human nature felt no temptation to take a chance, no satisfaction (profit apart) in constructing a factory, a railway, a mine or a farm, there might not be much investment merely as a result of cold calculation" (p. 150). This is possible, but it is hard to say whether it is probable. It is not easy to imagine precisely what would happen if human nature and human motives were entirely different from what they are.

But then Keynes begins to expatiate upon all the dire consequences which follow from "the separation between ownership and management which prevails today" (p. 150), and all the evils which follow from the opportunities which organized stock markets give to the individual to revise his commitments. He does this by creating a number of fictions. One is that people know nothing about the future, and chronically guess wildly. Another is that those who buy and sell shares on the market are ignorant of the companies in whose shares they deal, and that only the "professional entrepreneur" has "genuine" knowledge. Still another fiction is that professional speculators are not concerned with the real prospective yields of investments, but merely with their ability to pass shares on at a higher price to "gulls" among the public, or even to gulls among themselves! Expectation comes to mean expectations regarding expectations: "We have reached the third degree where we devote our intelligences to anticipating what average opinion expects the average opinion to be" (p. 156).

In this chapter Keynes is still satirizing the New York stock market of 1928 and 1929. Today, of course, it is not hard to see in retrospect that optimism then went to excessive lengths. Hindsight is always clearer than foresight; and Keynes seems to be preening himself on how much better his hindsight of 1936 is than the foresight of the speculative community of 1929. But was Keynes sure enough of his ground *in early 1929* to sound a clarion warning, or to sell short and make a killing (and incidentally confer a social benefit by helping to mitigate excessive optimism)? Apparently not; but he explains that there were certain difficulties. Before we go into his further rhetoric, however, it may be advisable here to make a simple point. Whenever men are allowed liberty, and freedom of choice, they will make mistakes. Liberty is not a guarantee of omniscience. But neither are the mistakes of free men a valid excuse to take away their liberty, and impose government controls in its stead, on the ground that all wisdom and disinterestedness resides in the people who are going to do the controlling.

I have pointed out before that Keynes disdains to offer serious statistical evidence for statements that could easily be supported or disproved by available statistics. For example:

> Day-to-day fluctuations in the profits of existing investments, which are obviously of an ephemeral and non-significant character, tend to have an altogether excessive, and even an absurd, influence on the market. It is said, for example, that the shares of American companies which manufacture ice tend to sell at a higher price in summer when their profits are seaonably high than in winter when no one wants ice. The recurrence of a bank holiday may raise the market value-

tion of the British railway system by several million pounds (pp. 153-154).

Let us take these statements as they occur. Contrary to Keynes's first assertion, what nearly always surprises daily market commentators and outside observers is how *little* attention the market usually pays to non-significant day-to-day fluctuations in profits. A strike in the steel industry may be front-page news in every newspaper in the country, but shares of steel companies may not go down at all, or only by a tiny fraction. On the day that the strike is *settled,* however, and the whole country is breathing an audible sigh of relief, the steel stocks may go *down.* This is always ridiculed in letters to the editor as "illogical"; but it may happen because, though operations are being resumed, the higher wage-cost involved in the settlement may be regarded as threatening a reduction of profits *in the long-term.*

Notice how Keynes's second assertion above begins. "It is said." Is such hearsay Keynes's notion of evidence? Apparently it is; for he offers nothing else. In these days of electric refrigerators, his illustration of ice-manufacturing companies may seem obsolescent; but I have succeeded in digging up two American ice companies, and I print in Appendix B [1] the high, low, and average prices for each of them in the mid-winter period January-February for each of the twenty-five years from 1932 to 1956, inclusive, compared with the high, low, and average prices of the same shares in the mid-summer period July-August, as registered on the New York Stock Exchange. In the final column the July-August average is presented as a percentage of the January-February average.

What do these comparisons show? They show that the shares of the American Ice Co. averaged higher in summer than in winter in fourteen of these twenty-five years, but actually averaged lower in summer than in winter for nine

1 See p. 445.

of them. The shares of City Products Co. (formerly City Ice & Fuel Co.) averaged higher in summer than in winter in twelve of those years, but lower in summer than in winter for nine of them. Out of fifty cases, in short, the shares of these companies sold higher in summer than in winter only twenty-six times—about as often as a penny might come heads instead of tails in fifty throws.

The results here, it may be said, are inconclusive because summer ice companies were usually also in the winter fuel business. This is true; but it merely emphasizes the frivolous and apocryphal nature of Keynes's undocumented illustration.

Keynes's third assertion, about bank holidays, lends itself more easily to statistical verification or disproof. In Appendix C [2] I present a table comparing the closing bid-and-asked prices of the Southern Railway Company's deferred ordinary shares on two specific days out of every year for the twenty-five years from 1923 to 1947, inclusive. The Southern Railway Co. has been chosen because it was one of the "Four Main Line Railway Companies" and did not have dividends falling due in August. The twenty-five years from 1923 to 1947 were chosen because amalgamation of the British Railways took effect as from the first of January, 1922, when the "Four Main Line Railway Companies" came into being, and because nationalization of the principal railway undertakings was effected on the first of January, 1948, when they were vested in the British Transport Commission and shareholders received compensation by way of a fixed interest stock (guaranteed as to principal and interest by the British Treasury), and its market prices were not therefore influenced by earnings.

Now the most famous English Bank Holiday (which bears that specific name) is the one that falls on the first Monday in August. This is the one most likely to show the effect of Bank Holidays on the quotations of British Railways.

2 See p. 447.

Therefore the table in Appendix C compares the closing bid-and-asked prices of Southern Railway shares on the last business day in February (chosen as being furthest away from the August Bank Holiday and also reasonably away from the Christmas-New Year holidays) with the closing bid-and-asked prices on the first business day after the August Bank Holiday.

And what do the results show? Comparing the price on each of the two days, we find that in only seven of the twenty-five years was the price of these railway shares higher on the day after the August Bank Holiday than on the last day of February, whereas in eighteen of the twenty-five years it was actually *lower* right after the August Bank Holiday.[3]

From Keynes's point of view this is simply bad luck. On the mere law of averages, assuming that the Bank Holiday did not affect the value of railway shares one way or the other, Southern Railway shares should have been higher at Bank Holiday time about as often as they were lower. I attach no significance to the fact that the result turns out to be exactly the reverse of that of Keynes's unsupported statement. But the actual comparison is a good lesson against making sarcastic gibes at the expense of the speculative community on the basis of unconfirmed and, as it may turn out, quite false information.

Keynes next attacks professional speculators: "They are concerned," he writes, "not with what an investment is really worth to a man who buys it 'for keeps,' but with what the market will value it at, under the influence of mass psychology, three months or a year hence" (p. 155). And this behavior is an "inevitable result" of the mere freedom to buy and sell securities: "For it is not sensible to pay 25 for an investment of which you believe the prospective yield to justify a value of 30, if you also believe that the market will value it at 20 three months hence" (p. 155).

[3] Though the figures are not shown in Appendix C (p. 447), I found that the results were exactly the same if the day chosen for comparison was the last business day *before* the August Bank Holiday.

Such reasoning on the part of a professional speculator is of course *possible,* but it is preposterous to regard it as *usual.* It assumes a speculator saying to himself something like this: "I know from my own sources of information that this stock I can buy now for 25 is really worth 30, on the basis of what it is going to earn; but I have a hunch that some apparently bad news is going to break within the next few months, and though *I* know that this will not adversely affect the *real* value of this stock, *other* people, who constitute the *majority,* will be foolish enough to be influenced by this news, and therefore they will push the quotation of this stock down to 20, even though *more* people by that time will know as I do that the stock is *really* worth 30 on the basis of yield," etc., etc.

It is a byword in Wall Street that people who turn this number of mental somersaults to arrive at a conclusion quickly go broke. Contrary to what Keynes supposes, it is the speculators who try to figure what the real future values of stocks are going to be who are most likely to come out best in the long run. Many seasoned speculators got out of the market in 1928, for the sound reason that stocks were selling too high in relation to existing or likely earnings. Then, seeing the market still going up, some of them decided to jump in again, on the assumption that "the others" were not only crazy, but could be safely counted upon to go still crazier. It was the speculators who threw away their own sensible calculations, in a cynical effort to beat the mob psychology, who got caught.

But Keynes is firmly convinced of the opposite: "Investment based on genuine long-term expectation is so difficult today as to be scarcely practicable. He who attempts it must surely lead much more laborious days and run greater risks than he who tries to guess better than the crowd how the crowd will behave" (p. 157). Keynes apparently believes this precisely because it is so implausible.

> It is the long-term investor, he who most promotes the public interest, who will in practice come in for most criticism,

> wherever investment funds are managed by committees or boards or banks. . . . If he is successful, that will only confirm the general belief in his rashness; and if in the short run he is unsuccessful, which is very likely, he will not receive much mercy (pp. 157-158).

To one who, like the present writer, spent many years writing daily on the stock market for New York newspapers, the foregoing sounds suspiciously familiar. It sounds like a man who once gave investment advice that turned out to be wrong, and who is looking for an alibi. It is the system that made the mistake, not he. The stock he recommended should in all logic have gone up to 108, even though it never did. . . . But such suspicions are unworthy, and I shall return to the merits of the argument.

3. *Gambling, Speculation, Enterprise*

What is it that Keynes is trying to prove? He is trying to prove that "liquidity" is wicked; that the freedom of people to buy and sell securities in accordance with their own judgment ought not to be allowed; and that their money ought to be taken from them and "invested" by bureaucrats, omniscient and beneficent by definition:

> Of the maxims of orthodox finance none, surely, is more anti-social than the fetish of liquidity, the doctrine that it is a positive virtue on the part of investment institutions to concentrate their resources upon the holding of 'liquid' securities. It forgets that there is no such thing as liquidity of investment for the community as a whole (p. 155).

It is true that there is no such thing as liquidity of investment for the community as a whole. (But only if this means the *world* community. The British, for example, can relieve a crisis by selling their American shares. Any individual country can sell or buy gold or dollars, etc.) But even if we grant that there is no such thing as liquidity of investment for the world considered as one big community, this does not mean that "liquidity" cannot still be of considerable advantage to individual countries, individual banks, individual corporations, or individual persons—and *therefore* of advantage to the community as a whole.

On the same kind of reasoning as he used in this instance, Keynes could have argued that fire insurance is worthless because *someone* must bear the loss of the fire. It is true that someone must bear the loss; but the whole purpose of insurance is to distribute and diffuse the loss. And this is what "liquidity" also serves to do. It is easy to see how much good can come, and it is difficult to see how much harm can come, from allowing an individual to sell his securities to others. Others are not forced to buy them. They buy them only at a price that they regard as advantageous to themselves; and they may turn out to be better judges than the seller.

This is why there is no point to Keynes's complaint that: "The actual, private object of the most skilled investment today is 'to beat the gun,' as the Americans so well express it, to outwit the crowd, and to pass the bad, or depreciating, half-crown to the other fellow" (p. 155). This is a peculiarly unfortunate image for Keynes, the advocate of government spending, deficit financing, and inflation, to have used. For if the half-crown is depreciating, it is depreciating because the politicians are printing too much money, and if the half-crown can be passed on, despite the other fellow's unwillingness to take it, it is because the politicians have made it legal tender. Keynes forgets that what he is describing is not merely the purpose of stock-market speculation, but the purpose of enterprise as well. For the entrepreneurs who make the greatest profits will be the minority who first and best anticipate the wants of consumers, who, if Keynes wishes to put it that way, 'beat the gun' as compared with the majority of their competitors.

Keynes once derided economists who worried about results "in the long run." "In the long run," he said cynically, "we are all dead." It is amusing to find the same man complaining here that long-run considerations are minimized because "human nature desires quick results, there is a peculiar zest in making money quickly, and remoter gains are discounted by the average man at a very high rate" (p. 157). But for Keynes, *any* stick was apparently good enough to beat the capitalist system with.

In attacking "speculation" in Wall Street, Keynes forgets that *all* enterprise, *all* human activity, inextricably involves speculation, for the simple reason that the future is never certain, never completely revealed to us. Who is a greater speculator than the farmer? He must speculate on the fertility of the acreage he rents or buys; on the amount and distribution of rainfall over the coming crop season; on the amount of pests and blight; on the final size of his crop; on the best day to sow and the best day to harvest and his ability to get help on those days. And finally he must speculate on what the price of his crop is going to be when he markets it (or at what day or price to sell for future delivery). And even in deciding how much acreage to plant to wheat or corn or peanuts, he must guess what *other* farmers are going to plant, and how much they are going to harvest. It is one speculation after another. And he and every entrepreneur in *every* line must act in relation to some guess regarding the actions of other entrepreneurs.

When all this is kept in mind, Keynes's attack on "speculation" begins to look pretty silly. His contrast between "speculation" and "enterprise" is false. If he is merely attacking *bad* speculation, then it is bad by definition. But intelligent speculation, as economists and market analysts have pointed out over and over, mitigates fluctuations, broadens markets, and increases production of the types of goods that consumers are most likely to want. Intelligent speculation is an indispensable and inherent part of intelligent production.

But Keynes deplores human freedom; he seems to deplore practically all the financial progress of the last two centuries:

> Speculators may do no harm as bubbles on a steady stream of enterprise. But the position is serious when enterprise becomes a bubble on a whirlpool of speculation. When the capital development of a country becomes a by-product of the activities of a casino, the job is likely to be ill-done. The measure of success attained by Wall Street, regarded as an institution of which the proper social purpose is to direct new investment into the most profitable channels in terms of future yield, cannot be claimed as one of the outstanding triumphs of *laissez-faire* capitalism (p. 159).

This tirade, which treats speculation as merely a synonym for gambling, reflects the prejudices of the man in the street. The difference between gambling and speculation is clear: in gambling, the risks are arbitrarily invented or created; in speculation, the risks *already exist,* and *somebody* has to bear them.

In gambling one man wins $1,000 and another loses it, depending on whether a ball falls into an odd or even number on a roulette wheel or on which horse comes in first on a race track. But the wheel could be spun and the race could be run without the betting, without either losses or gains. The world would probably be richer rather than poorer if gambling casinos and race tracks did not exist at all.

But it is not so with the great organized exchanges, either for commodities or for securities. If these did not exist, the farmer who raises wheat would have to speculate on the future price of wheat. But as they do exist, the farmer or miller who does not wish to assume this risk can "hedge," so passing the risk on to a professional speculator. Similarly, a corporation manager who knows how to make air conditioners, but does not wish personally to assume all the financial risks involved from the vicissitudes of competition and of changing market conditions for air conditioners, may offer stock on the market and let investors and professional speculators assume those financial risks. Thus each job is done by a specialist in that job, and is therefore likely to be better done than if either the producer or the speculator tried to do both jobs.

The market, consisting of human beings, unable to foresee the future with certainty, will make mistakes—and some of them in retrospect will look like incredible mistakes. Yet Wall Street, notwithstanding its academic and political detractors, *can* be claimed as one of the outstanding triumphs of *"laissez-faire"* capitalism. The results speak for themselves. The United States has achieved the greatest volume of investment, the greatest capitalistic development, the greatest volume of production, the greatest economy of manpower, the highest standard of living that the world has ever known. And it has been able to do this in an important degree precisely *because* of the help rendered by the marvelous financial organization centered in Wall Street and not in spite of it. Surely it should have struck Keynes and his followers as worthy of notice that the country with the greatest "gambling casinos" and the greatest "liquidity" was also the country with the world's greatest capital development and the highest average standard of living!

But Keynes carries his hostility to freedom to the point where he suggests "the introduction of a substantial Government transfer tax on all transactions" as "the most serviceable reform available" (p. 160). Continuing, he declares: "The spectacle of modern investment markets has sometimes moved me towards the conclusion that to make the purchase of an investment permanent and indissoluble, like marriage, except by reason of death or other grave cause, might be a useful remedy for our contemporary evils" (p. 160).

He draws back from this totalitarian suggestion for a moment, only to work himself up again: "So long as it is open to the individual to employ his wealth in hoarding or lending *money*, the alternative of purchasing actual capital assets cannot be rendered sufficiently attractive" (p. 160). "The only radical cure for the crises of confidence . . . would be to allow the individual *no choice* [my italics] between consuming his income and ordering the production of [a] specific capital-asset" (p. 161). For people don't know what they are doing anyway. "Most, probably, of our decisions to do something positive . . . can only be taken as a result of animal spirits—of a spontaneous urge to action rather than inaction, and not as the outcome of a weighted average of quantitative benefits multiplied by quantitative probabilities. Enterprise only pretends to itself to be mainly actuated by the statements in its own prospectus" (pp. 161-162). Free private investment depends upon "the nerves and hysteria and even the digestions" of private investors (p. 162), on "whim or sentiment or chance" (p. 163).

And what is all this leading up to? The denouement comes in the final paragraph of the chapter:

> For my own part I am now somewhat sceptical of the success of a merely monetary policy directed towards influencing the rate of interest. I expect to see the State, which is in a position to calculate the marginal efficiency of capital-goods on long views and on the basis of the general social advantage, taking an ever greater responsibility for directly organizing investment (p. 164).

So there you have it. The people who have earned money are too shortsighted, hysterical, rapacious, and idiotic to be trusted to invest it themselves. The money must be seized from them by the politicians, who will invest it with almost perfect foresight and complete disinterestedness (as illustrated, for example, by the economic planners of Soviet Russia). For people who are risking their own money will of course risk it foolishly and recklessly, whereas politicians and bureaucrats who are risking *other* people's money will do so only with the greatest care and after long and profound study. Naturally the businessmen who have earned money have shown that they have no foresight; but the politicians who haven't earned the money will exhibit almost perfect foresight. The businessmen who are seeking to make cheaper and better than their competitors the goods that consumers wish, and whose success depends upon the degree to which they satisfy consumers, will of course have no concern for "the general social advantage"; but the politicians who keep themselves in power by conciliating pressure groups will of course have *only* concern for "the general social advantage." They will not dissipate the money for harebrained peanut schemes in East Africa; or for crop supports that keep submarginal farmers in business and submarginal acreage in cultivation; or to build showy dams and hydroelectric plants that cannot pay their way but can swing votes in the districts where they are built; or to set up Reconstruction Finance Corporations or Small Business Administrations to make loans to projects in which nobody will risk his own money. There will never be even a hint of bribery, or corruption, or the gift of a mink coat to a minor official by the beneficiary of the loan. . . .

This is the glorious vista that Keynes unveils. *This* is "the new economics."

Chapter XIV

"LIQUIDITY PREFERENCE"

1. *No "Liquidity" Without Saving*

We now come to three chapters and an appendix that it seems most convenient to treat as a unit. These are the chapters in which Keynes unfolds his famous concept of "liquidity-preference" as an explanation (in fact as the *sole* explanation) of the rate of interest, and in which he dismisses the alleged "classical" theory of the rate of interest as altogether inadequate and mistaken. We shall first take up the concept of liquidity-preference, to find what is wrong with it, and then see to what extent, if any, Keynes's criticisms of the "classical" theory of interest are warranted.

Just before he gets to his own explanation of the rate of interest, Keynes uses casually, and in passing, the phrase "the psychological time-preferences of an individual." Except for the adjective "psychological," which in this context is quite unnecessary, the concept of time-preference, as we shall see, is essential to any theory of interest. Though Keynes constantly uses this concept *implicitly,* he either ignores or repudiates it *explicitly.* But here I wish merely to call attention to the phrase itself, because it probably suggested to Keynes his own phrase "liquidity-preference" which, as we shall see, happens to be both unhelpful and inappropriate.

Let us begin with his definition. Keynes begins by admitting time-preference into his analysis under the name of "propensity to consume," which "determines for each individual how much of his income he will consume and how much he will reserve in *some* form of command over future consumption" (p. 166). This decision having been made, the individual must then decide:

> in *what form* he will hold the command over future consumption (p. 166). Does he want to hold it in the form of immediate, liquid command (*i.e.,* in money or its equivalent)? Or is he prepared to part with immediate command for a specified or indefinite period, leaving it to future market conditions to determine on what terms he can, if necessary, convert deferred command over specific goods into immediate command over goods in general? In other words, what is the degree of his *liquidity-preference*—where an individual's liquidity-preference is given by a schedule of the amounts of his resources, valued in terms of money or of wage-units, which he will wish to retain in the form of money in different sets of circumstances? (p. 166).
>
> [Keynes goes on:] It should be obvious that the rate of interest cannot be a return to saving or waiting as such. For if a man hoards his savings in cash, he earns no interest, though he saves just as much as before. On the contrary, the mere definition of the rate of interest tells us in so many words that the rate of interest is the *reward for parting with liquidity* for a specified period. . . . Thus the rate of interest at any time, *being the reward for parting with liquidity,* is a measure of the unwillingness of those who possess money to part with their liquid control over it. (My italics, pp. 166-167.)

There are several odd things about this passage. Keynes begins by denying what nobody of sense asserts. Of course the rate of interest is not a return merely for "saving or waiting *as such.*" But the saving or waiting is the necessary means to obtain the funds to be invested at interest.[1]

Nor, on the other hand, is the rate of interest the "reward" for parting with liquidity. The economic system is

[1] Jacob Viner has made this point neatly: "By analogous reasoning [Keynes] could deny that wages are the reward for labor, or that profit is the reward for risk-taking, because labor is sometimes done without anticipation or realization of a return, and men who assume financial risks have been known to incur losses as a result, instead of profits. *Without saving there can be no liquidity to surrender.* [My italics.] . . . The rate of interest is the return for saving without liquidity." *Quarterly Journal of Economics,* LI (1936-1937), 157.

not a Sunday school; its primary function is not to hand out rewards and punishments. Interest is paid, not because borrowers wish to "reward" lenders, but because borrowers expect to earn a return on their investment greater than the interest they pay for the borrowed funds. The lender is also free to invest his own funds directly rather than to lend them to someone else for investment; and the rate of interest that he is offered may often decide which of these two things he will do.

But let us, in order to look into the matter, provisionally accept Keynes's definition that interest is "the reward for parting with liquidity"—in other words, for overcoming the individual's "liquidity-preference."

We may note in passing that it is rather odd that Keynes did not make the overcoming of "liquidity-preference" the explanation not only of the rate of interest, but of any price whatever. If you wish to sell me tomatoes, for example, you will have to offer them at a sufficiently low price to "reward" me for "parting with liquidity"—that is, parting with cash. Thus the price of tomatoes would have to be explained as the amount necessary to overcome the buyer's "liquidity-preference" or "cash preference." Perhaps this way of describing the matter might serve to make the man who is being induced to buy tomatoes look slightly ridiculous for preferring "liquidity" or cash, and if the purpose was ridicule of the purchaser's mental processes, in needing to have an inducement to buy tomatoes, it might do well enough for that purpose. But as a serious explanation for the market prices of commodities, I do not believe it would have any advantages over the present more orthodox explanations of economists, and it is easy to see some very serious disadvantages. It is hardly an illuminating phrase. If I wish to hold cash rather than invest it at the moment, this may of course be called cash preference or liquidity-preference. But preference over *what?* If I am offered $20,000 for my house and turn the offer down, this could be described in Keynesian language as house-preference. But if I am offered

$21,000 and take it, this would have to be called liquidity-preference. Yet it is merely the preference of $21,000 over $20,000. It is a little hard to see what advantage this Keynesian phrase has over orthodox economic terms.

2. *Money is a Productive Asset*

Now what are the motives for "liquidity-preference"? In separate chapters Keynes gives two different sets. In Chapter 13, "The General Theory of the Rate of Interest," he tells us:

> The three divisions of liquidity preference which we have distinguished above may be defined as depending on (i) the transactions-motive, *i.e.,* the need for cash for the current transaction of personal and business exchanges; (ii) the precautionary motive, *i.e.,* the desire for security as the future cash equivalent of a certain proportion of total resources; and (iii) the speculative motive, *i.e.,* the object of securing profit from knowing better than the market what the market will bring forth (p. 170).

But in Chapter 15, "The Psychological and Business Incentives to Liquidity," Keynes gives us a further breakdown of the "transactions-motive" into the "income-motive" and the "business-motive."

Now the transactions-motive and the precautionary-motive Keynes seems to respect and almost to approve: "In normal circumstances the amount of money required to satisfy the transactions-motive and the precautionary-motive is mainly a resultant of the general activity of the economic system and of the level of money income" (p. 196). But the speculative-motive arouses his derision and anger. And also his reforming zeal: "It is by playing on the speculative-motive that monetary management . . . is brought to bear on the economic system" (pp. 196-197).

According to Keynes, holding cash for the "speculative-motive" is wicked. This is what the Monetary Authority must stop. It is Keynes's usual trick of giving the dog a bad name as an excuse for shooting him. But it is a nice question whether those who hold cash because they distrust the prices of investments or of commodities are holding cash in order to speculate or in order *not* to speculate. They hold cash (beyond the needs of the transactions-motive) because they distrust the prices of investments or of durable consumption goods; they believe that the prices of investments and/or of durable consumption goods are going to fall, and they do not wish to be caught with these investments or durable goods on their hands. They are seeking, in short, *not* to speculate in investments or goods. They believe that next week, next month, or next year they will get them cheaper.

This may be called speculating in money, as Keynes calls it; or it may be called a refusal to speculate in stocks, bonds, houses, or automobiles. The real question to be asked about it, however, is not whether or not this is "speculation," but whether it is wise or unwise speculation. It is usually most indulged in after a boom has cracked. The best way to prevent it is not to have a Monetary Authority so manipulate things as to force the purchase of investments or of goods, but to prevent an inflationary boom in the first place. However, I am anticipating.

Perhaps we may get a little more light on this subject if we turn for a moment from the *General Theory* to an answer made by Keynes in the *Quarterly Journal of Economics* (1937) to four discussions of his *General Theory*.[2]

> Money, it is well known, serves two principal purposes. By acting as a money of account, it facilitates exchanges without its being necessary that it should ever itself come into the picture as a substantive object. In this respect it is a convenience which is devoid of significance or real influence. In the second place, it is a store of wealth. So we are told, without a smile on the face (pp. 186-187).

[2] Reprinted as Chapter XV in *The New Economics*, ed. by Seymour E. Harris, (New York: Alfred Knopf, 1952).

This is an extraordinary perversion of classical doctrine. The most usual statement in the orthodox economic textbooks is that money serves first of all the function of a *medium of exchange.* And according to some economists, this function includes and subsumes all its other functions—such as "money of account," "standard of value," and "store of value"—which are merely the qualities of a satisfactory or ideal medium of exchange.

But to continue the quotation from Keynes that we had just started:

> It is a store of wealth. So we are told without a smile on the face. But in the world of the classical economy, what an insane use to which to put it! For it is a recognized characteristic of money as a store of wealth that it is barren; whereas practically every other form of storing wealth yields some interest or profit. Why should anyone outside a lunatic asylum wish to use money as a store of wealth? (p. 187).

Perhaps, with a little patience, we could have helped Keynes to understand. They wish or hope or believe that the thousand dollars they earn today will have at least as much purchasing power (whether in cash or as face value of a bond) a year from now or twenty years from now. They do not wish to have to become speculators. If "it is a recognized characteristic of money as a store of wealth that it is barren," this "recognition" is mistaken, in spite of the fact that so many economists have been guilty of it. As W. H. Hutt has pointed out, money "is as productive as all other assets, and *productive in exactly the same sense.*" "The demand for money assets is a demand for *productive resources.*" [3] Failure to recognize this is the source of one of Keynes's greatest fallacies.

Before we go on to explain the theoretical reasons why Keynes's liquidity-preference theory is wrong, we must first point out that it *is* clearly wrong. It goes directly contrary

[3] W. H. Hutt, "The Yield from Money Held," *On Freedom and Free Enterprise: Essays in Honor of Ludwig von Mises* (Princeton: Van Nostrand, 1956), p. 197 and p. 216.

to the facts that it presumes to explain. If Keynes's theory were right, then short-term interest rates would be highest precisely at the bottom of a depression, because they would have to be especially high then to overcome the individual's reluctance to part with cash—to "reward" him for "parting with liquidity." But it is precisely in a depression, when everything is dragging bottom, that short-term interest rates are *lowest*. And if Keynes's liquidity-preference were right, short-term interest rates would be lowest in a recovery and at the peak of a boom, because confidence would be highest then, everybody would be wishing to invest in "things" rather than in money, and liquidity or cash preference would be so low that only a very small "reward" would be necessary to overcome it. But it is precisely in a recovery and at the peak of a boom that short-term interest rates are highest.[4]

It is true that in a depression many long-term bonds tend to sell at low capital figures (and therefore bear a high nominal interest yield), but this is entirely due, not to cash preference as such, but to diminished confidence in the continuation of the interest on these bonds and the safety of the principal. In the same way, in the early and middle stages of a recovery, many bonds will rise in price and the yield they bear will therefore decline. But this will not be the result of diminished cash preference, but simply the result of increased confidence in the continuance of the interest and the repayment of the principal.

It is true again that when a boom has just busted, then in the crisis of confidence short-term interest rates will rise and sometimes soar. But the common-sense explanation of this is not merely a rise in cash preference on the part of lenders, and a compensation for increased risks, but a greatly increased demand for loans on the part of borrowers to protect security margins, and to carry unsold and temporarily unsaleable inventories of finished goods.

[4] See Appendix D, p. 448.

3. *Interest Is Not Purely Monetary*

The reader will notice that in the paragraphs above I have frequently substituted the term "cash preference" for Keynes's "liquidity-preference." I do not think that either term is helpful or necessary; they throw considerably more confusion, and considerably less light, on the condition to be analyzed than the traditional terms that Keynes rejects. But as between the two, cash preference is much to be preferred to liquidity-preference, not only because it is less vague, but because it does not, like liquidity-preference, make Keynes's doctrine self-contradictory. For if a man is holding his funds in the form of time-deposits or short-term Treasury bills, he is being paid *interest* on them; therefore he is getting interest and "liquidity" too. What becomes, then, of Keynes's theory that interest is the "reward" for "*parting* with liquidity"?

Even if a man carries his liquid funds, not in the form of cash under the mattress, but in the form of a demand bank deposit, the bank is lending out, say, some four-fifths of this, and therefore in combination they are getting the better of both worlds. For he still has the "liquidity" and the bank has the interest. One of the most unrealistic aspects of his wholly unrealistic theory is Keynes's singular blindness to the fact that banks lend out the great bulk of their demand deposit liabilities, put them to work, and draw interest on them. If Keynes had confined his "liquidity-preference" theory to a *pure* cash-preference theory, he would have had to confine his theory to pocketbook cash and under-the-mattress cash, plus the cash reserves of banks. For these are the only unused "hoards" in the system. And the great bulk even of these would have to be set down, even by Keynes, as cash kept for "the transactions-motive."

Now Keynes's theory of interest is a *purely monetary* theory. Keynes, in fact, ridicules all theories of interest that bring in "real" factors. His attack on Alfred Marshall's theory is typical:

> The perplexity which I find in Marshall's account of the matter is fundamentally due, I think, to the incursion of the concept 'interest,' which belongs to a monetary economy, into a treatise which takes no account of money. 'Interest' has really no business to turn up at all in Marshall's *Principles of Economics,*—it belongs to another branch of the subject (p. 189).

This is to throw out cavalierly not only Marshall but practically all the "classical" and "neo-classical" economists —in fact, all the economists who have made any contribution to the subject since the Middle Ages. Interest, of course, is normally paid in money. But so is rent; so are profits; so are prices; and so are wages. They all, like interest, "belong to a monetary economy." On this reasoning we would take no account of real factors whatever but throw the analysis of everything into the books devoted purely to money.

Keynesians might go on to object that interest is paid not only *in* money but *for* money; that in this sense the phenomenon of interest is "purely monetary," and is merely to be explained in terms of the supply of, and demand for, loanable funds. This type of supply-and-demand theory, often met with in current economic textbooks, is not incorrect, but it is superficial and incomplete. When we go on to ask what in turn *determines* the supply of, and demand for, loanable funds, the explanation must be made largely in real terms. But Keynes explicitly denies the relevance of these real factors.

A sufficient judgment on Keynes's theory of interest was pronounced by Ludwig von Mises at least twelve years before Keynes's theory was even published. The following passage is from page 133 of Mises' *The Theory of Money and Credit.* This book was published in the American edition (New York: Harcourt, Brace) in 1935. But this is a translation from the second German edition, published in 1924:

To one group of writers, the problem appeared to offer little difficulty. From the circumstance that it is possible for the banks to reduce the rate of interest in their bank-credit business down to the limit set by their working costs, these writers thought it permissible to deduce that credit can be granted gratuitously or, more correctly, almost gratuitously. In drawing this conclusion, their doctrine implicitly denies the existence of interest. It regards interest as compensation for the temporary relinquishing of money in the broader sense—a view, indeed, of insurpassable naiveté. Scientific critics have been perfectly justified in treating it with contempt; it is scarcely worth even cursory mention. But it is impossible to refrain from pointing out that these very views on the nature of interest hold an important place in popular opinion, and that they are continually being propounded afresh and recommended as a basis for measures of banking policy.

And this, in fact, is the judgment of other competent economists. Frank H. Knight writes:

> The most essential fact is that there is no functional relation between the price level and any rate of interest. Consequently, no monetary change has any direct and permanent effect on the rate. On this point such writers as Keynes and [J. R.] Hicks fall into the simple methodological fallacy dealt with in the early part of this paper—confusion of the power to 'disturb' another value magnitude with a real functional connection of causality. Keynes bases his whole argument for the monetary theory of interest on the familiar fact that open-market operations can be effective. Hicks makes the error more palpable. . . . Hicks assumes without qualification or reservation a definite (inverse) functional relation between the quantity of money and the interest rate.
>
> It is a depressing fact that at the present date in history there should be any occasion to point out to students that this position is mere man-in-the-street economics.[5]

[5] *On the History and Method of Economics,* (University of Chicago Press, 1956), p. 222.

It is true that interest is paid in money, and on a capital sum usually specified in money, and that therefore monetary factors have to be considered, especially when considering dynamic changes in the rate of interest. Keynes's fallacy consists in assuming that because monetary factors can be shown to affect the rate of interest, "real" factors can safely be ignored or even denied.

Whatever is true in Keynes's theory of interest was discovered long ago by the Swedish economist Knut Wicksell, and is fully taken account of in the works of Ludwig von Mises, F. A. Hayek, and others.

But an account of the real factors which govern the rate of interest will be reserved for the next chapter.

Chapter XV

THE THEORY OF INTEREST

1. *An "Unsettled Problem"*

After presenting his own theory of interest, which he complacently calls "the *general* theory of the rate of interest," Keynes devotes a chapter to a criticism of what he calls "The Classical Theory of the Rate of Interest," together with an appendix to this chapter.

It is a mark of the curious intellectual provincialism of Keynes in economics, as I have already pointed out, that whenever he talks about the "classical" theory he seems to have in mind principally or solely Alfred Marshall and A. C. Pigou (though with occasional sarcastic sideswipes at Ricardo). This is not merely an Anglo-centric, but a Cantabrigia-centric view of economic history and theory. But Keynes does make occasional references to other writers, and in a sense he deals impartially with all: he distorts or caricatures, or quotes misleading excerpts from, the views he is ostensibly presenting.

Unfortunately, and despite the title and assumptions of Keynes's Chapter 14, there simply is no accepted "classical theory" of the rate of interest. As Gottfried Haberler has written (*Prosperity and Depression,* 1941, p. 195): "The theory of interest has for a long time been a weak spot in the science of economics, and the explanation and determination of the interest rate still gives rise to more disagreement among economists than any other branch of general economic theory." Though great progress has been made in the last eighty years or so (principally beginning with Jevons and Böhm-Bawerk), almost every writer on interest has his own theory, or at least his own special emphasis.

But we may divide current theories of interest into three broad categories: (1) productivity theories, (2) time-preference theories, and (3) theories which combine productivity and time-preference concepts. A fourth category (which, however, overlaps on all of these) consists of productivity, time-preference, or combined theories that also take account of disturbances caused by monetary factors. But the kind of purely monetary theory represented by Keynes is *pre*-classical, mercantilistic, and man-in-the-street economics.

It is clear that if *any* of these three types of "orthodox" interest theory is right (if we are to lump under "orthodox," as Keynes does, whatever is non-Keynesian) Keynes's purely monetary theory must be wrong. It is, of course, not a sufficient criticism of Keynes's theory to point this out. We should show that at least one of these "orthodox" theories is in fact correct. This forces us into a digression on positive theory. While I dislike to rush into territory where geniuses and angels have stumbled, I am afraid we have no choice. But we shall venture into the field by examining in turn each of three principal types of "real" interest theories, as expounded by their ablest spokesmen, and try to assess the strengths and weaknesses of each.

2. *Productivity Theories*

Let us begin by examining the productivity theory as expounded by Frank H. Knight:

> The peculiar feature of interest which makes it a special problem for economics is that it is not a rent paid directly for the use of property in the concrete sense but is a repayment for the use of money (and as such takes the form of an abstract number, a ratio, or percentage). Yet while the borrower obtains and repays a money loan, it is the use of goods which the borrower wants and gets by means of the loan. If loans for consumption are left out of account, as they may well be since

> under modern conditions their terms depend upon those of loans for productive purposes, the rental or yield of goods the use of which is obtained by means of the loan provides under normal conditions the income paid out in the form of interest. Competition tends to bring about equality of return from equal investments; the ratio of this equalized return to investment is the rate of interest.[1]

This at first blush is a very persuasive statement, but it fails to explain the central problem of the rate of interest, which can only be answered by a recognition of the existence of time-preference. Professor Knight, in the article just quoted, goes on to discuss time-preference theories:

> The competition of buyers and sellers [according to these theories] will set on income-yielding wealth a price which makes the amount demanded equal to the amount offered at that price. This price involves a uniform market rate of discounting future values. Thus if at the equilibrium point it takes $1 in hand to buy $1.05 payable one year from date, it will also take $20 to buy a piece of property yielding a perpetual income of $1 per year; all other income bearers will be valued on the basis of the same arithmetical proportion and the rate of interest will be 5 per cent. . . .
>
> The productivity theorists . . . do not question the validity of the time-preference reasoning but find that it lacks finality as an explanation under actual conditions. . . .[2]

Knight's discussion, here and elsewhere, seems to me to admit the need of time-preference as at least part of the explanation of interest, but to give it at best a subordinate role and to admit it through the back door. At times he explicitly repudiates it even while his general discussion implies it.

Nonetheless, it seems to me that a productivity theory of interest can be defended, at least partly, against one fre-

[1] *The Ethics of Competition, and Other Essays,* Article on "Interest," (University of Chicago Press, 1935), pp. 257-258. (Originally printed in *The Encyclopaedia of the Social Sciences,* 1932.)

[2] *Ibid.,* p. 258.

quent criticism. This is made by Keynes in the *General Theory:*

> Nor are those theories more successful which attempt to make the rate of interest depend on 'the marginal efficiency of capital.' It is true that in equilibrium the rate of interest will be equal to the marginal efficiency of capital, since it will be profitable to increase (or decrease) the current scale of investment until the point of equality has been reached. But to make this into a theory of the rate of interest or to derive the rate of interest from it involves a circular argument, as Marshall discovered after he had got half-way into giving an account of the rate of interest along these lines. For the "marginal efficiency of capital" partly depends on the scale of current investment, and we must already know the rate of interest before we can calculate what this scale will be. The significant conclusion is that the output of new investment will be pushed to the point at which the marginal efficiency of capital becomes equal to the rate of interest; and what the schedule of the marginal efficiency of capital tells us, is, not what the rate of interest is, but the point to which the output of new investment will be pushed, given the rate of interest (p. 184).

There are two errors in this criticism. The first, an error of phraseology, leads to the second, an error of logic. If Keynes is really speaking about "the *marginal* efficiency of capital" (the actual phrase he uses), then he is speaking only of a *point* on the curve or schedule of the efficiency or yield of capital. If the marginal efficiency of capital at any moment is conceived (as with any precise usage of terms it should be) merely as a *point* on the curve of the yield of capital, then the argument that Keynes is criticizing is indeed "circular," and Keynes's criticism is altogether valid.

But we have seen that Keynes uses his key terms very loosely and carelessly. Most of the time, when he refers to "the marginal efficiency of capital," he does not mean the *marginal* efficiency of capital at all, but merely the efficiency of capital. (Or, technically, the curve of the-yield-of-capital-

and-quantity-demanded.) In fact, as we have already had occasion to note, Keynes uses the marginal efficiency of capital as a synonym for "the investment demand-schedule": "We shall call this the investment demand-schedule; or, alternatively, the schedule of the marginal efficiency of capital" (p. 136).

Now if, in the passage I have quoted above from page 184 of the *General Theory,* we substitute (except in the second sentence) the phrase "investment demand-schedule" for "marginal efficiency of capital," we find that the argument that Keynes is criticizing is not circular but merely incomplete. For the market rate of interest would then be at the point at which the investment demand-schedule (or curve) intersected the savings supply curve. The investment demand-schedule would then influence (though not by itself determine) the rate of interest just as would the supply of savings.

Keynes was led into his error by following his master Marshall. On pages 139-140 he quotes a passage from Marshall's *Principles* (6th ed., pp. 519-520) in which Marshall tries to show (and Keynes agrees) that attempting to arrive at a theory of interest by taking into account the productivity of capital goods is "reasoning in a circle." But having accepted this reasoning as applied to the interest rate, Keynes draws back from applying it also, as Marshall does, to wages. "But was he not wrong," asks Keynes in a worried footnote (p. 140), "in supposing that the marginal productivity theory of wages is equally circular?"

Marshall was, indeed, wrong in both cases. To argue that the expected yield from new investments, or the investment demand-schedule, doesn't affect the interest rate is like arguing that buyers don't affect the price of a commodity; they merely decide how much to buy at that price! Of course we cannot determine the price of a commodity *merely* by knowing the "demand curve"; we must *also* know the supply curve. It is too often forgotten that the full name of the "demand curve" (which Wicksteed called "an elliptical, ambiguous, and misleading phrase")[3] is "the curve of price-and-quantity demanded," as the full name of the supply curve is "the curve of price-and-quantity-offered." It is the point of *intersection* of these curves that determines price. Similarly (to anticipate), the investment demand curve, the savings supply curve, and the interest rate, are interdependent.

The real weakness of the naive productivity theories of interest is that they misconceive the relationship between "capital" and "yield." As Irving Fisher has put it: "The statement that 'capital produces income' is true only in the physical sense; it is not true in the value sense. That is to say, *capital value does not* produce income value. On the contrary, income value produces capital value. . . . The orchard is the source of the apples; but the value of the apples is the source of the value of the orchard."[4] If I may add another illustration, the hen produces the eggs, but the (discounted) value of the eggs produces the value of the hen.

People in the investment market, in fact, talk habitually more as economists talk. They recognize that the capital value is determined by the "yield," not the other way round. Let us say that a (perpetual) bond is issued at a par value of $1,000 and pays interest of $40 a year, when the going long-term interest rate is 4 per cent. If the going long-term interest rate rises to 5 per cent, the market price of the bond will fall to $800. If the going long-term interest rate falls to 3 per cent, the market price of the bond will rise to $1,333.

3. *Time-Preference Theories*

But recognition of this relationship still does not solve the major problem of interest. This is to determine precisely why these particular relationships come to exist be-

3 Philip Wicksteed, *The Alphabet of Economic Science*, 1888, (New York: Kelley & Millman, 1955), p. 97.

4 *The Theory of Interest* (New York: Kelley & Millman, 1954), p. 55.

tween capital values and yields. And in the solution of this problem the concept of time preference is essential. As Mises phrases it:

> For the economist a problem is presented in the determination of prices for land, cattle, and all the rest. If future goods were not bought and sold at a discount as against present goods, the buyer of land would have to pay a price which equals the sum of all future net revenue. . . .
>
> If the future services which a piece of land can render were to be valued in the same way in which its present services are valued, no finite price would be high enough to impel its owner to sell it.[5]

Mises espouses a pure time-preference theory:

> Time preference is a category inherent in every human action. Time preference manifests itself in the phenomenon of originary interest, *i.e.*, the discount of future goods as against present goods. . . .
>
> Originary interest is the ratio of the value assigned to want-satisfaction in the immediate future and the value assigned to want-satisfaction in remoter periods of the future. It manifests itself in the market economy in the discount of future goods as against present goods. It is a ratio of commodity prices, not a price in itself. There prevails a tendency toward the equalization of this ratio for all commodities. . . .
>
> Originary interest is not a price determined on the market by the interplay of the demand for, and the supply of, capital or capital goods. Its height does not depend on the extent of this demand and supply. It is rather the rate of originary interest that determines both the demand for, and the supply of, capital and capital goods. . . .
>
> People do not save and accumulate because there is interest. Interest is neither the impetus to saving nor the reward or the compensation granted for abstaining from immediate consumption. It is the ratio in the mutual valuation of present goods as against future goods.
>
> The loan market does not determine the rate of interest. It

[5] Ludwig von Mises, *Human Action* (New Haven: Yale University Press, 1949), pp. 522-523.

adjusts the rate of interest on loans to the rate of originary interest as manifested in the discount of future goods.[6]

This is so opposed to the layman's ordinary way of thinking, and so opposed to what is found in the great majority of economic textbooks, that most readers will find the theory difficult to assimilate.

But it should be obvious that interest is peculiarly concerned with *time*. Contrary to Keynes's belief, it is at least as much through the rate of interest as through the anticipated yield of new capital goods that "the expectation of the future influences the present" (p. 145). The rate of interest is involved in every price in which the time element enters. The price of a house is the discounted value of its future income. As Irving Fisher has insisted: "The rate of interest is the most pervasive price in the whole price structure."[7] In fact, it is almost supererogatory to say that time-preference (or, if we prefer that term, time-discount) *causes* the rate of interest. Time-preference or time-discount *is* the rate of interest, looked at from another side. If I borrow $100 for one year at 5 per cent, this is another way of saying that I value $100 *now* more than $105 (which I then expect to surrender) one year from now. The interest rate may be stated, not only as an annual monetary payment which is a certain percentage of a loaned capital sum, but as a *ratio* between present and future capital sums. If people valued future goods as much as present goods, one would have to pay an infinite sum for the right to receive $5 a year *perpetually*. But as a matter of fact, if the current long-term interest rate is 5 per cent, one can buy the right to an infinite series of $5 a year for only $100.

Insurance companies are quite used to looking at the question of interest, not in terms of an annual rate of payment, but as a ratio between present and future sums. As-

[6] *Ibid.*, pp. 521, 523, 524.
[7] *The Theory of Interest*, p. 33.

suming a current long-term interest rate of 5 per cent, one can pay only $61.39 for the right to receive $100 ten years from now; only $37.69 for the right to receive $100 twenty years from now; only $8.72 for the right to receive $100 fifty years from now, and so on.

A simple and striking form of the time-preference theory is put forward by the Mexican economist, Faustino Ballvé:

> If the entrepreneur obtains money, he is able to have today what he could otherwise not have until tomorrow. When he obtains a loan, *he buys time*: the interest that he pays is the price of the advantage he obtains from having at his disposal immediately what he would otherwise have to wait for.[8]

Of course the borrower does not *literally* buy or borrow time. Each of us is allotted just twenty-four hours a day, and can neither buy nor sell any of it—at least not in its pure form. But the borrower does buy, or "hire," the *use* of money (or of the assets that he can obtain with the money), and this use is of course *use-in-time*—the time for which the loan runs.

Other names for interest, therefore (or for the thing for which interest is paid), might be *time-valuation, time-use, or time-usance.* The old word *usury,* which originally meant merely interest, was, therefore (until it got its evil connotation of *exorbitant* interest), etymologically more descriptive than its modern substitute.

We are now in a better position to realize the fallacy of Keynes's rejection of the "real" factors that determine the interest rate. The borrower pays interest not merely for money but usually for the assets he can obtain with money. He will therefore decide, in accordance with the interest rate that he is asked for money, whether, say, he will *rent* a house or borrow money and *buy* a house and pay interest on the purchase price. The person from whom he borrows

[8] My own translation from *L'Economie Vivante,* (Paris: SEDIF, 1957), p. 84. Dr. Ballvé wrote me (shortly before his untimely death) that a literal translation from the 1955 Mexican edition of the key sentence here would read: *"Therefore, when he borrows money he is, in fact, borrowing time."*

is also free to decide whether he will himself use his funds to buy a house or lend the money out at interest on a mortgage to somebody else who wants to buy a house. There will thus tend to be an equilibrium between interest rates and rents of houses (minus depreciation and maintenance costs); or rather among the price of houses, the level of (net) rents and the level of interest rates; and each will affect the other.

4. *Combined Interest Theories*

This brings us to the third type of interest theory, which seeks to combine productivity and time-preference factors.

This third type of theory is sometimes disparagingly called "eclectic." But the adjective is not justified if it is meant to imply that those who hold it select a little from the productivity theories and a little from the time-discount theories and fail to give any consistent explanation of interest. On the contrary, this third type of theory is really a *combined* theory. It seeks to *unify* what is true in the productivity theories with what is true in the time-discount theories. In the same way as the price of a commodity is explained as the point of intersection of the supply curve and the demand curve, so one form of the combined theory explains the interest rate as the point of intersection of the curve of supply of savings with the curve of investment demand.

The combined theory of the interest rate reached its highest and most elaborate expression in Irving Fisher's great work *The Theory of Interest* (1930). Schumpeter called this "a wonderful performance, the peak achievement, so far as perfection within its own frame is concerned, of the literature of interest." [9] It is not hard to understand his enthusiasm. Few persons, after reading Fisher, can fail to find Keynes's discussion of interest superficial, haphazard, and even amateurish.

[9] Joseph A. Schumpeter, *Econometrica,* Vol. 16, No. 3, July, 1948.

Fisher marshals the interplay of innumerable factors governing the rate of interest around two pillars of explanation: "Impatience" (time discount) and "Investment Opportunity" ("the rate of return over cost").

F. A. Hayek has followed the Fisher theory in its general outlines, and explains the relation of the productivity factor to time-preference as follows:

> The most widely held view is probably that, as in Marshall's two blades of the scissors, the two factors [productivity and time-preference] are so inseparately bound up with each other, that it is impossible to say which has the greater and which the lesser influence.
>
> Our problem here is indeed no more than a special case of the problem to which Marshall applied that famous simile, the problem of the relative influence of utility and cost on value. The time valuation in our case corresponds of course to his utility, while the technical rate of transformation is an expression of the relative costs of the commodities (or quantities of income at two moments of time).[10]

A complete positive theory of interest would have to take into account more factors than can be adequately discussed in a single chapter. If the market interest rate, for example, were in "complete" equilibrium, here are some of the things that would have to be equated:

1. The supply of, with the demand for, capital (*i.e.*, the supply of savings with the demand for investment).
2. The price of capital instruments with their cost of production.
3. The income from capital goods with their price and their cost of production.
4. The "marginal yield of capital" with the rate of time-discount (time-preference).
5. The supply of loanable (monetary) funds with the demand for loanable funds.

If we wished to illustrate these complex relationships graphically, we would produce an unintelligible maze of

[10] *The Pure Theory of Capital* (London: Macmillan, 1941), pp. 420-421.

lines unless we were willing to use a set of diagrams rather than any single diagram. But the graph on the next page will illustrate one set of major relationships. The vertical line OY represents the interest rate; the horizontal line OX represents the annual volume of savings or investment demand measured, say, in billions of dollars. The curve ID represents investment demand. The lower the interest rate the greater the volume of investment demand; the higher the interest rate the less the volume of investment demand. The curve SS represents the supply of savings. As drawn, it assumes *some* savings even at a zero interest rate. The tendency of higher interest rates will be, within limits, to encourage a greater volume of savings.

But the slope and shape of the savings curve is more debatable than that of the investment demand curve. Some economists would maintain that within a wide range of interest rates the savings curve should be vertical—in other words, that the volume of savings is not greatly influenced by interest rates. Other economists would say that higher interest rates, within a certain range, might encourage more savings, but that above a certain rate the line should actually curve backwards toward the line OY—in other words, that very high interest rates may actually discourage saving because a high income from interest could be obtained from comparatively little saving.

Though the rate of interest and the supply of savings will of course influence each other, we must remember that the supply of savings may be to a large extent independent of the interest rate, just as the interest rate may be to some extent independent of the supply of savings. There would be *some* savings (as a reserve against contingencies) at a zero interest rate. Perhaps the most important line on this chart so far as the rate of interest is concerned is not, in the long run, either ID or SS, but *td,* the line of time-discount. For it is this, in the long run, that may *determine,* rather than be determined by, both the supply of savings and the investment demand.

In the diagram as drawn, the market rate of interest is in equilibrium with the time-discount rate at 3½ per cent. The supply of savings and investment demand are also in equilibrium at that point. In any *short-run* period we may think of these quantities as all *interdependent,* rather than as determined primarily by the time-discount rate.

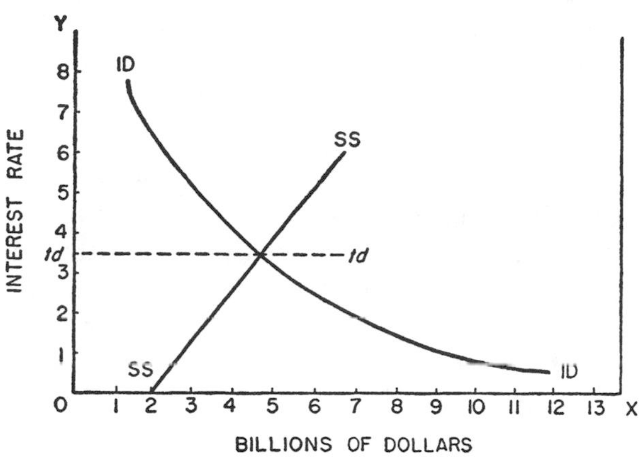

Some readers may think that in the graph the investment-demand curve and the savings-supply curve are together sufficient to determine the interest rate at their point of intersection, and that there is no need or legitimate place for a third line, whether it is called time-discount or anything else. From the standpoint of the orthodox supply and demand curves they are right. (*All* diagrams of this sort are mere aids to thought, efforts to visualize hypothetical relations, never to be taken too literally.) But a supply-and-demand analysis of the interest rate, or of any competitive price whatever, while correct, is superficial, a mere first step. The next step is always to inquire what the particular supply and demand forces are and what *causes* them to be what they are.

Let us, as an illustration, take securities on the stock market. A stock, let us call it American Steel, is selling at 50 on the market. Why is it selling at that particular price?

One answer, of course, is because "supply" and "demand" are at equilibrium at that price. But this only pushes the problem back a stage; it only poses it in another form. Why are supply and demand at equilibrium *at that particular price?* The answer is that the composite *valuations* put upon the stock by *both* buyers and sellers center for the moment at that point. Another way of putting this is that the valuations put on the stock by the marginal buyer and the marginal seller cross at that point. The last buyer must have valued the stock at *more* than $50, the last seller must have valued it at *less* than $50.

Now let us say that American Steel closes at 50 on Monday, but that after the close of the market the board of directors unexpectedly fails to declare the regular quarterly dividend. On Tuesday morning the stock opens 5 points down, at 45. It can be said, of course, that American Steel has fallen because the "supply" of the stock has increased and the "demand" has diminished. But obviously this is not the *cause* of the stock's fall in value, but the *consequence*. Physically, there are no more shares of American Steel outstanding on Tuesday than there were on Monday. Physically, the number of shares bought and the number of shares sold exactly equal each other on Tuesday as they did on Monday. There were no transactions in the stock between the closing price of 50 on Monday and the suddenly lower opening price of 45 on Tuesday. The value of the stock has not fallen because of a change in the amount offered and the amount demanded. It is "supply" and "demand" that have changed because the value of the stock has fallen!

Putting the matter in another way, the individual valuations set upon the stock by *both* sellers and buyers have fallen because of the (generally) unexpected passing of the previous regular dividend.

The matter could, of course, be diagrammatically represented by the usual supply and demand curves crossing each other on Monday, with the demand curve moving to the left and the supply curve moving to the right on Tuesday. (Actually, the supply curve in this case is merely the demand curve of the present holders of the stock. The situation could be represented by placing the valuations of both holders and potential holders on a single demand curve on Monday and lowering the whole curve on Tuesday. However, as the price would be the point at which the valuations of the marginal seller and the marginal buyer crossed each other, it is graphically better to have a "supply" curve as well as a "demand" curve.) These curves indicate relationships, but not necessarily causation. It is the lowered valuation of the stock in the minds of both buyers and sellers that causes the change in the "supply" and "demand," rather than the change in amount supplied and amount demanded that causes the lowered valuation.

In the same way, it is the composite time-preference or time-discount schedule in the minds of both borrowers and lenders that determines the rate of interest, the position of the investment demand curve and the position of the supply-of-savings curve, rather than the supply and demand curves which determine the composite time-preference point.

It may help some readers (even though the parallel is misplaced) to think of "normal" time-discount as the main factor governing the long-run "normal" rate of interest (rather than the ever changing constellation of day-to-day market rates of interest) much in the same way as cost-of-production "determines" the relative "normal" prices of commodities rather than their short-run market prices. In modern theory, of course, its cost of production does not "determine" the "normal" price of a commodity, but relative costs of production are part of the interdependent relationships among relative prices. As Wicksteed has put it: "One thing is not worth twice as much as another because it has twice as much 'labor' in it, but producers have been willing to put twice as much 'labor' into it because they know [expect] that when produced it will be worth twice as much, because it will be twice as 'useful' or twice as much desired." [11]

The same sort of cause-and-effect amendment that Wicksteed makes in the classical theory of the relation of cost of production to price must be made also in Böhm-Bawerk's concept of the lengthening of the period of production. The fact that certain capital goods take longer to produce than others does not necessarily increase their value or productivity; but the expectation that certain capital goods will be more valuable or productive makes producers willing to undertake a longer period of production, if necessary, to secure them.

Each saver's and entrepreneur's time-preference or time-discount (including his estimate of the composite time-preference or time-discount of the community as a whole) will help to determine the current rate of savings or the current investment demand; but at any given moment the points of intersection of these supply and demand curves will "determine" market rates of interest.

5. *Real Plus Monetary Factors*

After this long excursion into positive theory, we can recognize much more clearly the nature of the fallacies in Keynes's theory of interest. His main fallacy consists in ignoring or denying the determining influence of "real" factors on the rate of interest. It is true that the error of many of the classical economists was the opposite of this. In looking beyond "the monetary veil" at the real factors underneath, they forgot that both short-term and long-term loans consist after all, in money, and that both interest and principal are payable in money. This means that the theory of capital and interest must be understood in terms of money as well as in "real" terms, and that the monetary influences on the interest rate must be studied as well as

[11] Philip H. Wicksteed, *The Alphabet of Economic Science,* 1888. (New York: Kelley & Millman, 1955), p. 117.

the real influences. But Keynes made no new contribution when he jumped to the conclusion that therefore the interest rate is a *purely* monetary phenomenon. He merely returned to the *pre*-classical assumption of the mercantilists (as he himself, in his final chapters, came to recognize) and to what has always been the assumption of the man in the street.

Nor would he have been the first to discover, if he *had* discovered it, that *both* sets of influences, real and monetary, had to be recognized and reconciled in any complete theory of interest. That glory belongs to the Swedish economist, Knut Wicksell. The great contribution which Wicksell made to interest theory was to reconcile the "real" theories of interest as developed by the classical economists and amended by Jevons and Böhm-Bawerk, with what actually happens to interest rates in the day-to-day money market as the banker or the security investor confronts it. The real factors act *through* the monetary factors. Wicksell's really *general* theory of interest (real-cum-monetary) was carried further by Irving Fisher and receives its most mature exposition in the work of Ludwig von Mises.[12]

Wicksell saw that it was both theoretically and actually possible for the Central Bank temporarily to depress interest rates by what are called "open-market operations." When the Central Bank wishes to reduce interest rates it buys short-term (and sometimes long-term) obligations in the market and creates deposits or bank notes against them. By buying these short-term obligations and raising their capital value, it directly reduces market interest rates, and by creating bank deposits or even "cash," it creates additional monetary funds to be thrown on the loan market, thus further tending to reduce interest rates. By doing this, in fact, the Central Bank could apparently reduce interest rates down to any figure where they were high enough to pay the mere operating costs of the banks.

[12] Cf. *Human Action,* Chaps. 18, 19, and 20.

This is the one germ of truth in Keynes's purely monetary theory of interest rates. "Open market operations" are certainly practicable for bringing about temporary (which may sometimes mean rather prolonged) reductions in interest rates.

But Wicksell (and more clearly those who followed him) also recognized that the process did not end there. Interest rates are depressed, it is true, by buying short- and long-term obligations, by creating deposits—in brief, by manufacturing money. But this sets in train a series of forces which act the other way. The market interest rate for money can be kept below the "natural" rate only by continuous additions to the supply of money and credit. But these continuous additions to the money and credit supply eventually raise prices of commodities. And when these prices are raised, the larger amount of money now in circulation is needed to finance the same volume of physical transactions and production as was previously financed by the smaller volume of money. So the new money supplies are all used up in current production. If the attempt is made to issue new money still faster than the older supplies are already raising prices, the result might only be to raise prices (through general fear of inflation) even faster than the new money supplies were put out. In any case, lenders, fearing that further inflation was in the offing, would demand a higher interest return to insure them against the possible loss of the real capital value on their original loan.

So the process by which the Central Bank originally was able to *lower* interest rates, will now simply serve to *raise* them. And if the bank stops the open-market and other operations by which it lowered interest rates, the adjustment of prices to the new volume of money and credit will restore interest rates to the "natural" level and probably even beyond.

This is a brief, oversimplified, and inadequate description of the process. But it is sufficient to show that everything that is true in the Keynesian monetary theory of interest was already recognized by Wicksell, Fisher, Mises, Hayek, and others before Keynes wrote.

Keynes was undoubtedly acquainted with Wicksell's work. He refers to it frequently in his *Treatise on Money*. Even in the *General Theory* he devotes one footnote of a couple of lines to "the 'natural' rate of Wicksell" (p. 183), and another couple of lines to him in connection with the "natural" rate of interest (p. 242). But, mysteriously, he never mentions Wicksell at all when he is making the same criticisms of the "classical" theory of interest as Wicksell had made a generation before the appearance of the *General Theory*. And in his left-handed reference (on p. 183) he alludes to Wicksell and Hayek with the disdainful intimation that they are much too subtle. He quotes from Ibsen's *Wild Duck:* "The wild duck has dived down to the bottom —as deep as she can get—and bitten fast hold of the weed and tangle and all the rubbish that is down there, and it would need an extraordinarily clever dog to dive after and fish her up again" (p. 183).

But a theory is not necessarily wrong because it was too deep and subtle for Keynes. In his own theory of interest he certainly did not dive deep; he merely muddied shallow waters.

I am tempted to say that in rejecting *both* productivity *and* time-preference theories, or any combination of them, Keynes was left with no real theory of interest. But on second thought it is clear that he *was* flirting with the oldest theory of all—the *Exploitation Theory*. This was once described by Irving Fisher as the persistent idea that "to take interest is, necessarily and always, to take an unfair advantage of the debtor. This notion is something more than the obviously true idea that the rate of interest, like any other price, may be exorbitant. The contention is that there ought to be no interest at all." After tracing the persistence of this notion through primitive societies, ancient

Rome, and the Middle Ages, Fisher declared that, "Today the chief survival of the exploitation idea is among Marxian Socialists."[13] But Fisher wrote this some years before Keynes attempted still another revival in "modern" guise.

[13] *The Theory of Interest,* 1930, pp. 48-49.

Chapter XVI

CONFUSIONS ABOUT CAPITAL

1. *On Going Without Dinner*

As we advance in the *General Theory,* the fallacies seem to be crowded in more tightly, and in Chapter 16, "Sundry Observations on the Nature of Capital," they become particularly thick.

"An act of individual saving means—so to speak," Keynes begins—"a decision not to have dinner today." The matter is obviously put this way in order to make an act of saving appear to be inherently absurd. The truth is that an act of individual saving means, for the overwhelming majority of savers, merely a decision not to have *two* dinners today. It is much more sensible all around to put aside enough to make sure that one also has a dinner tomorrow.

But let us resume the quotation:

> An act of individual saving means—so to speak—a decision not to have dinner today. But it does *not* necessitate a decision to have dinner or to buy a pair of boots a week hence or a year hence or to consume any specified thing at any specified date. Thus it depresses the business of preparing today's dinner without stimulating the business of making ready for some future act of consumption. It is not a substitution of future consumption demand for present consumption demand,—it is a net diminution of such demand (p. 210).

On the basis of Keynes's own formal definitions of saving and investment earlier in the *General Theory,* according to which "they are necessarily equal in amount, being, for the community as a whole, merely different aspects of the same thing" (p. 74), this whole passage is nonsensical and self-contradictory. We can make sense of it only if we re-define saving merely as *non-spending* of *money*. Even then the passage is (conditionally) true only in a very restricted sense. In order to make it true, we must throw our italics, not on the word *not*, but on the word *necessitate*. An act of saving does not *necessitate* a future act of consumption—particularly if it is accompanied or followed by an equivalent act of deflation (*i.e.*, an actual cancellation or disappearance of the amount of money saved), and if prices and wages are rigid.

But in the modern economic-world, an act of saving, if it is not followed within a month or so by an equivalent spending, is almost invariably accompanied or followed by an act of investment. This is merely a way of saying that people in a modern economic community do not simply hoard money in a sock or under the mattress. Even if they merely deposit it in a checking account, the great bulk of it is immediately loaned out by the bank. If they deposit it in a savings account the whole of it is invested for them.

> Moreover [Keynes continues], the expectation of future consumption is so largely based on current experience of present consumption that a reduction in the latter is likely to depress the former, with the result that the act of saving will not merely depress the price of consumption-goods and leave the marginal efficiency of existing capital unaffected, but may actually tend to depress the latter also. In this event it may reduce present investment-demand as well as present consumption-demand (p. 210).

Even Keynes, one might suppose, would have stopped at this point to re-examine either his premises or his paradoxical conclusion. For what he is saying is that though saving and investment are "necessarily equal," *increased* saving may mean *decreased* investment!

Before we examine the basic fallacy here, however, we may pause a moment to point out a secondary fallacy. In the passage just quoted Keynes is tacitly assuming, not merely that there have been acts of saving, but that there has *suddenly* been *more* saving than in the immediate past. For if, let us say, people in a given community had previously spent 90 per cent of their incomes on consumption and set aside 10 per cent for savings-investment, both consumption-goods and production-goods entrepreneurs would have adjusted their operations to this distribution. Consumption-goods producers would have expected to sell, say, only 90 units of goods in a given period while capital-goods producers were selling 10 units. Saving at the same rate as in the past would do nothing to disturb the existing balance. Only if savings, say, were suddenly doubled, and consumers only bought 80 units of consumption-goods where they had previously bought 90, would the consumption industries be disturbed.

The assumption of a sudden *increase* in saving, in fact, is the only one that makes sense out of Keynes's conclusions. That this is what he does tacitly assume is brought out by a remark on the following page: "An individual decision to save does not, in actual fact, involve the placing of any specific forward order for consumption, but merely the *cancellation* of a present order." (My italics, p. 211.) As John Stuart Mill pointed out more than a century ago in dealing with precisely this fallacy about saving: "This is confounding the effects arising from the mere suddenness of a change with the effects of the change itself." [1]

But even this assumption of a net increase in the rate of saving (or rather of a net decrease in the rate of consumption) is not enough to make sense out of Keynes's conclusion. We must also assume that what is saved is not invested, as it normally would be. For if, in the new situation, only 80 per cent of income were spent on consumption, but 20 per cent, instead of 10, went into investment, the capital-goods industries would be stimulated sufficiently to absorb any unemployment in the consumption-goods in-

[1] *Principles of Political Economy,* Book I, Chap. V, § 9. (Eighth Edition), p. 104.

dustries. And *future* income would be even greater than otherwise. The only assumption on which Keynes's conclusion can be justified is that the increased savings would mean merely increased money hoardings (accompanied by rigid prices and wage-rates). And this would happen only in a period when the *expectations* of consumers were *bearish,* either regarding the future price of durable consumer goods, or their own prospects of continued employment, or both.

> The absurd, though almost universal, idea that an act of individual saving is just as good for effective demand as an act of individual consumption, has been fostered by the fallacy, much more specious than the conclusion derived from it, that an increased desire to hold wealth, being much the same thing as an increased desire to hold investments, must, by increasing the demand for investments, provide a stimulus to their production; so that current investment is promoted by individual saving to the same extent as present consumption is diminished (p. 211).

Now this "absurd idea" is, in fact, a true description of what normally happens, because normally an act of saving *is* an act of investment. If a man does nothing else than deposit his weekly salary check in his commercial bank account, for example, and draw out only part of the amount to pay his bills and meet his current expenses, the bank will normally lend out at short term, say, about four-fifths of the deposit. If the same man deposits part of his weekly salary in a savings account, the savings bank will lend out at long term almost the entire deposit. Saving and investment (using both terms in their unsophisticated senses) normally go together, and are normally part of the same completed transaction.

In trying to prove that this is not so, Keynes resorts to reasoning so tortured that it becomes almost impossible to follow it. "This fallacy," he tells us, "comes from believing that the owner of wealth desires a capital-asset *as such,* whereas what he really desires is its *prospective yield*" (p. 212). This distinction, in connection with this particular line of argument, has more subtlety than point. It is equivalent to observing shrewdly that what a concert audience really goes to hear is not the piano but its sound. The distinction is no less true, in fact, of consumption than of capital goods. We buy or rent a house, an automobile, or a piano for the services we get out of it. And the "yield" of capital goods, like the "yield" of consumption goods, is not necessarily a *physical product,* but a "service," a *value.* The yield of a railroad or a truck, like the yield of a pleasure car, consists in the value added by transportation. The yield of an office building, like the yield of a residence, consists in shelter, heat, convenience of location, attractiveness and impressiveness of appearance, and other services, both tangible and intangible. Capital goods "yield" a *money* income; consumer goods directly yield an *enjoyment* income.

One of Keynes's own major fallacies is his assumption that "yield" must mean a *physical* yield rather than a *value* yield. That is why he embraces the medieval notion that money is "barren." That is why he persistently fails to recognize that people wish to hold cash, not because of some wholly irrational or anti-social "liquidity-preference," but because of the *yield* they expect from holding cash. This yield may consist in the ability not only to make immediate purchases but to take advantage of future opportunities. Or cash may be held speculatively in the expectation of a rise in the purchasing power of money (or, what is the same thing, in the expectation of a fall in the price of durable goods).

Nor is this speculative holding of money, as Keynes constantly implies, wicked or anti-social simply because it does not go immediately into purchasing consumption goods at excessive prices or making unprofitable investments. If the speculative holders of money are *right* in their expectations, they perform a social function by refusing to waste resources unprofitably and by forcing a quicker return to more realistic and workable price and wage relationships. It is those who persist in holding wage-rates and prices at excessive and unworkable levels who are acting anti-socially.

After telling us that the owner of wealth does not desire a capital asset "as such," but only its "prospective yield," Keynes goes on: "Now, prospective yield wholly depends on the expectation of future effective demand in relation to future conditions of supply. If, therefore, an act of saving does nothing to improve prospective yield, it does nothing to stimulate investment" (p. 212).

This is a strangely inverted argument. An act of saving is not undertaken to "improve" prospective yield, but *to take advantage of* prospective yield. Saving (somewhere) is *indispensable* to equivalent investment. Saving represents the *supply* of the funds needed to satisfy investment *demand.* Every manufacturer or seller knows that when by production or offer he increases the *supply* of a commodity he does not thereby raise its *price* or increase the *demand* for it. The supplier is merely taking advantage of the existing price and demand; he is helping to *meet* the existing demand. The actual effect of his own action, indeed, is to tend to *lower* the price and to *reduce* the amount of demand that remains unsatisfied. Earlier in the *General Theory,* as we have seen, Keynes compares saving and investment to selling and buying respectively, and reminds us of the elementary proposition that "there cannot be a buyer without a seller or a seller without a buyer" (p. 85). But in the foregoing argument from page 212 he does in fact assume that there can be selling without buying, saving without investment.

Keynes's argument on this point shuttles back and forth so much, in fact, and seems to reverse its direction so often, that the task not merely of answering it, but even of saying what it *is,* often appears hopeless. Immediately after he has treated saving, in effect, as a one-sided operation, like selling without buying, he insists with his own italics on calling it *"two-sided."* But "two-sided" in a rather strange way. To quote:

> Moreover, in order that an individual saver may attain his desired goal of the ownership of wealth, it is not necessary that a *new* capital-asset should be produced wherewith to satisfy him. The mere act of saving by one individual, being *two-sided* as we have shown above, forces some other individual to transfer to him some article of wealth old or new. Every act of saving involves a "forced" inevitable transfer of wealth to him who saves, though he in turn may suffer from the saving of others. These transfers of wealth do not require the creation of new wealth—indeed, as we have seen, they may be actively inimical to it. (His italics, p. 212.)

I find it impossible to make head or tail of this argument, or to read any sense into it. Every sentence of it seems to be wrong. An act of *net* saving by any individual *must* involve the creation of a new capital asset. If it fails to do so, if it is in fact a mere *transfer* of an existing capital-asset (say a stock or a bond), then the only reason it does not lead to the creation of a new capital asset is that it must be offset by an exactly equivalent act of *dissaving* on the part of some other individual—either the person who sells the saver the existing capital-asset, or some other person. But if there is no offsetting act of dissaving elsewhere, then a net *addition* to saving by anybody *must* mean the creation of a new capital asset.

It is, moreover, impossible to see how a saver "forces" some other individual to transfer some article of wealth old or new. A man who earns a wage of $100 a week and saves $10 out of it has not "forced" his employer to transfer this $10 to him. He has earned it for his services; he has produced an *equivalent* value in return. And if he has not "forced" this $10 out of his employer, it is impossible to say from whom he has forced it. If he has not stolen it, he has given an equivalent. The buyer does not "force" a transfer of goods from the seller; the seller does not "force" a transfer of money from the buyer. It is impossible to make any sense out of such a form of statement.

But if it is impossible to say with confidence what Keynes means in this paragraph, it is not impossible to guess. His errors come mainly from using the terms "saving" and "investment" in many different senses, several of which are mutually contradictory. If we define saving and investment as Keynes formally defines them in Chapter 6 of the *General Theory,* in which *both* terms mean merely *unconsumed output,* then they are not merely equal but identical, and the whole of Keynes's subsequent discussion of the difference between them is invalid. If saving, however, is thought of purely in terms of hoarded *money,* and investment is thought of purely in terms of *capital goods* (excluding money), then there is of course a difference between them. But it does not follow that Keynes's reasoning even on these foregoing definitions (which he never makes *explicitly*) is valid. For Keynes (1) constantly writes as if the man who holds money holds nothing of "real" value; (2) never tells the reader whether in any particular case he is assuming a constant or a changing money supply; and (3) never tells the reader whether in any particular case he is assuming flexible or rigid prices and wage-rates.

2. *Saving, Investment, and Money Supply*

If Keynes is assuming a constant money supply, then an "act of saving" by any individual or group (when "saving" means solely *money* saving) must necessarily be offset by an act of "dissaving" by some other individual or group. For if the money supply is constant, the *average* cash holding cannot be increased. If, under such conditions, the majority of people suddenly *attempt* to save more, then the initial result must be that producers (and nearly all families are producers as well as consumers) will buy less of each other's goods. It is *only* in these suddenly changed specific conditions, and for such an assumed *initial* period, that the predicted Keynesian result of unemployment would take place as a consequence, not of "saving," but of *attempted* saving.

And even this consequence is possible *only under the further assumption* that prices or wage-rates are "sticky" or inflexible in a downward direction. For if prices and wage-rates are fluid in both directions, the immediate response to a falling off in the desire to buy goods or to hire workers would be a lowering of prices or wage-rates to a point where people would cease to attempt to save more than before and would consent to make their usual purchases again. In any case, the reduced supply of money offered would now be sufficient to buy the previous volume of goods and to employ the previous number of workers at the now lower prices and wages.

But this analysis reminds us that even when the "Keynes unemployment effect" takes place, Keynes is accusing the wrong factor of being the culprit. The real culprit is not saving, but wages and prices that are inflexible in a downward direction. And even the "saving" of which Keynes complains is not saving or even an attempt to save in the ordinary sense; it is an attempt to hold *money* rather than *goods,* in the expectation that the purchasing power of money will go up (*i.e.,* that the price of goods will go down).

But even here it is not the attempted saving (or rather the attempted hoarding) that is the cause of the downturn; *it is the expectation of the downturn that causes the attempted hoarding.* And the expectation of the downturn is caused, in turn, by the belief that prices or wage-rates or both are excessive at levels unlikely to be maintained. Keynes's sarcastic shafts, however, are never directed against inflexible or excessive wage-rates, but only against the attempted "saving" that they provoke.

We must come to the conclusion, then, that under the assumption of a constant money supply, saving and investment are necessarily at all times equal, and grow *pari passu.* Savers invest either directly or indirectly. They either use their savings to buy stocks or bonds or mortgages or houses or other durable goods; or they deposit their funds in savings or checking accounts which the banks invest for them or lend out on short term. Some savers may, of course, "invest" in more pocketbook cash, but only at the expense of others. Under the assumption of a constant money supply, there cannot be a net increase in *average* cash holdings.

Yet many modern economists do distinguish between saving and investment, and do talk of inequalities between saving and investment. And this distinction, when properly made and understood, is not only valid, but constitutes an important and necessary tool of analysis. The best way to show this is to analyze Keynes's argument denying it.

Keynes, as we have seen, is bewilderingly inconsistent on this point, assuming in Books III, IV, V, and VI, and in a grossly exaggerated degree, the very difference he has been at such pains to deny in Book II. In Book II he explicitly rejects "the new-fangled view that there can be saving without investment or investment without 'genuine' saving" (p. 83). The argument by which he does this is lengthy and complex, but a few quotations will indicate its nature:

> The prevalence of the idea that saving and investment, taken in their straightforward sense, can differ from one another, is to be explained, I think, by an optical illusion due to regarding an individual depositor's relation to his bank as being a one-sided transaction, instead of seeing it as the two-sided transaction which it actually is. It is supposed that a depositor and his bank can somehow contrive between them to perform an operation by which savings can disappear into the banking system so that they are lost to investment, or, contrariwise, that the banking system can make it possible for investment to occur, to which no saving corresponds. (P. 81.)

Now this is precisely what a depositor and his bank *can* contrive to do. The way in which "the banking system can make it possible for investment to occur, to which no saving corresponds" is easier to describe, so we shall begin with it. A big manufacturer comes to his bank with a proposition to put up a new plant; and the bank, because it has faith in his judgment or shares his optimism, advances him $1,000,000 toward it. It does this by creating a deposit credit of $1,000,000 against which he is free to draw. Thus $1,000,000 of monetary purchasing power has been *newly created.* Let us assume that it constitutes a new addition to the outstanding supply of money and bank credit. This sum is invested in the plant. "Investment" has increased by $1,000,000. This increase is represented by a physical asset, which we shall assume is a net addition to the supply of capital instruments. The increase in "investment," then, is real. But there has also suddenly come into being $1,000,000 of new "cash." Is this a genuine saving? Keynes insists that it is:

> The notion that the creation of credit by the banking system allows investment to take place to which 'no genuine saving' corresponds can only be the result of isolating one of the consequences of the increased bank-credit to the exclusion of the others. . . . The savings which result . . . are just as genuine as any other savings. No one can be compelled to own the additional money corresponding to the new bank-credit, unless he deliberately prefers to hold more money rather than some other form of wealth (pp. 82-83).

But this is a very Pickwickian definition of "genuine" savings. The bank creates a "cash" balance by writing a credit on its books—and lo! this becomes "new" savings, and "just as genuine as any other savings," because somebody must hold the new cash balance! On this definition, we create "new" savings, "as genuine as any other savings," simply by expanding the credit supply. On the same reasoning we can create any amount of new "savings" we wish overnight, simply by printing that amount of new paper money, because *somebody* will necessarily hold that new paper money!

It is only by rejecting this whole perversion of words and meanings that we are able to make any sense at all of the

General Theory after Book II. For then we find that Keynes's fear of "savings" and praise of "investment" follow because of his constant assumption that these two words not only refer to two quite distinct things, but that savings and investment are constantly likely to be *unequal.* And when we analyse how this inequality can come about, we uncover the hidden assumption that gives to the Keynesian system whatever plausibility it may have.

Under the assumption of a constant money supply, as we have seen, saving and investment are necessarily at all times equal, and move together. But when new money and bank credit are created (by, say, new bank borrowings to construct new plants) *investment* increases without any corresponding increase in ordinary saving. This may be put the other way. When investment exceeds genuine saving, *it is because new money and bank credit are being created.* In short, when investment exceeds genuine saving, *it is because we are in a period of inflation.* Contrariwise, in a crisis, or period of liquidation, bank loans are being repaid and not renewed; the money supply is shrinking, and ordinary saving exceeds subsequent investment.[2] In short, when genuine saving exceeds investment, it is because we are in a period of *deflation.*

To put it still another way, an excess of *prior* saving over *subsequent* investment (when we use these terms in their monetary or monetary-value sense, and not both in the technical sense of "unconsumed product") is but another way of describing *deflation,* and an excess of investment over prior saving is but another way of describing *inflation.* As long as there is an equality of genuine saving and investment

[2] I have made no use in my exposition of such technical terms, so fashionable in recent literature, as *ex-ante* saving or investment vs. *ex-post* saving or investment. I find these adjectives vague and confusing. Obviously they mean, respectively, *before* or *after* something has happened, but few of those who use them ever trouble to specify clearly before or after *what.* Sometimes *ex-ante* is used merely to mean *intended* and *ex-post* to mean *realized.* But it is much less confusing to use these established English adjectives, when they express the meaning, than the new-fangled Latin coinages. After all, a mere *intention* to save is not saving, and a mere *intention* to invest is not investment.

(using both terms in their monetary or monetary-value sense) there is neither inflation or deflation.

Of course, there is always, and under *all* conditions, *simultaneous* equality of "saving" and "investment," *i.e.*, equality *at any one moment of time.* But there is often *inequality* between *prior* saving and *subsequent* investment (using both terms in a monetary or monetary-value sense). And this inequality between saving at one moment and investment at another moment is usually the *consequence,* rather than the *cause* of, the monetary deflation or inflation that must necessarily accompany it.

So the harmfulness of "saving," on which Keynes expatiates so often, and the blessings and necessity of "investment," on which he is equally eloquent, do not follow from the absolute amount of either savings or investment in themselves, but from the unstated assumption that one exceeds the other. If an excess of saving over investment *means* deflation, then there is no trick (and no revolutionary "new" economics) in "proving" that it *causes* deflation. And if an excess of investment over saving *means* inflation, it is supererogatory to prove that it causes inflation.

The whole Keynesian policy is a policy of averting, at any cost, deflation of any amount, and courting almost any risk of perpetual inflation in order to maintain perpetual "full employment." And the whole Keynesian theoretical system rests, among other tricks or errors, on ignoring the fact that with a constant money supply all saving implies an equal amount of investment, and assuming, instead, that there is a constant tendency for saving to exceed investment unless the government bureaucracy as constantly steps in to dream up and order enough "investment" to "fill the gap."

3. *Roundabout Production*

Section II of Chapter 16 contains a number of curious *non sequiturs* which it hardly seems profitable to stop to straighten out. The section is noteworthy chiefly because it repeats the criticism that Marshall made of Böhm-Bawerk in a footnote.[3] I have already anticipated this criticism in my previous chapter (p. 212); but it may be worth while to examine it in the form in which it is stated by Keynes.

"It is true," he writes, "that some lengthy or roundabout processes are physically efficient. But so are some short processes. Lengthy processes are not physically efficient because they are long" (p. 214).

This is true. But, first of all, what counts in economics is not *physical* efficiency or productivity but *value* productivity. And because the precise causal relationship between roundabout processes and production was sometimes misleadingly stated by Böhm-Bawerk, it does not follow that the "length" or "roundaboutness" of the productive process is *irrelevant* or that the Böhm-Bawerkian analysis is "useless," as Keynes (p. 176) and Marshall supposed. It is the expected greater (value) productiveness of certain more lengthy or roundabout processes of production that makes producers willing to undertake them. The causation is the reverse of what Böhm-Bawerk sometimes implied.

But if the length or roundaboutness of various periods of production is to be thrown out as *irrelevant* to a discussion of saving and investment or capital and interest, then consistency would force us also to throw out all considerations of relative costs of production in a discussion of prices of consumer or capital goods. For Böhm-Bawerk's analysis of the length or roundaboutness of production periods is only a special case of relative-cost-of-production analysis in connection with the valuation or pricing process, with particular emphasis on the cost of *time*. Now both Marshall and Keynes, far from ignoring or rejecting considerations of costs of production, constantly emphasize them in their discussion of prices. And Keynes, especially, constantly falls into the very cause-and-effect-reversal error in connection with production costs and prices of which he accuses Böhm-

[3] Alfred Marshall, *Principles of Economics,* (Eighth edition), p. 583.

Bawerk in connection with roundabout processes and productivity.

4. *Abundance Unlimited*

Sections III and IV of Chapter 16 are so fantastic in their assumptions and reasoning that it is difficult to know where to start picking up the fallacies and misstatements.

Keynes begins with the bland statement: "We have seen that capital *has to be kept scarce enough* in the long-period to have a marginal efficiency which is at least equal to the rate of interest" etc. (My italics, p. 217.) This is much as if he had written: "We have seen that commodities have to be kept scarce enough to give them a price." This statement embodies the insinuation both that the rate of interest is a purely artificial and unnecessary thing and that capitalists have to conspire to "keep" everything scarce so that somebody or other can make a profit.

Keynes then goes on to speculate upon what would happen in "a society which finds itself so well equipped with capital that its marginal efficiency is zero and would be negative with any additional investment" (p. 217). And this is not merely a hypothetical assumption for the purpose of deducing hypothetical consequences, nor even an assumption which is not supposed to be realized for an indefinitely remote future. If

> State action enters in . . . to provide that the growth of capital equipment shall be such as to approach saturation point at a rate which does not put a disproportionate burden on the standard of life of the present generation . . . I should guess that a properly run community equipped with modern technical resources, of which the population is not increasing rapidly, ought to be able to bring down the marginal efficiency of capital in equilibrium approximately to zero within a single generation (p. 220). [And, going further:] If I am right in supposing it to be comparatively easy to make capital-goods so abundant that the marginal efficiency of capital is zero, this may be the most sensible way of gradually getting

> rid of many of the objectionable features of capitalism (p. 221).

Nonsense could hardly be carried further. The central problem with which economics deals, the problem with which mankind has been struggling since the beginning of time, is the problem of scarcity, and this problem is assumed away in a few blithe words. It is "comparatively easy to make capital-goods so abundant that the marginal efficiency of capital is zero."

Did Keynes stop to think for a moment what this would imply? It would imply that capital goods were so abundant that they had no exchange value! And if they had no value, they would be as free as air or (most) water or other goods without scarcity. It would be worth nobody's while to keep such capital goods in repair (unless it cost nothing, not even anybody's labor, to keep them in repair). There would be no problem even of replacement. For as soon as there were a problem of replacement, it would mean that capital goods once more had a value and cost something to produce: therefore, presumably, capital goods would cost nothing to produce.

Moreover, if the marginal efficiency of capital were zero, it would also mean that no *consumer goods* would have any scarcity, price, or exchange value. For as long as any consumer goods anywhere failed to reach the point of satiation, and had a price or a value, then capital to help produce these consumer goods would have *some* marginal yield above zero.

A marginal efficiency of zero for capital would mean, in brief, such an abundance of *everything* that neither capital goods nor consumers goods would have any scarcity, any price, or any exchange value. In such circumstances the rate of interest, of course, would also fall to zero—not only because the rate of interest and the marginal yield of capital tend toward equality, but because it is one of the implications of a zero marginal yield for capital that no one would want to borrow money for investment. If someone did want to borrow money for investment (enough to pay *anything* for the privilege), it would imply that to this borrower, at least, capital *did* have a marginal yield above zero.

Capital will continue to have a marginal yield above zero, in brief, as long as it continues to help in the production of consumer goods that have a price above zero. And if these consumer goods have a price above zero, it will be not only because they fill human wants, but because their supply is not unlimited and because they cost *something* to produce. And it is this cost of production (and not some wicked conspiracy of the capitalists) that keeps them scarce.

The capitalist system, in fact—which is the system of free, private, competitive enterprise—has been doing more to reduce production costs, and to relieve scarcity, than any system in history. It is because America has come nearer to adopting a full free private enterprise system that it has done more to relieve scarcity than any other nation in history. But as human wants are insatiable, and as both consumer and capital goods will always, to repeat, cost *something* to produce, the day when capital will cease to have any yield at all, and when consumer goods cease to have a price, and when no scarcity of any kind exists, is still far, far off. All talk of making capital so plentiful as to reduce its marginal efficiency to zero "within a single generation" is the purest moonshine.

No doubt Keynes's "system" owes part of its popularity to the impression that he has at last provided not only that Economics of Abundance,[4] of which the Utopians have been dreaming from time immemorial, but has combined with it a Conspiracy Theory according to which the Moneylenders keep everything scarce in order that they may continue to receive Interest. But if *everybody* could have Complete Abundance of everything simply by ceasing to "keep capital scarce," then this Conspiracy must certainly

[4] *Cf.* F. A. Hayek, *The Pure Theory of Capital* (London: Macmillan, 1941), p. 374

be the most stupid and pointless in history. Did Keynes seriously believe all this?

Having announced this triumphant fallacy Keynes proceeds to draw some triumphant corollaries from it:

> The post-war experiences of Great Britain and the United States are, indeed, actual examples of how an accumulation of wealth, so large that its marginal efficiency has fallen more rapidly than the rate of interest can fall in the face of the prevailing institutional and psychological factors, can interfere, in conditions mainly of *laissez-faire,* with a reasonable level of employment and with the standard of life which the technical conditions of production are capable of furnishing (p. 219).

This little passage contains four major fallacies:

(1) It is based, not on a *cyclical* theory of depression, but on a *secular* theory. It contains the seeds of the Stagnationist Theory of a Mature Economy which the Keynesian disciples in the United States, notably Alvin H. Hansen, did so much to develop. This theory has been so thoroughly disposed of by George Terborgh in his *The Bogey of Economic Maturity* (Chicago: Machinery and Allied Products Institute, 1945) that I shall not deal with it here. It rests on the assumption that a nation goes into an economic tailspin because it becomes too rich for its own good. The tremendous growth of the American economy (and even of the British economy) since Keynes's paragraph was written is a sufficient refutation in itself.

(2) It assumes that the interest rate is not only a merely monetary phenomenon but a purely arbitrary one. Both of these fallacies have already been sufficiently discussed.

(3) It shares with the Technocrats and similar crank groups the naive belief that production is being held down to existing levels, not by limited capital and labor, but by some sort of Conspiracy or Perversity in the "System."

(4) It reveals Keynes's bias against economic freedom and in favor of statist controls. As we shall see later, his whole theory is based on the tacit assumption that neither busi-

nessmen, bankers, speculators, investors, nor consumers can be expected to act rationally in their own self-interest, but that government bureaucrats can always be depended upon to act with great rationality and disinterested regard for the public good. On the same page, in fact, from which the foregoing quotation is taken, Keynes expresses the fear that nations "will suffer the fate of Midas" if "the propensity to consume and the rate of investment are not deliberately controlled in the social interest but are mainly left to the influences of *laissez-faire*" (p. 219).

Keynes's hostility to the rich and to the capitalist system breaks out in sarcasms reminiscent of Marx:

> Insofar as millionaires find their satisfaction in building mighty mansions to contain their bodies when alive and pyramids to shelter them after death, or, repenting of their sins, erect cathedrals and endow monasteries or foreign missions, the day when abundance of capital will interfere with abundance of output may be postponed (p. 220).

Such sentences throw considerably more light on Keynes's emotional attitudes than they do on the process of economic production.

One is moved to wonder, in fact, whether the popularity of the *General Theory* among government bureaucrats and in many academic groves doesn't rest precisely on its anti-business bias.

Chapter XVII

"OWN RATES OF INTEREST"

1. *Speculative Anticipations are not "Interest"*

Chapter 17 of the *General Theory,* "The Essential Properties of Interest and Money," is dull, implausible, and full of obscurities, *non sequiturs,* and other fallacies. Even Alvin Hansen, Keynes's leading American disciple, has written:

> Immediately after the appearance of the *General Theory* there was a fascination about Chap. 17, due partly no doubt to its obscurity. Digging in this area, however, soon ceased after it was found that the chapter contained no gold mines. . . . In general, not much would have been lost had it never been written. . . . Keynes's discussion in Sec. I., Chap. 17, is confused and of no real importance.[1]

I am tempted to let the matter go at this; but some of the fallacies that appear in this chapter are worth analysis both in the interests of thoroughness and for the light the analysis may throw on the rest of the *General Theory.*

It is in this chapter that Keynes toys with the strange notion of "own rates of interest":

> The money-rate of interest—we may remind the reader—is nothing more than the percentage excess of a sum of money contracted for forward delivery, e.g. a year hence, over what we may call the 'spot' or cash price of the sum thus contracted for forward delivery. It would seem, therefore, that for every kind of capital-asset there must be an analogue of the rate of interest on money. For there is a definite quantity of (e.g.)

[1] *A Guide to Keynes,* pp. 159-160.

> wheat to be delivered a year hence which has the same exchange value today as 100 quarters of wheat for 'spot' delivery. If the former quantity is 105 quarters, we may say that the wheat-rate of interest is 5 per cent per annum; and if it is 95 quarters, that it is *minus* 5 per cent per annum. Thus for every durable commodity we have a rate of interest in terms of itself,—a wheat-rate of interest, a copper-rate of interest, a house-rate of interest, even a steel-plant-rate of interest (pp. 222-223).

Of all the confusions in the *General Theory* this is one of the most incredible. Even such loyal Keynesians as Hansen and Lerner [2] boggle at it.

> The own rate of interest—the house rate, the wheat rate, and the money rate [Hansen insists] is in fact the marginal efficiency of a unit whether that unit be a house, a bushel of wheat, or a sum of money. . . . The all-embracing term for the so-called own rate of interest is the *marginal efficiency* rate, or the rate of return over cost from investment in an increment of the capital asset in question.[3]

Now this is only a little less nonsensical, a little less violent misnomer, than Keynes's own term. What Keynes is talking about is certainly not an "interest rate" of any kind. Nor is it, as Hansen supposes, a "marginal efficiency rate." It is not merely that it would be confusing and silly to talk of a "marginal efficiency rate" of a bushel of wheat. This "marginal efficiency rate" would often be a *negative sum.* And if the "marginal efficiency" of a bushel of wheat were negative, the *price* of a bushel of wheat would also be negative, or at least zero.

Now an interest rate is at least a *rate.* If it amounts to r for one year, then it is $2r$ for two years, $3r$ for three years, $\frac{1}{2}r$ for one-half year, and so on. On such an analogy one might perhaps talk of the (net) rent of a house as a house-rate-of-interest. But what Keynes is talking about is not even

[2] A. P. Lerner, "The Essential Properties of Interest and Money," *Quarterly Journal of Economics,* May, 1952.

[3] Alvin H. Hansen, *A Guide to Keynes,* p. 160.

a *hiring* rate, which would at least have some reasonable analogy with an interest rate. He is talking merely of *speculative anticipations of price changes,* which may change from day to day, hour to hour, or minute to minute.

Keynes should have had some intimation that he was talking nonsense, one would suppose, when he was explaining "own-rates of interest" to the reader: "Let us suppose," he writes, "that the spot price of wheat is £100 per 100 quarters, that the price of the 'future' contract for wheat for delivery a year hence is £107 per hundred quarters, and that the money-rate of interest is 5 per cent; what is the wheat-rate of interest?" (p. 223). After a slight calculation he concludes that in this case "the wheat-rate of interest is *minus* 2 per cent per annum." And he adds, in a footnote, "This relationship was first pointed out by Mr. Sraffa, *Economic Journal,* March, 1932" (p. 223).

Now a negative interest rate is in itself a foolish and self-contradictory conception,[4] for it is impossible to imagine any sane person *lending* any amount of wheat or money or anything else in order to make a *foreseen* loss; and the term "interest rate" implies that the rate is *foreseen* if it implies anything. The term "interest rate," again, implies that something is being *lent* by one party to the transaction and *borrowed* by the other, and that the principal sum (or object) is being *returned* by the *borrower* to the *lender* at the end of the contractual period.

But no "lending" or "borrowing" of wheat occurs in the transaction described by Keynes, but merely a purchase and sale. And if a "rate of interest" is being paid, it is impossible to figure *from* whom *to* whom. It is even impossible to know, from the illustration Keynes gives, whether the purchaser of the future contract for wheat has made a profit or a loss. To know *that,* one would also have to know the spot

[4] Unless one considers the amount one pays to a warehouse for storing cotton, wheat, or furniture, or to a safe-deposit vault owner for storing one's jewelry, securities or cash, a "negative rate of interest." But to call a charge for storage or the service of safe-keeping a "negative interest rate" is deliberately to court needless confusion.

price for wheat *when the year was up,* and compare it with the £107 that the purchaser of the future contract had to pay.

We cannot even say, in the illustration given, that the *seller* of the 100 quarters of wheat is £2 better off than if he had *not* sold the wheat but had borrowed £100 at 5 per cent to carry it; because this would depend entirely upon the spot price he would have to pay for the same amount of wheat when the year was up. Similarly, we cannot even say that the *buyer* of the "future" contract for wheat is £2 worse off than if he had not bought the forward contract but had lent out his £100 at 5 per cent for a year instead. To answer either question we must know what the spot price of wheat is at the time that the "future" contract falls due. If the price of spot wheat is then £114, the previous seller of the wheat is £9 worse off than he might have been if he had held his wheat, and the buyer of the forward wheat is £9 better off than he would have been if he had not bought the forward contract. Similarly, if the spot price of wheat at the end of the year is still £100, then the seller of the wheat is £5 better off than if he had held his wheat and paid £5 interest to carry it, and the buyer is £5 worse off than if he had not bought the future contract but had merely lent out his money at 5 per cent instead.[5] But in neither case, of course, are we talking about a "wheat-rate of interest."

The whole illustration, in fact, leads one to question how much Keynes knew about actual transactions in the speculative commodity markets. I pick up the newspaper as of the day I am writing this, and quote some illustrations as I find them. As of Aug. 8, 1957, then, the opening price of Chicago wheat (new contract) for September delivery was $2.14 a bushel; for December delivery $2.19½ a bushel; for the following March, $2.21¾; but for the following May, $2.16⅞, and for the following July, $2.03¾. How could one figure from this the "wheat-rate of interest"? There is, of course,

[5] I have not gone into the question of what would be involved if this were merely a "hedging" operation. That consideration is here irrelevant.

a premium of 5½ cents for December wheat over September, and a premium of 7¾ cents of March over September, and of 2¼ cents of March over December. If one finds such confusion amusing, one could treat these sums as a "negative wheat-rate of interest." Even here, however, one would be hard put to it to explain why the negative wheat-rate of interest was so much lower for six months than for three months. But what is one to do when one gets to the May and July deliveries, and finds the situation completely reversed, so that one can buy a bushel of wheat for delivery eleven months off for 10¼ cents *less* than one pays for delivery next month? Here are all sorts of positive and negative "rates of interest" for the same commodity on the same day!

If we turn to Chicago corn (also on Aug. 8, 1957), we find exactly the reverse situation. There the price of a bushel of corn for September delivery is \$1.30⅞; for December delivery \$1.26⅞; for March delivery \$1.31⅛, and for May delivery \$1.33⅞. So the "corn-rate of interest," unlike the "wheat-rate of interest," for the first three months is a "positive" rate (talking in Keynesian terms) but for six and eight months suddenly becomes a "negative" rate!

If we throw out all such nonsense, stop calling apples cherries and triangles squares, and ask what really happens, we find that the difference between spot prices and future prices, or between one future price and another, is merely the result of differences in *speculative anticipations.* The speculative community, in other words, is putting a separate guess on the probable supply and demand situation regarding each commodity at each of a series of delivery dates in the future. Unlike the situation with regard to (riskless) money-lending, the profit or loss from these transactions cannot be known in advance. (Unless they are "hedging" operations designed to *avoid* a speculative risk by taking the risk both ways.)

This does not mean that the going short-term interest rate (on money) does not play a part in speculative prices.

Where the wheat that is being sold for forward delivery must meanwhile be carried by the seller in storage, the seller will mentally deduct the prospective storage, insurance, and other carrying-charges (including the interest he has to pay to borrow the money to carry it) in figuring what he is "really" getting for his wheat; and the buyer will mentally add these carrying charges in figuring what he is "really" paying.

But both are in fact betting on what they expect the *spot* price to be for wheat on the day of delivery. The buyer thinks he will be getting the wheat cheaper (or at least avoiding the risks of loss), by buying it now at the existing "futures" price than by paying the spot price as he expects it to be six or nine months hence. The seller thinks he is getting more (or avoiding risk) by selling at the "futures" price now than by waiting to sell and taking a chance on the spot price six or nine months hence. Buyer and seller, in short, have different estimates; each is betting against the judgment of the other. There is no need for any concept of a "wheat-rate of interest" in understanding such a transaction; there is no real analogy with any rate of interest, and nothing but confusion can result from introducing a spurious analogy.

2. *Impossible Miracles*

Because there is no validity at all in the idea of "own-rates of interest," I shall spare the reader an analysis of the pretentious algebraic notation ("$q - c + l$," etc.) that Keynes introduces to explain the differences between the "own-rates of interest" of different goods. It is curious, in fact, how Keynes himself pursues this and other of his own ideas to the point of *reductio ad absurdum* while seeming to remain completely blind to the absurdity. At one point he even introduces the idea that each *national currency* must have a different "own-rate of interest": "Here also the difference between the 'spot' and 'future' contracts for a foreign money in terms of sterling are not, as a rule, the same for different foreign moneys" (p. 224). Of course not; and the reason is clearly that, as long as most national currencies remain on a mere paper basis, there is bound to be a different speculative guess (changing daily) concerning the future value of every national currency. To call these different speculative guesses "rates of interest" is merely silly.

On the same page, Keynes, in illustrating own-rates of interest theory, writes: "To illustrate this let us take the simplest case where wheat, one of the alternative standards, is expected to appreciate at a steady rate of *a* per cent per annum in terms of money" (p. 224). The illustration is absurd and impossible. Never in history has wheat been "expected to appreciate at a steady rate of *a* per cent per annum in terms of money." And it is impossible to imagine without self-contradiction the conditions under which such an expectation could exist. One would be the expectation of an absolutely fixed "objective" value for a bushel of wheat each year (month, day, and hour), combined with a steady annual (also monthly, weekly, and daily) depreciation in the value of the currency unit. Such an expectation, if general, would be falsified because speculative transactions would anticipate it immediately. Another condition would be one in which the value of the dollar would be expected to remain absolutely fixed while the value of a bushel of wheat appreciated at a steady rate annually (and presumably monthly, weekly, and daily). For such an anticipation to exist, we should have to imagine a condition in which everybody miraculously expected the demand for wheat to increase with complete regularity (and without speculative anticipation!) while the supply for equally miraculous reasons remained rigid; or one would have to imagine so finely adjusted a decline in the production of wheat as to make a steady appreciation in value at the same uniform rate possible. One would have to imagine a universally shared expectation upon which no speculator, no buyer or seller, acted! But the assumptions are too self-contradictory to pursue further.

Yet it is always instructive, in analyzing a fallacy, to try to discover what it was that led its author to embrace it. As with so many other fallacies of Keynes, we find that even this one was not original with him. Irving Fisher, in *The Theory of Interest* (1930), played with the idea for a few sentences: "No two forms of goods can be expected to maintain an absolutely constant price ratio toward each other. *There are, therefore, theoretically just as many rates of interest expressed in terms of goods as there are kinds of goods diverging from one another in value.*" (His italics, p. 42.) But this idea is then almost immediately dropped. I think this was because Fisher's common sense recognized that the free convertibility at all times of money into goods (at market prices) and of goods into money, brought about, in effect, a single uniform interest rate, *"the"* interest rate, expressed in money. The constant fluctuations over time in the prices of individual goods can hardly, therefore, be treated as changes in individual "interest rates." They are speculative oscillations. *"The"* common interest rate is diffused through the whole price system.

3. *Ought Wages to be Rigid?*

I shall have to skip over whole nests of minor fallacies and confusions in the later part of Keynes's Chapter 17 in order to concentrate upon a few major ones. One of the most important is his contention not only that money-wages are "sticky," but that they *ought* to be. In other words, Keynes contends not only that money wage-rates fail to respond to changes in supply and demand but that it would unstabilize the economy if they did so. It is a very good thing that they are unresponsive:

> If money-wages were to fall easily, this might often tend to create an expectation of a further fall with unfavorable reactions on the marginal efficiency of capital (p. 232).

> Professor Pigou (with others) has been accustomed to assume that there is a presumption in favor of real wages being more stable than money-wages. But this could only be the case if there were a presumption in favor of stability of employment. . . . If, indeed, some attempt were made to stabilize real wages by fixing wages in terms of wage-goods, the effect could only be to cause a violent oscillation of money-prices. For every small fluctuation in the propensity to consume and the inducement to invest would cause money-prices to rush violently between zero and infinity. That money-wages should be more stable than real wages is a condition of the system possessing inherent stability (pp. 238-239).

A full analysis of such passages will be postponed until we come to consider Keynes's Book V on "Money-Wages and Prices." Here it is enough to notice that Keynes is against (1) flexibility and adjustment of money-wages; and (2) against *stability* of real wages (because it would "cause money-prices to rush violently between zero and infinity").

Evidently the man is going to be hard to satisfy. Also, because these positions are mutually contradictory, it is going to be hard to know which is Keynes's "real" position when it comes to analyzing his doctrine. I may anticipate our conclusion to the extent, however, of pointing out that the belief that a subsequent adjustment of "real" wage-rates to a *prior* change in money-prices "would cause money-prices to rush violently between zero and infinity" is such furious nonsense that no analysis could render it more ridiculous than it is on its face.

4. *We Owe Our Lives to Saving*

It is already clear that Keynes is determined, with no matter what argument or assertion, to exculpate excessively high wage-rates from all blame for unemployment and to pin that blame on to the demand of lenders for the payment of interest on their loans. Thus there is no real difference of doctrine, but merely one of obscurity, complexity, and intellectual pretentiousness, between the contentions of the

General Theory and the baldest and most demagogic propaganda of union leaders. One difference is, indeed, that Keynes is more openly cynical in his proposals and more openly contemptuous of everyone who does not accept his doctrine. He is also more openly contemptuous of "the public" generally:

> Unemployment develops, that is to say, because people want the moon;—men cannot be employed when the object of desire (*i.e.* money) is something which cannot be produced and the demand for which cannot be readily choked off. There is no remedy but to persuade the public that green cheese is practically the same thing and to have a green cheese factory (*i.e.* a central bank) under public control (p. 235).

The theory embodied in this paragraph is that the public is irrational, that it can be easily gulled, and that the object of government is to be the chief party to the swindle.

The results of turning central banks into green cheese factories to deceive the public will be examined in a later chapter. Here I wish to analyze a typical paragraph in which Keynes seeks to put the blame for almost everything that has gone wrong in history on his great bête noir, "liquidity-preference":

> That the world after several millennia of steady individual saving, is so poor as it is in accumulated capital-assets, is to be explained, in my opinion, neither by the improvident propensities of mankind, nor even by the destruction of war, but by the high liquidity-premiums formerly attaching to the ownership of land and now attaching to money. I differ in this from the older view as expressed by Marshall with an unusual dogmatic force in his *Principles of Economics*, p. 581:—
>
> "Everyone is aware that the accumulation of wealth is held in check, and the rate of interest so far sustained, by the preference which the great mass of humanity have for present over deferred gratification, or, in other words, by their unwillingness to 'wait' " (p. 242).

Once more Keynes has managed to pack an astonishing number of misstatements and fallacies into a small space.

No doubt the world is still far poorer in "accumulated capital-assets" than it desires to be. How "poor" it is compared with what it might have been under ideal conditions is, of course, a matter of pure speculation. But Keynes's statement that the world is poor in accumulated capital assets, even as compared with the past, is subject to statistical test.

There is not space here to go into this matter in great detail. The reader is referred to the appropriate historical and statistical material.[6] But aside from the notorious fact that the condition of the masses is enormously better than it was two centuries ago, just before the Industrial Revolution (*i.e.,* the birth of modern capitalism), there is the still more notorious fact that the population of the world since then has increased three-fold or four-fold. It was capital accumulation that made this possible. This means that at least two out of every three of us owe our very existence to the savings and investments of our forebears (in spite of "high liquidity-premiums") and to the capitalist system. What assurance has any of us that he is the one person in every three or four that would have come into the world anyway, without this capital accumulation? Could Keynes or anyone else afford to be patronizing about it?

The gain in capital accumulation is not to be measured, of course, merely by number of factories or amount of machinery. The gain in world population implies the erection of an enormous amount of housing. And it has involved, in fact, the continuous *qualitative* improvement in housing, tools, machinery, and every sort of capital asset.

It is the *qualitative* improvement in capital assets, which is certainly no less important than the quantitative increase, that Keynes constantly ignores. Perhaps the greatest single form of capital investment in the world, in fact, is represented by the *improvement in land,* to make it more get-at-able, usable, tillable, fertile, attractive, productive in every

[6] See e.g., *Capitalism and the Historians,* (ed.) F. A. Hayek, (University of Chicago Press, 1954), and Ludwig von Mises, *Human Action,* (New Haven: Yale University Press, 1949), pp. 613-619.

way. This has involved an immense amount of leveling, road-making, road improvement, canal-digging, forest-clearing, draining, irrigation systems; river improvement and flood-control systems; plowing, fertilizing, and, in cities, of street-laying, street-widening, sewerage systems, the laying of pipes and wires and sidewalks, and so *ad infinitum.* Once this work has been *done,* the casual or careless observer is apt to take most of it for granted, as if it had always been that way, or all been provided by "nature." The careless economist is apt to call it simply "land," and to forget that, in all civilized countries, it is land to which an enormous amount of capital improvement has been applied.

It might be added also that the growth of capital accumulation is *accelerative.* This acceleration has been most pronounced since the beginning of the Industrial Revolution—that is to say, since the repeal of the mercantilistic restrictions, the trade barriers, and above all of the usury laws—those laws against high interest rates that Keynes thinks so wise.

The next thing to notice, in the passage I have quoted from p. 242, is that, after greatly underestimating the existing amount of world capital accumulation, Keynes speaks of the "high *liquidity-premiums* formerly attaching to the ownership of land." Now no doubt in the pre-capitalistic period land-ownership represented usually the chief form of wealth-ownership. But how Keynes figures that land ever bore a "*liquidity*-premium" is a mystery. Land is proverbially, and has nearly always been, probably the most *illiquid* possession that a man can hold. It was usually much *more* illiquid in the past than it is today, when its liquidity is for practical purposes greatly increased by numerous real estate agents, by newspaper advertising, and by an organized mortgage market. It has become less illiquid with the development of capitalism; for in the pre-capitalistic period land was usually inherited and commonly entailed. A rich man's relatively *liquid* possessions consisted of the precious metals, jewelry, works of art, cattle (once even a medium of exchange), and non-perishable crops, such as tobacco (once also a medium of exchange).

Finally, we must notice in the passage quoted that Keynes not only rejects the time-preference theory of interest, but even time-preference, "impatience" or "waiting" as an important *element* in the theory of interest. And he does this without deigning to offer any argument whatever, but simply by the *ex cathedra* statement that "I differ in this from the older view." It may be pointed out, however, that he differs in this also from his *own* previous acknowledgment in the *General Theory* itself of the way in which "the psychological time-preferences of an individual" (p. 166) affect his decisions as between present and future consumption, and from his own frequent use (e.g., p. 135) of the term "rate of discount" in connection both with the interest rate and the marginal efficiency of capital. "The rate of discount" is a meaningless concept except in relation to time-preference. It is, in fact, merely another name for the rate of interest.

5. *Keynes vs. Wicksell*

Section VI of Chapter 17 contains a short discussion of Knut Wicksell's concept of a "natural" rate of interest. Keynes discusses it only to dismiss it. Here again his dismissal is not based on anything that can properly be called an analysis, but simply on his personal "opinion":

> I am now no longer of the opinion that the concept of a 'natural' rate of interest, which previously seemed to me a most promising idea, has anything very useful or significant to contribute to our analysis. It is merely the rate of interest which will preserve the *status quo;* and, in general, we have no predominant interest in the *status quo* as such (p. 243).

It is hard to call this anything else than a deliberate misrepresentation. The implication of Keynes's statement is that what the "natural" rate of interest would preserve is the existing distribution of wealth or income, or the existing level of production or employment. But the only thing that the "natural" rate of interest would preserve, on Wicksell's definition, is the established pre-existing average of prices. What Wicksell meant by the "natural" rate of interest, in other words, was the rate of interest that would be *neither inflationary nor deflationary*. He saw that if the rate of interest were pushed *above* this level, it would unduly discourage borrowing, cause a contraction in the volume of money and credit, and hence a fall in prices, activity, and employment. But if the rate of interest fell or were held down *below* the "natural" level, it would lead to overstimulation of borrowing, and hence to an inflationary expansion in the volume of money and credit.

Though it was defective in some respects (as pointed out by Ludwig von Mises and others who improved upon it), Wicksell's discussion of the interest rate, and of its relations to changes in the volume of money and credit, marked a great forward step in economic analysis. While Wicksell correctly saw (unlike Keynes) that the rate of interest is primarily determined by "real" factors, he took full account of the disturbances caused (and he even to some extent exaggerated the disturbances caused) by changes in the volume of money and credit.

Thus Wicksell took full account of the one germ of truth in Keynes's otherwise naive and false theory of interest—the truth that *changes* in the volume of money and credit have something to do with changes in the interest rate. But Wicksell saw clearly that in the absence of changes in the quantity of money and credit the interest rate would be determined by "real" factors, and that changes in the quantity of money act only as *disturbing* factors which only *transitionally* and *temporarily* affect the interest rate.

That Keynes's purely monetary theory of interest is quite naive and completely fallacious we have already seen in Chapters XIV and XV. But we may notice again here that, though Keynes's few references to Wicksell's contribution to the theory of interest are all disparaging (telling us merely that he *rejects* it), they reveal that he was *acquainted with* Wicksell's contribution. Yet in his chapter on "The Classical Theory of Interest" Wicksell's name appears only once, and then merely in a three-line footnote (p. 183). The reader unacquainted with the literature of the subject would get no hint that Wicksell had fully anticipated the only valid point in Keynes's discussion of the "classical" theory of interest, viz., that some account must be taken of the relation of interest rates to changes in the money supply. Even his disciple, Alvin H. Hansen, calls Keynes to task for this injustice:

> With respect to another subsidiary point Keynes is clearly wrong. He calls attention to the failure of the classical school to bridge the gap between the theory of the rate of interest in Book I dealing with the theory of value and that in Book II dealing with the theory of money. This is formally correct, at least with respect to many writers, but then he adds the opinion that also the *neoclassical* school had made a muddle of its attempt to build a bridge between the two. Now this certainly could not be said of Wicksell. This paragraph (p. 183) is far from convincing.[7]

It is hard to escape the conclusion that Keynes, in order to try to prove his own originality and the wrongness of everybody before him, failed to give a clear account of Wicksell's contribution and sought to salve his conscience by a disparaging reference to it.

6. *"Equilibrium" of an Ice Cube*

While Keynes persistently refuses to acknowledge that the rate of interest has anything to do with the real factors that control it, such as investment opportunity and time-preference, he just as persistently seeks to relate it (in Sect. VI of Chap. 17 and elsewhere) to "the level of employment":

7 *A Guide to Keynes,* pp. 151-152.

> I had, however [in the *Treatise on Money*], overlooked the fact that in any given society there is, on this definition, a *different* natural rate of interest for each hypothetical level of employment. And, similarly, for every rate of interest there is a level of employment for which that rate is the "natural" rate, in the sense that the system will be in equilibrium with that rate of interest and that level of employment. . . . I had not then understood that, in certain conditions, the system could be in equilibrium with less than full employment (pp. 242-243).

This entire passage is pure nonsense. It is absurd, as I have frequently pointed out before, to talk of "equilibrium with less than full employment" because this is simply a contradiction in terms. The absence of full employment negates the very concept of equilibrium.

Perhaps an analogy will help to make clearer not only why this concept is self-contradictory but why Keynesians nonetheless persist in accepting it. Drop a cube of ice into a bowl of water. The cube will cause a splash and other disturbances in the water level. It will plunge toward the bottom of the bowl, then rise to the top, and settle with about nine-tenths of its bulk below the water level and the remaining tenth above. When it has settled there, and the water is once more calm, there is, true enough, something resembling a position of "equilibrium"—or, shall we say, *partial* equilibrium. But the reason part of the ice cube remains above the water level for a time is because it is *frozen*. *Complete* equilibrium is not established until the ice cube has melted, and the water is all at one level. Frozen wage-rates cause frozen unemployment. When wage-rates become fluid again, "full" employment is restored.

It is, perhaps, not too difficult to account for Keynes's misuse of the term "equilibrium" and for the uncritical acceptance of this misuse by so many writers. The older economists thought of equilibrium as an actual state of affairs. They contrasted "stability" with "disturbance," a "period of equilibrium" with a "period of transition." But any living economy is *always* in "transition"—and fortunately so. An economy that had reached completely "stable equilibrium" would be an economy that had not only stopped growing but had stopped going.

The only kind of equilibrium worth trying for is the *dynamic* equilibrium that is approached through competition and fluid prices and wage-rates. This must not be conceived of as a position that is ever reached, but as ever-changing positions that are *approached* or *passed through* —as the pendulum of a clock constantly approaches or passes through the vertical equilibrium position but never rests there as long as the clock is running.

Paraphrasing and reversing Grover Cleveland's famous aphorism, we may say regarding economic equilibrium that it is a *concept* that confronts us, not a condition. Yet this concept is not unrelated to reality. It is a limiting notion. There is always a *tendency* toward equilibrium. An economy can get stuck for a long period at a point of unemployment, as a clock can get stuck if someone puts chewing gum in the works. But in neither case should the result be called "equilibrium."

There is, finally, no such functional relationship between the level of interest and the level of employment as Keynes assumes. (He offers, in fact, neither statistical nor plausible logical grounds for this assumption.) The really significant relationship, which Keynes persistently ignores or denies, is that between the level of wages and the level of employment.

The rate of interest and the level of employment are related in any actual situation only in the sense that there is *some* interconnection among *all* economic phenomena.

Chapter XVIII

THE GENERAL THEORY RESTATED

1. *Economic Interrelationships*

Keynes's Chapter 18 is called "The General Theory of Employment Restated." The "restatement" turns out to be confusion worse confounded.

On the assumption that "we have now reached a point where we can gather together the threads of our argument," Keynes thinks "it may be useful to make clear which elements in the economic system we usually take as given, which are the independent variables of our system and which are the dependent variables" (p. 245).

Now economics is concerned with human valuations, human decisions, and human action. *Everything* in the system is a variable. No relationship (unless it is merely two ways of saying the same thing) is a constant. Nothing is permanently "given." Almost anything can be an "independent" variable, in the sense that a change can originate at that point. When a change has originated at any point, then the relationship of nearly all the factors is one of *mutual* dependence, of *interdependence*.

> We take as *given* [Keynes continues] the existing skill and quantity of available labor, the existing quality and quantity of available equipment, the existing technique, the degree of competition, the tastes and habits of the consumer . . . the social structure including the forces . . . which determine the distribution of the national income. This does not mean that we assume these factors to be constant; but merely that, *in this place and context, we are not considering or taking*

> *into account* the effects and consequences of changes in them. (Italics supplied, p. 245.)

David McCord Wright contends that this is actually the first point in the *General Theory* where Keynes states "the basic assumptions of his fundamental model"; and he uses the foregoing italics to stress the point that *"in the basic model"* on which Keynes's system rests, "virtually *all the dynamic social forces are omitted."* [1]

Frank H. Knight, after quoting the same passage, as well as a passage on the following two pages (246-247), in which Keynes declares: "Thus we can sometimes regard our ultimate independent variables as consisting of" . . . etc., follows his quotations by a sweeping comment on the whole Keynesian system:

> It would surely appear that if one is willing to make assumptions of this sort—along with those already pointed out, namely, that there *is* unemployment, that wages and prices cannot fall (but are free to rise), that wages are uninfluenced by the supply-offering of labor, that the price of capital-service is dependent only on the speculative attitude of the public toward money (*i.e.*, toward general prices) and the quantity of money fixed by the arbitrary fiat of a central banking authority entirely uninfluenced either by saving or by the demand for capital—one should indeed find little difficulty in revolutionizing economic theory in any manner or degree or in rationalizing any policy which one might find appealing.[2]

On the same page, Keynes continues: "The division of the determinants of the economic system into the two groups of given factors and independent variables is, of course, quite arbitrary from any absolute standpoint" (p. 247). This is entirely true; and if Keynes had recognized this clearly and consistently, the whole *General Theory* might not have been written. What is "given," what is an

1 *Science,* November 21, 1958, p. 1259.

2 *The Canadian Journal of Economics and Political Science,* February, 1937, pp. 120-121.

"independent variable," and what is a "dependent variable," depends entirely on the problem with which we are dealing.

Economic analysis continually involves the setting up and testing of *hypotheses*. It asks, for example, if *a* and *b* are given, what will be the value of *c*, or if *a* and *c* change, what will be the effect on *b*, etc.

The basic illustration is, of course, the relationship of supply, demand, and price. If "supply" is used in the sense of quantity supplied, and "demand" in the sense of quantity demanded, then a change originating in any one of these three factors will change another. In other words, *if* any two of these three factors are, by *hypothesis* or by *assumption,* the "independent variables," then the other becomes, for the purpose of solving the particular problem under consideration, the "dependent variable."

If supply is used in the sense of supply "schedule" or "curve," and demand in the sense of demand "schedule" or "curve," then orthodox economic analysis would say that a change in either one does not necessarily change the other, though a change in either would change price; and that under conditions of perfect competition price could not change independently, but only as a consequence of a change in the supply curve, or the demand curve, or both. This, it may be pointed out, is merely a consequence of the *meaning* of our terms. The *full* name for the "demand curve," for example, is the curve of price-and-quantity-demanded.

In any case, it is characteristic of economic problem-solving that what is "given" is determined by the nature of the problem. Conclusions regarding what is dependent and what is independent, what is cause and what effect, are determined by our arbitrarily selected starting point.

In commenting upon Keynes's Chapter 18, therefore, I shall not make again any detailed analysis of the factors that Keynes regards as "independent variables" and "dependent variables" respectively, what he regards as cause and what effect. It is enough merely to make the general point that his analysis is arbitrary and implausible, and sometimes clearly reverses cause and effect.

A few comments upon some particular sentences or passages, however, seem called for.

> Within the economic framework which we take as given, the national income depends on the volume of employment, *i.e.* on the quantity of effort currently devoted to production, in the sense that there is a unique correlation between the two (p. 246). Our present object is to discover what determines at any time the national income of a given economic system and (which is almost the same thing) the amount of its employment (p. 247).

The national income is certainly not the same thing as the amount of employment. Nor is there a "unique correlation" between them. The United States with heavy unemployment would have an immensely higher income, either total or per capita, than India or China with full employment. And even within the same nation, say the United States, employment and income do not necessarily rise and fall proportionately. As employment gets fuller, production per man employed tends to fall. As unemployment rises, production per man employed tends to rise. This is partly because, when unemployment sets in, it is the least efficient workers that tend to be dropped first, and when employment rises, it is the less efficient (than those already employed) that must be hired. Moreover, when employment is assured, and other jobs are easy to obtain, there tends to be relaxation of effort on the part of workers, whereas when jobs are insecure, there is an increase of individual effort.

Again, either insistence on excessive wage-rates, or new inventions and improvements, may force the substitution of machinery for workers. In one case there may be a temporary fall in employment without any corresponding fall in production (or total income). In the other case there may be no net change in employment but a significant rise in production (and real income). The "volume of employment" does *not* necessarily mean "the quantity of effort currently devoted to production." Part of "the effort devoted to production" consists in capital improvement, better management, a better balance of production, etc. "Full employment" can conceal gross inefficiencies in production, malinvestment, unbalanced output of consumer goods, and laxity. All of which Keynes consistently ignores.

"Changes in the rate of consumption are, in general, *in the same direction* (though smaller in amount) as changes in the rate of income." (Keynes's italics, p. 248.) In other words, when a man's income rises, he consumes more; the more his income rises, the more he tends to consume; and when a man's income falls, he consumes less! Tremendous discovery, which deserves all the italics that Keynes can give it.

2. *"Stable" Unemployment*

Keynes's reasoning leads to the logical conclusion that there must be violent fluctuations in prices and employment. But these violent fluctuations do not, in fact, seem to occur. Instead of concluding, however, that there must be something wrong in his own analysis, Keynes concludes that there must be something illogical about economic realities. He develops a theory of mysterious stabilizing forces.

> In particular, it is an outstanding characteristic of the economic system in which we live that, whilst it is subject to severe fluctuations in respect of output and employment, it is not violently unstable. Indeed it seems capable of remaining in a chronic condition of sub-normal activity for a considerable period without any marked tendency either towards recovery or towards complete collapse. Moreover, the evidence indicates that full, or even approximately full, employment is of rare and short-lived occurrence (pp. 249-250).

This is a sweeping generalization from a comparatively short and special experience. The condition of comparatively "stabilized unemployment" existed in the United States from about 1931 to 1939. It began sooner in Britain, from about 1925. And in both cases the reason was the same. The British pound sterling, off gold, had fallen from a parity of $4.86 to a low of $3.18 in February of 1920; it had recovered strongly and in late 1924 and early 1925 stood at approximately 10 per cent below the gold parity. Prices and wages had adjusted themselves upward, however, to a lower value for the pound. In April of 1925 Britain decided to return to a gold standard at the old parity of $4.86. This decision would not have been disastrous if British business and labor had recognized its implications, which was that wage-rates and prices would have to readjust downward again to compensate for the domestic and international rise in the value of the pound. But organized labor in Britain remained adamant against accepting any cut in wage-rates. It was precisely because organized labor in Britain followed the very course during and after 1925 that Keynes applauds in the *General Theory* that it brought about the "stable unemployment" that he deplores and regards as a permanent attribute of "the economic system in which we live."

The same thing is true in the United States. Prolonged mass unemployment was specifically a phenomenon of the 1930's. As a result of the inflation of World War I, wholesale prices in May of 1920 had reached a peak at 248 per cent of the 1913 level. Then came the most violent price break on record for such a period. By August of the following year, 1921, the index of wholesale prices had dropped to 141. This resulted, temporarily, in heavy unemployment. But wage-rates were fortunately still flexible. As compared with wholesale prices, their decline was indeed comparatively small. If we compare average wholesale prices with average hourly wages in 1920 and 1922, we find that whereas prices fell an average of 38 per cent between

1920 and 1922 hourly wages fell an average of only 11 per cent. But this was enough to permit readjustment. By the spring of 1923 the United States had reached new high levels in industrial production and there were labor shortages in many lines.[3]

In brief, the "stabilized" unemployment in the United States in the thirties, and in Britain in the late twenties and the thirties, was not a permanent characteristic of "the economic system in which we live." It was a temporarily frozen situation due to the very wage-inflexibility-downwards that Keynes advocates. It was not the result of *laissez faire,* but the result of labor-union policy supported by government policy. And it was not an "unemployment equilibrium," which is a contradiction in terms, but an unemployment frozen by policy, by a refusal to adjust.

3. *The Demand for Labor is Elastic*

"When there is a change in employment, money-wages tend to change in the same direction as, but not in great disproportion to, the change in employment; *i.e.* moderate changes in employment are not associated with very great changes in money-wages" (p. 251).

This is a typical instance of Keynes's reversal of typical or normal cause and effect. The significant thing, in most situations, is the effect of changes *in* wage-rates *on* employment. Looked at from this side, employment tends, of course, to change in the *opposite* direction from wage-rates. If there has been prolonged mass unemployment, as a result of labor-union insistence on excessive hourly wage-rates (in relation to prices and marginal labor productivity), then a *fall* of these wage-rates toward the equilibrium point will mean a *rise* in employment. If, of course, it is *prices* rather than wage-rates that have been above the equilibrium

3 For a fuller account of what happened to prices, wages, and production in both Britain and America in the twenties and the thirties, the reader may consult Benjamin M. Anderson, *Economics and the Public Welfare* (New York: Van Nostrand, 1949).

level, or if for some reason wage-rates have temporarily fallen below the equilibrium level, then an increase in the demand for goods due to a fall in prices, or some other change, or an increase in the demand for labor due to the low wage-rate, will mean an increase in *both* employment and wage-rates. In this special case the relationship stated above by Keynes would hold. But this is a comparatively rare and short-lived situation. Much more frequently, it is a *downward* adjustment in wage-rates (or a gradual rise in man-machine-hour productivity) that will bring a *rise* in employment.

What will happen, in short, depends upon the initial situation from which we start; upon the assumptions we make regarding the previous state of disequilibrium. But Keynes almost never explicitly states his initial assumptions. He persistently treats abnormal situations as normal ones, or hopelessly confuses everything by calling a state of disequilibrium a state of equilibrium.

Keynes is correct, though not for the reasons he gives, in declaring that "moderate changes in employment are not associated with very great changes in money-wages" (p. 251). A much more enlightening way to state this is to say that moderate changes in wage-rates can bring about much larger changes in employment. Paul Douglas, as a result of elaborate statistical studies, came to the conclusion that the demand for labor is highly elastic—that a 1 per cent *decline* in wages can mean a 3 or 4 per cent *increase* in employment, when wages have been held above the point of marginal productivity.[4] (This could mean, conversely, that a *rise* of 1 per cent in wage-rates, under similar conditions, could mean a 3 or 4 per cent *decrease* in employment.) A. C. Pigou independently came to a similar conclusion.[5]

(I do not personally believe that it is possible to measure, either by statistics or mathematical deduction, the precise

[4] Paul H. Douglas, *The Theory of Wages* (New York: Macmillan, 1934), pp. 113-158 and 501-502.

[5] A. C. Pigou, *The Theory of Unemployment* (London: Macmillan, 1933).

"elasticity" of demand for any service or commodity. A better name for "elasticity" of demand is *responsiveness* of demand. The latter phrase at least makes it clearer that what we are talking about is the decisions and actions of employers or consumers, and not some inherent quality in the service or commodity itself. But as changes in price can never be assumed to be the *sole* reason for changes in the quantity demanded, and as "other conditions" [including the "demand curve" itself] can never safely be assumed to be precisely the same for any two years, two days, or two moments in succession, it follows that the "elasticity" or responsiveness of demand is never precisely measureable. On what reasonably appear to be fairly persistent relationships, however, we may be reasonably justified in basing practical policies.)

4. *Stabilize Wage-Rates—or Employment?*

> If competition between unemployed workers always led to a very great reduction in money-wage, there would be violent instability in the price level. . . . The wage-unit might have to fall without limit until it reached a point where the effect of the abundance of money in terms of the wage-unit on the rate of interest was sufficient to restore a level of full employment (p. 253).

There are more fallacies in this passage than the reader is likely to have patience to examine. Keynes is apparently trying to prove that if there were free competition among workers, instead of union-enforced or law-enforced inflexibility downwards, the result would be intolerably and limitlessly violent oscillations in prices.

The proposition is just as absurd as it sounds. Price changes normally come first, and determine wage-rate changes, rather than *vice versa.* It is far better, when the choice must be made, to have wide oscillations in prices than wide oscillations in production and employment. The attempt to "stabilize" farm prices at levels above those that would be set by a free, competitive market, as American experience has so dramatically proved, merely leaves unsold farm "surpluses" that pile up in government warehouses. The attempt to stabilize wages at levels above those that would be set by a free, competitive market leaves unemployed surpluses of labor that pile up on government unemployment insurance or relief rolls. We do not stabilize the economy by trying to hold up wages regardless of what happens to prices. We unstabilize it, and create the very mass unemployment that Keynes professes to wish to cure.

It is significant that the Keynesians do not dare to apply their theory both ways. They do not urge that wage-rates be held down when prices soar, in order to stabilize prices by bringing them down again.

Keynes's wage theories are useful only as labor-union propaganda. Their "scientific" pretensions are pure quackery.

In the passage quoted above from page 253 of the *General Theory,* Keynes drags in the effect of a reduction of wage-rates on the interest rate. Of course, the interconnection of all prices (and both wage-rates and interest rates are "prices" in the broadest sense) is such that there is *some* interrelationship between wage-rates and interest rates. But the interrelationship is so complex and for the most part so indirect that a lengthy discussion of this point would be largely irrelevant digression.

We have already seen that Keynes had a false theory of interest. We shall soon see that he had also a false theory of wage-rates, a false theory of money and credit, and a false theory of prices.

Chapter XIX

UNEMPLOYMENT AND WAGE-RATES

1. *Unemployment is Caused by Excessive Wage-Rates*

If I were put to it to name the most confused and fantastic chapter in the whole of the *General Theory,* the choice would be difficult. But I doubt that anyone could successfully challenge me if I named Chapter 19, on "Changes in Money-Wages."

Its badness is after all not surprising. For it is here that Keynes sets out to challenge and deny what has become in the last two centuries the most strongly established principle in economics—to wit, that if the price of any commodity or service is kept too high (*i.e.,* above the point of equilibrium) some of that commodity or service will remain unsold. This is true of eggs, cheese, cotton, Cadillacs, or labor. When wage-rates are too high there will be unemployment. Reducing the myriad wage-rates to their respective equilibrium points may not in itself be a *sufficient* step to the restoration of full employment (for there are other possible disequilibriums to be considered), but it is an absolutely *necessary* step.

This is the elementary and inescapable truth that Keynes, with an incredible display of sophistry, irrelevance, and complicated obfuscation, tries to refute.

He begins, as is his habit, by affecting to state the "classical theory" of the matter; and, as is also his habit, he misstates it. Then he discovers this theory to be question-begging and "fallacious." Next he applies his "own method of analysis."

I spare the reader the quotation, but if he is interested in reading an argument that outdoes Humpty-Dumpty's best efforts in Alice in Wonderland or the complicated and bewildering chain of causation of a Rube Goldberg cartoon, I direct his attention to the long paragraph beginning at the top of page 261 and ending at the top of page 262. Instead of trying to unsnarl this Gordian knot one loop at a time, and calling attention to each fallacy and irrelevance, which would only take us over ground we have already covered, we shall economize time by by-passing it for the moment, as well as the whole chapter and most of its appendix, and by quoting a couple of paragraphs from the last two pages of the appendix in which Keynes contrasts his own views with those of A. C. Pigou:

> The difference in the conclusions to which the above differences in assumptions and in analysis lead can be shown by the following important passage in which Professor Pigou sums up his point of view: "With perfectly free competition among workpeople and labor perfectly mobile, the nature of the relation (*i.e.* between the real wage-rates for which people stipulate and the demand function for labor) will be very simple. There will always be at work a strong tendency for wage-rates to be so related to demand that everybody is employed. Hence, in stable conditions everyone will actually be employed. The implication is that such unemployment as exists at any time is due wholly to the fact that changes in demand conditions are continually taking place and that frictional resistances prevent the appropriate wage adjustments from being made instantaneously." [1]
>
> He concludes (*op. cit.*, p. 253) that unemployment is primarily due to a wage policy which fails to adjust itself sufficiently to changes in the real demand function for labor.
>
> Thus Professor Pigou believes that in the long run unemployment can be cured by wage adjustments; whereas I maintain that the real wage (subject only to a minimum set by the marginal disutility of employment) is not primarily determined by "wage adjustments" (though these may have repercussions) but by the other forces of the system, some of which

[1] A. C. Pigou, *The Theory of Unemployment*, p. 252.

(in particular the relation between the schedule of the marginal efficiency of capital and the rate of interest) Professor Pigou has failed, if I am right, to include in his formal scheme (pp. 277-278).

There is a double advantage in starting our discussion of Chapter 19 with this quotation. (1) Instead of giving us Keynes's misstatement, which would first have to be corrected, of the "classical theory" of the relation of wage-rates to unemployment, it at least gives us Pigou's statement of the "classical" view in his own words; and (2) it contains the most compact and lucid statement that Keynes gives of his own views on the subject.

Pigou's statement is the correct one. Keynes's view is clearly incorrect, though it does contain one grain of truth in a bushel of errors. This grain of truth, it may be added, is not original with Keynes.

Let us begin by seeing what qualifications are necessary in the Pigou statement.[2]

When Pigou speaks of "everybody" or "everyone" being employed, the word "everybody" must clearly be interpreted in a restricted sense. He cannot be speaking of those who do not need or do not want to work, or of children, or of the physically handicapped, or of criminals or lunatics, or those who are so incompetent, stupid, reckless, or slovenly that they destroy more value than they produce, so that an employer would be out of pocket even if he could hire them for nothing. By "everybody" he must mean employable persons who actually wish to work, and it would probably be better if he had used this phrase.

Again, when Pigou declares that "in *stable* conditions

[2] The present book is a discussion of Keynes's views, not of Pigou's. The comments here are meant to apply merely to the passage quoted, not to the whole of Pigou's views in his *Theory of Unemployment* or in later work, in which he revised and restated his earlier views as a result of Keynes's criticisms. Pigou's so-called "conversion" as a result of Keynes's criticisms is probably one of the principal reasons for the present intellectual fashionableness of the Keynesian doctrines. But we shall do better to ignore this *ad hominem* argument and confine ourselves to the objective merits of the issue.

everyone will actually be employed" he must have meant to say in *equilibrium* conditions. It is not stability but the speed and precision of wage adjustments that Pigou is really emphasizing. Relatively "stable" *un*employment is possible with a "stable" or frozen *dis*equilibrium, as was shown both in Britain and the United States in the period between 1925 and 1939. (Keynes capitalized on this, as we have seen, by giving it the self-contradictory name of "unemployment equilibrium.") The equilibrium that we should keep in mind need not be "stable" in the sense of static. That is to say, it need not refer merely to the kind of equilibrium postulated in a "stationary" or evenly rotating economy. It can refer to a dynamic equilibrium postulated as being achieved by instantaneous and precise adjustments to changing conditions, or constantly being *approached* in practice in a free competitive economy.

Finally, while maladjustments in wage-rates are usually the *principal* reason for unemployment, and *can* be the sole reason, *other* maladjustments can also cause unemployment, including maladjustments among particular prices and (here is the one germ of Keynesian truth) even (though improbably) maladjustments in interest rates.

Suppose now, for the sake of clarity, we rephrase Pigou's summary in a more satisfactory form, retaining his own phrasing wherever that is acceptable: With perfectly free competition among workpeople and labor perfectly mobile, there will always be at work a strong tendency for wage-rates to be so related to demand that all employable persons who desire jobs are employed. Hence, in conditions of equilibrium all such persons will actually be employed. The implication is that such unemployment as exists at any time is due wholly to the fact that changes in demand conditions are continually taking place and that frictional resistances prevent the appropriate wage, price, and other (even interest-rate) adjustments from being made instantaneously.

Now if Keynes had been content to make merely these

revisions, if he had been content merely to deny, in his quotation from Pigou, the implication that wage adjustments are the *sole* adjustments needed to retain or restore full employment, his objection would have been correct even if not original. But Pigou's position as summarized by Keynes, that most often "unemployment is *primarily* due to a wage policy which fails to adjust itself sufficiently to changes in the real demand function for labor" (my italics, p. 278) is correct. Keynes explicitly denies even this. Keynes is definitely wrong, in short, when he maintains "that the real wage . . . is not *primarily* determined by 'wage adjustments' . . . but by the other forces of the system." (My italics, p. 278.) These other "forces," it is true, even maladjustments in the interest rate, must be taken into account whenever there is heavy unemployment. But they are usually secondary to the unemployment caused by maladjustments in wage rates.

2. *Wage-Rates Are Not Wage Income*

With this correct positive doctrine in mind, it may be worth while to examine some of the major fallacies which led Keynes to his false conclusions.

Perhaps the first and most important of these fallacies is Keynes's habitual confusion between hourly wage-*rates* and total wage *payments*. In common with, I fear, most writers on economics, he uses the loose word "wages" sometimes to mean wage-*rates* and sometimes to mean total *payrolls,* or total wage *income*. The reader is seldom sure in which of these two radically different senses Keynes is using the word; and Keynes seldom seems to be sure himself. I do not mean to imply that he *always* falls into this confusion. Sometimes the distinction is clear enough in his mind and explicit in the examples that he cites. The confusion is none the less frequent enough to account for many of the otherwise inexplicable conclusions in the *General Theory*.

This confusion is one of the prices that writers on economics pay for trying to use simple, popular language. It never occurs when they are discussing the prices of commodities. It would not occur to even a moderately competent economist to assume that if an entrepreneur raised the price of his product 20 per cent, his gross income would increase 20 per cent. If an individual entrepreneur, engaged in the production of a homogeneous competitive product, such as copper, were arbitrarily to raise his price 20 per cent above that of his competitors, his gross income, instead of increasing 20 per cent, would probably disappear entirely. None of his product would be sold. And even if the entrepreneur were a monopolist, or if all the entrepreneurs in the same industry uniformly raised their prices by 20 per cent, even the man in the street knows that (assuming no other change in the supply or demand "curve") there would be a decline in the volume of sales. The gross income of the individual entrepreneur would not increase in proportion to the price rise; it might even fall *below* its previous level. In short, as far as commodities are concerned, there is no confusion in the popular mind between prices, volume of sales, and gross income. But in writing on labor, even many professional economists constantly confuse "prices" with total income because they call both by the same name—"wages." [3]

Many economists (and this partly derives from Keynes) put forward a curious argument in attempting to justify their double standard, or double set of economic principles, in the discussion of prices and wages respectively. They tell us, without a smile, that "wages" cannot be treated like other costs or other prices, because "wages" are the workers' *income,* and if we cut this income we are not only being cruel and inhuman, but we correspondingly reduce "pur-

[3] In my own discussion I have tried to avoid the ambiguous word "wages" altogether, distinguishing constantly between hourly wage-*rates* and total payrolls, total wage payments, or total labor income. Where I do occasionally use the word "wages" (to escape the appearance of pedantry) I should be understood always to refer to hourly wage-rates and never to total payrolls except when these are explicitly specified.

chasing power" and send the economy into a downward spiral.

Now whatever is true in this statement is true not only of "wages" but of all costs and all prices. Everybody's (monetary) cost is somebody else's income. The price of finished steel is a motor-car manufacturer's cost but (multiplied by tonnage) the steelmaker's income. The price of iron ore or scrap steel is the finished steelmaker's cost but the iron mine's or scrapdealer's income. But if wage-rates or steel prices or scrap prices are too high in relation to other prices, or to supply or demand, an increase in such wage-rates or prices will *not* lead to a corresponding increase in the total income of workers, or of steelmakers, or of scrap-dealers; and it may easily lead to a *decrease* in that total income, through unemployment or a decline in sales more than proportionate to the increase in price.

It is not merely a fallacy, therefore, but a sham humanitarianism, and a cruel deception, always to insist on wage-rate increases whether or not conditions justify them, and always to resist wage-rate reductions whether or not conditions require them.

3. *"Elasticity" of Demand for Labor*

A second fallacy of Keynes's is that, even when he does explicitly distinguish between wage-rates and total wage income, he raises the question whether the demand for labor is really "elastic" or not, or whether its "elasticity" can be greater than "unity." Now Paul Douglas and A. C. Pigou, as I have already pointed out in another connection, had independently, before the appearance of the *General Theory,* attempted a statistical answer to this question, and had come with surprising agreement to the conclusion that the elasticity of the demand for labor is about —3. This means that a 1 per cent reduction in wages can mean a 3 per cent increase in employment, if wages have previously been above the marginal productivity of labor, or, conversely, that a 1 per cent increase in wages can mean a 3 per cent reduction in employment if wages are above the marginal productivity of labor.

I have already pointed out that it is not possible to measure the "elasticity" of the demand for labor (or for anything else) statistically or mathematically. "Elasticity" of demand is merely a misleading and unfortunate name for *responsiveness* of demand. It is obviously impossible to know in advance precisely how the demand for any commodity or service will respond to a change in its price. There are too many factors in the situation, and these factors can never be assumed to be precisely the same for two successive months or minutes.

The concept of a measureable "elasticity" of demand (or of a *predictable* responsiveness of demand) is based on the tacit assumption that when the price of a commodity or service changes, or is changed, the demand "curve" *remains exactly where it was.* It can never, of course, be known whether this is in fact true. A price may have gone up *because the demand curve itself has gone up*—in which case there may be no decrease in the amount demanded. There may even be an *increase* in the amount demanded. Or a price may have gone down *because the demand curve itself has gone down*—in which case there may be no increase in the amount demanded, and there may even be a *decrease* in the amount demanded.

Now as the very existence of a demand "curve" (or demand "schedule") is purely hypothetical, as the "slope" or "shape" of this curve can never be in fact known, and as it can never be known precisely how much it has risen or fallen (or, in the fashionable technical jargon, "moved to the right" or "to the left"), it follows that the "elasticity" of demand for any commodity or service can never be determined by comparing changes in the amount sold with changes in price. For these changes have occurred between two or more periods or moments of time, and we can have no assurance whatever that the demand "curve" has itself remained the same between those periods or moments of time. The demand "curve" may meanwhile have "shifted" from one position to another, or changed its "shape," or we may be on a different "section" of it.

There are still other dangers in the application of the elasticity-of-demand concept to labor. We cannot legitimately speak, for example, of "the" elasticity of the demand for labor, for this will vary with every different kind of labor, almost with every firm, and with every different set of conditions. The responsiveness of employment of all building workers collectively to changes in wage-rates, for example, may be very high, whereas the responsiveness of employment of electrical installation workers alone to changes in their wage-rates may be very low, because the demand for electricians is a joint demand with that for other building workers. To speak of "the" elasticity of the demand for "labor," therefore, may be to speak of an almost meaningless average.

If its dangers and limitations are kept constantly in mind, however, the "elasticity" of demand (or better, the responsiveness of demand) can be a useful tool of thought. The statistical investigations of Douglas and Pigou seem to raise at least a presumption in favor of a (usually) high responsiveness of employment to changes in wage-rates.

In any case, there is the strongest possible presumption in favor of letting free competitive market forces decide the question. When *un*employment exists, it exists because there is *dis*equilibrium somewhere. The most likely place is in the wage-rates of the occupations in which the unemployment exists. This presumption is enormously increased when such wage-rates are arbitrarily held at their existing level by labor-union insistence, which prevents free competitive market forces from operating in those occupations. And this presumption must hold either until free competition (for jobs and for workers) is restored in those occupations or until the unions concerned have consented to a provisional reduction in wage-rates to see whether such a reduction is followed by an increase in employment.

Of course unemployment *could* be caused in one occupation by an excessive wage-rate in another. (For example, some construction workers could be unemployed because wages [and prices] in the steel industry were too high.) It is even theoretically conceivable (to make every concession to Keynes) that the disequilibrium causing unemployment might be in some relationship among prices or even in interest rates. But this is highly improbable unless such inappropriate prices are monopolistically controlled, or unless interest rates have been made excessive as a result of governmental monetary mismanagement.

Another type of error that runs through Keynes's Chapter 19 is his consistent failure to state all the relevant assumptions in the hypothetical illustrations that he sets up, and then to come to a conclusion that could only be warranted on the basis of an assumption (and often a self-contradictory one) that he has failed to state. When we are dealing with unemployment, for example, we must assume that there is a reason for the unemployment. The most probable reason is that wage-rates are too high—*i.e.* that they are *above* the point of equilibrium. This may not be so; but it is certainly one of the hypotheses, if not the *first* hypothesis, that ought to be considered. Keynes never considers it. His examples tacitly assume that wage-rates are already at, or even *below,* the point of equilibrium. Only on that assumption could he reach the conclusion, as he does, that a reduction of wage-*rates* would mean a reduction of wage *income,* either by not increasing employment in the least, or by actually reducing it further. Of course if wage-rates are already at, or below, the point of equilibrium, it would be an act not only of injustice but of sheer folly to reduce them further. But if, as it is enormously more plausible to assume, there is unemployment because wages are *above* the point of equilibrium, then reduction of wage-rates to the point of equilibrium would both restore full employment and *increase* payrolls and the total income of the community.

4. *Fallacies of "Aggregative" Economics*

At the very beginning of Chapter 19 Keynes professes to find a great invalid assumption at the heart of the "classical theory" that a decline in wage-rates (that have been above the equilibrium point) will restore employment. He states the "classical" argument of how this will happen in a particular "industry." (He wrongly states it by giving only a special case, not the general theory.) Then he pauses. The classical theory, he says, has no way of extending its conclusions "in respect of a particular industry to industry as a whole" except by a false "analogy" (p. 260). Therefore "it is wholly unable to answer the question what effect on employment a reduction in money-wages will have" (p. 260).

Where's the catch? Keynes explains:

> The demand schedules for particular industries can only be constructed on some fixed assumption as to the nature of the demand and supply schedules of other industries and as to the amount of the aggregate effective demand. It is invalid, therefore, to transfer the argument to industry as a whole unless we also transfer our assumption that the aggregate effective demand is fixed. Yet this assumption reduces the argument to an *ignoratio elenchi*. For, whilst no one would wish to deny the proposition that a reduction in money-wages *accompanied by the same aggregate effective demand as before* will be associated with an increase in employment, the precise question at issue is whether the reduction in money-wages will or will not be accompanied by the same aggregate effective demand as before measured in money, or, at any rate, by an aggregate effective demand which is not reduced in full proportion to the reduction in money-wages (*i.e.* which is somewhat greater measured in wage-units). (Keynes's italics, pp. 259-260.)

Now the only reason this tangled argument is worth noticing at all is that such a tremendous to-do has been made about it by the Keynesians, many of whom, indeed, think that this is *the* great flaw that Keynes has found in "classical" economics, and *the* great contribution that he has made to economics. "Aggregate" or "aggregative" economics, they tell us, has displaced "special" or "partial" economics, or "the economics of the firm." The "macroscopic" view has displaced the "microscopic" view.

Keynes's whole argument on this point is so confused that the chief difficulty in answering it is the difficulty of discovering just what the argument is.

Let us begin by looking again at the Keynesian term "effective demand." We have seen that there is no need for the adjective. It implies that there are two kinds of demand—"effective" and ineffective. Ineffective demand could then only mean desire unaccompanied by monetary purchasing power. But economists have never called this demand. The term "demand" as used by economists has always meant effective demand, and nothing else. Inserting the adjective, then, adds nothing but confusion.[4]

How, then, about the term "aggregate demand"? Aggregate demand may be thought of in two senses—in terms of commodities or in terms of money. Abstracting from money, the aggregate demand for commodities is ultimately the aggregate supply of commodities. The supply of one commodity is the demand for another, and vice versa. We are back to "Say's Law." And Say's Law is always true (in fact it is a truism) when we assume prices and production to be in equilibrium. Under such conditions, aggregate demand follows from aggregate supply. But Keynes and the Keynesians reject aggregative economics in the one sense in which it is both true and useful.

If the aggregate demand is thought of in terms of money, then it tends to change only with the supply of money.

[4] As we have remarked before, Keynes often succeeds in being technical and pedantic without being precise.

If it is invalid, as Keynes contends, to argue from what happens in a particular "industry" to industry as a whole, then it is no less invalid to argue from what happens in a particular firm to what happens in a whole "industry."[5] But, as a matter of fact, the invalidity exists only in Keynes's mind and is a result of the confusion in his own thinking.

Let us begin with a single "industry" and see what happens. There are two main cases to be considered. The first is that in a "closed" domestic industry in which prices are too high because wage-rates are too high, and therefore the market is contracted and there is unemployment. Suppose wage-rates are reduced enough to allow prices to be reduced enough to restore the market and restore full employment in that industry. There is then both more employment in that industry and more production; therefore more total wages and more gross income; therefore more purchasing power for the goods of other industries. So restoring employment in that industry through cutting wage-rates (*i.e.*, cutting them just enough to make the re-employment possible) has not merely left "aggregate effective demand" where it was; it has *increased* it by raising the "effective" demand of the workers and entrepreneurs in the industry involved while doing nothing whatever to reduce the effective demand of the workers and entrepreneurs in other industries.

Let us call this Industry A. Suppose, now, that the same thing happens in Industry B. Then the increase in the

[5] Keynes's argument does not seem to recognize that an "industry" is not only itself an aggregate, but a purely conventional or arbitrary aggregate without definite boundaries. As of Jan. 1, 1957, for example, there were at least 241 U.S. companies engaged in one or more processes of making steel products. But 23 were "integrated," 60 were "semi-integrated," and 147 were "non-integrated." Some companies, for example, owned their own coal mines and railroads and made their own coke. Were they in the steel industry, the coal industry, the railroad industry, or the coke industry? The U.S. Steel Corporation has a subsidiary that builds bridges. Is it in the steel industry or the construction industry? Some companies make both steel pipe and plastic pipe. Are they in the steel industry or the plastic industry or the pipe-making industry? Firms concerned with different processes, from coke-making to cold finishing, sell to and buy from each other. Just where does "the steel industry" begin and end?

effective demand of Industry B for the products of all other industries, including A, must add still further to the aggregate effective demand. And so, also, if we go on to consider Industries C, D, E . . . N. Keynes has simply raised a pseudo-problem.

The other case, which Keynes does not consider, would be in an "open" international industry as, for example, copper. Here the price would be fixed internationally (with allowance for transportation costs) by the state of international supply and demand. The American copper industry would not be able to lower the world price (proportionately or perhaps even significantly) by lowering its own wages. But if there were unemployment in the American copper industry, it would be (assuming the mines themselves were not inferior to those elsewhere) because wage-rates were too high. They would have to be cut to make employment and the reopening of the mines possible. If a cut in wages *did* (proportionately or more than proportionately) restore employment in the American copper industry, however, obviously the effect would be to increase the effective demand of the workers and owners in that industry for the products of other American industries. Again Keynes's problem becomes a pseudo-problem, created merely by his own confusion, not by some gap or missing link in classical theory.

5. *The Attack on Flexible Wage-Rates*

But the chapter on wages is crammed with confusions and fallacies. One of the most incredible is Keynes's argument against permitting flexibility of wage rates. This flies in the face of everything that has been learned about economics, and the advantages of a free economy, in the last two centuries:

> To suppose that a flexible wage policy is a right and proper adjunct of a system which on the whole is one of *laissez-faire,* is the opposite of the truth. It is only in a highly authori-

tarian society, where sudden, substantial, all-around changes could be decreed that a flexible wage-policy could function with success. One can imagine it in operation in Italy, Germany or Russia, but not in France, the United States or Great Britain (p. 269).

Such a statement fairly takes one's breath away. *Laissez faire* means non-adjustment! *Laissez faire* means inflexibility! Authoritarianism means flexibility! Flexibility means rigidity! One thinks of George Orwell's *Nineteen Eighty-Four,* where war is peace, ignorance is strength, and freedom is slavery.

Nor is the implied approval in the foregoing quotation of totalitarian economic controls to be dismissed as a mere momentary fancy. In the preface that Keynes wrote in September, 1936, to the German edition of his *General Theory,* he tried to "sell" his system to Nazi Germany by writing:

> The theory of aggregate production that is the goal of the following book can be much more easily applied to the conditions of a totalitarian state than the theory of the production and distribution of a given output turned out under the conditions of free competition and of a considerable degree of *laissez-faire.*[6]

Keynes, in brief, does not believe in a free market, does not believe in a free and flexible economy. In his eyes the very virtues of a free economy become its vices:

> Except in a socialized community where wage-policy is settled by decree, there is no means of securing uniform wage reductions for every class of labor. The result can only be brought about by a series of gradual, irregular changes, justifiable on no criterion of social justice or economic expediency (p. 267). If important classes are to have their remuneration

6 The German text reads: "Trotzdem kann die Theorie der Produktion als Ganzes, die den Zweck des folgenden Buches bildet, viel leichter den Verhältnissen eines totalen Staates angepasst werden als die Theorie der Erzeugung and Verteilung einer gegebenen, unter Bedingungen des freien Wettbewerbes und eines grossen Masses von laissez-faire erstellten Produktion."

> fixed in terms of money in any case, social justice and social expediency are best served if the remuneration of *all* factors are somewhat inflexible in terms of money (p. 268).

Now in a free (non-statist, non-socialist, non-totalitarian) economy, wages do not and cannot adjust themselves *en bloc,* as a unit, by some neat, fixed, round, uniform percentage. Nor do prices adjust themselves *en bloc,* by a uniform percentage or as a unit. Nor does production adjust itself *en bloc* or as a unit. In a free economy there are literally millions of different prices,[7] millions of individual wage-rates, thousands of *classes* of wage-rates, prices of hundreds of thousands of different commodities of different grades and at different points. In a free economy there are millions of daily adjustments of one wage-rate to another, of one price to another, of this wage-rate to that price, of that price to this wage-rate. There is constantly going on in a free economy, in brief, an almost infinite number of mutual adjustments. This is how the economy works. This is how its keeps in dynamic equilibrium. This is how the balance of production is maintained among thousands of different goods and services to meet the changing needs and desires of millions of different consumers.

But all this conflicts with the simplistic theories of Keynes. He thinks in aggregates, in averages, in abstractions which are mental constructs that have lost touch with reality. He thinks, in short, in lumps. He deals only in his own lump-concepts like average-"level"-of-wages, average-"level"-of-prices, aggregate demand, aggregate supply. Production itself is regarded as being divided only into a few big lumps called "industries." Sometimes production is even regarded as one big homogeneous lump. Keynes cannot understand a free economy precisely because it does not consist of such lumps. Having reduced everything to aver-

[7] One price controller found, for example, that there were actually 350,000 separate prices in the United States for coal alone. (Testimony of Dan H. Wheeler, director of the Bituminous Coal Division. Hearings on extension of the Bituminous Coal Act of 1937.)

ages, he cannot understand any adjustment, he is even *against* any adjustment, that is not a uniform adjustment of each of these averages, blocks, lumps, to the other.

In denouncing such a free and flexible adjustment of individual prices and wage-rates and outputs as "unjust" and "inexpedient," Keynes does not seem to realize that he is by implication accepting as both economically and ethically "right" the *previous* interrelationship of prices and wage-rates. If only "a simultaneous and equal reduction of money-wages in all industries" (p. 264) is to be tolerated, if "a series of gradual, irregular" changes in wages is "justifiable on no criterion of social justice or economic expediency" (p. 267), then it must be because the *previous* relationship of wage-rate to wage-rate was precisely what it ought to have been. This is defending the status quo with a vengeance!

In brief, Keynes forms a ridiculously oversimplified theory of how a free enterprise economy ought to work, and because it does not work that way, he denounces it. Then he goes on to self-contradictory arguments to prove that reducing wage-rates to bring them more into line with economic realities would reduce or "violently" disturb prices and production, and that the way to stabilize the economy is to refuse to allow free or piecemeal adjustments to take place (p. 269).

6. *Inflation vs. Piecemeal Adjustment*

Having decided that piecemeal adjustment of wage-rates is unjust, Keynes decides that the best way to get a uniform reduction of wage-rates is by a little deception—*i.e.*, by inflating or debasing the money supply so as to raise prices. It appears that "only a foolish person . . . would prefer a flexible wage policy to a flexible money policy" (p. 268), and "it can only be an unjust person who would prefer a flexible wage policy to a flexible money policy" (p. 268). In brief, a person must be both foolish and unjust not to prefer inflation (*i.e.*, debasement of the monetary unit) to adjustment of individual wage-rates to a change in prices or conditions of supply and demand. And one of the advantages of a "flexible money policy" is that one can thereby systematically cheat creditors and so reduce "the burden of debt" (p. 268). And, of course, "having regard to the excessive burden of many types of debt, it can only be an inexperienced person" (pp. 268-269) who would hesitate to fleece creditors by paying them off in a debased currency rather than make honest wage adjustments.

Because Keynes, with his lump, aggregate thinking, is opposed to restoring employment or equilibrium by small, gradual, piecemeal adjustments, he can only advocate sudden, over-all, violent adjustments. Either we must simultaneously, he argues, slash the wages of everybody by a flat, uniform percentage, in totalitarian fashion, or we must achieve the same result by inflating the money supply and raising the price level, so that everybody's *real* wages are slashed by the same percentage. But the irony of this is that, if only a small specific adjustment is needed in one sector of the economy, the violent remedy that Keynes recommends will be quite ineffective.

Let us assume a situation, for example, in which all wage-rates are at equilibrium levels except wages in the building trades, which are 10 per cent above equilibrium levels. There will then probably be unemployment, not only in the building trades themselves, but also, say, in the steel, cement, brick, and lumber industries, because of the falling off in demand from the building trades. And there will be some unemployment in the television, camera, clothing, and other trades because of the unemployment in the building trades and the consequent fall in retail business.

The whole situation could be cured by a 10 per cent cut in building wages alone (which would show up in the average for all industry, say, as a cut of less than 1 per cent in wage-rates). But such a cut in building wages alone, in Keynesian theory, would be "gradual" and "irregular" and hence "unjust" and "inexpedient." For Keynesian theory is not interested at all in *particular* adjustments. It sees them merely as disturbing factors. Therefore Keynes's remedy would be a 10 per cent debasement of the monetary unit to raise prices and living costs. In other words, he would wish to raise *all* prices 10 per cent, and cut *everybody's* real wage about 10 per cent.

But if he could succeed in doing this, the outcome would not cure the situation. For after all these adjustments had been made, wages in the building trades would still be 10 per cent too high in terms of all other wages and prices. When the temporary effects of the inflation had worked themselves out, the unemployment would return, because the same maladjustment *within* the wage-price structure would exist.

I began the last paragraph by saying, "if he could succeed in doing this." I meant, if he could succeed in his declared goal of cutting all *real* wage rates by a uniform 10 per cent. But, of course, this is not what inflation of the money supply would be likely to do. Unless the inflation were brought about chiefly by an increase in loans or subsidies to the construction industry itself, a more probable effect of a general monetary inflation would be to increase *other* wages and prices to bring them approximately "abreast of," that is to say, more nearly in equilibrium with, wages and prices in the construction industry. This is what would happen, that is, if the Keynesian scheme worked as planned.

But even if it did, what would this mean? If wages in the construction industry constitute 9 per cent of all wages, then the Keynesian remedy, at its best, would involve raising 91 per cent of all money wages 10 per cent in order to avoid asking the receivers of 10 per cent of money wages to accept a 10 per cent cut. The Keynesian remedy, in short, is like changing the lock to avoid changing to the right key, or like adjusting the piano to the stool instead of the stool to the piano.

And even so, it is unlikely to be more than temporarily successful. For new maladjustments and disequilibria would be almost certain to occur at the higher scale of price. These, under the Keynesian ground rules, would have to be corrected by still further inflation, and so *ad infinitum.*

Always what is relevant to economic equilibrium and full employment is the relationship of particular wages-rates to other wage-rates, of particular prices to other prices, and of particular wages to particular prices; never of averages to averages, or of the wage "level" to the price "level." Such mathematical averages or average levels do not exist in the real world. They are mental constructs; [8] they are fictions; they conceal the real maladjustments in any given economic situation, or make them appear to cancel out.

They do not really cancel out, however. If we use an index number of 100 to represent each equilibrium wage-rate, respectively, in four different industries, then if Industry A has a wage-rate index of 80, Industry B of 90, Industry C of 110, and Industry D of 120, their average index number would be 100. A Keynesian statistician, relying on averages and aggregates, would declare "wages" to be in equilibrium. Yet the wage-rate of none of the four industries would be in equilibrium. The solution, for a restoration of equilibrium and full employment, would be a mutual and multiple adjustment of particular wage-rates. It would not be to raise the whole level to an index number of 120 so as not to hurt the feelings or disturb the prejudices of the union leaders in Industry D.

It is important, finally, to point out that no real adjustments of wages or prices are ever made, upward or downward, in the flat uniform simultaneous way in which Keynes implies they are made or ought to be made.

I present, on pp. 284 and 285, two charts prepared for a

[8] Cf. F. A. Hayek, *Prices and Production,* (London: George Routledge, 1935, 2nd ed., rev.), pp. 4-5, and Louis M. Spadaro, "Averages and Aggregates in Economics," in *On Freedom and Free Enterprise: Essays in Honor of Ludwig von Mises* (ed.) Mary Sennholz, (Princeton: Van Nostrand, 1956).

1948 publication,[9] by the National Industrial Conference Board. These show the percentage changes in average hourly earnings of workers in twenty-five manufacturing industries over two different periods.

Let us see first of all what happened in the earlier period when wages were falling. (Chart 1.) In the period from 1929 to 1932, there was an *average* decline in hourly earnings in all twenty-five industries of 15.6 per cent. *But the decline was different in each of the twenty-five industries,* ranging from only 2.1 per cent in the least affected to 29 per cent in the most affected.

Turn to Chart 2, and let us see what happened in the longer period from 1929 to 1939, when wages were dominantly rising. In this period the *average* rise in all twenty-five industries was 22 per cent. But the rise was different in each of the twenty-five industries, ranging from 3.6 per cent in the least affected to 37.1 per cent in the most affected.

It is worth making some additional observations about these charts. The range of changes in *individual* hourly earnings is even greater than the charts show. Each of the twenty-five solid lines on each chart *is itself an average* of hourly earnings in a particular industry, and conceals the range within that industry.

Keynesians will no doubt be quick to point out that the decline in hourly earnings between 1929 and 1932 did not prevent (and they will no doubt contend that it even intensified) the decline in employment and output in that period. But several points may be made on the other side.

First, there is nothing in the charts to show that the declines were greatest in the industries where they were most needed to restore employment and production.

Secondly, changes in hourly *earnings* are likely to be much greater than changes in hourly wage-*rates*. This is because, when volume of business is low, *overtime* rates tend to disappear, and when volume of business is high,

9 Jules Backman and M. R. Gainsbrugh, *Behavior of Wages* (New York), pp. 16, 18.

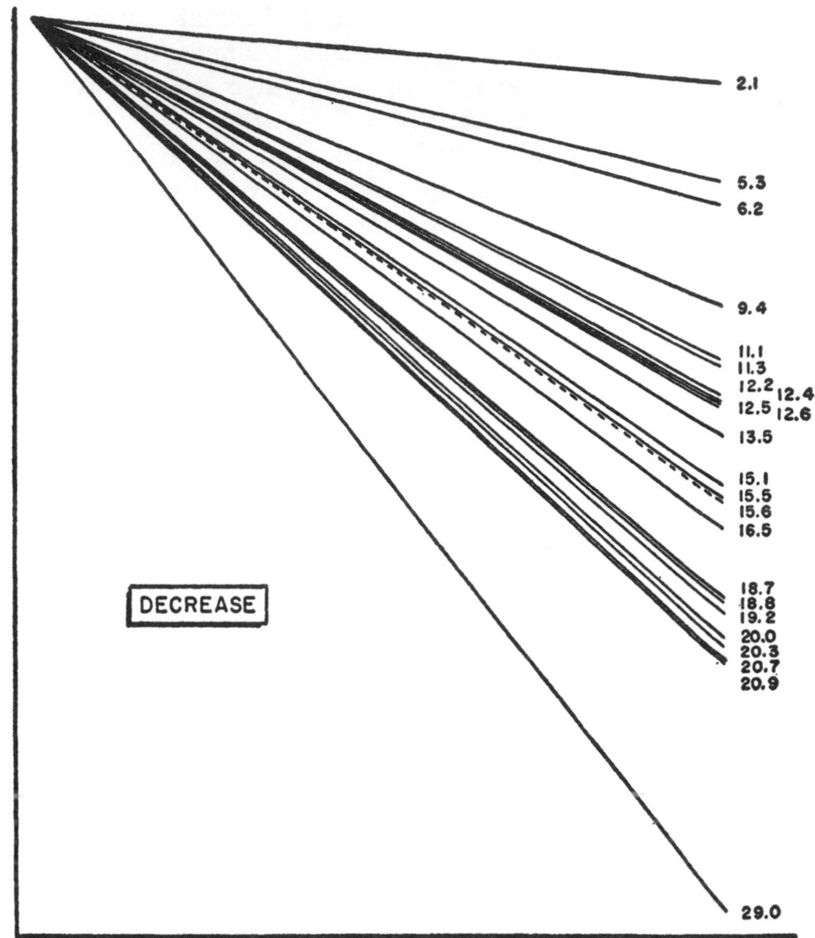

Chart I: Percentage Change in Average Hourly Earnings, 25 Manufacturing Industries, 1929 to 1932. Broken line represents 25 manufacturing industries.

overtime rates tend to pile up. This gives an exaggerated impression, both ways, of changes in standard-time wage-rates. In fact, the hourly earnings may change widely in either direction without any change in standard wage-rates.

Thirdly, wage-rates are not the *only* factor governing the volume of employment at any moment. Possibly from a

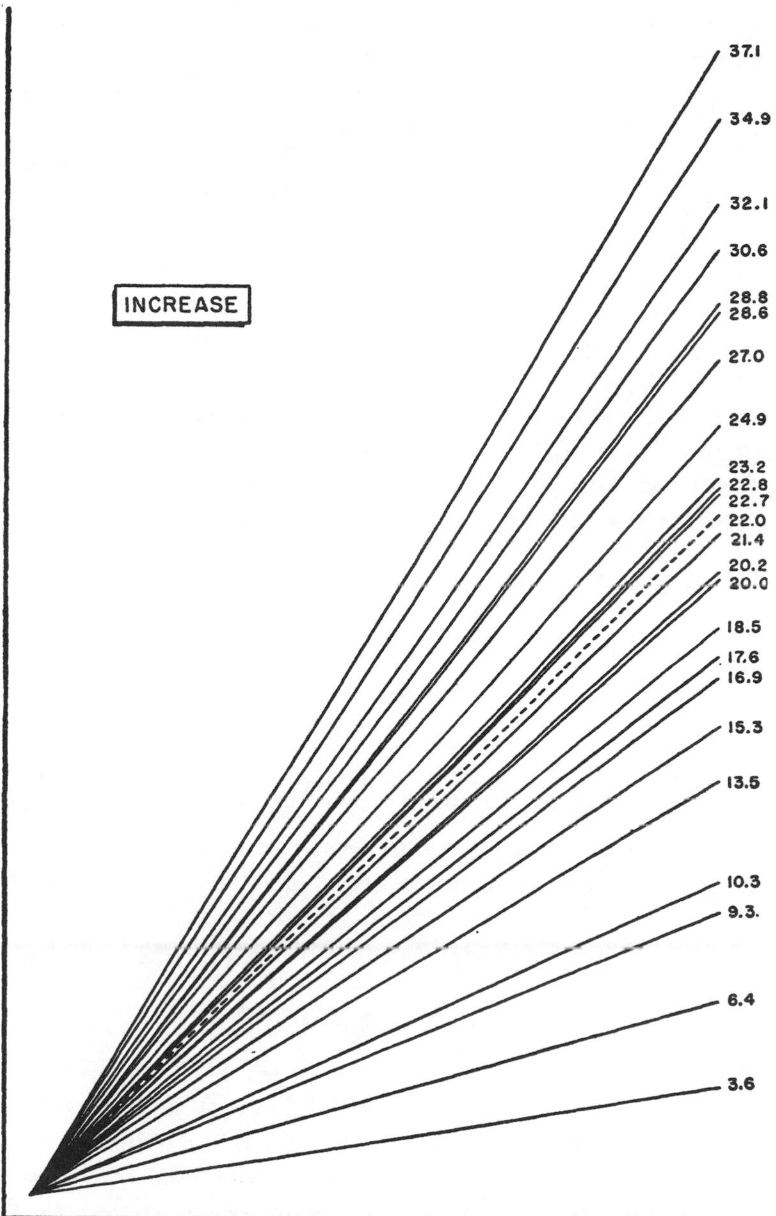

Chart II: Percentage Change in Average Hourly Earnings, 25 Manufacturing Industries, 1929 to 1939. Broken line represents 25 manufacturing industries.

purely hypothetical point of view there is always some wage-rate, however low, capable of assuring full employment under almost any condition. But in practice, supplementary adjustments will be necessary. In practice, also, no adjustment can be instantaneous, or sufficiently quick to assure full employment at all times, even with assumed flexible wage-rates.

Finally, the striking *increase* in hourly earnings between 1929 and 1939 (which of course meant an even more striking increase between 1932 and 1939) certainly did not wipe out unemployment or bring full recovery. On the contrary, the period was one of continued mass unemployment. (In the ten years from 1931 to 1940 there was average unemployment of ten million, or 18.6 per cent of the total working force.)

7. *A Class Theory of Unemployment*

Keynes's preference for general monetary inflation over piecemeal wage and price adjustments is the result of still other major fallacies. He does not realize that the government cannot cheat creditors through inflation if the creditors have full advance knowledge of the government's intentions. He does not realize that a *planned* inflation cannot be gradual or controlled, but will get out of hand the moment the plan is known. And he does not realize that when prices are falling *because costs of production are falling,* the price fall does not endanger profit margins or employment.

And bound up with these is still another major fallacy. Though Keynes has poured more derision on Ricardo than perhaps on any other economist, he has himself adopted a primitive "Ricardian" cost-of-production theory of prices according to which a nation can artificially hold up its "price-level" by holding up its "wage-level." (Cf. pp. 268 and 271.) To explain this fallacy (after Menger, Jevons, Böhm-Bawerk, Wicksteed, Knight, Mises) would take too long. It is better to refer the Keynesians to some good modern textbook.

Nor shall I go at length into the reasons why unemployment is *not* caused, as Keynes insists, primarily by maladjustments between the rate of interest, the marginal efficiency of capital and investment. It is sufficient to point out not only that his theory of interest is completely false, but that interest rates are extremely fluid and flexible, that they are determined by full competition among lenders as well as borrowers, and not held rigid by compulsory collective bargaining, union monopolies and mass picket lines.

It is more instructive to inquire *why* Keynes put forward this extremely complicated and implausible theory. And here we may have to answer that, siding as he did with the immemorial labor-union insistence that employment is not caused by excessive wage-rates, he had to come up with *some* theory as to what does cause it. And as he couldn't blame the labor-union leaders, what more natural (and politically convenient) than to blame the moneylenders, the creditors, the rich? Like Marxism, this is a class theory of the business cycle, a class theory of unemployment. As in Marxism, the capitalists become the scapegoats, with the sole difference that the chief villains are the moneylenders rather than the employers.

And that, I suspect, rather than any new discoveries of technical analysis, is the real secret of the tremendous vogue of the *General Theory*. It is the twentieth century's *Das Kapital*.

Chapter XX

EMPLOYMENT, MONEY, AND PRICES

1. *An Unproved "Functional" Relationship*

I hope I have not said it too often, but as we advance in the *General Theory,* the confusions and fallacies become progressively denser, and crowd up to a point where the task of disentangling the traffic snarl begins to look utterly hopeless.

This is not surprising. In Chapters 20 and 21, for example, which we shall now consider together, "Keynes applied to the theory of money and prices," as one Keynesian has put it, "the tools of analysis which he had developed earlier" in the book. But as these "tools of analysis," as we have seen, nearly all consisted of faulty and confused concepts, a discussion of their supposed interaction merely compounds the confusion. As we have already analyzed these basic confusions, I need not repeat the analysis, though it may be necessary to remind the reader from time to time of these basic confusions in calling attention to the additional and derived confusions that arise when these fallacious concepts are made the basis of further reasoning concerning their alleged interrelationships.

The substance of Chapter 20, "The Employment Function," need not detain us long. It is an effort to work out a series of mathematical equations concerning "the employment function." Keynes offers an alleged "definition" of "the employment function" on page 280, but what he really gives us is, as in other cases, an equation without a definition. He does tell us, however, that

> the *object* of the employment function [is] to relate the amount of the effective demand, measured in terms of the wage-unit, directed to a given firm or industry or to industry as a whole with the amount of employment, the supply price of the output of which will compare to that amount of effective demand (p. 280).

The reader may make whatever he can of this; but a few hints will probably economize his time and mental effort. The first thing he can do is to put aside the phrase "measured in terms of the wage-unit." Though Keynes defined the "wage-unit" as a "quantity of employment" (p. 41), his explanation showed that he really defined it as meaning merely a quantity of *money* paid to persons employed. In fact, it seems to mean merely the average national hourly wage-rate at any moment as measured in shillings or dollars.

But in accordance with the philosophic principle of Occam's razor, that entities should not be multiplied unnecessarily, it is better to think in any given context either of the number of man-hours worked, or the number of men employed, or total wage payments, and to omit the merely confusing hybrid concept of "wage-units." If these mean nothing more than the average national hourly wage-rate, and if this is, say, $2, then it is easy to convert total wage payments into total man-hours worked, or vice versa, if we know one sum or the other. Then we shall at least know whether what we are talking about is total man-hours worked, or average hourly wage-rates in dollars, or total wage payments in dollars—and we shall be at least one step nearer to clarity of thought.

When a few other such simplifications have been made, we shall find that all Keynes is talking about is the relation of "effective demand" (another confused conception—"the aggregate income [or proceeds] which the entrepreneurs *expect* to receive" [p. 55]) to the amount of employment. But without analyzing this further, what reason is there to suppose that this relationship is a "functional" relationship at all—that there is any such thing as "the employment function"? Keynes never condescends to offer any statistical evidence that any such "function" exists (or, for that matter, that any of his other "functions" exist), and certainly he does not offer any plausible deductive proof that it exists.

We touch here upon an economic error that long antedates Keynes. It can be traced back as far as Cournot (1838) and was revived in its modern form chiefly by Jevons (in 1871); it is the basis today of a huge literature of "mathematical economics." When an empiric or presumptive relationship seems to exist between one economic "quantity" and another, so that one seems to vary proportionately, or increasingly, decreasingly, or inversely, with another, some economists have fallen into the habit of calling the first a "function" of the second. This suggests a mathematical analogy; and perhaps little harm is done as long as it is treated merely as an analogy, as a figure of speech. It is unobjectionable to say, for example, that, other things remaining unchanged, the demand for a commodity (in the sense of the amount bought) *seems to* vary *almost as if* this demand were a decreasing function of the price of the commodity. But the moment we put this in the form of a mathematical expression—the moment, we write, for example:

$$D = f(p)$$

or use some similar notation to stand for such a relationship, we are in danger of making an illicit leap. We have *assumed* in our formula that this mathematical relationship exists. We can of course assume such a relationship *by hypothesis,* but this can never yield anything better than a *hypothetical* conclusion. We no more *prove* that a relationship exists by expressing it in a mathematical equation than by expressing the same assumption in words. We are merely more in danger of deceiving ourselves, because we have made our assumption precise, though it may be precisely wrong.

Let us remind ourselves, for example, of exactly what a

"function" is. Once more I take the definition: "If a variable y is related to a variable x in such a way that each assignment of a value to x *definitely determines* one or more values of y, then y is called a FUNCTION of x." [1] (My italics.)

That a given value of x, in any assigned meaning, definitely determines one or more values of y, is something that we must prove to be true, not something that we make true simply because we have assumed it.

Section I of Chapter 20 on "The Employment Function" consists of a set of equations concerning this alleged function. Keynes assumes that the functional relationship exists, but never attempts to prove it. There is, in fact, no good reason whatever to assume that any functional relationship exists between "effective demand" and the volume of employment. Everything depends, in fact, upon the interrelationships of wage-rates, prices, and the money supply. No matter how low total monetary demand falls, full employment could exist at the appropriate relationship of wage-rates to prices. No matter how high total monetary demand is pushed, unemployment will exist if an unworkable relationship exists between wage-rates and prices.

But even Keynes does not seem to take his mathematical explorations very seriously. At the beginning of Section I he remarks in a footnote: "Those who (rightly) dislike algebra will lose little by omitting the first section of this chapter" (p. 280).

2. *General Value Theory vs. Monetary Theory*

As all the other major questions raised by Chapter 20 are also raised by Chapter 21 on "The Theory of Prices," we may proceed to the latter forthwith.

Keynes opens this chapter with a long paragraph that is worth quoting in full:

> So long as economists are concerned with what is called the Theory of Value, they have been accustomed to teach that

[1] Gerald E. Moore, *Algebra* (New York: Barnes & Noble, 1951), p. 50.

> prices are governed by the conditions of supply and demand; and, in particular, changes in marginal cost and the elasticity of short-period supply have played a prominent part. But when they pass in volume II, or more often in a separate treatise, to the Theory of Money and Prices, we hear no more of these homely but intelligible concepts and move into a world where prices are governed by the quantity of money, by its income-velocity, by the velocity of circulation relatively to the volume of transactions, by hoarding, by forced saving, by inflation and deflation *et hoc genus omne;* and little or no attempt is made to relate these vaguer phrases to our former notions of the elasticities of supply and demand. If we reflect on what we are being taught and try to rationalize it, in the simpler discussions it seems that the elasticity of supply must have become zero and demand proportional to the quantity of money; whilst in the more sophisticated we are lost in a haze where nothing is clear and everything is possible. We have all of us become used to finding ourselves on the one side of the moon and sometimes on the other, without knowing what route or journey connects them, related, apparently, after the fashion of our waking and our dreaming lives (p. 292).

This satire would have had considerably more point if it had been made a generation earlier. It sounds, indeed, suspiciously like a sly allusion to Keynes's own teacher, Alfred Marshall. But at the time it appeared, in 1936, it no longer applied, at least to the pioneers of economic thought. Knut Wicksell's *Lectures on Political Economy,* in two volumes (Vol. I: *General Theory,* Vol. II: *Money*) appeared in an English edition in 1934 and 1935. They had existed in German since 1901 and 1906. These lectures made giant strides toward a reconciliation and unification of "value" theory and monetary theory. Ludwig von Mises' *Theorie des Geldes und der Umlaufsmittel,* which carried this unification even further, appeared in its first German edition as early as 1912, and in its second in 1924; it had been translated into English as *The Theory of Money and Credit* in 1934. In America, Benjamin M. Anderson's *The Value of*

Money, which appeared first in 1917, was in large part a protest against the tradition and practice of putting general economic theory and monetary theory in separate compartments. Anderson's book had appeared in a second edition in 1936.

Was Keynes aware of all this? If so, why did he ignore it all in the paragraph just quoted? One dislikes to write of him, as Wicksell wrote of Gustav Cassel, that he ignored those who had anticipated him because he desired "at all costs to be esteemed an original and even path-breaking theorist." [2] But one must choose between this explanation or the explanation of sheer ignorance. And Keynes (even in the *General Theory*) makes references (though largely disparaging) to the work of both Wicksell and Mises.

But perhaps the dichotomy between general value theory and monetary theory was never quite as sharp as Keynes's satiric portrait assumes. Scientific progress in all fields is made by isolating a problem; by studying the effect of one force or factor at a time. In the physical sciences this is done through the method of hypothesis tested by experiment. In the social sciences experiment in any meaningful scientific sense is impossible,[3] and the method of isolating hypotheses must be the chief reliance. Keynes himself admits this in Chapter 20:

> The object of our analysis is . . . to provide ourselves with an organized and orderly method of thinking out particular problems; and, after we have reached a provisional conclusion by isolating the complicating factors one by one, we then have to go back on ourselves and allow, as well as we can, for the probable interaction of the factors amongst themselves (p. 297).

This was the method originated by the classical economists, and specifically by Keynes's *bête noire,* Ricardo.

[2] Knut Wicksell, *Lectures on Political Economy,* (London: George Routledge, 1934), I, 220.

[3] Cf. John Stuart Mill, *A System of Logic,* Vol. II, Book VI, Chap. VII, Sect. 2, for an illuminating discussion that is far from being out of date.

They *abstracted,* among other things, from money, in order to simplify and make manageable the problem of value. In a perhaps unfortunate phrase of Mill's, they tried to "look behind the monetary veil." Their mistake was not in doing this, but in later forgetting that they *had* abstracted from money, and that their conclusions were therefore oversimplified and more hypothetical than realistic. And when they reintroduced money, or discussed monetary problems, they made the further mistake of forgetting what they had learned when they had abstracted from money. They failed, in short, to put the two sets of problems together; or rather, their solutions were merely pasted together, not unified. "Monetary economists" and "general economists" worked within separate frames of reference, and both lost by the separation.

Curiously enough, Keynes does much the same thing. His own effort at unification of monetary theory and general value theory, as well as of "static" and "dynamic" theory, is unsuccessful. It is unsuccessful because of a number of specific errors, some of them astonishing.

Keynes's general method, in Chapter 20, of introducing a number of simplifying assumptions in the theory of value and money and prices and then reintroducing "the possible complications which will in fact influence events" is correct in principle. But he is unsuccessful in result because some of his simplifications and complications are the wrong simplifications and complications, and because some of his fundamental concepts are either misleading or false.

In discussing money, for example, he tells us in italics: *"The importance of money essentially flows from its being a link between the present and the future"* (p. 293). And again: "Money in its significant attributes is, above all, a subtle device for linking the present to the future" (p. 294).

Now I should say, on the contrary, that the importance of money flows essentially from its being a medium of exchange, and that its most significant attribute is that it functions as the medium of exchange. In performing this function, it is true, money does, incidentally, serve as a "link" between present and future; but so do all sorts of other things. Money is far from unique in this respect. It may be doubted whether, in economic life, it serves even as the *chief* link between the present and the future. That honor should preferably be reserved for *the rate of interest* (which is not, Keynes's theories notwithstanding, a purely monetary phenomenon). Another link between the present and the future is the system of "forward" and "future" prices on the organized exchanges. All prices, in fact, even present prices of securities and commodities, are links between the present and the future, because they embody and reflect the anticipations of buyers and sellers respecting the future.

It is true that such prices happen to be expressed in terms of money; but they would anticipate the future just as much if they were expressed in terms of each other—if the price of wheat were expressed in terms of cotton or of cotton in terms of wheat. Of course, prices expressed in terms of money *also* reflect anticipations regarding the future value of the monetary unit itself. But money, as such, has no unique quality in reflecting anticipations regarding the future. It is, in fact, men's anticipations regarding the future, and not the particular material terms in which these anticipations are expressed, that constitute the real "link" between the present and the future. Men constantly act with an eye on the future; and their actions and valuations express their anticipations regarding that future.

Chapter XXI

PRICES AND MONEY

1. *"Costs" are Prices*

Another strange thing about Keynes's Chapter 21 is that though it is called "The Theory of Prices," it is hardly a theory of *individual* prices at all, or even of *relative* prices, but merely a theory of changes in the price *"level."* Keynes even specifically declares: "The Theory of Prices, that is to say, the analysis of the relation between changes in the quantity of money and changes in the price-level with a view to determining the elasticity of prices in response to changes in the quantity of money . . ." (p. 296). Now unless one has a correct theory of *individual* prices and of *relative* prices one is unlikely to have a correct theory of the price *"level"* which is merely an average made up of individual prices. But when we try to analyze Keynes's theory of individual prices and of relative prices, we encounter so many confusions and contradictions that the task of straightening them out becomes next to hopeless.

> In a single industry [we are told] its particular price-level depends partly on the rate of remuneration of the factors of production which enter into its marginal cost, and partly on the scale of output. There is no reason to modify this conclusion when we pass to industry as a whole (p. 294).

Let us notice first of all a couple of the minor ambiguities in these two sentences. We have already seen that "a single industry" involves an arbitrary classification without definite boundaries. Notice also that even in speaking of "a single industry" Keynes speaks of its "price-*level*," which is already a collective concept involving an average. What he probably meant to say—or in any case what would have been theoretically more defensible—is that "The particular price of a single homogeneous product depends partly," etc.

But this minor difficulty surmounted, we find that what we have here is a crude Ricardian cost-of-production theory of prices in which the marginal *utility* of a particular commodity, or the relative marginal utility of two or more commodities, is not even mentioned.

Keynes continues: "The general price-level depends partly on the rate of remuneration of the factors of production which enter into marginal cost and partly on the scale of output as a whole, *i.e.* (taking equipment and technique as given) on the volume of employment" (p. 294).

Here "the general price-level" is explained by "rates of remuneration" and "marginal costs," but wage-rates and costs arc not explained at all. They are simply taken for granted. Yet wage-rates and costs are *prices*. Marginally speaking, they are the price of an extra hour's labor, or an extra unit of raw materials, or an extra increment of equipment, etc.

In modern marginal theory, prices and costs *mutually determine* each other; there is no one-way causation. Wicksell, endorsing the mathematical formulation of Walras, put it forcibly:

> As soon as we have more than one factor of production (e.g. simple manual labor), and in fact wc havc hundreds of different kinds, the principle that costs of production determine the exchange value of a product can no longer be maintained. These costs become quite simply the *prices* of the factors of production, which are necessarily determined in combination with the prices of commodities in a single system of simultaneous equations.[1]

Relative costs of production may legitimately play a part in modern economics when we are dealing with the problem

[1] Knut Wicksell, *Lectures on Political Economy,* I, 225.

of relative price formation. Here costs may be said to "determine" prices, not directly, but by their influence on relative supply and hence on relative marginal utilities.

It is true that Keynes finally does bring in the effect of demand on "the general price-level," but what he discusses is merely the effect of *changes* in demand:

> It is true that, when we pass to output as a whole, the costs of production in any industry partly depend on the output of other industries. But the more significant change, of which we have to take account, is the effect of changes in *demand* both on costs and on volume. It is on the side of demand that we have to introduce quite new ideas when we are dealing with demand as a whole and no longer with the demand for a single product taken in isolation, with demand as a whole assumed to be unchanged (pp. 294-295).

All that Keynes does at this point, however, is to consider the effect on "the general price-level" of an increase in the money supply. But here his confusions simply increase. He has presented no theory at all, or at best only a circular theory, of what determines a particular price or the relationship of particular prices to each other. But he proceeds to explain why the *average* of *all* prices (*i.e.*, the general price-level) rises or falls. (Perhaps what he is really talking about is the average of *retail* commodity prices, as he seems to consider "costs" and wage-rates to be somehow outside of "the general price-level.") What makes prices rise, according to Keynes, is a rise in Aggregate Effective Demand, and aggregate or effective demand turns out to be, for all practical purposes, synonymous with the money supply.

Keynes is right in not accepting "the crude Quantity Theory of Money," but his treatment of the whole subject is superficial and confused. He does draw a distinction between "effective demand" and the quantity of money: "Effective demand will not change in exact proportion to the quantity of money" (p. 296). But two pages later he makes the astonishing statement that "The primary effect of a change in the quantity of money on the quantity of effective demand is through its influence on the rate of interest" (p. 298). This is like asserting that a circuitous detour is the shortest distance between two points. By "effective demand" Keynes seems to mean little more than total *monetary* demand; therefore doubling the quantity of money, say, directly doubles the "effective demand" because the two terms practically mean the same thing.

Keynes is also right (though not for the reasons he gives) in pointing out that if we begin with a condition of underemployment, a given increase in the quantity of money will probably not raise prices proportionately but will spend itself partly in raising employment. But though he almost invariably assumes a condition of underemployment, he just as consistently fails to recognize or acknowledge the real reason for this underemployment when it exists. That reason is almost invariably the existence of excessive wage-rates in relation to prices. To put the matter in another way, some wage-rates are above the point of equilibrium. If, now, we pour an increased supply of money into the system, and if the effect of this is to raise wholesale and retail prices *without raising the excessive wage-rates proportionately,* then the result will be increased employment; and the consequent increased supply of goods will make the general price rise lower than it would otherwise have been. But Keynes gets to this conclusion by a set of artificial assumptions and arbitrary reasons that have little relation to economic realities.

2. *The Positive Theory of Money*

Instead of making a detailed criticism of Keynes's implied theory of money, it would effect a considerable economy of time and space if I said a few words at this point concerning what I believe to be the correct theory of money. These remarks must necessarily be sketchy; and as they will often give conclusions without the underlying argument, they may sometimes unintentionally sound dogmatic.

The quantity of money is always a relevant consideration in determining the value of the monetary unit, just as the total supply of wheat is relevant in determining the value of a bushel of wheat. But the value of the monetary unit is not necessarily in exact inverse proportion to the quantity of money (as held by the rigid or Mechanical Quantity Theory) any more than the value of a bushel of wheat is necessarily in exact inverse proportion to the supply of wheat.

The inflexible Quantity Theory of Money tacitly assumes that the "elasticity of demand" for money is unity. This proposition has never been proved, and receives little statistical support. The value of the monetary unit is determined not merely by the quantity of money but by the *quality* of that money. Putting the matter another way, the value of the monetary unit is not determined merely by the *present* quantity of money but by people's expectations concerning the *future* quantity, and by such other factors as the assumed integrity or stability of the issuing government or banks. Hence it is typical at the beginning of any inflation to find that prices rise *less* than the increase in the money supply, and that in the later stages of an inflation prices rise *more* than the increase in the money supply.

It must be borne in mind furthermore that an increase in the quantity of money, no matter by how much it may raise the *average* of prices, never results in an exactly proportionate increase in each price. It is only, in fact, because Keynes and other inflationists tacitly assume that an increase in the quantity of money will raise some prices more than others (particularly retail prices more than "costs" and wage-rates) that they conclude that inflation will cure unemployment.

I have said nothing above about the much-discussed "velocity-of-circulation" of money, and its supposed effect on prices. This is because I believe the term "velocity-of-circulation" involves numerous irrelevancies and confusions.

Strictly speaking, money does not "circulate"; it is exchanged against goods. A house that frequently changes hands does not "circulate." A man can only spend his monetary income once. Other things remaining equal, "velocity-of-circulation" of money can increase only if the number of times that goods also change hands (say stocks or bonds or speculative commodities) increases correspondingly. The annual rate of turnover of demand bank deposits is normally twice as great in New York City as in the rest of the country. In 1957, for example, it was 49.5 in New York and averaged only 23.0 in 337 other reporting districts. This is because New York is the speculative center.

An increase in the "velocity-of-circulation" of money, therefore, does not necessarily mean (other things remaining unchanged) a corresponding or proportionate increase in "the price-level." An increased "velocity-of-circulation" of money is not a *cause* of an increase in commodity prices; *it is itself a result* of changing valuations on the part of buyers and sellers. It is usually a sign merely of an increase in speculative activity. An increased "velocity-of-circulation" of money may even accompany, especially in a crisis at the peak of a boom, a *fall* in prices of stocks or bonds or commodities.[2]

3. *What Theory of Prices?*

Though I shall elaborate upon this at a later point, it follows from the above that inflation is (1) a *dangerous* "remedy" for unemployment, because the inflation may get out of hand and will in any case create great injustices; (2) an *unnecessary* remedy for unemployment, which can be cured simply by the appropriate (free market) adjustment

[2] This section is inserted merely to indicate the point of view from which Keynes's monetary theories are here being criticized. Obviously this is not the place to elaborate a complete positive theory of money and credit, but some positive theory must necessarily be implied in all criticism. The author's views on monetary theory correspond most closely with those of Benjamin M. Anderson, *The Value of Money* (1917, 1934) and of Ludwig von Mises, *The Theory of Money and Credit* (English edition, 1934) to both of which I am heavily indebted.

and coördination of wage-rates and prices to each other and to the existing money supply; and (3) an *uncertain* remedy for unemployment, because the unemployment will either continue or be resumed if wage-rates go up to the same extent as prices so that the maladjustment which caused the unemployment is after all not corrected.

I have already pointed out that though Keynes calls Chapter 21 "The Theory of Prices" he *defines* the theory of prices (p. 296) as "the analysis of the relation between changes in the quantity of money and changes in the price-level." This, as I have remarked, is merely a theory of *changes* in a statistical *average* of prices. It therefore omits any analysis or explanation of (1) what determines any one particular price (say the price of eggs), and (2) what determines the *relation* of individual prices to each other. But these are the really fundamental problems involved. Until we have solved them we cannot go on to any rational discussion of why individual prices *change,* and why the "price-level" (which is a purely statistical construct put together from individual prices) changes. But Keynes simply takes these fundamental problems for granted. It is hard to escape the verdict of Hayek:

> Although the technocrats, and other believers in the undoubted productive capacity of our economic system, do not yet appear to have realised it, what [Keynes] has given us is really that economics of abundance for which they have been clamoring so long. Or rather, he has given us a system of economics which is based on the assumption that no real scarcity exists, and that the only scarcity with which we need concern ourselves is the artificial scarcity created by the determination of people not to sell their services and products below certain arbitrarily fixed prices. These prices are in no way explained, but are simply assumed to remain at their historically given level, except at rare intervals when 'full employment' is approached and the different goods begin successively to become scarce and to rise in price.

Now if there is a well-established fact which dominates

economic life, it is the incessant, even hourly, variation in the prices of most of the important raw materials and of the wholesale prices of nearly all foodstuffs. But the reader of Mr. Keynes' theory is left with the impression that these fluctuations of prices are entirely unmotivated and irrelevant, except towards the end of a boom, when the fact of scarcity is readmitted into the analysis, as an apparent exception, under the designation of 'bottlenecks.' [3]

Let us look at Keynes's strange picture of the economic world a little more closely:

> But, in general, the demand for some services and commodities will reach a level beyond which their supply is, for the time being, perfectly inelastic, whilst in other directions there is still a substantial surplus of resources without employment. Thus as output increases, a series of 'bottle-necks' will be successively reached, where the supply of particular commodities ceases to be elastic and their prices have to rise to whatever level is necessary to divert demand into other directions (p. 300).

Some of the shortcomings in this picture have already been pointed out in the quotation from Hayek above. There are assumed to be, as a usual and virtually a "normal" condition, all sorts of "unemployed resources" kicking around, including, apparently, surplus raw materials, so that for a long time increase in demand does not lead to increase in price. Increasing costs are not regarded as typical but as exceptional, and then only because "bottlenecks" are created. And "bottlenecks" themselves are treated as exceptions, instead of as the outcome of varying degrees of scarcity and varying but inevitable lags in the responsiveness of demand.

This brings us to an aspect of Keynes's thought that has seldom been recognized, even by his critics. A surprisingly large number of his errors spring, not from his heterodoxies, but from his uncritical acceptance of certain "classical"—or,

[3] Friedrich A. Hayek, *The Pure Theory of Capital*, (University of Chicago Press, 1941), p. 374.

it would be better to say, Marshallian—doctrines, concepts, or terms. One of these concepts, now used almost universally, is that of the "elasticity"—of demand, supply, price, or what-have-you.

The concept—or rather the term—owes its present great vogue to Marshall. It is a very useful concept, but it can also be a deceptive one, particularly when, as in the last thirty years, a whole literature develops around it that combines oversimplification with a spurious precision. This latter development is mainly the result of the use of the dubiously appropriate term *elasticity*. I have previously adverted to the misleading quality of this term, but it is now worth scrutinizing even more closely.

Responsiveness, as I shall try to show, is a term that not only expresses more clearly and directly what is meant but avoids most of the pitfalls of *elasticity*. It is an ironic misfortune in the recent history of economic thought that though Marshall himself suggested this alternative, he immediately dropped it and used the term "elasticity" instead.

> We may say generally [he wrote] that the *elasticity* (or *responsiveness*) *of demand* in a market is great or small according as the amount demanded increases much or little for a given fall in price, and diminishes much or little for a given rise in price. [His italics. And he continues in a footnote]: We may say that the elasticity of demand is 1, if a small fall in price will cause an equal proportionate increase in the amount demanded: or as we may say roughly, if a fall of 1 per cent in price will increase the sales by 1 per cent; that it is 2 or ½, if a fall of 1 per cent in prices makes an increase of 2 or ½ per cent respectively in the amount demanded; and so on.[4]

But there are serious drawbacks to the term "elasticity." (1) The mechanical analogy on which it rests is somewhat forced and far-fetched, and does not suggest what happens as directly and simply as "response" or "responsiveness" does. (2) It leads easily to the false assumption that the

[4] Alfred Marshall, *Principles of Economics,* (Eighth edition), p. 102.

"elasticity of demand" for a commodity is something *built into the commodity* rather than merely the response of *consumers* to a change of price. (3) It has led to a literature of mock precision (and at the same time of oversimplification) to which the term "response" or even "responsiveness" is unlikely to lead.

Our present purpose, however, is not to elaborate in general upon each of these drawbacks, but merely to show how Keynes's thought and writing were vitiated both by his use of the term "elasticity" and by his careless concept of it. It constantly leads him into tautology. "They may also have different elasticities of supply in response to changes in the money-rewards offered" (p. 302). But as "elasticities of supply" *means* "response" this could have been written more briefly, simply and clearly: "The response of their supply to changes in price may also be different." Again, "the elasticity of effective demand in response to changes in the quantity of money" (p. 305) could be at once clarified and shortened by writing "the response of demand to changes in the quantity of money," etc. And still again, "the elasticity of money-prices in response to changes in effective demand measured in terms of money" (p. 285) could have been phrased simply "the response of prices to changes in demand."

It is largely on such pretentious pleonasms and circumlocutions that Keynes's reputation for profundity seems to rest.

4. *Another Digression on "Mathematical" Economics*

Keynes devotes a whole section of Chapter 21 to a statement of his price theories in mathematical form. But we have even Keynes's word for it that we lose practically nothing if we bypass these equations:

> It is a great fault of symbolic pseudo-mathematical methods of formalizing a system of economic analysis, such as we shall set down in section VI of this chapter, that they expressly

> assume strict independence between the factors involved and lose all their cogency and authority if this hypothesis is disallowed; whereas, in ordinary discourse, where we are not blindly manipulating but know all the time what we are doing and what the words mean, we can keep 'at the back of our heads' the necessary reserves and qualifications and the adjustments which we shall have to make later on, in a way in which we cannot keep complicated partial differentials 'at the back' of several pages of algebra which assume that they all vanish. Too large a proportion of recent 'mathematical' economics are mere concoctions, as imprecise as the initial assumptions they rest on, which allow the author to lose sight of the complexities and interdependencies of the real world in a maze of pretentious and unhelpful symbols (pp. 297-298).

This is admirably said; but Keynes himself does not seem to have realized the full force of it. It is hard otherwise to account for the "maze of pretentious and unhelpful symbols" that he himself uses. Even after he has used them in section VI he declares:

> I do not myself attach much value to manipulations of this kind; and I would repeat the warning, which I have given above, that they involve just as much tacit assumption as to what variables are taken as independent (partial differentials being ignored throughout) as does ordinary discourse, whilst I doubt if they carry us any further than ordinary discourse can. Perhaps the best purpose served by writing them down is to exhibit the extreme complexity of the relationship between prices and the quantity of money, when we attempt to express it in a formal manner (p. 305).

Do such symbols and manipulations, however, in fact usually serve this purpose? Or do they not much more frequently deceive the writer who uses them (and many of his readers) into supposing that he has discovered something; that it will now be easy (or at least possible) to ascertain and substitute real numerical values for his algebraic symbols and hence determine real relationships or make precise predictions that apply to the real world?

The majority of Keynesians undoubtedly believe this; and the master has encouraged the belief: "Nevertheless, if we have all the facts before us, we shall have enough simultaneous equations to give us a determinate result" (p. 299). Of course if we have all the facts we shall have all the facts. If we already know the future we can predict it. But when Keynes leads his readers to suppose that they can make real economic predictions or solve practical problems of economic policy if they only pull enough simultaneous equations together, if they only make sure to have "as many equations as unknowns," he reminds one, by contrast, of the much sounder warning of Irving Fisher. Fisher, though he used even more mathematics in his *Theory of Interest* than Keynes does in his *General Theory,* had a much surer sense of the limitations of the algebraic method:

> In science, the most useful formulas are those which apply to the simplest cases. For instance, in the study of projectiles, the formula of most fundamental importance is that which applies to the path of a projectile in a vacuum. Next comes the formula which applies to the path of a projectile in *still* air. Even the mathematician declines to go beyond this and to take into account the effect of wind currents, still less to write the equations for the path of a boomerang or a feather. . . . At best, science can only determine what *would* happen under *assumed* conditions. It can never state exactly what does or will happen under actual conditions.[5]

Keynes's mathematical equations on pages 304-306 are peculiarly suspect because they are all concerned with "elasticities"—of prices, "wage-units," output, "effective demand," employment, etc. Some of these concepts (e.g. "output") are obviously too heterogeneous and hazy to be capable of statement in useful or valid mathematical form. But my present purpose is simply to ask whether "elasticity" itself is a precise enough concept to justify its use in a mathematical equation.

[5] *The Theory of Interest,* 1930. (New York: Kelley & Millman, 1954), pp. 316-317.

Marshall himself had great doubts on the matter. After a long section on "elasticity of supply" and "supply schedules," he writes:

> But such notions must be taken broadly. The attempt to make them precise over-reaches our strength. If we include in our account nearly all the conditions of real life, the problem is too heavy to be handled; if we select a few, then long-drawn-out and subtle reasonings with regard to them become scientific toys rather than engines for practical work.[6]

Frank H. Knight points out that:

> Serious embarrassment arises from the fact that there is no conceivable way of determining the elasticity of either demand or supply with reference to any particular time period. . . . The conditions underlying either curve will never actually remain constant. . . . As to the chance of making any estimate or calculation of elasticity for any real period, the possibilities in the abstract are limited enough on the supply side, but are virtually zero on that of demand.[7]

We may surely carry our doubts further than Marshall carried his. Even to speak of "the elasticity of demand" for a commodity is to imply, as we have seen, not only that this "elasticity" is *a quality of the commodity* but that there is something *fixed* or *constant* about it, at least within a given price range. To speak merely of the *response* of demand to a change in price is to make neither of these tacit assumptions. We realize then that we are merely speaking of the response of *buyers or consumers* to a change of price under a whole complex set of concrete conditions at one moment of time, without jumping to any tacit conclusions regarding what the response would be to a still further change of price of that commodity in the same direction, or even to precisely the same change of price of the same commodity under another set of concrete circumstances at another moment in time.

6 Alfred Marshall, *Principles of Economics*, Eighth Edition, pp. 460-461.
7 *The Economic Organization*, (New York: Augustus M. Kelley, 1951), p. 176.

5. *"Elasticity" of Demand Cannot be Measured*

In spite of many ambitious efforts in recent years,[8] "elasticity" of demand is not only difficult but impossible to measure. We can collect plenty of statistics, approaching infinity, but we can never be sure which to take and how to interpret them.

To glimpse some of the real difficulties: The closing price of a bushel of ordinary hard wheat at Kansas City on Oct. 2, 1957 was \$2.10¼, and x bushels were sold there on that day. On Oct. 3 the closing price was \$2.10, and y bushels were sold. On Oct. 3, 1956 the closing price was \$2.25½, and z bushels were sold. Assuming that we knew the values of x, y, and z—that is, the total amount sold at Kansas City on each of these days—the data would still tell us nothing whatever about elasticity of demand. The price of wheat fluctuated greatly on each of these three days. To get an accurate average price a statistician would have to know how many bushels sold at each different price (there is an eighth-of-a-cent difference between prices), and make up a weighted average for the day. But this average would already begin to conceal what the statistician was trying to find out. For a different amount of wheat was sold at each eighth-of-a-cent's difference. He would have to chart these and draw a (very irregular) curve. This information would in turn be valueless because it would tell us only what went on at Kansas City on three days.

Suppose, disregarding the enormous difficulties and complexities, we could find out and chart the amounts of ordinary hard wheat sold at each different price on every business day of 1956 and 1957 everywhere in the United States; and even that we could do the same for the preceding fifty years. Would we *even then* be able to measure "the elasticity of demand" for wheat? The figures would still be worthless because the price of and demand for wheat are

[8] Cf. e.g, Henry Schultz, *The Theory and Measurement of Demand*, (University of Chicago Press, 1938).

influenced in the United States (in spite of controls and price supports) by the total world supply and total world demand for wheat. Assuming we could collect world prices and world sales, and translate them in acceptable statistical ways into terms of the American dollar, would we *still* be able to measure the "elasticity of demand" for wheat?

Putting aside the enormous and practically insurmountable difficulties in the way of collecting and arranging statistics of any real precision (for the "annual" price of "wheat," as obtainable in any existing statistical compilation, is merely the average of an enormous number of different daily and hourly prices of several different grades of wheat), we come up against the basic insoluble problem. *When the price of a commodity changes, and the amount of it that is bought also changes, we are never able to say with confidence whether the amount bought changed because the price was at a different point on the same "demand curve," or whether the amount bought changed because the demand curve itself "shifted."* And this is true whether we are talking about different prices and different amounts sold from one year to another, from one month to another, from one day to another, or from one hour to another.

What economists do in practice is usually *to beg the question.* If the price is lowered, and the amount of the product bought is increased, they say this proves that the demand for the product is "elastic." If the price is lowered, and the amount of the product bought is not increased, they say this proves that the demand for the product is "inelastic." But if the price is lowered, and the amount sold *also* declines (the kind of thing that happens on the commodity and stock exchanges every day of the week), they say this proves that the "demand curve" itself has fallen, or, in the professional jargon, has "shifted to the left."

And when we turn to "elasticity of supply" our difficulties of measurement increase rather than diminish. For both elasticity of demand and elasticity of supply have a *time* dimension. As applied to supply, this time dimension is somewhat different for every commodity. Yet nothing is more frequent than to find *lags* in adjustment confused with *lack* of adjustment. The supply of coffee, for example, is called "inelastic," when what is meant is that it takes about five years for newly planted coffee trees to mature and bear. Therefore, if there is a rise in the demand for coffee, and a consequent rise in the price, *this* year's supply and even *next* year's supply may prove "inelastic"; but the supply *five years' from now* may prove to be only too responsive to this year's increase in demand (which may not be permanent).

Again, to take an imaginary commodity, we may find that the "elasticity" of supply in response to an increase in price, as measured in Marshallian terms, is 1½ the first month (because the increased price brings forth speculative holdings of the commodity), then only ¼ the second month, $\frac{1}{16}$ the third month, zero for the next nine months, and then suddenly "unity" or better, as a new crop comes on the market or a new plant comes into production. But what, then, is *"the"* elasticity of supply of that commodity?

I have not entered upon this long digression to attempt to discredit the concept of "elasticity" of demand or supply, or demand or supply "schedules" or "curves." These are useful diagrammatic analogies, concepts, and tools of thought when employed with moderation and humility. But they have become the basis for an enormous (and pretentious and cocky) literature of "mathematical economics" which parades and manipulates a maze of algebraic symbols which are assumed to have "scientific" and even predictive value, but for which it would be impossible in practice to ascertain or assign real numerical values.

One reason for this is not merely that these values cannot really be known, but that they are oversimplified (and hence falsified) even in concept. Demand responds to changes in price. Supply responds to changes in price. But there is no reason to suppose that any scientifically *predeterminable* response of demand or supply attaches under all conditions to any given change in price. To the practical businessman or entrepreneur this is and must remain a matter of guesswork. He can find out what has happened to that commodity or similar commodities in the past; but this is no sure guide to the future. The mathematical economist cannot give him any sure-fire formula.

Keynes, it is true, has no unique guilt for the mathematical part of the *General Theory*. His mathematics are comparatively modest in extent. His claims for the usefulness of his equations are far more modest than those of the present school of "mathematical economists." But it is just as well to point out that nearly all the mathematics employed in the *General Theory,* insofar as practical application or even theoretical illumination is concerned, is empty and useless.

6. *Sacrosanct Wage-Rates, Sinful Interest Rates*

Keynes ends Chapter 21 in a burst of pure demagogy reminiscent of Marx. It is impossible to treat this final section as serious economics. It is designed to prove (1) that it would be harmful or dangerous to reduce almost any wage-rate, and (2) that it would be beneficial to reduce almost any interest rate.

The confusions in this section are almost hopeless. Some of them are foreshadowed a few pages ahead: "The cost-unit, or . . . the wage-unit, can thus be regarded as the essential standard of value; and the price-level, given the state of technique and equipment, will depend partly on the cost-unit and partly on the scale of output . . ." (p. 302).

Now to say that the *wage-unit* is the *essential standard of value* is to say that the *price* in dollars, and moreover the *average* price in dollars, of a heterogeneous good or service is the "essential standard of value," *and not the dollar in terms of which the price is expressed.* For the "wage-unit," let us remember, is the "money-wage" of "an hour's employment of ordinary labor" (p. 41). In other words, Keynes is saying that the dollar in which the price of labor is expressed is *not* the "essential standard of value," but that this average price *is* the "essential standard of value." Logically, this is something like saying that the foot is not the standard of length, but that the "arm-unit" (the length of the "ordinary" man's arm) is the essential standard of length. It is like saying that the pound is not the standard of weight, but that the "ordinary" beefsteak (which, say, now happens to average 2½ pounds) is the "essential" standard of weight.

I am not myself arguing that the dollar *is* the "standard of value" in the United States. All prices are *expressed* in dollars, and when two or more prices are compared with each other, they are compared *in terms of* dollars, and are in that sense "measured" in dollars. But the dollar, or any other monetary unit, is not the "standard of value" in the sense that the foot is a standard of length or the pound a standard of weight. For (so far at least as practical life is concerned) the foot and the pound are not relative but absolute; they remain unchanged. But the value of the dollar, or of any other monetary unit, is itself constantly changing. Its value is itself "measured" in terms of its "purchasing power"—*i.e.*, by the varying amounts of goods and services against which it is exchanged. "Economic value," in short, cannot be measured in absolute terms. Market value can be expressed only as a comparison, as a *ratio* of exchange. But it is the *dollar* (or other monetary unit) in terms of which all economic values are commonly *expressed*.

The dollar, then, is not the "essential standard of value." But this only multiplies the absurdity of regarding the *dollar price of an hour's "ordinary" labor* as the "essential standard of value." One might say that this was a return to the crude value theories of Ricardo and of Marx. But it is logically even more indefensible, because in regarding "an hour's ordinary labor" as the "standard of value," Ricardo and Marx were trying to set this standard in *real* terms, whereas Keynes *rejects* the monetary unit as the standard of value and fails to see that its value is inevitably involved in the "essential standard of value" he chooses. For the "wage-unit," being merely the average hourly wage in terms of dollars, is itself *merely the temporary average ratio of exchange between the currency unit and a "labor-unit."*

And when Keynes declares that "the price-level . . . will depend partly on the cost-unit" (p. 302), he is saying that the average of all prices is determined and caused by a single price. Modern economic theory has made it clear not only that "costs" are themselves prices, but that "costs" and "prices" *mutually determine* each other.

How did Keynes come to slip into these logical monstrosities, these apparently quite gratuitous absurdities? The answer is that he considered these absurdities essential to this central thesis that it is always harmful even to think about reducing wage-rates: "If . . . money wages were to fall without limit whenever there was a tendency for less than full employment . . . there would be no resting-place below full employment until either the rate of interest was incapable of falling further or wages were zero" (pp. 303-304).

The hysterical supposition that any attempt to adjust wage-rates to bring them into equilibrium with other prices would cause wages to "fall without limit" and go to zero is a bugaboo that could scare only mental children. It is just what it sounds like—howling nonsense.

7. *Monetary Inflation Preferred to Wage Adjustment*

Section VII of Chapter 21 is chiefly given over to the proposition that whenever there is unemployment "the escape will be normally found in changing the monetary standard or the monetary system so as to raise the quantity of money, rather than in forcing down the wage-unit and thereby increasing the burden of debt" (p. 307). In other words, unemployment should always be cured by further monetary inflation, never by adjusting wage-rates that have got out of line. The piano must be adjusted to the stool, not the stool to the piano.

We have already dealt with the folly of all this, but a

further point should be expanded upon here. Keynes speaks of "forcing down *the* wage-unit." But we have seen that this "wage-unit" is, in fact, an *average* of hourly wage-rates. Now this average is a statistical construct, not a concrete fact, and not necessarily a relevant fact. Unemployment at any given time may be cured, not by reducing *average* wages, but by reducing certain *specific* wage-rates, and probably by diverse percentages. Reducing these specific wage-rates will, of course, necessarily also reduce the average; but it is the specific adjustments, and not the resulting average adjustment, that are relevant to curing the unemployment.

I have already shown, in the illustration of what happened in twenty-five different industries (pp. 284-285) that it is by widely varying specific changes that wage adjustments are actually made. But we may make the principle clearer by a hypothetical illustration. Let us say that we have two commodities, gadgets and widgets, each of which sells for $2.50. The marginal unit-cost of each consists chiefly of labor cost. At a wage of $2 an hour, say, the total marginal unit-cost of each would be equal to the price, $2.50. But the wage-rate in the gadget industry happens to be $1.40 an hour, and the wage-rate in the widget industry $2.60 an hour. The average wage-rate in both industries together is then $2. This *average* is not excessive in relation to the demand for, and the price of, each commodity. But this average is no consolation to the widget industry, which cannot make a profit. In a closed economy, and with no acceptable substitute, the widget industry could raise its prices; but this would reduce the demand for its product and hence would create unemployment in the industry. In an open economy—in which, say, the Japanese industry could still sell widgets in New York at $2.50, the American widget industry would have to close down entirely, throwing all previous workers in the industry out of employment. There might continue to be full employment in the gadget industry, which would be able to lower prices and might even expand; but not enough (at least not for a long time) to absorb the unemployment in the widget industry.

The illustration is perhaps lengthy. But it is apparently necessary to spell it out to make clear the meaninglessness of averages and aggregates when we are trying to discuss realistically the maladjustments in the economy which lead to unemployment. Keynes's insistence on lumped thinking, on dealing with the economy in such (unacknowledged) averages and aggregates and "mixed bags" as "*the* wage-unit" and "the price-*level,*" results in systematically missing the very problems to be solved.

8. *Those Arbitrary Moneylenders*

Keynes's discussion of interest rates is, as we have seen, even more demagogic than his discussion of wage-rates. "Today and presumably for the future the schedule of the marginal efficiency of capital is, for a variety of reasons, much lower than it was in the nineteenth century" (p. 308). Here is a sweeping generalization based on conditions in 1935, the year in which Keynes was composing the *General Theory,* and on the four or five years preceding. There is no reason for supposing it to be true. It seems merely quaint in the nineteen fifties, in a world of inflation, full employment, overemployment, and unparalleled capital investment plans everywhere.

> The acuteness and peculiarity of our contemporary problem arises, therefore, [Keynes continues] out of the possibility that the average rate of interest which will allow a reasonable level of employment is one *so unacceptable to wealth-owners* that it cannot be readily established merely by manipulating the quantity of money. . . . But the most stable, and the least easily shifted, element in our contemporary economy has been hitherto, and may prove to be in future, the minimum rate of interest *acceptable to the generality of wealth-owners.* (My italics, pp. 308-309.)

Here everything that has been discovered about economics since the Middle Ages, when all interest was called "usury" and considered wholly unjustified, is thrown out the window. Interest rates, we are to understand, unlike everything else in the market, are fixed merely by one party to the transaction, by the seller or the lender, by sheer arbitrary determination, custom or extortion. We are back to a crude Exploitation Theory of interest. Everything depends on what lenders will "accept," and nothing on what borrowers will offer, or *why they will offer it.* Neither the current yield of direct capital investments nor the expected yield of direct capital investments (the "marginal efficiency of capital") is supposed to have any influence on the interest rate. The borrowers and the lenders are supposed to be a different *class* of people (presumably the poor and the rich), and never the same person, say, who is trying to decide whether it is to his advantage to lend his money to someone else for an interest rate, or to invest it directly in some project for a return and perhaps even to borrow more. If A is thinking of buying a stock that is currently yielding 5 per cent a year on its price, it is presumably an outrage for B to ask 5 per cent interest if A wants to borrow the money to buy the stock.

All this is, of course, nonsense. *The rate of interest is a market price like any other market price.* It is as flexible (on new loans) as any other price (as any historic comparisons will show) and much more flexible over short periods (especially in the downward direction) than wage-rates. Moreover, in the modern capitalistic economy the lenders (owners of bonds, of saving deposits, and life insurance policies) are as a rule not the "rich," and the borrowers (owners of common stock, of private firms, and of real estate) not the "poor."

Interest rates are related to other prices and are constantly adjusting to other prices, as other prices are to them. Wage-rates are related to other prices and (when not fixed by government or union coercion) are constantly adjusting to other prices, as other prices are to them. When both adjustments are right, when there is full price, wage, and interest-rate coördination, there is full employment and maximum balanced production.

But Keynes treats both interest rates and wages as if they were completely outside of the price system, or at least as if they ought to be. Government must constantly step in to keep up wage-rates and to push down interest rates. This, of course, is a naked class theory of the business cycle and of unemployment, strikingly similar to Marxist theory. As with Marxism, the tacit assumption is that these government policies are necessary to protect the poor and discomfit the rich. But as also with Marxism, there is the pose that morality has nothing to do with it; that the existing "system" just won't work and must break down.

The chief difference between Marxism and Keynesism is that for the former the employer is the chief villain, and for the latter the lender, with his nasty and pointless liquidity-preference.

Chapter XXII

THE "TRADE CYCLE"

1. *A "Sudden Collapse" of the "Marginal Efficiency of Capital"?*

Keynes begins his Chapter 22, "Notes on the Trade Cycle," by telling us that if his theory of what determines the volume of employment is right, it "must be capable of explaining the phenomena of the Trade Cycle." Though this chapter professes to be merely an application of the theories hitherto expounded, it actually adds many new errors.

I doubt whether many avowed Keynesians have ever really worked through the *General Theory;* but most of them have probably read this chapter (which is one of the least technical in the book) or at least popularizations of it. It contains the essence of those practical recommendations that have done so much harm.

> The essential character of the Trade Cycle [Keynes begins by telling us] and, especially, the regularity of time-sequence and of duration which justifies us in calling it a *cycle,* is mainly due to the way in which the marginal efficiency of capital fluctuates. The Trade Cycle is best regarded, I think, as being occasioned by a cyclical change in the marginal efficiency of capital . . . (p. 313).

Now, as we have already pointed out, "the marginal efficiency of capital," like most of the key Keynesian terms, is vague, and is used by Keynes in several different senses.[1] At

[1] Cf. B. M. Anderson, *Economics and the Public Welfare,* p. 403: "It goes through more metamorphoses than even Ovid knew about!"

one time it seems to mean the actual present yield of capital assets; at another time the *expected future* yield of specific capital assets; and at still another time it seems to mean merely the outlook for business profits, regardless of the specific return to a specific capital asset. If we give "the marginal efficiency of capital" this broad meaning, it does not make much difference whether we say that changes in the marginal efficiency of capital cause the trade cycle, or that changes in the trade cycle cause changes in the marginal efficiency of capital, because in this broad sense changes in the marginal efficiency of capital and changes in the business outlook turn out to mean pretty much the same thing. If, however, Keynes's proposition were that Trade Cycle movements are caused, initiated, and led by (independent) changes in the specific returns to specific capital assets it would be too implausible on its face to be worth disproving.

Keynes's belief that "there is some recognizable degree of *regularity* in the time-sequence and duration of the upward and downward movements" (p. 314) of the business cycle is debatable. The closer the investigation the less "regular" the duration that seems to emerge.

The first problem is that of agreeing upon any specific way of *measuring* the length of business cycles. The possible indices or combinations thereof are infinite. Taking coke production as one index, Burns and Mitchell [2] found that, from 1914 to 1932, the length of the "expansion phase" of what they distinguished as five distinct cycles varied between 15 and 44 months, of the "contraction phase" between 10 and 37 months, and of the "full cycle" between 26 and 57 months. These ranges would no doubt be greater if more cycles were studied. Moreover, the peak and trough months of these "cycles" do not correspond very closely if we shift to other indices, such as coal production, steel production, petroleum output, cotton stocks at mills, calves slaughtered under Federal inspection, etc.

2 Arthur F. Burns and Wesley C. Mitchell, *Measuring Business Cycles,* (New York: National Bureau of Economic Research, 1946) pp. 27, 119.

Passing over these difficulties, what seems to be true is that business cycles are phenomena that occur typically over a period of a few years rather than over a period measured in days or weeks on the one hand, or decades on the other. This is partly because this is the amplitude and type of fluctuation we have arbitrarily decided to *call* the "trade cycle" or "business cycle," and partly because there is a certain *viscosity* in the economic system, so that changes at any point normally take a certain time to make their effects felt more generally.

There are exceptions even to this. A labor strike, or an enemy bombing, or a flood or a fire or an earthquake, or even a holiday, may bring business almost to a halt, in a single day, from a period of great activity; and activity may just as promptly be restored. But we ordinarily do not count such changes when we study "business cycles." Keynes's belief in the "regularity" of duration of trade cycles, however, is an important part of the theory he puts forward to explain them.

"A more typical, and often the predominant, explanation of the crisis is," he declares, "not primarily a rise in the rate of interest, but a sudden collapse in the marginal efficiency of capital" (p. 315).

Now the truth or importance that we attach to this statement depends once more upon the interpretation we give to Keynes's ambiguous term, "the marginal efficiency of capital." If it means merely the outlook for business profits (which in this context it does seem to mean), then it is true but obvious. For a collapse in the outlook for business profits is in turn merely another name for a collapse of confidence. A collapse in the state of confidence is, of course, an inherent part of the crisis. But this merely raises the question: What caused confidence to collapse? What caused the outlook for profits to turn sour? What brought on the sudden collapse in "the marginal efficiency of capital"?

This is merely one more illustration of the confusions Keynes gets into through the ambiguity of his own terms.

If "the marginal efficiency of capital" means the *expected* yield of capital assets (as Keynes frequently tells us it does) then it is an *expectation,* a *psychological* phenomenon, dependent on the general outlook for business profits as businessmen estimate that outlook, correctly or incorrectly. If the "marginal efficiency of capital" means (as it seems on its face to mean) the present *physical productivity* of capital assets, then clearly it is not *this* that "collapses" in the crisis, either as cause or consequence. If, finally, "the marginal efficiency of capital" means the present *monetary value* of the goods that capital instruments help to produce, then a collapse in that monetary value may cause a collapse in the marginal efficiency of capital. But the causation is not the other way round.

In sum, Keynes's explanation of the crisis as a sudden collapse of the marginal efficiency of capital is either a useless truism or an obvious error, according to the interpretation we give the phrase "the marginal efficiency of capital."

2. *When Governments Control Investment*

It is significant that Keynes's explanation of the crisis exonerates a rise in the rate of interest as the chief culprit, in spite of his tendency elsewhere to make excessive interest rates and "liquidity-preference" the main cause of unemployment.

> We have been accustomed in explaining the 'crisis,' [he writes] to lay stress on the rising tendency of the rate of interest under the influence of the increased demand for money both for trade and speculative purposes. At times this factor may certainly play an aggravating and, occasionally perhaps, an initiating part (p. 315).

But when this happens, he neglects to point out (or perhaps does not understand) that it is precisely because the rate of interest had previously been kept too *low,* and credit had been freely extended to marginal and other dubious projects incapable of earning a realistic rate of interest or surviving except under conditions of inflation. The high rate of interest then gets the blame for the collapse of the marginal or unsound projects that were launched only under the illusions created by the preceding inflationary low rate of interest.

Insofar as Keynes presents any clear theory of the trade cycle whatever, it is the theory that the economy cannot be trusted to private hands, cannot be trusted to the free play of the market, but must be put in the hands of government bureaucrats, who are apparently to be regarded as *ex officio* perfectly rational, completely informed, incorruptible, and free from any taint of political interest.

His distrust of a free economy is unconcealed:

> It is of the nature of organized investment markets, under the influence of purchasers largely ignorant of what they are buying and of speculators who are more concerned with forecasting the next shift of market sentiment than with a reasonable estimate of the future yield of capital-assets, that, when disillusion falls upon an over-optimistic and over-bought market, it should fall with sudden and even catastrophic force (pp. 315-316). It is not so easy to revive the marginal efficiency of capital, determined, as it is, by the *uncontrollable* and *disobedient* psychology of the business world. It is the return of confidence, to speak in ordinary language, which is so *insusceptible to control* in an economy of individualistic capitalism. (My italics, p. 317.)

One incidental point brought out in this passage is that it extends the phrase "the marginal efficiency of capital" to the point where it means, "in ordinary language," merely *confidence!* But what the passage reveals most of all, in the words I have italicized, is the essentially authoritarian nature of Keynes's thought. In free markets purchasers are "largely ignorant of what they are buying." The business world is "uncontrollable" and "disobedient," like a naughty child. Obviously in such a world investors cannot be trusted to invest their own money, or entrepreneurs to make their own decisions. Keynes does not flinch from drawing the logical conclusion: "I conclude that the duty of ordering the current volume of investment cannot safely be left in private hands" (p. 320).

Whoever controls investment controls the direction and nature of production—decides what is to be made and sold and what is not, what consumers are to be permitted to have and in what volume. And Keynes does not shrink from this corollary either (except for a certain lack of clarity and candor) but begins to talk lightly of supporting "all sorts of policies for increasing the propensity to consume" (p. 325), and redistributing the wealth. "In existing conditions . . . where the volume of investment is unplanned and uncontrolled, subject to the vagaries of the marginal efficiency of capital as determined by the private judgment of individuals ignorant or speculative" the least he would support is "a socially controlled rate of investment" (pp. 324-325).

All this implies, once more, not only that entrepreneurs, businessmen, investors, and speculators are ignorant, mercurial, and irresponsible, but that there exists a class of people (perhaps economists very much resembling Lord Keynes) who are completely informed, rational, balanced, wise, who have means of knowing at all times exactly how much investment is needed and in exactly what amounts it should be allocated to exactly which industries and projects, and that these managers are above corruption and above any interest in the outcome of the next election.

Great Britain, unfortunately, decided to try the Keynesian remedy. The results are now known. I present herewith an analysis by Professor Ely Devon of the University of Manchester which appeared in Lloyd's Bank Review of London for July, 1954:

> It is now generally acknowledged that there are no objective criteria by which the Government can decide what is the right amount of investment in total. But it is still sometimes argued that it is possible by statistical analysis to decide on the distribution of investment. If the Government in its control over investment merely wants to imitate market procedure

and to select the lines of investment that will pay best, then it might try to work out rates of return on the various projects submitted to it and use such rates as the criteria for selecting which to approve. Even on this basis, however, prospective rates of return could be calculated only with very wide margins, representing the essential risks involved in such forecasting and, as with estimates of future coal and steel requirements, statistical investigation might expose and illustrate these risks but is unlikely to narrow them.

Usually, Government control of investment does not merely try to imitate market procedures; indeed, the very purpose of Government control is to prevent ordinary market forces being the criterion of distribution. The controlling authority tries to select on the basis of the public interest or of social priorities. It is extremely difficult to see how social priorities or social rates of return can be measured statistically. How does one compare statistically the social rate of return from building more houses with the social rate of return from more investment on road building and repair? Or compare the social rate of return from additional investment in the coal industry with investment in engineering or textiles?

Whether or not it is possible to measure social rates of return statistically, there is in any case little evidence that such calculation ever played an important role in the deliberations of the Capital Issues Committee and the Investments Program Committee. Little has been published about the proceedings of these two important committees and the criteria which they used in arriving at their decisions, but I suspect that the allocation of investment is much better thought of as the result of political and administrative struggles and pressures, than as a rational choice determined by the statistical measurement of rates of social return.

Each industry or line of investment is the administrative responsibility of some Government department, and in the argument about the investment program, each department would fight for the interests for which it was responsible. Every argument would, of course, be used to demonstrate that the investment being sponsored is vital to the economy, because it would relieve a potential bottleneck, result in export expansion or dollar saving. The strength of this case, the efficiency with which it is presented, the power and energy of the Minister in charge, public pressure, and generally accepted but vaguely expressed ideas of what is 'essential and inessential,' would all go to determine how each particular request for inclusion in the investment program was treated.

No doubt argument before these committees would be dressed up in statistics, since every official knows that a statistical case always makes an impression. And if all those concerned play the statistical game correctly—especially if they are not sure that they are playing a game—then an apparent air of deciding the issues rationally in terms of quantitative estimates of the results of alternative lines of action may easily be maintained.

3. *The Life of Durable Assets*

So much for one of the main economic policies which Keynes advocated. Now let us return to some of the technical economic analysis upon which his astonishing conclusion was based.

Keynes, as we have seen, believed in regularity in the duration of the business cycle. Specifically, he believed that "the duration of the downward movement" had "an order of magnitude which is not fortuitous," but "which shows some regularity of habit between, let us say, three and five years" (p. 317). Characteristically, he presents no statistical evidence of this, nor does he refer to any source where the statistical evidence can be found.

The extreme difficulty even of measuring business cycle durations is brought out by Burns and Mitchell in *Measuring Business Cycles.* Table 56 on page 221 of that volume shows that the contraction phase of fifteen American cycles as measured by monthly pig iron production between 1879 and 1933 ranged from five months to forty-four months, as compared with Keynes's "three to five years."

Geoffrey H. Moore, continuing these statistical studies of the National Bureau of Economic Research, finds that the *average* duration of the downward movement of the twenty-four cycles in the period from 1854 to 1954 was just twenty months.

But this statistical average conceals a wide range of duration. The contraction beginning in August 1918 lasted only seven months; that beginning in October 1873 lasted sixty-five months. In spite of Keynes's impression of regularity, here is a difference in duration of almost ten times as much in one case as in another.

Had Keynes been discussing the average duration of the whole cycle, instead of merely the downward phase, his guess would have come near the mark. The expansion and contraction phase together, of the twenty-four cycles, add up to just fifty months, or slightly over four years. But this average again conceals wide differences. For whereas the *average* expansion phase of the twenty-four cycles lasted thirty months, the *range* was from as low as ten months to as long as eighty months.

Now Keynes tries to explain his assumed "regularity" by "the influences which govern the recovery of the marginal efficiency of capital" (p. 317). But here he shifts once more from the wider interpretation of that phrase as equivalent merely to "the state of confidence," to the narrow interpretation of the specific productivity of specific capital assets. He concludes that the "duration of the slump" has "a definite relationship to the length of life of durable assets" (p. 318) and also to "the carrying costs of surplus stocks" (p. 317).

Here again, no statistical evidence is offered, and it may be questioned whether any is possible. There is no meaningful "average" length of life of "durable assets" and no meaningful "average" period for getting rid of "surplus stocks." Every capital instrument has a different *economic* life span (not necessarily coincident with its *physical* life span). Even durable assets of approximately the same life span were bought and installed at different times, and therefore need replacement at different times. The average life expectation of a human being is, say, seventy years, but under normal conditions approximately the same percentage and numbers of men and women die and are "replaced" each year, at a fairly even rate. They do not die all at once and get replaced each seventieth year.

Keynes has not only got his elementary arithmetic mixed up, but has reversed economic cause and effect. The amount of new and durable assets or current inventories purchased depends on the state of expectations, the state of confidence, rather than the other way round. Whether a manufacturer keeps his old equipment for another year or two, or buys new equipment, depends less upon the physical age of his equipment than upon his expectations regarding the future of sales, costs, and prices. Whether people keep their old automobiles or buy new ones depends more upon their own present income or estimate of future income than upon the precise age of their old car. There is no point at which people are "compelled" to buy new cars or at which a manufacturer is "compelled" to buy new equipment. This depends chiefly upon his estimate of future conditions in his business.

The same reasoning applies even more to inventories. There is no meaningful "average" time for getting rid of them. Nothing is gained by averaging the time it takes a department store to get rid of an excess inventory of bed sheets with the time it takes a Cadillac dealer to get rid of an excess stock of cars. And in any case each specific time-period depends more upon the purchasing power and state of expectations of buyers, and upon the willingness of sellers to cut prices for "clearance," than upon the "need" of buyers to replace their own stocks.

In brief, while "the length of life of durable assets" perhaps has *some* relation to the duration of a slump, it is only one of many factors, and seldom the most important. Nor does there appear to be any statistical way of determining its exact relationship or relative importance.

4. *A Policy of Perpetual Inflation*

Keynes's theory of the crisis, like his theory of so many other things, consists merely in a *contra-mundum* attitude, a denial of nearly every doctrine that is "orthodox" or established. If one truth concerning economic crises has been established in recent years, it is that they are typically brought on by cheap-money—*i.e.,* low interest-rate—policies that encourage excessive borrowing, excessive credit-expansion, imprudent speculation, and all the distortions and instabilities in the economy that these finally bring about. It follows that such crises can be prevented by keeping money sufficiently "tight" so that credit expansion, reckless speculation, and hare-brained ventures are not encouraged in the first place. It follows also that when such symptoms of an inflationary boom appear, a timely increase in money-rates can prevent them from running too far, and dampen down the boom before it has run to excessive lengths.

All this, of course, Keynes rejects. He treats the whole thing as a strange and perverse theory: "It may appear extraordinary that a school of thought should exist which finds the solution for the trade cycle in checking the boom in its early stages by a higher rate of interest" (p. 326). Keynes professes to be totally incapable of understanding the reasoning of this "school of thought," and this profession seems to be sincere.

> The only line of argument, along which any justification for this policy can be discovered, is that put forward by Mr. D. H. Robertson, who assumes, in effect, that full employment is an impracticable ideal and that the best that we can hope for is a level of employment much more stable than at present and averaging, perhaps, a little higher (pp. 326-327).

Now whether "full employment," *as conceived by the Keynesians,* is a practicable or even a *definable* ideal is a question that we shall later examine. And whether or not Keynes correctly states Roberston's argument is a question with which we are here not concerned. We need merely point out that this is *not* the real line of argument for checking the boom in its early stages by a higher rate of interest. The real objection to keeping rates of interest too low too long is that they encourage excessive borrowing, inflationary price and wage rises, speculative projects that cannot pay their way, and illusions, instabilities, and distortions throughout the economy that are bound to lead eventually to a crash.

But Keynes professes to believe that those who are opposed to inflationary bubbles are opposed to full employment: "The austere view, which would employ a high rate of interest to check at once any tendency in the level of employment to rise appreciably above the average of, say, the previous decade, is, however, more usually supported by arguments which have no foundation at all apart from confusion of mind" (pp. 327-328).

Now I know of no one who advocates or ever advocated raising the rate of interest *in order to lower the level of employment.* If Keynes knew of such an economist he should have quoted him. Economists have advocated raising the rate of interest in order to slow down, or to halt, or to prevent in the first place a money-and-credit *inflation,* with the instabilities and final crisis to which such an inflation always leads. They want the rate of interest raised to a non-inflationary level so as not to be confronted with a crisis and heavy unemployment when the inflationary bubble bursts.

Keynes's economics is the economics of wish fulfillment, the economics of the Land of Cockaigne, where every problem can be solved by rhetoric:

> Thus the remedy for the boom is not a higher rate of interest but a lower rate of interest! For that may enable the so-called boom to last. The right remedy for the trade cycle is not to be found in abolishing booms and thus keeping us permanently in a semi-slump; but in abolishing slumps and thus keeping us permanently in a quasi-boom (p. 322).

This sounds more like the wind-up speech of a political candidate at the final rally of a campaign than like the statement of a serious economist. Of course the economic ideal is to keep maximum production and even "full employment" (sensibly defined) all the time. But Keynes proposes to do this, in effect, by a policy of perpetual inflation, of keeping the interest rate low by a constant expansion of the money-and-credit supply (for that is what a policy of perpetual cheap money means). But this would not bring maximum balanced production of the products that consumers most wanted, nor steady employment. It is a policy of boom-and-bust, with the method correctly described.

And Keynes solves the trade-cycle problem rhetorically by the simple device of never once mentioning in this chapter the level of wage-rates! Never once does he ask what would happen if wage-rates, in this full employment boom, started racing ahead of prices and wiping out profit margins. Never once does he say what he would do to stop this from happening. In the Keynesian system, the level of wage-rates, and their effect on employment, is The Great Unmentionable.

Keynes's theory of the trade cycle, including his theory of interest-rate policy, is crowded with contradictions. The rate of interest, according to him, should be low in the depression, low in the boom, and low in the crisis. His "remedy" is to keep the boom going by encouraging over-investment and malinvestment, and then, when the boom cracks, to keep it going by lowering the rate of interest still more to encourage still more over-investment and malinvestment. He refused to recognize the rate of interest as a payment for anything real—whether the productivity or rental-value of the capital assets that could be bought with the borrowed funds, or the payment for generalized time-usance. He failed to recognize that the rate of interest is a market phenomenon like any other. He was opposed to "clapping on a high rate of interest which would probably deter some useful investments" (p. 321); forgetting that any market price for anything cuts off all the possible purchasers who are unwilling or unable to pay that price; but if the total supply is sold, the commodity nonetheless goes into presumably its most productive uses. What confused Keynes was the belief that "money" was not anything real, but merely pieces of paper that could be turned out at will by the printing press. He was capable of writing, for example:

> Or, again, the evil is supposed to creep in if the increased investment has been promoted by a fall in the rate of interest engineered by an increase in the quantity of money. Yet there is no special virtue in the pre-existing rate of interest, and the new money is not 'forced' on anyone. . . . (P. 328).

Here Keynes clearly acknowledges that he favors artificially cheap money even if it is brought about by direct monetary inflation. As a matter of fact, this is the only way in which a cheap money *policy* can be made effective. Either the supply of money (and/or credit) has to be increased to keep the interest rate down, or the artificially low interest rate (if it is effective at all) will stimulate increased borrowing and a consequent increase in the money-and-credit supply. True, there is "no special virtue in the *pre-existing* rate of interest," but there is at least a negative virtue in a rate of interest which is not inflationary.

5. *More Carts Before Horses*

There are some incidental fallacies in Section VI of Chapter 22 that are worth noticing chiefly as an index to the unreliability and slovenliness of Keynes's thought. He dismisses "the belief that in a boom investment tends to outrun saving" on the ground that it "implies that saving and investment can be unequal, and has, therefore, no meaning until these terms have been defined in some special sense" (p. 328).

This is disingenuous; not only because Keynes himself defined investment and savings in this "special sense" in his

Treatise on Money, but because, notwithstanding his formal definitions of saving and investment in Section II of Chapter 6, according to which they must always be equal, the whole thesis of the *General Theory,* which makes "saving" sinful and "investment" virtuous, depends constantly on the tacit assumption that one can in fact occur without the automatic occurrence of an equal amount of the other.

(The truth, as we saw in our Chapter XVI, is that in a boom [monetary] investment *can* outrun *previous* genuine saving *provided new money or bank credit has been meanwhile created*—provided, in other words, there is monetary inflation.)

Again, Keynes makes some astonishing statements on page 328. "In the short period supply price usually increases with increasing output, on account either of the physical fact of diminishing return or of the tendency of the cost-unit to rise in terms of money when output increases." But in the typical "Keynesian" situation, after there has been unemployment and unused capacity, unit costs of production *fall* when output increases because of the reduction of unit overhead costs.

"The rise of prices is merely a by-product of the increased output." But increased output, demand remaining unchanged, means a *fall* of prices.

"No one has a legitimate vested interest in being able to buy at prices which are only low because output is low." This is a reversal of cause and effect. When output is low it is usually because prices are low because demand is low.

When statements about elementary economic relationships are so slovenly and confused, it is hardly surprising that we should encounter so much confusion and fallacy in the discussion of more complicated problems.

6. *Sun-Spots Before the Eyes*

The final section of Chapter 22, on the supposed connection of the size of crops with the business cycle, is irrelevant to the main themes of the *General Theory,* and need detain us only as a further illustration of the slipshod and offhand theorizing that Keynes seemed to think good enough for economics.

Keynes takes off from the theory of W. Stanley Jevons (presented in 1878) that the trade cycle was primarily due to the fluctuations in the bounty of the harvest, and these in turn to a sun-spot cycle. Keynes restates and defends the theory in this form:

> When an exceptionally large harvest is gathered in, an important addition is usually made to the quantity carried over into later years. The proceeds of this addition are added to the current incomes of the farmers and are treated by them as income; whereas the increased carry-over involves no drain on the income-expenditure of other sections of the community but is financed out of savings. That is to say, the addition to the carry-over is an addition to current investment. This conclusion is not invalidated even if prices fall sharply. . . . Thus it is natural that we should find the upward turning-point to be marked by bountiful harvests and the downward turning-point by deficient harvests (pp. 329-330).

Now such a theory, to be even superficially plausible, calls first of all for inductive or statistical support. It would be necessary to show: (1) a direct correspondence, or at least a positive correlation, simultaneous or lagging, between the size of crops and the degree of prosperity; (2) at least an approximate correspondence between the total size of crops and the size of the carry-over from them; (3) at least an approximate correspondence between the total size of a crop and the volume of bank loans for carrying the carry-over; and (4) a correlation between the annual changes in the volume of agricultural loans for carrying crops and the annual changes in the *total* volume of bank loans for all purposes.

Not one of these statistical comparisons is made by Keynes or even suggested. Yet these statistics are all easily available, at least on a national scale; and some of them are directly contrary to the theory. The total monetary value of a crop (and there is no other practicable way of measuring the value except in monetary terms) bears no direct correspondence with the size of the crop. Thus in the decade 1876-1885 (to take figures from Jevons's own period) the annual production of wheat in the United States averaged 448,337,000 bushels, and the annual farm value averaged $413,730,000. But in the decade 1886-1895 the annual average production of wheat in the U.S. rose to 526,076,000 bushels, whereas the annual average farm value *fell* to $356,288,000.[3] I could cite any number of similar falls in total farm value of crops when the crops themselves increased. Speaking broadly, in fact, the farmers' total income from crops does not vary either directly or inversely with the total size of the crops. The conditions of demand in any year, and changes in the value of the monetary unit itself, are just as important as changes in crop supply.

Secondly, there is no necessary correspondence between the total size of a crop and the size of its carry-over. Thus in the five years 1941-1945 the average size of the new American wheat crop was 984,580,000 bushels, and the average size of the carry-over was 389,099,000 bushels; whereas in the five years 1946-1950 the average size of the new American wheat crop rose to 1,184,749,000 bushels and the average size of the carry-over fell to 281,603,000 bushels. In 1948 the new wheat crop was 1,294,911,000 bushels, and the carry-over 307,285,000 bushels; in 1949 the new crop fell to 1,098,415,000 bushels, but the carry-over rose to 424,714,-000 bushels.[4]

I need not go on to show the lack of correspondence between the total size of crops or carry-overs with total bank loans year by year. After all, it is the business of the propounder of a theory to present at least the prima facie reasons that make it seem plausible before it becomes incumbent on anybody else to present an elaborate disproof.

[3] Statistical Abstract of the United States, 1953, p. 650.
[4] *Ibid.*, p. 655.

Keynes's deductive argument for his "modernized" version of the Jevonian trade-cycle theory is implausible even in the absence of statistical disproof. It is based on the tacit assumptions (never spelled out) that large crops lead to a corresponding automatic increase in the volume of bank loans; that this increase adds to the volume of monetary purchasing power; and also that, for some mysterious reason, none of this purchasing power is ever tied up by the holding of the crops themselves. In fact, Keynes contends that "the reduction of redundant stocks to a normal level" actually has a "deflationary effect"! (p. 331).

It is, on the contrary, surplus stocks hanging over the market that have the deflationary effect. Prices of any commodity tend to rise as such surplus stocks are worked off. These are facts known to every informed speculator or businessman, but they were apparently never called to Lord Keynes's attention.

Chapter XXIII

RETURN TO MERCANTILISM?

1. *"Let Goods be Homespun"*

I have had occasion to point out several times in the course of this book that the leading ideas put forward by Keynes in the *General Theory,* far from being advanced and original, were a reversion to much older and more primitive ideas. And though Keynes flattered himself in the Preface to the *General Theory* for "treading along unfamiliar paths" and for "escaping from the old" ideas, he began to recognize increasingly in the course of the *General Theory* that he was really moving back, in his essential notions, to pre-classical seventeenth-century thinking, and that his ideas bore a striking similarity to those of the mercantilists. In Chapter 23 he recognized these similarities frankly and explicitly; but treated them as confirmation of the correctness of his "new" views!

In rejecting the classical views on free trade, he thinks it "fairest" to point out the extent of his own conversion:

> So lately as 1923, as a faithful pupil of the classical school who did not at that time doubt what he had been taught and entertained on this matter no reserves at all, I wrote: "If there is one thing that Protection can *not* do, it is to cure Unemployment. . . . There are some arguments for Protection, based upon its securing possible but improbable advantages, to which there is no simple answer. But the claim to cure Unemployment involves the Protectionist fallacy in its grossest and crudest form" (p. 334).[1]

[1] The self-quotation is from *The Nation and the Athenaeum,* Nov. 24, 1923.

Keynes might have quoted a far more comprehensive endorsement of free trade that he made only a few months before this in the *Manchester Guardian Commercial Supplement* of Jan. 4, 1923:

> We must hold to Free Trade, in its widest interpretation, as an inflexible dogma, to which no exception is admitted, wherever the decision rests with us. We must hold to this even where we receive no reciprocity of treatment and even in those rare cases where by infringing it we could in fact obtain a direct economic advantage. We should hold to Free Trade as a principle of international morals, and not merely as a doctrine of economic advantage.[2]

These quotations are chiefly interesting as illustrations of Keynes's intellectual virtuosity and instability. He could be equally eloquent and brilliant on either side of a question. While he repudiates his free-trade views in the *General Theory,* published in 1936, he had repudiated them even more strongly in an article in the *Yale Review* in the summer of 1933. There he announced the abandonment of his former free-trade ideas and frankly sympathized "with those who would minimize rather than with those who would maximize economic entanglement among nations."

"Let goods be homespun whenever it is reasonably and conveniently possible," Keynes continued there, "and above all let finance be primarily national. . . . A greater measure of national self-sufficiency and economic isolation among countries than existed in 1914 may tend to serve the cause of peace rather than otherwise." (This last belief must have received something of a jolt with the outbreak of World War II six years later. It is an historic irony that Keynes wrote these words just when Nazi Germany was about to launch on its policy of autarky.)

In that 1933 article Keynes at least recognized that "national self-sufficiency and a planned domestic economy"

[2] Quoted in *Tariffs: The Case Examined,* by Sir William Beveridge and others. (London: Longmans, 1931), p. 242.

went logically together, whereas domestic planning and free trade or internationalism did not. In the *General Theory* this is less explicitly admitted.

As a further example of Keynes's intellectual instability, his admiring biographer speaks of "his reversion towards Free Trade at the end of his life." [3]

But our chief purpose here is not to point to Keynes's many inconsistencies, but to examine which of his ideas were right and which were wrong. And clearly the position he took in the *General Theory* on free trade versus mercantilism was untenable.

He begins by stating what seems to him "the element of scientific truth in mercantilist doctrine" (p. 335). He admits that "the advantages claimed [by the mercantilists] are avowedly national advantages and are unlikely to benefit the world as a whole" (p. 335). But he neglects to add that they are all beggar-my-neighbor policies, the total result of which, even on the mercantilists' own assumptions, could only *injure* the world as a whole if universally applied. And he refuses to recognize that the typical mercantilist policies —the chief of which is protection—hurt even (and most often, especially) the nation that tries them alone. For such a nation either forces its own consumers to pay more for the products they wish than they would otherwise have to pay, or deprives them of these products altogether. Protection creates home industries that are less efficient than the corresponding foreign industries, at the cost of injuring home industries that are more efficient than the corresponding foreign industries.

Keynes concedes this in a parenthetic and left-handed way: "The advantages of the international division of labor are real and substantial, even though the classical school greatly overstressed them" (p. 338). But he never tells the reader explicitly what these advantages are; for when they are spelled out it becomes evident that even some of the

[3] R. F. Harrod, *The Life of John Maynard Keynes,* (New York: Harcourt, Brace, 1951), p. 469.

authors of "the classical school" never really stressed them enough.

Keynes states and endorses practically all the ancient and long-exploded fallacies of the mercantilists. We may safely leave the refutation of these to Adam Smith, Ricardo, Bastiat, and Mill; or even to Henry George, William Graham Sumner, Taussig, and a hundred others. It really is not a task that needs to be done over and over again in every generation or decade.

Or is it? What keeps the mercantilist fallacies alive, in spite of a thousand refutations, is (1) the special short-run interests of particular producers within each country, who would always stand to benefit if competition *against them alone* could be kept out; and (2) the persistent inability or refusal, even of many "economists," to look for or understand the secondary and long-run effects of a proposed policy. The art of economics consists in looking not merely at the immediate but at the longer effects of any act or policy; it consists in tracing the consequences of that policy not merely for one group but for all groups.[4]

2. *Running Comment on Running Comments*

It may be well, then, to make a running comment on some of Keynes's running comments.

> The weight of my criticism [he tells us] is directed against the inadequacy of the *theoretical* foundations of the *laissez-faire* doctrine upon which I was brought up and which for many years I taught;—against the notion that the rate of interest and the volume of investment are self-adjusting at the optimum level, so that preoccupation with the balance of trade is a waste of time. For we, the faculty of economists, prove to have been guilty of presumptuous error in treating as a puerile obsession what for centuries has been a prime object of practical statecraft (p. 339).

What is to be said of this? In a free economy the rate of interest and the volume of investment are (in the absence of

[4] See the present author's *Economics In One Lesson,* (New York: Harper, 1946).

government tampering with the money-and-credit supply) just as much market phenomena as the price of milk and the quantity of milk sold. They are just as self-adjusting as any other price or any other volume of sales. They are just as self-adjusting in relation to current supply and current demand. Classical theory held that, in free markets, prices, wages, and interest rates, volume of sales and volume of investment, tended to move toward, or oscillate about (hypothetical and always changing) equilibrium levels. But good classical theory never assumed that they invariably adjusted themselves at the "optimum level"—if that phrase is used to mean some ideal level. That would require perfect foresight on the part of buyers and sellers, lenders, borrowers, and entrepreneurs. Sound classical theory never assumed perfect foresight. One may ask whether it is not Keynes who is guilty of "presumptuous error" in so cavalierly dismissing what the best economists have taught for two centuries.

Keynes's attack on free interest rates is really an attack on free markets and free enterprise generally. In the very next paragraph we find him describing free markets as "the operation of blind forces" (p. 339). "Recently," he continues, "practical bankers in London have learnt much, and one can almost hope that in Great Britain the technique of bank rate will never be used again to protect the foreign balance in conditions in which it is likely to cause unemployment at home" (p. 339).

By 1957, however, bankers had really learnt much. They had learnt that Keynes's theories didn't work. After twenty years of cheap-money policies they raised the discount rate of the Bank of England to 7 per cent—to halt inflation and to protect the foreign balance. But the world is only slowly beginning to realize that excessive wage-rates can cause unemployment under any conditions. And it is precisely at excessive wage-rates that Keynes forbids us to point an accusing finger. His whipping boy was the interest rate.

He even goes so far as to write, in a footnote: "The

remedy of an elastic wage-unit, so that a depression is met by a reduction of wages, is liable . . . to be a means of benefiting ourselves at the expense of our neighbors" (p. 339). Just how it injures our neighbors to offer them goods at lower prices, or just how it injures the great body of the workers to reduce wage-rates to the equilibrium point that maximizes employment and total payrolls, I leave to the Keynesians to explain. In any case, Keynes ends up with the mercantilist conclusion that markets must never be left free; that the government must control practically everything:

> There was wisdom in [the mercantilists'] intense preoccupation with keeping down the rate of interest by means of usury laws . . . and in their readiness in the last resort to restore the stock of money by devaluation, if it had become plainly deficient through an unavoidable foreign drain, a rise in the wage-unit, or any other cause (p. 340).

Practically all the Keynesian remedies, then—especially arbitrarily holding down interest rates and inflating the currency—were known to and practiced by the mercantilists of the seventeenth century and earlier, by Keynes's own admission.

The "new economics," in brief, turns out to be merely the exhumation of ancient and exploded fallacies.

3. *Wise Mercantilists, Stupid Economists*

Instead of becoming disturbed when he found that his "new" and "path-breaking" ideas had been anticipated by the seventeenth-century mercantilists, Keynes seems to have been reassured and delighted by the discovery:

> Mercantilist thought never supposed that there was a self-adjusting tendency by which the rate of interest would be established at the appropriate level. On the contrary they [sic] were emphatic that an unduly high rate of interest was the main obstacle to the growth of wealth; and they were even aware that the rate of interest depended on liquidity-prefer-

> ence and the quantity of money. They were concerned both with diminishing liquidity-preference and with increasing the quantity of money, and several of them made it clear that their preoccupation with increasing the quantity of money was due to their desire to diminish the rate of interest (p. 341).

Keynes was charmed to find that his own chief fallacies had been anticipated by the philosopher John Locke in 1692: "The great Locke was, perhaps, the first to express in abstract terms the relationship between the rate of interest and the quantity of money in his controversy with Petty" (p. 342). The reason Locke also mistook this relationship was that he too, like Keynes, assumed that the rate of interest was a purely monetary phenomenon. But Locke at least had the excuse of having lived and died not only before the appearance of the classical economists, or of the work of Böhm-Bawerk, or Irving Fisher, but even before the appearance of David Hume's essay "Of Interest" in 1741. The great Hume was, perhaps, the first to point out that "The rate of interest . . . is not derived from the quantity of the precious metals"—by which he meant the quantity of money.

> The mercantilists [continues Keynes] were under no illusions as to the nationalistic character of their policies and their tendency to promote war. It was *national* advantage and *relative* strength at which they were admittedly aiming. We may criticize them for the apparent indifference with which they accepted this inevitable consequence of an international monetary system. But intellectually their realism is much preferable to the confused thinking of contemporary advocates of an international fixed gold standard and *laissez-faire* in international lending, who believe that it is precisely these policies which will best promote peace (p. 348).

This is the beginning of a series of closely packed paradoxes and contradictions in which Keynes proceeds to prove triumphantly that nationalism is the best internationalism, that hostile policies bring peace, and friendly policies, war, that international currency stability and free trade bring instability and chaos, and that nationalistic and mutually hostile policies bring international stability and prosperity.

Having just implied, in the passage quoted above, that nationalistic and beggar-my-neighbor policies were "realistic," and that an international gold standard and freedom of lending and trade lead to war rather than peace, Keynes goes on:

"For in an economy subject to money contracts and customs more or less fixed over an appreciable period of time, where the quantity of domestic circulation and the domestic rate of interest are primarily determined by the balance of payments . . ." (p. 348). I must interrupt here to point out that this is an obvious confusion of cause and effect. The balance of payments is itself heavily influenced and largely determined by relative rates of interest in different nations, relative national changes in the quantity of money, and relative changes in national price averages, or, rather, in specific prices. The balance of payments, in fact, is far more often a consequence of one or more of these other changes than *they* are of the balance of payments.

Continuing from the point where I interrupted, Keynes goes on to declare that under these conditions

> there is no orthodox means open to the authorities for countering unemployment at home except by struggling for an export surplus and an import of the monetary metal at the expense of their neighbors. Never in history was there a method devised of such efficacy for setting each country's advantage at variance with its neighbors' as the international gold (or, formerly, silver) standard. For it made domestic prosperity directly dependent on a competitive pursuit of markets and a competitive appetite for the precious metals (pp. 348-349).

What this passage mainly illustrates is how thoroughly mercantilistic Keynes's assumptions had become, and how infirm and uncertain was his grasp of classical theory. Under an international gold standard and freedom of trade the import of gold by Alphavia is no more at the "expense" of Betavia, which exported the gold, than the import of wheat by Betavia is at the expense of Alphavia, which exported the wheat. Just as an individual merchant in either country may wish to exchange his money for wheat, or vice versa, so one merchant in Alphavia may wish to exchange his wheat for money and another merchant in Betavia may wish to exchange his money for Alphavian wheat. The transaction occurs because both parties to the transaction gain by it. It is at neither's "expense." To say that "Alphavia" gains gold and that "Betavia" loses gold is merely a mercantilist confusion. The transaction is between individual merchants. To assume that only the person who gets the money or gold "gains" and that the person who gets goods for it must "lose" is merely another puerile confusion.

True, free trade under an international gold standard involves a "competitive pursuit of markets." So does domestic trade. An American and a German steel company may bid against each other for a construction contract in Italy; but other American and German steel companies may also bid against their respective compatriots, either for domestic or for foreign business. It is precisely mercantilism, medieval and modern, that turns what ought to be competition between individuals or firms into competition between *nations*. It is precisely domestic currency manipulations, devaluations, exchange controls, import quotas, bilateral trade treaties, and high tariffs that create international antagonisms.

As for a "competitive appetite for the precious metals," one may just as well speak of a competitive appetite for Swiss watches, or for German cameras, or for French wines, or for English dinnerware, or for American typewriters and automobiles. If I want to buy anything at all, at home or abroad, my bid must compete with that of others who want it. Was Keynes against competition itself? If so, what did he propose to substitute? His actual proposals merely tend to substitute nationalized and politicalized competition for interpersonal or inter-firm competition. They would increase rather than reduce the pressure for beggar-my-neighbor policies and for trade wars and real wars.

"When by happy accident the new supplies of gold and silver were comparatively abundant," Keynes continues (without break from the foregoing quotation), "the struggle [for the precious metals] might be somewhat abated" (p. 349). Here is another glaring fallacy. If the precious metals had been *abundant,* they would not have been precious. If abundance of the monetary metal is what is needed, then the logical remedy would be a copper standard, or, still better, an iron standard. In the remark just quoted even the most elementary and basic economic principle, the relationship between value and quantity, is forgotten. (Unless, of course, Keynes's unstated argument is that it would have been precisely necessary to have a constant *cheapening* of the precious metals to perpetuate a rise of prices, a constant inflation.)

Keynes goes on, adding bad controversial manners to bad logic: "The part played by orthodox economists, whose common sense has been insufficient to check their faulty logic, has been disastrous to the latest act" (p. 349). Here is a wholesale gibe at Adam Smith, Ricardo, John Stuart Mill, Bastiat, Bastable, Marshall, and Taussig—at everyone who has contributed anything to the extension or clarification of the theory of foreign trade; and made by a man whose own common sense was insufficient to check his illogic. One begins to suspect that Keynes's reputation, like Shaw's, rests in large part on sheer impudence.

And what, in the place of the disastrous policies favored by the orthodox economists, does Keynes recommend? "The opposite."

> It is the policy of an autonomous rate of interest, unimpeded by international preoccupations, and of a national investment program directed to an optimum level of domestic employment which is twice blessed in the sense that it helps ourselves and our neighbors at the same time. And it is the

> simultaneous pursuit of these policies by all countries together which is capable of restoring economic health and strength internationally, whether we measure it by the level of domestic employment or by the volume of international trade (p. 349).

So this is what logic and common sense are supposed to look like. If each nation follows nationalistic policies, regardless of their effect on other nations, if each nation tries to maximize exports and to minimize or forbid imports, the volume of international trade will be greater than ever! If the bureaucrats seize our savings and forbid us to invest our own funds for fear that we would make a terrible mess of it, *they* will have the omniscience to know just when to invest it, and just where, and just how much to put into each venture, and just what ventures will succeed and what will not; and we shall all live forever in a perfectly regulated economic paradise.

(For further particulars see what happened to the British government investment program since the end of World War II and the history of our own Reconstruction Finance Corporation.)

4. *The Religion of Governmental Controls*

In Sections IV, V, and VI of Chapter 23, in his further onslaught on the doctrine of Free Trade and a free market rate of interest, Keynes continues to abuse the classical economists and to praise, in contrast, the medievalists and the present-day currency cranks.

The classical school created a "cleavage," he contends, "between the conclusions of economic theory and those of common sense. The extraordinary achievement of the classical theory was to overcome the beliefs of the 'natural man' and, at the same time, to be wrong" (p. 350).

Such epigrams came easily to Keynes. They are the chief source, I suspect, of his reputation among literary men as a great economist. But it is astonishing how much more appropriate they are when applied to Keynes's own theories than to those against which they were directed. Certainly there is a yawning gap between the conclusions of Keynesian theory and those of common sense. Keynes's own most extraordinary achievement was to overcome the beliefs of the 'natural man' and at the same time to be wrong. For the natural man, unconfused by Keynesian economics, assumes in theory, if not in practice, that thrift is better than squandering; and Robinson Crusoe took it for granted that the propensity to work was more essential to his survival than the propensity to spend.

"I remember Bonar Law's mingled rage and perplexity in face of the economists," writes Keynes in approval (of Bonar Law), "because they were denying what was obvious" (p. 350). That is, *they seemed to Bonar Law* to be denying what was obvious. Keynes might have done better to remember the remark by a character in Bernard Shaw's *Saint Joan* when told of the theory of Pythagoras that the earth is round and revolves around the sun: "What an utter fool! Couldn't he use his eyes?"

But Keynes goes gaily on: "One recurs to the analogy between the sway of the classical school of economic theory and that of certain religions" (pp. 350-351). It was Keynes's own great contribution to "exorcise the obvious" (p. 351) and to substitute the Religion of Spending, the Religion of Monetary Inflation, the Religion of Governmental Controls, with the government bureaucrats as the High Priests, regulating the volume, direction, and nature of Investment with infallible wisdom.

> There remains an allied, but distinct, matter where for centuries, indeed for several millenniums, enlightened opinion held for certain and obvious a doctrine which the classical school has repudiated as childish, but which deserves rehabilitation and honor. I mean the doctrine that the rate of interest is not self-adjusting at a level best suited to the social advantage but constantly tends to rise too high, so that a wise Government is concerned to curb it by statute and cus-

tom and even by invoking the sanctions of the moral law (p. 351).

Here Keynes entirely misconceives, or misstates, the classical theory of interest rates, indeed the classical theory of prices generally. That theory does not contend that whatever is, is right. It does not say that today's prevailing interest rate, arrived at in the free market, is always the "right" one, "best suited to the social advantage"—any more than it asserts that the price of a commodity, or of a share on the stock market, is at any moment the "right" one. The classical theory merely asserts that, *in the long run,* the unhampered market, reflecting the composite desires, valuations, and actions of the individuals composing it, is the best *method* for determining prices or interest rates, and while never infallible, is more calculated to bring optimum social advantage than any other method. Keynes's own tacit assumption is that he or his friends, or bureaucrats who would be necessarily politically motivated (by the desire to please the politically dominant groups and to stay in power) would be far better judges of the "right" interest rate than lenders and borrowers acting in accordance with their own judgment.

It is true, of course, that *borrowers* always consider interest rates too high, just as workers always think wages too low, producers always think prices too low, and consumers always think prices too high. But to appeal to these interested sentiments is political demagogy, not economics.

"Provisions against usury," continues Keynes, "are amongst the most ancient economic practices of which we have record" (p. 351). So indeed they are. And so are all forms of government price-control, from the Code of Hammurabi (circa 2000 B.C.), through the Edicts of the Roman Emperor Diocletian (245-313 A.D.), and through the dreadful Law of the Maximum in the French Revolution.[5] But

[5] See, e.g., Mary G. Lacy, "Food Control During Forty-six Centuries," *Scientific Monthly,* June, 1923, or the same author's *Price-Fixing by Governments, 424* B.C. *to 1926* A.D., 1926.

it is certainly strange to find the antiquity of a stupid economic prohibition put forward in 1936 as a serious argument for its revival.

"The destruction of the inducement to invest by an excessive liquidity-preference," continues Keynes, "was the outstanding evil, the prime impediment to the growth of wealth, in the ancient and medieval worlds" (p. 351).

Here is another striking illustration of the way in which Keynes's thought was distorted by an inappropriate vocabulary of his own coining. What is "excessive liquidity-preference" if it is not merely the *absence* of "inducement to invest"? Or just another name for that absence? The "inducement to invest," by Keynes's definition, is the inducement to buy capital goods or other investment assets. But no one would seriously think of saying that the inducement to buy (anything at all) is "destroyed" by a preference not to buy. An insufficient inducement to invest, or a more-than-sufficient "liquidity-preference," are merely two ways of saying the same thing. The second is not an *explanation* of the first. It is merely a repetition of it in different words.

Of course if we think of the investor and the lender as two different persons (as they sometimes are), then the inducement to invest of the borrower must be at least a tiny bit higher than the reluctance to lend of the lender before a transaction can take place. The two must agree upon an equating interest rate, in short, that is mutually satisfactory. But the like is true of any transaction in any commodity whatever. The inducement to buy of the buyer of shares on the Stock Exchange (or of anything else), must be high enough for him to offer a price sufficient to overcome the reluctance to sell of the seller; otherwise there is no transaction. If the reluctance of any merchant to sell his goods at a certain price is greater than the inducement of customers to buy at that price, then the goods will not be sold until the seller either lowers his asking price or the buyers overcome their reluctance to pay the existing price. My reluctance to buy a share on the Stock Exchange at 75 may be overcome by my inducement to buy it at 70. My reluctance to sell it at 70 may be overcome by my inducement to sell it at 75. Buying and selling, lending and borrowing, in short, can all be explained either in terms of inducement or in terms of reluctance. My desire to buy a Buick may be greater or less than my reluctance to part with the necessary cash.

But it does not constitute a new and revolutionary system of economics, or a more penetrating one, to explain the economic process in terms of reluctance rather than in terms of desire and inducement. The term "liquidity-preference" does not explain the level of interest rates a whit better than the term egg-preference would explain the price of eggs. And an explanation of the level of interest rates in terms of a reluctance to part with cash no more proves that interest rates are chronically too high than an explanation of the price of jewelry in terms of the holders' reluctance to part with the jewels would prove that jewelry is chronically priced too high.

I would blush to expound the obvious and elementary at this length, if it were not constantly denied for four hundred pages in a book hailed by the dominant academic economists today as the greatest economic revelation of the twentieth century.

> [Keynes resumes] I now read these discussions [of the Medieval Church] as an honest intellectual effort to keep separate what the classical theory has inextricably confused together, namely, the rate of interest and the marginal efficiency of capital. For it now seems clear that the disquisitions of the schoolmen were directed towards the elucidation of a formula which should allow the schedule of the marginal efficiency of capital to be high, whilst using rule and custom and the moral law to keep down the rate of interest (p. 352).

As Keynes merely returns here to one of the fallacies in his theory of interest, we need not repeat our analysis of it. It is simply necessary to point out that while the rate of interest is of course not *identical* with the marginal efficiency of capital, or even *caused* by it, the two are intimately related. The relationship is analogous to that between price and marginal cost of production. Though in the short-run these may often vary from each other in either direction, there is always a long-run tendency for them to come to equality. To treat interest rates and the marginal efficiency of capital not only as separate but as disconnected and without reciprocal influence is to be blind to one of the central relationships of economic life. Though time-preference (or the rate of time-discount) is primary, there is always a tendency for the rate of interest and the marginal yield of capital to come into equilibrium with each other. Keynes's belief that a special *deus ex machina,* or government bureaucrat, is necessary to adjust the rate of interest to the marginal efficiency of capital goes with the belief that a government price-controller is necessary to adjust prices to marginal production costs. What Keynes is proposing here is, in fact, government price-fixing in a special field. A free market can be counted on to make the appropriate adjustments infinitely better.

5. *Canonization of the Cranks*

Just as Keynes was astonished to find that his "new" opinions had been anticipated by the mercantilists of the seventeenth century, so he found that some of these opinions had also been anticipated by modern monetary cranks. But in the second case as in the first, instead of taking this as a warning to re-examine his assumptions and deductions, he greeted the agreement as a confirmation of his new doctrines.

And one of those whose reputation he tried to rehabilitate was "the strange unduly neglected prophet Silvio Gesell" (p. 353). Gesell had attracted some attention in the economic underworld by proposing a form of money that would automatically lose part of its value every month, like a rotting vegetable. His proposed method of achieving this was to require the holder of every currency note to have it stamped each month, with stamps purchased at the post office, in order to keep it good at its face value. This meant, in effect, that people would have to *pay* interest to the government for the privilege of holding their own money. Money held, without being stamped, would lose a fraction of its purchasing power every month. The purpose of this was to discourage people from saving; to make monetary saving practically impossible; to force everyone to spend his money, for no matter what, before it lost its value. Any one who was wicked enough to wish to put aside money against the contingency of illness in his family, for example, would thus be effectively frustrated.

It is obvious that such money would never freely circulate except in a community of idiots unless it were made legal tender and there was no choice but to accept it. There was in principle nothing original in the proposal. It did not differ essentially from the immemorial practice of coin clipping, except that it would have occurred much more systematically and much more often. It combined nearly all the evils of ordinary paper inflation with some special disadvantages of its own. Its sole advantage as compared with ordinary paper money inflation is that the holder would clearly recognize and identify the government tax, and know precisely what the incidence of that tax was on himself.

But Keynes takes it all very seriously, regrets that once, "like other academic economists, I treated [Gesell's] profoundly original strivings as being no better than those of a crank" (p. 353), and suggests exactly how much the monthly stamp tax ought to be. "It should be roughly equal to the excess of the money-rate of interest (apart from the stamps) over the marginal efficiency of capital corresponding to a rate of new investment compatible with full employment," and this figure could be determined "by trial and error" (p. 357).

We need not linger over this particular absurdity. Even

most Keynesians maintain an embarrassed silence about it. In this new wonderland into which Keynes has wandered, it was the classical economists who suddenly seemed stupid and lacking in common sense, and it was the works of the currency cranks (for Gesell was only one of scores with similar schemes) that were full of "flashes of deep insight."

I shall pause only to comment upon one sentence in the course of Keynes's discussion of Gesell's ideas: "The prime necessity is to reduce the money-rate of interest, and this, he pointed out, can be effected by causing money to incur carrying-costs just like other stocks of barren goods" (p. 357).

Thus Keynes endorses the medieval idea that money is "barren." But if money is "barren," and if (on Keynes's own theory) interest is paid only for money itself, and never for the yield of what it will buy, why are borrowers so foolish as to agree to pay interest for money, and why are lenders not happy to find themselves able to lend money at any rate whatever above absolute zero? Why do people insist either on borrowing or on holding on to something that yields them nothing whatever? Such questions have already been answered, not only in our previous chapters on the rate of interest, but specifically by W. H. Hutt in his essay "The Yield from Money Held," [6] in which he shows that money "is as productive as all other assets, and productive in exactly the same sense"; that its marginal productive yield is constantly being equated with that of all other assets; and that its yield, like the yield of so many other assets, consists precisely in its *availability* at the moment when it is wanted or needed. The reader may consult Hutt's essay for the expansion of this argument. It is simply necessary to point out here that the failure of Keynes and his followers to recognize the real yield enjoyed by the holder of money assets is one of the most serious fallacies in their theory of interest.

[6] Mary Sennholz (ed.), *On Freedom and Free Enterprise: Essays in Honor of Ludwig von Mises* (Princeton: Van Nostrand, 1956).

6. *Mandeville, Malthus, and the Misers*

Section VII of Keynes's Chapter 23 comprises a discussion of the anticipations by Bernard Mandeville, Thomas Malthus, and J. A. Hobson of Keynesian under-consumption theory. It opens, however, with a quotation from Professor E. Heckscher's *Mercantilism* on the sixteenth and seventeenth-century "deep-rooted belief in the utility of luxury and the evil of thrift. Thrift, in fact, was regarded as the cause of unemployment, and for two reasons: in the first place, because real income was believed to diminish by the amount of money which did not enter into exchange, and secondly, because saving was believed to withdraw money from circulation." [7]

Surely the Keynesians ought to conspire to suppress this quotation! It so perfectly and nakedly sums up Keynes's central "contribution" to economic thought.

Incidentally, though Keynes takes many quotations from Heckscher's two volumes, and holds them up for admiration of mercantilist thought, there are some passages in Heckscher's history that are conspicuously *not* quoted by Keynes. I take one as an example—a passage concerning French mercantilism during the seventeenth and eighteenth centuries:

> It is estimated that the economic measures taken in this connection cost the lives of some 16,000 people, partly through executions and partly through armed affrays, without reckoning the unknown but certainly much larger number of people who were sent to the galleys or punished in other ways. On one occasion in Valence, 77 were sent to the galleys, one was set free and none were pardoned. But even this vigorous action did not help to attain the desired end. Printed calicoes spread more and more widely among all classes of the population, in France as everywhere else.[8]

[7] E. Heckscher, *Mercantilism* (London: Macmillan, 1935), II, 208.
[8] *Ibid.*, I, 173.

Would Keynes have presented this as another example of the "realism" of mercantilist thought, "which deserves rehabilitation and honor"?

Keynes next launches upon an extended series of quotations from Bernard Mandeville's *Fable of the Bees; or Private Vices, Public Benefits,* which first appeared in 1714.

There is much wisdom in this remarkable poem, and much fallacy. Keynes likes the fallacious part, and quotes extensively from Mandeville's doctrine that prosperity is increased by expenditure and luxurious living, and reduced by thrift and prudence and saving. It is a little late to start answering this fallacy of Mandeville's; the classical economists did it quite adequately, and I shall excuse myself from repeating the task. Besides, we shall have a chance to answer the same doctrine as formulated (much more guardedly) by Malthus.

For after praising Petty for his statement in 1662 justifying "entertainments, magnificent shews, triumphal arches, etc." on the ground that their costs flowed back into the pockets of brewers, bakers, tailors, and shoemakers (p. 359), and after deprecating, by contrast, "the penny-wisdom of Gladstonian finance" (p. 362), Keynes comes to "the later phase of Malthus," where "the notion of the insufficiency of effective demand takes a definite place as a scientific explanation of unemployment" (p. 362). He quotes practically two full pages from Malthus, from which I shall take two passages; for it is instructive to distinguish what was right in Malthus's views from what was wrong:

> Adam Smith has stated that capitals are increased by parsimony, that every frugal man is a public benefactor, and that the increase of wealth depends upon the balance of produce above consumption. That these propositions are true to a great extent is perfectly unquestionable. . . .[9]

It is important to notice that Malthus, unlike Mandeville and Keynes, does not ridicule thrift *as such,* but only what he considers an unreasonable degree of it.

[9] Preface to Malthus's *Principles of Political Economy,* 1820, pp. 8-9.

> It is quite obvious [he continues] that they are not true to an indefinite extent, and that the principles of saving, pushed to excess, would destroy the motive to production. If every person were satisfied with the simplest food, the poorest clothing, and the meanest houses, it is certain that no other sort of food, clothing, and lodging would be in existence.[10]

In still another passage (which is notable for its failure to grasp the essential truth in Say's Law) Malthus asks: "What would become of the demand for commodities, if all consumption except bread and water were suspended for the next half-year?" [11]

Now the conclusions of Malthus just quoted are perfectly true, and even truisms, *if we accept the quite unrealistic assumptions on which they are based.* They tacitly assume that everyone has approximately the same income, and that everyone tries to produce more than he is interested in consuming. And they explicitly assume that *"every"* person is satisfied with the meanest house, etc. and that *"all* consumption except bread and water" is suspended.

But it is very difficult even to imagine a community in which everybody (or even any substantial percentage of the population) would act in so irrational a manner as the Malthus hypothesis assumes. It is true that there are nations and communities that are poor because most of the people are satisfied with low living standards. But these communities are poor not because they try to save too much out of what they produce, but simply because they fail to produce. Their characteristic mark is not thrift but laziness or improvidence. They live from day to day; they are racked periodically by disease and famine, because they do not produce enough in order to save enough to carry them through years of bad crops or other contingencies. The people in a community who produce above the subsistence level are in the overwhelming majority precisely the people who want to live and spend above the subsistence level. A community

10 *Ibid.*, pp. 8-9.
11 *Ibid.*, p. 363, footnote.

in which everybody strove to work enough and earn enough to live at ten times or even twice the subsistence level, but refused to live above a subsistence level, and insisted on saving the rest, would be a community possessed by a psychology so irrational and so difficult to imagine that the implications of the hypothesis are hardly worth working out in much detail.

But even if we assume such a community with such a psychology, it would at least be possible to imagine it surviving successfully for the six months assumed in Malthus's rhetorical question. For it could invest its money in capital goods, and these capital-goods industries would give the necessary employment to those laid off from employment on consumption goods, and the capital-goods industries would even earn a profit, *provided* they were capital goods for which there was a real demand, and the community at the end of the six months gave up its Spartan frugality and used its income to buy the added consumption goods that the new capital equipment was capable of producing. Many a country has done something closely equivalent to this in wartime, when it lived on a subsistence level of consumption in order to support armies and produce implements of war.

And if, moving from Malthus's violent hypothesis toward less unrealistic but still grossly oversimplified assumptions, we assume a community with only two income classes, in which the great mass, consisting of nine-tenths of the population, has a per-capita subsistence income of x dollars, and spends it all as it goes along, while the remaining tenth of the population has a per-capita income of $3x$ dollars, but consists entirely of misers who also spend only x dollars a year and save two-thirds of their income, or $2x$ dollars per capita, we have a community which (assuming that producers' expectations are based on this situation) would nonetheless progress and grow constantly richer. For the misers would invest their money in capital equipment. This would be used to increase production of consumer goods, to improve the quality of such goods, and to lower production costs. The real wages and income of both the Masses and the Misers would increase; and as the consumption of both the Masses and the Misers would increase by the hypothesis (for the Masses would always spend their whole incomes, and the rich Misers would individually spend as much as, though not more than, the poor Masses spent individually) consumption, production, and saving would all increase *pari passu.*

Suppose we change the names of our classes and call the upper 10 per cent, with the $3x$ incomes, the Capitalists, and the lower 90 per cent, with the x incomes, the Workers. Then it is the implied contention of the Mandevilles, Malthuses, and Keyneses that (assuming the Workers had no surplus incomes to save) the Capitalists would maximize prosperity by spending their full incomes, but produce depression by spending only as much as the Workers spend on consumption, and saving and investing (or vainly looking for investment "outlets" for) the other two-thirds of their incomes.

But nothing could be further from the truth. For if the Capitalists spent all their income on luxurious living there could be no capital investment. In that case there would be no increased production, and no lowering of production costs, hence no increase in the real wages or incomes of the Workers and no increase in their consumption. But if the Capitalists saved and invested the whole of the excess of their own incomes above the Workers' incomes, then all this investment would necessarily go into capital equipment for increasing the production of mass-consumption goods. The investment would not only produce jobs (which is the only consequence that Keynes seems to recognize), but *it would increase the average productivity of all jobs.* Hence it would increase the production of consumption goods, lower production costs, increase average marginal labor productivity and average real wages.

In brief, even if we make the extreme assumption that

the Capitalists, or upper income class, spend no more on consumption than the Workers, or lower income class, we find no necessary insufficiency of investment "outlets" or investment opportunities. Production will be increased by the new capital investment, real costs will be lowered by it; hence prices will be lowered (in the absence of inflation) and real wages will therefore increase to buy the additional product. (We are assuming by our hypothesis that there is no *sudden, uncaused,* or *irrational* saving, but that workers increase their consumption in proportion to their increase in incomes and that the Capitalists consume at least as much as the Workers.)

And directly contrary to the Mandeville-Malthus-Keynes thesis, this extreme thrift on the part of the Capitalists would not only not retard economic progress; it would maximize it. It would particularly maximize the progress of the Masses, because the Capitalists per capita would not be taking any more out of the consumption cake per capita than the Workers would. The surplus income of the Capitalists, instead of going for ostentation and wasteful sybaritic living, would be going into investment *to increase the production, reduce the cost, and improve the quality of consumption goods for the Masses.*

Incidentally, envy and hatred, which play such a large role behind the schemes of revolutionary economic reformers, would be minimized under such behavior by the Capitalists; for though there would be *in*equality of income there would be *equality* of consumption. Ostentatious and sybaritic living on the part of the rich, accompanied by Veblen's "conspicuous waste," which is recommended by implication by the Keynesians, is precisely the course most calculated to inflame envy and resentment and social discontent.[12]

[12] For an analysis of the respective effects of extravagance and thrift by the rich on the condition of the relatively poor, see Hartley Withers, *Poverty and Waste,* 1914, an excellent but neglected volume. Before World War I revived statism and inflationism, economists still dared to defend frugality. I cannot refrain quoting at this point, for example, from a little book by S. J. Chapman,

This is the conclusion that we get even when we make the extreme assumption of two income classes in which the higher income class saves the whole of its per capita excess of income above that of the lower income class. We can generalize this assumption, and bring it closer to reality, first by assuming n different income classes, instead of only two, with the poorest class having a mere subsistence per-capita income of x, the next worst off class an income of $x + 2y$, the third class from the botton an income of $x + 4y$, the fourth an income of $x + 6y$, etc. And instead of assuming that those with incomes above the minimum save the whole excess, we can assume that they save only half of it, and spend, respectively, $x + y$, $x + 2y$, $x + 3y$, etc. Or we can state our assumptions regarding saving and spending in the form of a continuous function, in which those with higher incomes not only save a continuously greater absolute amount than those with lower incomes, but a continuously greater percentage of their incomes. If there is no reason to fear an insufficiency of investment opportunities or "outlets" even under our preceding extreme assumption, there is of course still less reason to fear such an insufficiency under these more moderate and realistic assumptions.

7. *The Contribution of Mill*

So, when we look at the matter closely, we find that Gladstone and Benjamin Franklin, with their "penny-wisdom," were perhaps better economists after all, in every sense of

---

Political Economy, published in the Home University Library series in 1912. Chapman refers to the "outrageous fallacy" uttered by Marryat's hero, Mr. Midshipman Easy, in maintaining that the vice of extravagance "circulates money" and contributes to "the support, the comfort, and employment of the poor." "The fallacy betrays itself at once," comments Chapman, "when we remind ourselves that we cannot be ultimately dependent for employment on other people's wants, because we have all quite sufficient of our own to keep us fully occupied in satisfying them. Yet there are those today who . . . maintain that the excessive saving of the rich . . . is withholding employment from the poor. But saving which is not hoarding is indirect spending–spending on productive instruments which make things cheaper for the poor–and transparently more can be produced for the poor when their demand has to compete to a less extent with rich people's demand for consumers' goods" (pp. 224-226).

the word, than Petty with his "entertainments, magnificent shews, triumphal arches, etc.," or Mandeville with his liv'ries and coaches and mirac'lous palaces, or Keynes with his propensity to consume.

I do not wish to be understood as recommending Spartan living or parsimonious spending on the part of anybody who can afford better. On the contrary, I am inclined to agree with the conclusion of Malthus himself, which appears in the preface to his *Principles of Political Economy* just after the passage quoted a few pages back:

> The two extremes [prodigality and frugality] are obvious; and it follows that there must be some intermediate point, though the resources of political economy may not be able to ascertain it, where, taking into consideration both the power to produce and the will to consume, the encouragement to the increase of wealth is the greatest.

This exact optimum point could be achieved only on the assumption of perfect foreknowledge and wisdom on the part of investors, producers and consumers. But it may be approximated by the exercise of common prudence, civilized wants and tastes, and good sense. In any case, rational thrift is still a virtue, saving is not an economic crime, and no one has a *duty* to be a spendthrift. What is certain is that the optimum relationship between saving and spending will never be determined by algebra, by academicians, or by government bureaucrats. Consumers, following their own inclinations, will make mistakes, but are likely to come incomparably closer, on the average, to the optimum balance.

It is strange that in his sweeping historical review from the mercantilists, Mandeville and Petty through Malthus to J. A. Hobson and Major Douglas, Keynes never mentions John Stuart Mill. Yet in his *Principles of Political Economy* Mill wrote a passage that reads like a direct refutation of Keynes's spending theories. (It *was* a direct refutation of the immemorial fallacies that Keynes tried to revive.) Mill set himself to establish the "fundamental theorem" that "demand for commodities is not demand for labor." [13]

> This theorem, that to purchase produce is not to employ labor; that the demand for labor is constituted by the wages which precede the production, and not by the demand which may exist for the commodities resulting from the production; is a proposition which greatly needs all the illustration it can receive. It is, to common apprehension, a paradox; and even among political economists of reputation, I can hardly point to any, except Mr. Ricardo and M. Say, who have kept it constantly and steadily in view. Almost all others occasionally express themselves as if a person who buys commodities, the produce of labor, was an employer of labor, and created a demand for it as really, and in the same sense, as if he had bought the labor itself directly, by the payment of wages. It is no wonder that political economy advances slowly, when such a question as this still remains open at its very threshold. I apprehend, that if by demand for labor be meant the demand by which wages are raised, or the number of laborers in employment increased, demand for commodities does not constitute demand for labor. I conceive that a person who buys commodities and consumes them himself, does no good to the laboring classes; and that it is only by what he abstains from consuming, and expends in direct payments to laborers in exchange for labor, that he benefits the laboring classes, or adds anything to the amount of their employment.[14]

Present-day economists who are aware of this passage assume that it is wholly invalidated because it was based on the wages-fund theory, rather than on the marginal-productivity theory that has supplanted it.[15] Such a sweeping rejection, however, goes much too far.

It is of course true, notwithstanding Mill's argument, that $1,000 of saving and investment does not employ any *more* workers than $1,000 of consumer spending. But it

[13] *Principles,* Book I, Chap. V, § 9.

[14] *Loc. cit.*

[15] Cf., *e.g.,* A. C. Pigou, *Essays in Economics* (London: Macmillan, 1952), pp. 232-235 and Edwin Cannan, *A Review of Economic Theory,* p 109.

does help *to increase wage-rates,* because it helps to increase marginal labor productivity, whereas direct consumer spending does nothing in the long run to increase wage-rates, because it does nothing to increase productivity. If there had been nothing but consumer spending (plus mere capital replacement) since the seventeenth century, wages would still be at the miserable levels of that period, and two-thirds to three-quarters of the present world population would not have come into existence.

Mill, though much of his argument was mistaken, was right as against Keynes in at least emphasizing that "the demand by which wages are *raised*" is in the long run only investment demand, not consumer demand.

But I come now to a far more important quotation from Mill, a set of passages amazing in their anticipation of, and masterly answers to, the Keynesian fallacies. Mill was able to anticipate and answer these because, as we have seen, most of them are very old, dating back to the seventeenth century and earlier.

The book from which the following passages are taken is Mill's *Essays on Some Unsettled Questions of Political Economy.* These essays were actually written in 1829 and 1830 (when Mill was twenty-four), some eighteen years before the appearance of his *Principles of Political Economy* in 1848; but they were not published until 1844. Unlike the *Principles,* which has run into perhaps sixty editions,[16] these essays are difficult to come by. (In 1948 the London School of Economics included the work in its "series of reprints of scarce works on political economy" by making a photolithographic reproduction of the first edition of 1844.)

It is perhaps this lack of availability which accounts for the astonishing fact that in the whole of the Keynesian controversy of the last quarter century, Mill's remarkable essay, "Of the Influence of Consumption on Production,"

16 Cf. Michael St. John Packe, *The Life of John Stuart Mill* (New York: Macmillan, 1954), p. 310.

has not been quoted (so far as my knowledge goes) by either the "pro" or the "anti" Keynesians. To come upon it, after long trudging in the Keynesian bog, has something of the same excitement for the student of the "new economics" as Biblical scholars must have felt when they discovered and deciphered the Dead Sea scrolls. It is the rediscovery of a long-buried treasure.

Because this twenty-eight-page essay is so hard to come by, I shall quote from it at some length. But first I should like to advert once more to the curious intellectual paralysis that seems to seize so many contemporary economists where the theories of Keynes are concerned. When they find gross errors, they still cannot convince themselves that all the reputational smoke was without a justifying fire, and they try to find *some* original contribution that Keynes must have made. Even John H. Williams, after a very able critique of Keynes, in which he predicts that "the wave of enthusiasm for the 'new economics' will, in the longer perspective, seem to us extravagant," draws back, worries about his own "bias," tries "objectively" to appraise Keynes's contribution, and concludes: "Beyond question it was very great. . . . What he has given us, in particular, is a much stronger sense than we had before of the need for consumption analysis." [17]

Did we need this "stronger sense"? Let us listen to Mill in 1830:

> Among the mistakes [of the pre-classical writers] which were most pernicious in their direct consequences . . . was the immense importance attached to consumption. The great end of legislation in matters of national wealth . . . was to create consumers. . . . This object, under the varying names of an extensive demand, a brisk circulation, a great expenditure of money, and sometimes *totidem verbis* a large consumption, was conceived to be the great condition of prosperity.

[17] *American Economic Review,* May, 1948, p. 289.

> It is not necessary, in the present state of the science, to contest this doctrine in the most flagrantly absurd of its forms or of its applications. The utility of a large government expenditure, for the purpose of encouraging industry, is no longer maintained. . . .
>
> In opposition to these palpable absurdities, it was triumphantly established by political economists, that consumption never needs encouragement. . . . The person who saves his income is no less a consumer than he who spends it: he consumes it in a different way; it supplies food and clothing to be consumed, tools and materials to be used, by productive laborers. Consumption, therefore, already takes place to the greatest extent which the amount of production admits of; but, of the two kinds of consumption, reproductive and unproductive, the former alone adds to the national wealth, the latter impairs it. What is consumed for mere enjoyment, is gone; what is consumed for reproduction, leaves commodities of equal value, commonly with the addition of a profit. The usual effect of the attempts of government to encourage consumption, is merely to prevent saving; that is, to promote unproductive consumption at the expense of reproductive, and diminish the national wealth by the very means which were intended to increase it.
>
> What a country wants to make it richer, is never consumption, but production. Where there is the latter, we may be sure that there is no want of the former. To produce, implies that the producer desires to consume; why else should he give himself useless labor? He may not wish to consume what he himself produces, but his motive for producing and selling is the desire to buy. Therefore, if the producers generally produce and sell more and more, they certainly also buy more and more.

But then Mill, with characteristic conscientiousness, wants to make sure "that no scattered particles of important truth are buried and lost in the ruins of exploded error." He proceeds, therefore, to examine "the nature of the appearances which gave rise to the belief that a great demand . . . a rapid consumption . . . are a cause of national prosperity."

After a few pages, Mill makes the admission (which, according to the Keynesians, no classical economist ever made) that "at all times a very large proportion" of capital may be "lying idle. The annual produce of a country is never any thing approaching in magnitude to what it might be if all the resources devoted to reproduction, if all the capital, in short, of the country, were in *full employment*." (My italics.)

"This perpetual non-employment of a large proportion of capital," Mill continues, "is the price we pay for the division of labor. The purchase is worth what it costs; but the price is considerable."

After enlarging upon this for ten pages, Mill calls attention to the folly of the inflationary remedy:

> From what has been already said, it is obvious that periods of "brisk demand" are also the periods of greatest production: the national capital is never called into full employment but at those periods. This, however, is no reason for desiring such times; it is not desirable that the whole capital of the country should be in full employment. For, the calculations of producers and traders being of necessity imperfect, there are always some commodities which are more or less in excess, as there are always some which are in deficiency. If, therefore, the whole truth were known, there would always be some classes of producers contracting, not extending, their operations. If *all* are endeavoring to extend them, it is a certain proof that some general delusion is afloat. The commonest cause of such delusion is some general, or very extensive, rise of prices (whether caused by speculation or by the currency) which persuades all dealers that they are growing rich. And hence, an increase of production really takes place during the progress of depreciation, as long as the existence of depreciation is not suspected. . . . But when the delusion vanishes and the truth is disclosed, those whose commodities are relatively in excess must diminish their production or be ruined: and if during the high prices they have built mills and erected machinery, they will be likely to repent at leisure.

The believers in Say's Law, and the classical school generally, have been accused by the Keynesians of ignoring the very existence of business cycles. True, Mill did not have the phrase. But he points out how:

> Unreasonable hopes and unreasonable fears alternately rule with tyrannical sway over the minds of a majority of the mercantile public; general eagerness to buy and general reluctance to buy, succeed one another in a manner more or less marked, at brief intervals. Except during short periods of transition, there is almost always either great briskness of business or great stagnation; either the principal producers of almost all the leading articles of industry have as many orders as they can possibly execute, or the dealers in almost all commodities have their warehouses full of unsold goods.
>
> In this last case, it is commonly said that there is a general superabundance; and as those economists who have contested the possibility of general superabundance, would none of them deny the possibility or even the frequent occurrence of the phenomenon which we have just noticed, it would seem incumbent on them to show, that the expression to which they object is not applicable to a state of things in which all or most commodities remain unsold, in the same sense in which there is said to be a superabundance of any one commodity when it remains in the warehouses of dealers for want of a market.

He proceeds, then, to the following exposition of Say's Law (though he never mentions it by that name):

> Whoever offers a commodity for sale, desires to obtain a commodity in exchange for it, and is therefore a buyer by the mere fact of his being a seller. The sellers and the buyers, for all commodities taken together, must, by the metaphysical necessity of the case, be an exact equipoise to each other; and if there be more sellers than buyers of one thing, there must be more buyers than sellers for another.
>
> This argument is evidently founded on the supposition of a state of barter; and, on that supposition, it is perfectly incontestable. When two persons perform an act of barter, each of them is at once a seller and a buyer. He cannot sell with-

out buying. Unless he chooses to buy some other person's commodity, he does not sell his own.

If, however, we suppose that money is used, these propositions cease to be exactly true. . . . Interchange by means of money is therefore, as has been often observed, ultimately nothing but barter. But there is this difference—that in the case of barter, the selling and the buying are simultaneously confounded in one operation; you sell what you have, and buy what you want, by one indivisible act, and you cannot do the one without doing the other. Now the effect of the employment of money, and even the utility of it, is, that it enables this one act of interchange to be divided into two separate acts or operations; one of which may be performed now, and the other a year hence, or whenever it shall be most convenient. Although he who sells, really sells only to buy, he need not buy at the same moment when he sells; and he does not therefore necessarily add to the *immediate* demand for one commodity when he adds to the supply of another. The buying and selling being now separated, it may very well occur, that there may be, at some given time, a very general inclination to sell with as little delay as possible, accompanied with an equally general inclination to defer all purchases as long as possible. This is always actually the case, in those periods which are described as periods of general excess. And no one, after sufficient explanation, will contest the possibility of general excess, in this sense of the word. The state of things which we have just described, and which is of no uncommon occurrence, amounts to it.

For when there is a general anxiety to sell, and a general disinclination to buy, commodities of all kinds remain for a long time unsold, and those which find an immediate market, do so at a very low price. . . . There is stagnation to those who are not obliged to sell, and distress to those who are. . . .

In order to render the argument for the impossibility of an excess of all commodities applicable to the case in which a circulating medium is employed, money must itself be considered as a commodity. It must, undoubtedly, be admitted that there cannot be an excess of all other commodities, and an excess of money at the same time.

But those who have, at periods such as we have described,

> affirmed that there was an excess of all commodities, never pretended that money was one of these commodities; they held that there was not an excess, but a deficiency of the circulating medium. What they called a general superabundance, was not a superabundance of commodities relatively to commodities, but a superabundance of all commodities relatively to money.

Mill then discusses "liquidity preference" (once more without benefit of having the phrase):

> What it amounted to was, that persons in general, at that particular time, from a general expectation of being called upon to meet sudden demands, liked better to possess money than any other commodity. Money, consequently, was in request, and all other commodities were in comparative disrepute. In extreme cases, money is collected in masses, and hoarded; in the milder cases, people merely defer parting with their money, or coming under any new engagements to part with it. But the result is, that all commodities fall in price, or become unsaleable. . . .
>
> It is, however, of the utmost importance to observe that excess of all commodities, in the only sense in which it is possible, means only a temporary fall in their value relatively to money. To suppose that the markets for all commodities could, in any other sense than this, be overstocked, involves the absurdity that commodities may fall in value relatively to themselves.

Mill next turns to the Keynes-Hansen bogey of a "mature economy," though he had perhaps the good fortune not to know that phrase. He treats it as a fallacy discredited at least a generation before 1830:

> The argument against the possibility of general overproduction is quite conclusive, so far as it applies to the doctrine that a country may accumulate capital too fast; that produce in general may, by increasing faster than the demand for it, reduce all producers to distress. This proposition, strange to say, was almost a received doctrine as lately as thirty years ago; and the merit of those who have exploded

it is much greater than might be inferred from the extreme obviousness of its absurdity when it is stated in its native simplicity. It is true that if all the wants of all the inhabitants of a country were fully satisfied, no further capital could find useful employment; but, in that case, none would be accumulated. So long as there remain any persons not possessed, we do not say of subsistence, but of the most refined luxuries, and who would work to possess them, there is employment for capital. . . . Nothing can be more chimerical than the fear that the accumulation of capital should produce poverty and not wealth, or that it will ever take place too fast for its own end. Nothing is more true than that it is produce which constitutes the market for produce, and that every increase of production, if distributed without miscalculation among all kinds of produce in the proportion which private interest would dictate, creates, or rather constitutes its own demand.

This is the truth which the deniers of general over-production have seized and enforced. . . .

And in a final paragraph, Mill sums up:

The essentials of the doctrine are preserved when it is allowed that there cannot be permanent excess of production, or of accumulation; though it be at the same time admitted, that as there may be a temporary excess of any one article considered separately, so may there of commodities generally, not in consequence of over-production, but of a want of commercial confidence.

If Keynes and the Keynesians had known of this essay, and read and pondered it in time, we might have been spared the dreary and sterile economic "revolution" of the last quarter-century.

8. *J. A. Hobson and Major Douglas*

Only a comparatively short discussion is now required on the ideas of J. A. Hobson, from whom Keynes next quotes extensively. Hobson, fortunately, states his theory so clearly that his errors are easily detected and answered: "I hardly realised that in appearing to question the virtue of unlimited thrift I had committed the unpardonable sin" (p. 366). Of course *unlimited* thrift, if words have any meaning, would mean that nobody would spend any part of his income at all—an adventure in race suicide which no sane man has ever recommended. In the problem of the optimum relationship of saving to spending, what we are discussing is ratios and quantities, and none of these are specified in any of the quotations from Hobson that Keynes presents. Hobson habitually attacks "an *undue* exercise of the habit of saving" (p. 367), "any *undue* exercise of this habit" (p. 367), "*undue* saving" (p. 368, my italics); and of course whatever is "undue" is condemned by the adjective itself. If by "undue" saving Hobson means *sudden, unusual,* and *unexpected* saving, to which the previous volume or balance of production was unadjusted, then such saving is of course unsettling. But even here we do not know whether this sudden saving is the real cause of the harm done unless we know whether it is completely irrational and *uncaused,* or whether it is itself a natural or rational consequence of some *preceding* disturbing factor.

In any case, it is clear that Hobson believes in the existence of "*general* overproduction" (p. 367). And it is Say's Law, properly understood, which tells us that *general* overproduction is impossible. What is possible is only *unbalanced* production, *misdirected* production, production *of the wrong things.* But we have now been over this point too often to need to elaborate upon it once again.

This Section VII of Chapter 23 might have been entitled by Keynes: *Myself and Some Eminent Predecessors Who Have Never Understood Say's Law.*

Keynes closes with a few words on Major Douglas: "Since the war there has been a spate of heretical theories of underconsumption, of which those of Major Douglas are the most famous" (p. 370). Of course since the appearance of the *General Theory* the most famous heretical theory of underconsumption is Keynes's own. But Keynes goes on: "The detail of [Douglas's] diagnosis, in particular the so-called A + B theorem, includes much mere mystification" (p. 371).

And is there no needless mystification in the Keynesian I + C theorem, or in the S = Y — C theorem, or in the Z = ø(N) theorem, or in the $\Delta N = k\Delta N_2$ theorem, etc., etc.?

Chapter XXIV

KEYNES LETS HIMSELF GO

In his final chapter—"Concluding Notes on the Social Philosophy Towards Which the General Theory Might Lead"—Keynes really lets himself go. Here he assumes that all his previous propositions have been proved, and draws his triumphant and sweeping conclusions. This chapter, therefore, is even more tightly packed with fallacies and unwarranted deductions than any of the others. But it has the advantage of stating its fallacies in relatively clear and untechnical language, and it will therefore give us the opportunity also of reviewing them in clearer and less technical language than heretofore.

1. *Inequalities of Income*

"The outstanding faults of the economic society in which we live," Keynes begins, "are its failure to provide for full employment and its arbitrary and inequitable distribution of wealth and incomes" (p. 372).

There are four chief things wrong with this statement:

(1) The vagueness of Keynes's "full employment" concept (to which we shall return later for closer examination).

(2) Prolonged mass unemployment is not the fault of our economic "society," but of governmental interventions in labor-management relations, wage-rates, and money and banking policy—the very kind of intervention that Keynes wished to increase.

(3) The distribution of wealth and incomes is in the main neither "arbitrary" nor "inequitable" in a competitive free market system. As John Bates Clark showed so

brilliantly in "The Distribution of Wealth" (1899) "free competition tends to give to labor what labor creates, to capitalists what capital creates, and to entrepreneurs what the coordinating function creates." Individual inequities are bound to occur, but they are not systematic. Capitalism itself tends constantly to reduce them by its rewards to production. If we are looking for really "arbitrary" and "inequitable" distribution, we can find it in the East, or in backward and "underdeveloped" countries, or in Communist Russia and China—in short, in either pre-capitalistic or socialist societies.

(4) It is even a misnomer in capitalist countries to call this process "distribution." Income and wealth are not "distributed" but produced, and in general go to those who produce them.

But even if all this were not true, there is no reason to suppose that the Keynesian nostrums would remedy the situation.

Keynes next goes on to praise the "significant progress" brought about by the progressive income tax and death duties (a "progress" that economists are coming increasingly to doubt).

> Up to the point where full employment prevails [he tells us], the growth of capital depends not at all on a low propensity to consume but is, on the contrary, held back by it (pp. 372-373). An increase in the habitual propensity to consume will in general (*i.e.*, except in conditions of full employment) serve to increase at the same time the inducement to invest" (p. 373). The growth of wealth, so far from being dependent on the abstinence of the rich, as is commonly supposed, is more likely to be impeded by it. One of the chief social justifications of great inequality of wealth is, therefore, removed (p. 373).

How marvelous is the Keynesian world! The more you spend the more you save. The more you eat your cake, the more cake you have. The less you save the more inducement you have to invest. But there is, perhaps, a flaw in this logic. Even Keynes has insisted that saving and investment must be equal. As you can only invest what you save, the less you save the less you are able to invest—no matter how great the "inducement" to invest. Moreover, it is not excessive saving that creates unemployment, but excessive wage-rates—wage-rates, that is, above the marginal-productivity point. But we have been over and over all this ground before.

There follows a long paragraph in which Keynes concedes that "there is social and psychological justification for significant inequalities of incomes and wealth, but not for such large disparities as exist today" (p. 374). It appears that "there are valuable human activities which require the motive of money-making," but "much lower stakes will serve the purpose equally well," and "the task of transmuting human nature must not be confused with the task of managing it."

This paragraph is revelatory. It betrays the totalitarian touch. It shows Keynes in the role of "father knows best." He and his friends know, just by personal judgment, exactly what rewards and penalties are necessary. The people are to be "managed" by the Keynesian elite. A man does not have a right to keep what he earns; but allowing him to keep *some* of it is a gracious privilege in which a government clique of omniscient Keynesians may indulge him, like allowing a child to have just a little candy.

Just what (except expediency) prevented Keynes from announcing himself a complete socialist I do not know. What he seemed to want was a government-managed economy that would *imitate* some of the features of capitalism.

2. *The Euthanasia of the Rentier*

Keynes next turns back to his theory of the rate of interest.

> The justification for a moderately high rate of interest has been found hitherto in the necessity of providing a sufficient

inducement to save. But we have shown that the extent of effective saving is necessarily determined by the scale of investment and that the scale of investment is promoted by a *low* rate of interest. . . . Thus it is to our best advantage to reduce the rate of interest to that point relatively to the schedule of the marginal efficiency of capital at which there is full employment. There can be no doubt that this criterion will lead to a much lower rate of interest than has ruled hitherto . . . (p. 375).

Now many (non-Keynesian) economists are not sure that the inducement to save increases in direct proportion to the rate of interest. We need not go into the pros and cons of this argument, except to point out that a certain *minimum* interest rate is necessary to induce, if not saving, at least *investment,* which Keynes tells us is his main interest. (Keynes persistently thinks of investment as merely what a borrowing entrepreneur puts into his own business; I am here using the term to mean also any loan that a man makes with his savings, the purchase of a bond, etc.)

When Keynes tells us that "the scale of effective saving is necessarily determined by the scale of investment," he forgets that the primary causation is the other way round. Saving determines investment. Without saving, there is nothing to invest. Even on Keynes's own definitions, investment cannot come into being without equivalent savings. To say that "the scale of investment is promoted by a *low* rate of interest" is to look at the matter solely from the point of view of the borrower, and to forget the point of view of the lender.

Suppose we applied Keynes's dictums to buying and selling. We would then write something like this: "Buying is not determined by purchasing power, but effective purchasing power is determined by the scale of buying; and the scale of buying is promoted by *low* prices." This would be immediately recognized as nonsense. Even a Keynesian might be expected to see that the scale of *selling* (or of *producing* for sale) is promoted by *high* prices which give the highest inducement to produce. Of course, in practice, the maximum production, buying, and selling are achieved by the right *equilibrium* price—the price which does most to harmonize the desires and incentives of producers, sellers, buyers, and consumers respectively.

So it is with interest rates. The interest rate that promotes the maximum saving, lending, borrowing, and investment is neither the highest interest rate nor the lowest interest rate, but an *equilibrium* interest rate at which the greatest numbers of desires and incentives of both lenders and borrowers are reconciled.

Keynes's theory of the interest rate, like his emphasis on the monetary income of consumers and on the "propensity to consume," is purely a *demand* theory. Just as he seems to think in terms solely of the propensity to spend and buy, and not of the propensity to work or produce or sell, so he thinks solely of the incentive to borrow, and ignores the need of the incentive to save and to lend. When he takes account of the latter incentive, he does so only to denounce it as anti-social and wicked.

How does Keynes know that "there can be no doubt" that a rate of interest fixed in accordance with "the marginal efficiency of capital at which there is full employment" will be "a much lower rate of interest than has ruled hitherto"? Apparently because his personal feelings tell him so. "I feel sure that the demand for capital is strictly limited in the sense that it would not be difficult to increase the stock of capital up to a point where its marginal efficiency had fallen to a very low figure," where the return from capital instruments "would have to cover little more than their exhaustion by wastage and obsolescence" (p. 375).

Insofar as there is any argument at all for the conclusion on page 375, it seems to rest on the question-begging assumption that unemployment is the result of excessive interest rates rather than excessive wage-rates. Keynes does not appear to understand even the main purpose of capital and capital goods. That purpose is not merely to increase output, and to produce consumer goods that could not otherwise be produced, but to reduce costs of production.

Why would anybody invest in capital goods if he got no net return worth speaking of? Let us take, for example, a house that costs $20,000 to build. One can understand that a man might build such a house to live in himself. One can understand that he might build it to rent out to someone else—provided, of course, that he got a good deal more rent than simply enough to cover exhaustion by wastage and obsolescence. But suppose he were asked, instead, to lend a mortgage for the full value of such a house, to enable someone else to build it to rent out to still a third person. It is obvious that, in order to induce him to do this, the interest offered would have to be equal to the presumptive rent of the house minus the annual estimated depreciation, compensation for the worry and trouble of management (the landlord function), and relative protection against the risks of vacancy and of real estate speculation. The mortgagee's return, in short, is intimately connected with the prospective return of the legal owner of the building.

This is merely a special case of the constant close relationship between the rate of interest and the marginal yield of specific capital goods. If the intended mortgagee were not offered such a return, he would not lend the money; if the builder of the house were not allowed to charge a rent making it worth while, he would not build houses, either with his own money or somebody else's.

How, then, would Keynes force down interest rates and even the return to the entrepreneur and still get his saving, investment, and production? What he really has in mind, apparently, is *seizing the money through taxation and creating forced "investment" through the government.*

Does my assumption go too far? Then listen to this:

> Though this state of affairs [just about enough return to cover cost of capital replacement] would be quite compatible with some measure of individualism, yet it would mean the

euthanasia of the rentier, and, consequently, the euthanasia of the cumulative oppressive power of the capitalist to exploit the scarcity-value of capital (pp. 375-576).

For the light it throws on the heart of Keynes's message and on the popularity of his ideas among leftists, this sentence is one of the most revealing in the book. Notice how patronizingly individualism (*i.e.*, individual liberty) is treated. Keynes would graciously allow "some measure of" it. But he insists on "the euthanasia of the rentier." Euthanasia means painless death. That is, the death of the rentier would be painless to *Keynes*. There is an old proverb that if you want to hang a dog you must first call him mad. If you want to knock a man down you should first give him a bad name. So Keynes uses the French *rentier* as a smear word. The rentier is the terrible fellow who saves a little money and puts it in a savings bank. Or he buys a bond of United States Steel, and uses his cumulative oppressive power as a capitalist to exploit the U. S. Steel Corporation.

All this is demagogy and claptrap. It differs from the Marxist brand only in technical detail.

3. *Robbing the Productive*

Interest today [Keynes goes on] rewards no genuine sacrifice, any more than does the rent of land. The owner of capital can obtain interest because capital is scarce, just as the owner of land can obtain rent because land is scarce. But whilst there may be intrinsic reasons for the scarcity of land, there can be no intrinsic reasons for the scarcity of capital. . . . Even so, it will still be possible for communal saving through the agency of the State to be maintained at a level which will allow the growth of capital up to the point where it ceases to be scarce (p. 376).

How does Keynes know that interest rewards no genuine sacrifice? Certainly savers in moderate circumstances are constantly making sacrifices of immediate gratifications in order to save for a home, for the education of their children, or against possible ill-health. What does Keynes know about the individual sacrifices, abstentions, and choices of individual savers?

And does the rent of land reward no genuine sacrifice? Doesn't Keynes know that the capital and rental value of most land in the civilized world today is in large part the result of the capital that has gone into the roads and other communications that lead to it, as well as the clearing, leveling, draining, irrigation, plowing, fertilization, and building that have been put into it—all at a capital cost?

What does Keynes mean when he declares that "there are no intrinsic reasons for the scarcity of capital"? Isn't the greatest and sufficient intrinsic reason the fact that (in America, for example) there was no capital at all when we got here, and all of it had to be created by somebody? By some people's work and saving, even if some of them wouldn't have been admitted into the Bloomsbury circle? There is still scarcity of capital simply and solely because not enough of it has been created by work and saving.

Incidentally, people are not rewarded in economic life for "sacrifice," but simply for producing something that somebody else wants enough to be willing to pay for. I don't pay the General Motors Corporation $3,000 to reward its "sacrifice" in producing an Oldsmobile; I pay it because I want the Oldsmobile. If a man turns out something that you or I don't want, we are not interested in how much sacrifice his product cost him; it is not up to us to reward him for producing something for which we can find no use. In Keynes's topsy-turvy economics, in which only "genuine sacrifice" is rewarded, we would pay nothing to an inventor, musical composer, artist, or author unless he could prove that he didn't actually *enjoy* inventing, composing, painting, or writing.

To say that the owner of capital or the owner of land exploits "scarcity" is merely an ominous way of saying that *all* economic value is scarcity value. A market price for anything whatever can be obtained only because that thing is relatively scarce, in the sense that it is not a free gift of nature.

Keynes's economics of abundance for capital goods could be set down as a dream world, if it were not for the final sentence from Keynes quoted above. There he tacitly admits that savings and capital will not be forthcoming on the practically non-existent return that he proposes. But then, ah! the State steps in, the magical State, *seizes* the capital through taxation and does its own "investing."

Only the long-run result of this, of course, would be to reduce production and to make real capital scarcer than ever.

Keynes goes on: "I see, therefore, the rentier aspect of capitalism as a transitional phase which will disappear when it has done its work" (p. 376). This sentence implies the Hegelian-Marxian "stage" theory of history—except that nothing previous in the theory of Keynes explains what the work of the "rentier aspect" actually was. According to his theory, the rentier *always* demanded a rate of interest that was too high, and for some inscrutable reason was able to get it. As the rentier, in brief, according to Keynesian theory, never had any excuse for existing in the first place, he never did any work except to hold up economic progress and produce unemployment.

> And with the disappearance of its rentier aspect [Keynes goes on] much else in it besides will suffer a sea-change. It will be, moreover, a great advantage of the order of events which I am advocating, that the euthanasia of the rentier, of the functionless investor, will be nothing sudden, merely a gradual but prolonged continuance of what we have seen recently in Great Britain, and will need no revolution (p. 376).

This is all very reassuring. The rentier will be killed off quietly, because he will be unable to offer any resistance, and Britain will enjoy that marvelous prosperity (?) that followed her adoption of the Keynesian remedies. (Although after years of cheap money following the appearance of the *General Theory*—a bank rate of 2 per cent in 1937, 1948, 1950, etc.,—the Bank of England was finally forced to tighten up to a discount rate of 7 per cent in September of 1957.)

But what about "the functionless investor"? Here, I think, Keynes's pen inadvertently slipped. The *investor* (by his previous definition) has hitherto been his hero, his entrepreneur, exploited by that real villain, the *saver*. Did not the investor serve a function by earning and saving enough to become an investor? Did he not serve another function by making a choice of which project or firm to invest in and which not to invest in? But Keynes is really waxing eloquent now, and we should not interrupt him by these trivial questions.

> [He goes on] Thus we might aim in practice (there being nothing in this which is unattainable) at an increase in the volume of capital until it ceases to be scarce, so that the functionless investor will no longer receive a bonus; and at a scheme of direct taxation which allows the intelligence and determination and executive skill of the financier, the entrepreneur *et hoc genus omne* (who are certainly so fond of their craft that their labor could be obtained much cheaper than at present), to be harnessed to the service of the community on reasonable terms of reward (pp. 376-377).

In reply, it may be pointed out that capital will cease to be "scarce" only when it ceases to have value, so that anybody will be willing to give it away. It will cease to have value only when it either costs nothing to produce, or when its application ceases to reduce the costs (including time) of production of anything, or when the consumer goods that it helps to turn out themselves cease to be "scarce" and to have value—all of which conditions are impossible. The application of capital increases technological progress; and technological progress itself makes old machines and materials obsolete at the expense of new machines and materials. So capital, by aiding progress, automatically increases the need and value and "scarcity" of new capital for new applications.

Keynes's scheme of "direct taxation" is a scheme to rob the productive in order to reward the unproductive. It tries to exploit the fact that certain entrepreneurs (like certain poets, musicians, artists, scientists) are "fond of their craft." But the attempt to exploit these, to treat them like draft horses, to pay them just enough to keep them working, would have one flaw. Other entrepreneurs work primarily for the rewards in it, and when these are cut down below a sufficient inducement, they play golf or choose some other alternative—as the results of the expropriatory rates of the existing income tax are proving every day. It is obvious from Keynes's tone that he had an ill-concealed contempt, as befitted a member of the Bloomsbury circle, for the business entrepreneur.

Keynes concludes this section by writing: "It would remain for separate decision on what scale and by what means it is right and reasonable to call on the living generation to restrict their consumption, so as to establish, in course of time, a state of full investment for their successors" (p. 377). But people have already been deciding this question as *individuals* and *voluntarily,* and not by collective compulsion (except through progressive income and inheritance taxes and so-called State "investment"). Having rejected the voluntary solution, Keynes is forced to look for a solution through compulsion, such as that made by totalitarian governments.

Incidentally, "full investment," as we have seen, is a silly and meaningless phrase. It fails to recognize the illimitable improvements that are always possible in *quality,* and it is based on purely static assumptions. What becomes of "full investment" in a particular machine, for example, when a new machine or process is invented that makes the old one obsolete?

4. *The Socialization of Investment*

And now Keynes has a few kind and condescending words to say about a free and voluntary economic system. But beware of Keynes when he brings gifts! "In some other respects," he begins, "the foregoing theory is moderately conservative in its implications. . . . There are wide fields of activity which are unaffected" (pp. 377-378). Of course the state will have to increase "the propensity to consume" (*i.e.,* discourage saving), and it must fix (*i.e.,* lower) the rate of interest; and there must be "a somewhat comprehensive socialization of investment," but "beyond this no obvious case can be made out for a system of State socialism which would embrace most of the economic life of the community" (p. 378).

It is hard to believe that Keynes is as naive as he pretends, and that hc is not laughing up his sleeve. The rate of interest—the valuation of time and of all investments—is to be taken out of the market and put completely in the hands of the State. But Keynes ignores the complete interconnectedness of all prices. This especially includes the price of capital loans, any State tinkering with which must necessarily affect and distort all prices and price relationships throughout the economy. Through its socialized investment, moreover, the State would decide which firms or industries to expand and which to freeze or contract. Even though the State did not technically own the instruments of production, this would lead to a *de facto* socialism.

Keynes continues: "But if our central controls succeed in establishing an aggregate volume of output corresponding to full employment as nearly as practicable, the classical theory comes into its own again from this point onwards" (p. 378).

Let's see. The free market system (which is what Keynes means by "the classical theory") is incapable, according to him, of properly fixing the volume of money and credit, or the proper rate of interest, or the right volume and direction of investment, or the right volume of output, or adequate employment. But outside of that very little can be said against it! Yet Keynesians solemnly cite selected sentences of the sort I have just quoted in order to prove that Keynes was really a conservative, and aside from one or two minor reservations, a disciple of the classical economy!

It is worth noting that though he talks constantly in this chapter as in others of "full employment," he never mentions excessive wage-rates as a possible cause of unemployment or suggests any government interference with them. These are to be left, as before, to the labor-union leaders, which are to continue to enjoy legal privileges and immunities denied to all other groups.

> If we suppose the volume of output to be given, [Keynes continues] *i.e.*, to be determined by forces outside the classical scheme of thought, then . . . private self-interest will determine what in particular is produced, in what proportions the factors of production will be combined to produce it, and how the value of the final product will be distributed between them (pp. 378-379).

This passage is an obvious self-contradiction. If the State determines *how much* will be invested, *at what interest rate,* and just *where,* it necessarily determines what in particular is produced and with what factors. Keynes's scheme would take all of this out of private hands. He merely refuses to recognize the implications of his own proposals.

Keynes continues his patronizing attitude toward personal liberty: "There will still remain a wide field for the exercise of private initiative and responsibility. Within this field the traditional advantages of individualism will still hold good" (p. 380). I suppose one example of this would be the progressive income tax, so warmly approved by Keynes, which, in the United States, at the time of writing, rises to 91 per cent on the highest brackets. But the individual is still allowed to retain and spend 9 per cent of any additional money he earns (if it is not taken by state taxes) as a wide field for the exercise of his private initiative.

> Let us stop for a moment [Keynes goes on] to remind ourselves what these advantages are. They are partly advantages of efficiency—the advantages of decentralization and of the play of self-interest. The advantage to efficiency of the decentralization of decisions and of individual responsibility is even greater, perhaps, than the nineteenth century supposed; and the reaction against the appeal to self-interest may have gone too far (p. 380).

Well, after 379 pages talking about all the alleged damage done by individual responsibility and self-interest, it seems a little late, on the fourth page from the end, to begin a retraction. All this is, of course, only another self-contradiction. Government control of the volume of saving, of interest rates, and of investment, centralizes the *key* decisions, leaving only derivative and much less important decisions to individuals.

"But, above all," Keynes continues, "individualism, if it can be purged of its defects and its abuses, is the best safeguard of personal liberty in the sense that, compared with any other system, it greatly widens the field for the exercise of personal choice" (p. 380). This sententious declaration is mere tautology. Individualism not only "safeguards" personal liberty; it *means* personal liberty. And personal liberty means, of course, among other things, the freedom to exercise personal choice. The "abuses and defects" of which individualism is to be "purged" are, I presume, all the actions or decisions of which the bureaucrats happen to disapprove.

Keynes then goes on to praise, in a patronizing manner, "the variety of life, which emerges from this extended field of personal choice."

But this whole passage on page 380—and the whole chapter, in fact—is a series of self-contradictions. In it Keynes tries to get the best of both worlds—to insist on a government-controlled economy and to call it "individualism" and freedom of enterprise. As to his praise of "variety," why not competition and variety in interest rates, or competition and variety in investments? Why not "the exercise of personal choice" in making one's own investments with the money one has earned?

> Whilst, therefore [Keynes goes on], the enlargement of the functions of government . . . would seem to a nineteenth-century publicist or to a contemporary American financier to be a terrific encroachment on individualism, I defend it, on the contrary, both as the only practicable means of avoiding the destruction of existing economic forms in their entirety and as the condition of the successful functioning of individual initiative (p. 380).

In other words, the way to preserve individualism is to reject it, and in a central field. For investment is a key decision in the operation of any economic system. *And government investment is a form of socialism.* Only confusion of thought, or deliberate duplicity, would deny this. For socialism, as any dictionary would tell the Keynesians, means the ownership and control of the means of production by the government. Under the system proposed by Keynes, the government would *control* all investment in the means of production and would *own* the part it had itself directly invested. It is at best mere muddleheadness, therefore, to present the Keynesian nostrums as a free enterprise or "individualistic" *alternative* to socialism.

There follows a paragraph in which Keynes declares that

> if effective demand is deficient, not only is the public scandal of wasted resources intolerable, but the individual enterpriser who seeks to bring these resources into action is operating with the odds loaded against him. . . . The players *as a whole* will lose. . . . Hitherto the increment of the world's wealth has fallen short of the aggregate of positive individual savings; and the difference has been made up by the losses of those whose courage and initiative have not been supplemented by

exceptional skill or unusual good fortune. But if effective demand is adequate, average skill and average good fortune will be enough (pp. 380-381).

There is not a sentence in this quotation that is not based on some wrong assumption. Keynes's concept of "wasted resources," as W. H. Hutt has shown,[1] will not stand critical examination. There is much less real waste in frankly recognizing past malinvestment, and either scrapping it or allowing it to become periodically idle, than in trying to conceal its existence by a continuing inflation or by throwing good resources after bad. There is also, as Hutt has shown, a great deal of "pseudo-idleness," as in lawn mowers or phonographs or evening clothes which are used only occasionally, and whose services consist in their *availability*. Keynes particularly forgets this important "availability" service when he refers to cash balances as "hoarded" money.

Once again, net real "profits," by concept and definition, can go at best, under "normal" or static conditions, only to the more foresighted, skillful, or fortunate half of all entrepreneurs. The average entrepreneur tends to make just enough "profit" to compensate for the price of his own services if he worked for somebody else. The entrepreneurs with less than average foresight, skill, or luck will find themselves with losses. Only the better-than-average will achieve real profits.[2]

This general situation is not improved by continuous inflation, but merely concealed. The true situation is revealed again when allowance is made for the average lost purchasing power of money incomes received. Keynes offers no support whatever for his belief that the increment of the world's wealth has fallen short of the aggregate of positive individual savings. If this contention is true, it tends to show that the rate of interest, instead of being chronically too high, as Keynes never tires of repeating, has been chron-

[1] *The Theory of Idle Resources*, (London: Johnathan Cape, 1939).

[2] Cf. Frank H. Knight, *Risk, Uncertainty, and Profit* (Boston: Houghton Mifflin, 1921).

ically too *low* to compensate for risks. But the enormous increase in the world's wealth, and the vast accumulation of capital (say in America alone since the landing of the Pilgrims in 1620) hardly support his contention.

5. *The "Economic Causes of War"*

Keynes now follows with a section in which he offers his nostrum as a remedy for removing the alleged "economic causes of war." Strangely enough, he blames "domestic *laissez-faire* and an international gold standard" as the causes of "the competitive struggle for markets" (p. 382) between nations.

All this, of course, is the exact opposite of the truth. Under an international gold standard and freedom of trade, there was a competition between *individuals* or between *firms* for foreign and domestic business, but not between *nations* as such. Several American firms might bid against each other for a foreign contract, and if German firms were also bidding for it, they would be competing with each other as much as with the American firms. It is *nationalism,* it is the nonsensical concept of a "balance of trade" that does not take care of itself but can only be obtained by government intervention, that causes the *nationalistic* "struggle for markets."

Keynes denounces international trade as of the time that he was writing as "a desperate expedient to maintain employment at home by forcing sales on foreign markets and restricting purchases," whereas, under Keynesian economics, "if nations can learn to provide themselves with full employment by their domestic policy . . . there need be no important economic forces calculated to set the interest of one country against that of its neighbors" (pp. 382-383).

None of this bears much relation to the truth. Under a system of *laissez faire* (*i.e.,* free trade at home and free trade abroad) and an international gold standard, individuals buy what they need wherever they can get it cheapest. They sell in the best market. They do not think nationalistically. And so far as the international gold standard is concerned, nations can stay on it only by keeping their interest rates and their obligations in term of gold in equilibrium with those prevailing in the rest of the world. It is precisely the Keynesian system, with its *nationalistic* fixing of interest rates, with its domestic inflationism and its tricky devaluations of national currencies, that turns the struggle for a "favorable balance of trade" and for "foreign markets" into an *international* struggle. And it is precisely because this system seeks to maintain "full employment" by domestic-currency, interest-rate, and investment tricks, by disregarding the imbalance of production so brought about, and by disregarding the loss from failure to take full advantage of the international division of labor, that it is also a far less efficient system.

6. *The Power of Ideas*

We have been forced to be critical, and sometimes harshly so, about every chapter of Keynes's *General Theory* and every leading proposition it contains. I am sorry for this for more reasons than one. The present book would have been much shorter, the author would have been saved many dreary hours of analysis, and the reader's time would also have been economized, if there were fewer propositions and deductions in the *General Theory* with which one was forced to disagree. So it is with special pleasure that I turn to the final paragraph of the *General Theory,* for here at last we are able to say that Keynes has written something profoundly true and wise and memorably eloquent:

> The ideas of economists and political philosophers, both when they are right and when they are wrong, are more powerful than is commonly understood. Indeed the world is ruled by little else. Practical men, who believe themselves to be quite exempt from any intellectual influences, are usually the slaves of some defunct economist. Madmen in authority,

> who hear voices in the air, are distilling their frenzy from some academic scribbler of a few years back. I am sure that the power of vested interests is vastly exaggerated compared with the gradual encroachment of ideas. Not, indeed, immediately, but after a certain interval; for in the field of economic and political philosophy there are not many who are influenced by new theories after they are twenty-five or thirty years of age, so that the ideas which civil servants and politicians and even agitators apply to current events are not likely to be the newest. But soon or late, it is ideas, not vested interests, which are dangerous for good or evil.

And what a crowning irony that the "defunct economist," and "academic scribbler of a few years back," whose ideas are being applied by civil servants and politicians and agitators, should now be none other than John Maynard Keynes himself!

Chapter XXV

DID KEYNES RECANT?

1. *"The Classical Medicine"*

There is a persistent belief among many non-Keynesians that Keynes recanted the doctrines expounded in the *General Theory* toward the end of his life. The belief is based in part on reported conversations with friends, but the only public evidence I can think of is an article which appeared in the June, 1946, edition of *The Economic Journal* called "The Balance of Payments of the United States." Fifteen of its seventeen pages are concerned precisely with the subject of the title. They are a sympathetic study of the balance of payments of the United States and an attempt to forecast what it will be over the next five to ten years. We need not analyze either the arguments or the forecasts in these fifteen pages, which are either irrelevant to our present purpose or outdated. What concerns us are the final two pages. Here Keynes declares:

> I find myself moved, not for the first time, to remind contemporary economists that the classical teaching embodied some permanent truths of great significance, which we are liable today to overlook because we associate them with other doctrines which we cannot now accept without much qualification. There are in these matters deep undercurrents at work, natural forces, one can call them, or even the invisible hand, which are operating towards equilibrium. If it were not so, we could not have got on even so well as we have for many decades past.

This passage discloses a dawning suspicion on Keynes's part that the *General Theory* may have gone too far. But it still fails to show a real understanding of "the classical teaching." For there is nothing mysterious or occult about the forces which operate towards equilibrium. They are simply the result, in a system of freedom, of the efforts of producers to maximize their profits and the efforts of consumers to maximize their satisfactions.

Adam Smith's "invisible hand" was a brilliant metaphor but, rightly interpreted, nothing more than a metaphor. If the individual producer is free to try to maximize his profits, but legally and morally prohibited from doing so by force or fraud, then the only way that remains is for him to try to serve the wishes and needs of the consumer better than his competitors, by offering either better goods or the same goods at lower prices. The result of this free competition among producers and freedom of choice of consumers is to bring about a constant tendency toward equilibrium. And what applies to prices, producing, and consuming applies as well to wage-rates and employment, and to interest rates, saving, and investing.

"Admittedly, if the classical medicine is to work," Keynes continues, "it is essential that import tariffs and export subsidies should not progressively offset its influence." This surely looks like a withdrawal of his advocacy of mercantilist restrictions, economic nationalism, and management of "the domestic price level" at whatever cost to foreign trade.

Praising the "sincere and thoroughgoing proposals, advanced on behalf of the United States, expressly directed towards creating a system which allows the classical medicine to do its work," Keynes concludes: "It shows how much modernist stuff, gone wrong and turned sour and silly, is circulating in our system, also incongruously mixed, it seems, with age-old poisons, that we [the British] should have given so doubtful a welcome to this magnificent, objective approach." This looks like an almost savage rejection of the doctrines of the *General Theory*. But Keynes goes on:

I must not be misunderstood. I do not suppose that the classical medicine will work by itself or that we can depend on it. We need quicker and less painful aids of which exchange variation and over-all import control are the most important. But in the long run these expedients will work better and we shall need them less, if the classical medicine is also at work. And if we reject the medicine from our systems altogether, we may just drift from expedient to expedient and never get really fit again. The great virtue of the Bretton Woods and Washington proposals, taken in conjunction, is that they marry the use of the necessary expedients to the wholesome long-run doctrine. It is for this reason that, speaking in the House of Lords, I claimed that "Here is an attempt to use what we have learnt from modern experience and modern analysis, not to defeat, but to implement the wisdom of Adam Smith."

No one can be certain of anything in this age of flux and change. Decaying standards of life at a time when our command over the production of material satisfactions is the greatest ever, and a diminishing scope for individual decision and choice at a time when more than before we should be able to afford these satisfactions, are sufficient to indicate an underlying contradiction in every department of our economy.

2. *The Underlying Contradictions*

The greatest underlying contradiction, however, as this passage so clearly reveals, was in Keynes's own thought. In 1946, as in 1936, he was still trying to reconcile irreconcilables. By "the classical medicine" he could have only meant what Lionel Robbins has called "the System of Economic Freedom," which Robbins defines as "an urgent demand that . . . hampering and anti-social impediments should be removed and that the immense potential of free pioneering individual initiative should be released." [1] But Keynes wanted both freedom and controls. He wanted free trade

[1] *The Theory of Economic Policy in English Classical Political Economy*, (London: Macmillan, 1952).

and he wanted "exchange variation" and "over-all import control." That is, he wanted government currency manipulation, exchange control, import quotas and prohibitions which are the very negation of free trade and a free economy. He deplored "diminishing scope for individual decision and choice" at the same time as he continued to advocate all these restrictions on individual decision and choice and failed explicitly to repudiate even his scheme for government control and socialization of investment. He wanted to "implement the wisdom of Adam Smith" and yet to ignore the wisdom of Adam Smith.

What, then, can we say about this "recantation"? The great difficulty with Keynes is how to tell his recantations from his contradictions. His contradictions consisted of incompatible views that he held simultaneously. His recantations consisted of incompatible views that he recognized as incompatible and hence held only successively.

We saw in Chapter XXIII that he swung from free trade to hyper-protectionism (almost to autarky) and back again. In his 1946 article he seems to wish a little of each. In his *Treatise on Money* he gave definitions of saving and investment which he explicitly repudiated in the *General Theory* and then tacitly adopted anyway, because they were essential to his arguments. In *The Economic Consequences of the Peace,* in 1919, he wrote one of the most eloquent warnings against inflation on record,[2] only to advocate inflation, in the *General Theory,* as the standard recourse to cure all unemployment, if not as a permanent way of life. And in the *General Theory* itself (perhaps the central contention of which is that a cut in money-wage-rates cannot cure unemployment and will probably increase it) he blurts out a sentence like this: "When we enter on a period of weakening effective demand, a sudden large reduction of money-wages to a level so low that no one believes in its

2 This is the passage beginning with the oft-quoted sentence: "Lenin is said to have declared that the best way to destroy the Capitalist System was to debauch the currency" (pp. 235-237).

indefinite continuance would be the event most favorable to a strengthening of effective demand" (p. 265).[3]

So the 1946 article in the *Economic Journal* might be set down as just one more contradiction. True, Keynes says some patronizing things in it in favor of "the classical medicine," but he had already paid, as we have seen, many patronizing compliments to the classical system even in the *General Theory*.

And yet . . . There is that phrase, in the *Economic Journal* article, about *"much modernist stuff, gone wrong and turned sour and silly."* What could this refer to except Keynesian theory itself, as interpreted and applied by his more zealous disciples?

Was Keynes, then, in the last year of his life, at least on the verge of recantation? I spoke at the beginning of this chapter of reported conversations with friends or other economists. I shall cite but one:

> In my last talk with Keynes, a few months before his death, it was clear that he had got far away from his "euthanasia of the rentier." He complained that the easy money policy was being pushed too far, both in England and here, and emphasized interest as an element of income, and its basic importance in the structure and functioning of private capitalism. He was amused by my remark that it was time to write another book because the all-out easy money policy was being preached in his name, and replied that he did think he ought to keep one jump ahead.[4]

The situation reminds one of that in *The Brothers Karamazov,* in which Ivan Karamazov, who has preached a purely "philosophical" atheism and immoralism—"every-

[3] This sentence, of course, comes nearer to a correct analysis than the rest of the *General Theory;* but it cannot be accepted as it stands. A belief in the indefinite continuance of the lower wage-rates would *also* lead to a restoration of buying, production, and employment. All that is necessary to cure unemployment due to excessive wage-rates is individual (not necessarily general or uniform) wage-rate cuts just large enough to *destroy the conviction or fear that there may have to be still more cuts to come.*

[4] John H. Williams, *American Economic Review,* May, 1948, pp. 287-288n.

thing is permissible"—finds to his horror that his half-brother Smerdyakov, taking him at his word, has murdered and robbed their father. "I was only your instrument," says Smerdyakov, "your faithful servant, and it was following your words I did it. . . . 'All things are lawful.' That was quite right what you taught me . . . For if there's no everlasting God, there's no such thing as virtue, and there's no need of it."

Keynes was a brilliant man. Much of what he wrote he wrote with tongue-in-cheek, for the pleasure of paradox, to *épater le bourgeois,* in the spirit of Wilde, Shaw, and the Bloomsbury circle. Perhaps the whole of the *General Theory* was intended as a huge (400-page) joke, and Keynes was appalled to find disciples who took it all literally.

Wit and satire are dangerous weapons when not used in the service of good sense.

Chapter XXVI

"FULL EMPLOYMENT" AS THE GOAL

The "contribution" of Keynes that his disciples most often insist upon as valid and "permanent" is the substitution of "full employment" as the goal of economic activity rather than the "maximum production" of the classical economists.

We shall ask here three main questions about "full employment." 1. Is it definable? 2. Is it attainable? 3. Is it—at all times and under all conditions—even desirable?

1. *Is It Definable?*

Let us begin with the question of definition. The man in the street has few misgivings about this. "Full employment" means that "everybody" has a job. It means "jobs for all the people all the time."

This naive conception runs into immediate difficulties. Early in 1958, for example, the population of the United States was about 173 million. But there were only some 62 million employed. Therefore there must have been 111 million "unemployed"! Yet the official estimate was that there were at that time only 5 million unemployed.

For the government statisticians, the "unemployed" consist only of those in the "labor force" who are not employed. But just how was the line drawn between the 67.5 million who were counted as part of the labor force and the 105.5 million who were not? Here is how the U. S. Bureau of the Census described how it decided:

> Monthly estimates of the population of working age [14 years and over] showing the total number employed, the total

> unemployed, and the number not in the labor force are obtained from a scientifically selected sample of about 35,000 interviewed households in 330 areas throughout the country.

So the estimate of unemployed was in large part based on a sample of only one in every 1,400 households in the country.

My purpose here, however, is not to emphasize the probable error in such estimates, but to call attention to the necessarily arbitrary and in some cases purely subjective standards by which "unemployment" is officially determined.

The Bureau of the Census's explanation continues: "The unemployed total includes all jobless who were looking for work." How is the number of such persons estimated? From replies to the interviews. What constitutes realistically looking for work? The interviewers must rely in large part upon the realism of the replies. The labor force is not even a constant percentage of the total ("non-institutional") population. In July of 1957 it was 60.6 per cent; but in December only 58.1 per cent.

Some paradoxical results emerge. The monthly report for March of 1958, for example, opened as follows: "Employment rose by 300,000 between February and March . . . while unemployment was unchanged." How could that happen? The layman would naturally expect that if employment rose 300,000 in March unemployment would have dropped that much. The government statisticians' answer is that the "labor force" increased by that much.

The "labor force" increases partly by census estimates of the population reaching working age, etc., but also partly by changes in peoples' *decisions*. Suppose a man has a good job, with a wife at home and a son and daughter in college. He loses his job, whereupon not only he, but his wife, his son, and his daughter start looking for work. Because one person has lost his job, four persons are now "unemployed." So "unemployment" goes up faster than employment goes down.

Let's turn now to the explanations of the Department of Labor:

> Effective January 1957, persons on layoff with definite instructions to return to work within 30 days of layoff and persons waiting to start new wage and salary jobs within the following 30 days, are classified as unemployed. Such persons had previously been classified as employed. . . . The combined total of the groups changing classification has averaged about 200,000 to 300,000 a month in recent years.

So the "unemployed" increased about a quarter of a million simply by a change of definition!

We get into the same kind of problems and arbitrary decisions when we come to the matter of working hours. Obviously there cannot be jobs for "all the people all the time." We must deduct time for eating, sleeping, rest, and leisure. But how much time? It is customary to think of men being "partly unemployed" when they are laid off for two working days a week. But obviously they are as much unemployed if they work every day for correspondingly reduced hours. In the United States today, the standard full working week is forty hours, or five eight-hour days. This is shorter than the standard working week used to be, and in future it may be shorter still. Obviously the length of the working week that constitutes "full employment" is also a matter of arbitrary and conventional definition.

Let us see whether we can get some help from the academic economists, and first of all, of course, Keynes.

In the *General Theory,* Keynes gives us *two* definitions, neither of which seems to have much relation to the other. On page 15 he gives an involved definition of "involuntary" unemployment which, as I have already tried to show (p. 30), is invalid. From this he postulates a state of affairs in the absence of "involuntary" unemployment: "This state of affairs we shall describe as 'full' employment, both 'frictional' and 'voluntary' unemployment being consistent with 'full' employment thus defined" (p. 16). In other words, "full" employment is a state in which there can be both "frictional" and "voluntary" *un*employment! Full employment is not full.

Let's start again, this time with the definition on page 303:

> We have full employment when output has risen to a level at which the marginal return from a representative unit of the factors of production has fallen to the minimum figure at which a quantity of the factors sufficient to produce this output is available.

I confess I find it difficult to follow this jabberwocky; but I assume it implies that some sort of equilibrium has been reached. One is tempted to ask irreverently: Does this mean that Uncle Oscar has a job?

Let us turn to A. C. Pigou. Professor Pigou is aware of some of the difficulties we encounter when we try to define unemployment:

> A man is only unemployed when he is *both* not employed and *also* desires to be employed. Moreover, the notion of desiring to be employed must be interpreted in relation to established facts as regards (1) hours of work per day, (2) rates of wage, and (3) a man's state of health.[1]

This definition reveals that many subjective and arbitrary elements enter into the concept of "unemployment." But we shall see presently that there are many more difficulties than even Pigou's definition allows for.

After considerable discussion Pigou ends up with the conclusion that "The quantity of unemployment prevailing at any time is equal to the number of would-be wage-earners *minus* the quantity of labor demanded *plus* the number of unfilled vacancies." [2]

It is important to notice here that the "number of

[1] *The Theory of Unemployment,* (London: Macmillan, 1933), p. 3.
[2] *Ibid.,* p. 10.

would-be wage-earners" is not only largely a *subjective* rather than an *objective* quantity, but that "the quantity of labor demanded" and "the number of unfilled vacancies" are also largely subjective, rather than objective, because they depend on the changing intentions of employers. If I could get a man to mow my lawn at a certain hourly rate, there would be an "unfilled vacancy" at that rate, but if the professional gardeners available all demand more, I may decide either to mow my lawn myself, or to let it grow.

This principle applies throughout industry. Whether there are "unfilled vacancies" in a given firm may depend not only on the wage-rate at which the vacancies could be filled but whether employees with certain special qualities could be obtained.

In another place Pigou writes:

> A contrast is often drawn between situations in which there are more men available for jobs than jobs available for men and situations in which there are more jobs than men. In the former class of situation we have less than full employment, that is unemployment, in the latter more than full employment, that is over-full or, more briefly, over-employment.[3]

All this looks extremely simple. But the difficulty of statistical quantification, of deciding precisely what the numerical relationship is of "men available" to "jobs available," is precisely the difficulty of defining not only what is meant by "men *available*," but what is meant by a "job," particularly when it is "unfilled."

Let us try Sir William Beveridge. In his *Full Employment in a Free Society,* he defines full employment in his opening pages as "having always more vacant jobs than unemployed men. . . . The labor market should always be a seller's market rather than a buyer's market."

But this is obviously defining full employment as *over*-employment. (Incidentally, Sir William's demand that there must always be more vacant jobs than unemployed

[3] A. C. Pigou, *Essays in Economics,* (London: Macmillan, 1952), p. 108.

men is a demand that labor should be always *underpaid.* For this condition could only exist if the marginal product of labor were higher than its wage-rate, and labor, though "fully employed," would therefore be getting less than its full potential income.)

One of the most realistic discussions of the difficulties in the concept of full employment is that of Edwin G. Nourse, formerly Chairman of the President's Council of Economic Advisers. Commenting upon the declaration of policy in the American Employment Act of 1946, he writes:

> The phrase, "those able, willing, and seeking to work," does not define a labor force for whose optimum utilization the federal government can, in good economic conscience, pledge itself to "utilize all its plans, functions, and resources." In the absence of objective criteria, the word "able" becomes practically meaningless. Whether a given person is, in a commercial or industrial sense, able to work is a decidedly relative matter. Able to work steadily or only intermittently? At the kinds of work for which demand presently exists, only with other skills, or without any particular skill, aptitude, or even teachability? Able to work as determined by a doctor's certificate or by a foreman's report? Under standard shop or office conditions or only with special facilities or treatment? Equally rich in ambiguity is the companion term "willing." It was inserted as a gesture of reassurance to those who feared the camel of authoritarianism might be getting his nose under the tent of free enterprise. But does it mean willing to work at such jobs as are available or only at the job of one's dreams? Willing to work on a time schedule dictated by employers' needs or by workers' convenience? Seeking is, of necessity, the criterion relied on by the Census Bureau in giving us a monthly estimate of involuntary unemployment. But "wanting" would be a more apt term for our purpose since it is a commonplace in the experience of all who have dealt with the unemployed to find not a few persons who want work—may even need it desperately—and who yet are not actively seeking a job because they have become convinced that the search is hopeless.

The plain fact is that the size of our labor force is statistically determinate only within the limits of quite categorical definitions.[4]

When we speak of full employment, therefore, we would do better to use the term not as the Keynesian zealots use it, and not with any effort at an unattainable mathematical precision, but in a loose, common-sense way to mean merely the absence of substantial or abnormal unemployment.

If it be objected that this is not in fact a definition of *full* employment (and it is certainly not *brimful* employment), then I suggest that the term might be dropped entirely, and the term *optimum* employment used instead. This would have, among other advantages, that of reminding the user as well as his audience that employment is rather a means than an end, and that its optimum size is relative to other conditions or goals.

2. *Is It Attainable?*

Is "full employment" attainable? Here even those who favor the goal begin to waver. Alvin Hansen, in his definition of full employment in *Economic Policy and Full Employment* declares that: "In an economy as large as that of the United States, it is probable that at 'full employment' there would be at any one time between 2 and 3 million temporarily unemployed."[5] (About 4.5 per cent of the civilian labor force of 1945-47.)

Paul Douglas, commenting on Beveridge's use of a 3 per cent margin for seasonal and transitional unemployment, declared that such a criterion would be "fatal" in the United States: "To use deficit financing to drive unemployment down below 6 per cent is very dangerous. It will tend to do far more harm through inflation than the good it will do by

[4] "Ideal and Working Concepts of Full Employment," *American Economic Review,* May, 1957, p. 100.

[5] *Loc. cit.,* p. 19n.

absorbing those who are unemployed from seasonal and transitional causes." [6]

3. *Is It Unconditionally Desirable?*

So when "full employment" is seriously discussed, it turns out to be less than full employment. And the desirability of "full employment at whatever cost" [7] is gravely questioned.

Lionel Robbins,[8] quoting the Beveridge definition of full employment as "having always more vacant jobs than unemployed men," points out that: "A state of affairs in which, at current rates of wages, the demand for labor is continually greater than the supply, must be a state of affairs in which, in the absence of special restraints, the level of wage rates, and hence the level of prices, is tending continually to rise." He goes on to point out that even a full employment policy that tried to guarantee a mere *equality* of jobs and applicants would have to guarantee the trade unions that *"whatever [wage] rates they succeeded in getting, unemployment would not be permitted to emerge."* Professor Robbins concludes that Beveridgian full employment "tends to inflation, reduced adaptability, external disequilibrium and a most drastic curtailment of individual liberty."

Edwin Nourse, in the article from which I have previously quoted, declares that: "Ideally full employment would be such as promotes continuous maximization of production and real purchasing power for the people." But this definition recognizes that full employment is desirable, not as an end in itself, but only as a means to much broader ends. Even the "maximization of production" must be understood, not in the sense of the mere piling up of physical things, but in the sense of the maximization of consumer

6 *Economy in the National Government,* (1952), p. 253.

7 See Jacob Viner, *Quarterly Journal of Economics,* August, 1950.

8 *The Economist in the Twentieth Century* (London: Macmillan, 1956), "Full Employment as an Objective."

satisfactions. And this includes also, for example, the "production" (or "consumption"?) of more leisure at the cost of less desired (physical) things.

If we are talking not of unavoidable means but of desired ends, then we must recognize that the economic objective of mankind is not more work but less. I hope I may be forgiven for quoting what I have written in another place:

> The economic goal of any nation, as of any individual, is to get the greatest results with the least effort. The whole economic progress of mankind has consisted in getting more production with the same labor. It is for this reason that men began putting burdens on the backs of mules instead of on their own; that they went on to invent the wheel and the wagon, the railroad and the motor truck. It is for this reason that men used their ingenuity to develop a hundred thousand labor-saving inventions.
>
> All this is so elementary that one would blush to state it if it were not being constantly forgotten by those who coin and circulate the new slogans. Translated into national terms, this first principle means that our real objective is to maximize production. In doing this, full employment—that is, the absence of involuntary idleness—becomes a necessary by-product. But production is the end, employment merely the means. We cannot continuously have the fullest production without full employment. But we can very easily have full employment without full production.
>
> Primitive tribes are naked, and wretchedly fed and housed, but they do not suffer from unemployment. China and India are incomparably poorer than ourselves, but the main trouble from which they suffer is primitive production methods (which are both a cause and a consequence of a shortage of capital) and not unemployment. Nothing is easier to achieve than full employment, once it is divorced from the goal of full production and taken as an end in itself. Hitler provided full employment with a huge armament program. The war provided full employment for every nation involved. The slave labor in Russia had full employment. Prisons and chain

gangs have full employment. Coercion can always provide full employment. . . .

The progress of civilization has meant the reduction of employment, not its increase. It is because we have become increasingly wealthy as a nation that we have been able virtually to eliminate child labor, to remove the necessity of work for many of the aged and to make it unnecessary for millions of women to take jobs.[9]

[9] *Economics in One Lesson* (New York: Harper, 1946), pp. 68-70.

Chapter XXVII

"THE NATIONAL INCOME APPROACH"

No analysis of Keynesian economics would be complete without at least some discussion of what is variously called "aggregrative" economics, "macro-economics," and "the national income approach."

Many of his disciples are under the impression that it was Keynes who created "the national income concept." This is pure fantasy. Efforts to calculate the national income have a long history. Though Keynes does have a great deal to say about "aggregative" economics (which we have already analyzed), his discussion of the national income in the *General Theory* is confined, in fact, to two or three pages, which mainly refer to earlier studies by A. C. Pigou, Colin Clark, and Simon Kuznets.

Yet "the national income approach" owes at least part of its present vogue to Keynesian ways of thinking, and therefore a few words may properly be said about it here. A thorough discussion would call for a volume in itself, but I shall attempt no more than a few sketchy comments.

1. *Is National Income Determinate?*

The first thing to be emphasized about the national income is that it is an *arbitrary,* and from the standpoint of scientific precision an *indeterminate,* figure. The ablest students of the subject have recognized this. I need merely refer to the fine pioneering study of Simon Kuznets.[1]

[1] *National Income and Its Composition,* 1919-1938. (New York: National Bureau of Economic Research, 1941), 2 vols.

Kuznets devotes his entire first chapter, of fifty-seven pages, to a discussion of the problems embedded in the very concept of "national income." He begins:

> The statistician who supposes that he can make a purely objective estimate of national income, not influenced by preconceptions concerning the 'facts,' is deluding himself; for whenever he includes one item or excludes another he is implicitly accepting some standard of judgment, his own or that of the compiler of his data. There is no escaping this subjective element.

Kuznets goes on to show that estimates of the national income necessarily involve legal and moral considerations. Should we include "the compensation of robbers, murderers, drug peddlers, and smugglers"? And how shall we "draw a line between economic activity and economic goods on the one hand and active life in general and its stream of satisfactions on the other"? Should "washing, shaving, and playing for amusement on the piano" be treated as economic activity? "When judged by the attributes of satisfaction-yielding, scarcity, and disposability, they do not differ from the same activities carried on for money as services to other people (nursing, barbering, and giving concerts)."

And yet Kuznets decides to include only items that "are dealt in on the market." This of course excludes all do-it-yourself activities (which in total are probably enormous). It excludes all the products of the family economy, including all the activities of housewives. So we get to such paradoxes as these: When a man marries his cook, the value of her work disappears from the national income accounts. When an opera singer sings professionally, she is considered as adding the equivalent of her salary to the national income. When she sings for charity or for friends, it doesn't count.

How are we to prevent double counting at a hundred points? If we count the income of doctors and dentists, should we, or should we not, deduct it from the income of patients?

What is it that we are trying to measure, anyway? What is the difference between "economic activity" and "active life in general"? How, except by arbitrary "value judgments," do we distinguish between "productive" and "unproductive" activities? Are we trying to measure "national income *produced*," "national income *paid out*," "national income *spent*," or "national income *consumed*"?

No doubt today most laymen (and a large number of statisticians and economists!) assume that all these problems must have been satisfactorily solved, because they read daily in their newspapers official figures showing exactly what the national income, "personal income," "disposable personal income," and above all the "gross national product" or "GNP," were not only in past periods, but at what annual rate they are currently running. And these figures are presented with great precision, with decimal points. Few laymen are aware that these figures are made up not of definite items which can be lined up and counted, but in large part of *estimates* subject to error.

Let us take a few quite recent illustrations. The President's annual Economic Report of January, 1958, boasted in its opening paragraph that the nation's GNP, or output of goods and services, in 1957 totaled $434 billion, "5 per cent larger than in the preceding year." Only later in the report were we explicitly told that "four-fifths of this increase was accounted for by rising prices," and that therefore "in physical terms, the increase was only about 1 per cent." In July of 1958, however, the national income estimates received one of their periodic revisions, and the Department of Commerce statisticians decided that our GNP in 1957 was not $434 billion but $440 billion, and that our 1956 GNP was not $415 billion but $419 billion. Yet in "1957 prices," we were informed, our 1956 GNP was $435 billion.

This brings us to one of the great problems in estimating

national income. It is measured in a dollar which has itself no fixed value. In a period of inflation, all values are falsified. Today the most frequently cited over-all figure is not that of national income but of gross national product, or GNP. I shall therefore use this for purposes of illustration. For 1939 the GNP was estimated at $91.1 billion; for 1957 it was estimated at $440.3 billion. Here is an apparent quadrupling, or better, of the GNP. But when the government statisticians restate the figures in "constant dollars" (specifically in "1954 dollars"), they find that the GNP in 1939 has to be raised to $189.3 billion and that the 1957 GNP has to be lowered to $407 billion. In other words, "real" GNP did not quadruple but only about doubled in the 18-year period.

The government statisticians get this result by dividing actual dollar totals by an index number of prices for each year. They print, in fact, a separate table of "implicit price deflators" for the gross national product figures for each year based on an index number of 100 for 1954. The price deflator for 1939, on this basis, is 48.1, and for 1957 is 108.2. If we take the GNP in 1939 at the prices that prevailed in that year it comes, as we have seen, to $91.1 billion. But if we translate 1957 national income into 1939 prices, we get, instead of $440.3 billion, only $195.7 billion for 1957. This does not look nearly as impressive. If, again, we divide these figures by the population, we find a much lower rate of *per capita* growth than we are at all likely to gather from the crude over-all figures.

But though inflation and the changing value of the dollar make comparative over-all national income figures quite misleading, is it, in fact, possible to correct the comparison by applying "implicit price deflators"? Only approximately; never accurately. As Kuznets and every other serious student of index numbers has pointed out, goods never remain the same for two years in succession, either in relative quantities or in comparative quality, and no index number can be completely "scientific."

There is one further factor that distorts and falsifies comparative national income figures. It is a factor I do not recall ever having seen discussed in connection with these figures, yet it goes to the heart of the whole problem of measurability.

Larger crops often have a smaller total dollar value than smaller crops. (Hence crop-restriction schemes.) But this merely illustrates a wider principle. Economists have pointed out since the time of Adam Smith that it is not "value-in-use," but scarcity, that determines "value-in-exchange," or money price. Water is an indispensable commodity that ordinarily commands no price at all. If more and more things became plentiful (except dollars), the national income, as measured in dollars, might begin to *fall*. If we could imagine a situation in which everything we could wish for was in as adequate supply as air and water, we might have no (monetary) national income at all!

When one seeks to be clear about basic principles, it is never a bad idea (in spite of the ridicule that has been heaped upon it since the days of Karl Marx) to go back to "Crusoe economics." Suppose, then, we begin with a community of just two persons, one of whom raises beans (say 1,000 pounds) and the other of whom raises potatoes (also 1,000 pounds). This is their total wealth. The total wealth (or, if we wish, income) of the community is thus 1,000 pounds of beans plus 1,000 pounds of potatoes. But, someone may wish to know, which is the wealthier—Ben, who raises beans, or Peter, who raises potatoes? And what is the total wealth (or annual income) of the community expressed in terms of some common measure?

Suppose Ben and Peter exchange their beans and potatoes at a ratio of a pound for a pound (to such an extent as to bring the relative marginal utilities of each to both of them into equilibrium). And suppose we elect to regard the potatoes as the "medium of exchange" and the "money of account." Then the total income of the community is obviously 2,000 "pounds-of-potatoes," made up of 1,000 pounds of potatoes and 1,000 pounds of beans a year.

But now certain paradoxical results appear. Suppose Peter doubles the amount of potatoes he grows, while Ben raises only the same amount of beans. Then the income of the community has risen, in real terms, to 2,000 pounds of potatoes plus 1,000 pounds of beans. We might be tempted to conclude that, in terms of the common "standard-of-value," the income of the community was now 3,000 "pounds-of-potatoes." But because potatoes were now twice as plentiful, and beans were unchanged in supply, Ben might demand, and Peter be willing to pay, two pounds of potatoes for every pound of beans. But this would mean that the supply of beans was twice as valuable as before. Therefore the total income of the community, as expressed in potatoes, would not be 3,000 "pounds-of-potatoes," but 4,000.

Suppose, on the other hand, it was the supply of beans that had doubled, and Peter was able to demand and get two pounds of beans for every pound of potatoes. Then the income of the community, measured in "pounds-of-potatoes," would not be 3,000 "pounds" but only 2,000.

So our "national income" figure, expressed in a common medium of exchange or "money-of-account," does not express any *absolute* total at all, but merely *an internal relationship of marginal values* (times quantities). We could go on to illustrate this by a more complex "model," assuming, say, a hundred different commodities, one of which would be gold, and assuming that a certain weight of gold, a "dollar" (or one-thirty-fifth of an ounce), was the medium of exchange and the "money-of-account." It would then be easy to show that an increase in the other ninety-nine commodities would by no means mean a proportionate increase in the national income as measured in "dollars," and yet that a doubling of the amount of "dollars" alone might double the national income as expressed in dollars.

Nor would it be possible to "correct" for these paradoxical results, except in an inaccurate and untrustworthy fashion, by using "implicit price deflators" or inflators. And if the problem of translating money-value income into "real," or heterogeneous physical, income is insoluble, still more so is the problem of translating either into "psychic" or "enjoyment" income. Hence the impossibility of a "scientific" comparison of the income of "Russia" and the "United States."

In brief, national income estimates have a very limited value, a far more modest value than is now commonly supposed. They might have some value in comparing the national incomes of two different countries—*if* the figures in both countries were compiled by the same methods and (largely arbitrary or conventional) standards, *if* both countries had the same monetary standard (say gold), and *if* complete freedom of currency convertibility and of trade prevailed. Such comparisons have little value when currency ratios are fixed by government ukase or exchange control rather than by free markets or free convertibility into a common commodity.

2. *Its Dangers for Policy*

It is impossible, in sum, to arrive at a precise, scientific, objective, or absolute measurement of the national income in terms of dollars. But the assumption that we *can* do so has led to dangerous policies, and threatens to lead to even more dangerous policies.

Policy implications, in fact, are already found in the "national income approach." For this embodies an attempt to deal with economic problems starting from an arbitrarily constructed "whole," from a "collective," and not from acting individuals. This "macro-economic" as differentiated from the "micro-economic" approach raises first of all the question: Why is the "nation" considered the collective to be chosen and not the state (State of New York), the municipality (City of New York), the borough (Manhattan) or, on the other side, the continent (America)—or the whole world? The chief answer to this question is that the choice of the collective is determined mainly by political considerations. Many of our American "progressives" aim at an equalization of incomes within the United States, but not at a world equalization. This political tendency explains, also, why these people are always talking about the "distribution" of the national income and not about the contribution of the various individuals and groups of individuals to its coming into existence. Logically, the contribution problem ought to be considered first. Much of the "national income" discussion is dominated by the Marxian thesis according to which goods are "socially" produced and afterwards individually appropriated.

I have said that though the government compiles quarterly estimates both of gross national product and of national income, it is the former figure that is much more frequently cited. This is partly because it appears earlier (as a private firm knows its gross income before it knows its net income), and partly because it is the larger figure. National planners love big figures. We are constantly being told that "we" (the government) can easily afford to spend or give away (say, to foreign governments) this or that huge sum because it is after all only such-and-such a percentage of our gross national product. No one would dream of considering such reasoning valid as applied to a private firm. The average industrial company's net profit, for example, amounts (1956-7) to only 5 or 6 cents on every dollar of sales.

There are great deductions to be made from gross national product before we can estimate national income. For example, in 1957, gross national product was estimated at $440.3 billion, whereas national income was estimated at only $364 billion. In arriving at the latter figure some $34 billion was deducted for depreciation charges and some $38 billion for indirect business taxes. But depreciation charges are the result of estimates. The "right" amount of depreciation is never precisely known. Contrary to the belief of laymen (and even of many accountants) a depreciation charge is not so much an estimate of past deterioration as a forecast of future probabilities. It is never known, for example, when an old machine is going to be made obsolete by a new invention. And particularly in a period of monetary inflation, such as we have been undergoing for the last generation, depreciation charges are systematically underestimated, because they fail to allow for ever mounting replacement costs.

Another bad practice to which a too literal reliance on national income figures has led is that of insisting on the urgency of a certain "rate of growth" of the national income, no matter what level it has already reached. Thus a report of the Rockefeller Brothers Fund in 1958, looking ten years ahead, came up with the remarkable discovery that an economic "growth rate" of 5 per cent a year would lead to a bigger growth in ten years than a 3 per cent rate or even a 4 per cent rate.

This insistence on achieving or maintaining a certain "rate of growth" is the result of several misconceptions. Professor G. Warren Nutter has pointed out that there is "a long-run tendency . . . for the industrial growth rates to slow down, or retard, as the level of production gets higher." There are several basic explanations of this. One has to do with a trick of percentage figures. Another has to do with a physical satiety point in human needs. If only one family in a country has a bathtub, and the next year 50 families get one, the rate of growth is 5,000 per cent. But once everybody has a bathtub net growth stops. This principle applies to houses, automobiles, radios, television sets, etc.

In addition, as we have just noticed a little while back, as more and more things become plentiful (except dollars) there might even be a tendency for the national income figures to reflect this by *falling,* because prices might fall faster than output rose.

Still another practical danger of the religious use of national income figures is that it can lead to a confusion or reversal of economic cause and effect. The national income of a given year is *the total result* of all the production and transactions during that year. In this respect the national income figures are similar to the account books of a private firm. But more and more, in current discussion, one finds the national income figure treated as a *cause* of production. The national income is thought of as the purchasing power that automatically creates and buys the production. The truth is that the national income is the production itself, looked at from another side. Broadly speaking, national income does not cause national production, but national production causes national income. Insofar as the causation *is* the other way 'round, it is because of the truth in that very Say's Law that the Keynesians and national income addicts tell us has been discredited.

The national income figures seem to have given birth to all sorts of cause-and-effect fallacies. For example, if we look at the composition of the national income figures for, say, 1957, we find that part of the GNP total of $440.3 billion is arrived at by including $87.1 billion for "government purchases of goods and services." When the national income figures of $364 billion for that year are broken down into specific industries, we find that nearly $43 billion is accounted for by "government and government enterprises." It is easy to jump to the conclusion, which Keynesians do, that if it were not for these $87 billion of government purchases or these $43 billion of government payrolls and enterprises, the national income would be just that much less. People with a less favorable opinion of the role of government would point out that whatever the government spends it takes away from somebody in taxes. (This applies also to the hidden tax involved in monetary inflation.) Undoubtedly, such government employees as policemen, firemen, judges, and road-builders do increase (by an unascertainable amount) real national income. But it may be questioned whether such agencies as price controllers, rent boards, the Tariff Commission, the crop restriction agents of the Department of Agriculture, or the National Labor Relations Board do not bring about a net reduction of the real national income, in spite of the fact that they increase it according to the government figures.

If we think of the national income as a mere lump over-all sum in dollars, and it falls short of some "goal" by *x* billion dollars, it is a tempting step for economic planners to assume that the *x* billion dollars could be easily supplied by that much deficit spending, or even by printing that much money. This leads indirectly to inflation. For we can raise our national income to any figure we want simply by depreciating the dollar enough to raise prices to reach that income.

In Germany, in 1923, the national income (in marks) actually rose to hundreds of billions of times higher than its previous level, because the paper mark was depreciated to one-trillionth of its former purchasing power.

To be sure, when explicitly taxed with the point, economic planners will say that their goal is a national income of *x* billions "in dollars of present purchasing power." But they forget this qualification in actual practice. They are always citing the latest national income figures in terms of the latest and most inflated dollar. They do not stop to remind us, or even themselves, how much the national income would have to be written down to reflect the price level of, say, twenty years ago.

"The national income approach" has become one of the inportant incitements to inflation. For the easiest and surest way to get constantly bigger national income figures is not by increasing output and consumer satisfactions, but by constantly shrinking the measuring rod, by constantly depreciating the dollar.

It remains to be pointed out, finally, that economic forecasting based on "aggregative economics" or "the national income approach" has been a failure. David McCord Wright, who declares that: "In practical experience, the

Keynesian forecasters have quite a poor record," cites in evidence "the egregious failure of most Keynesian forecasts after World War II," which was "very largely due to an unexpected upward jump of the consumption level." Similarly, he adds, "in 1953 and again in 1958 the Keynesian models of mechanical interrelationships between investment and consumption did not work out." [2]

This judgment corroborates that of John H. Williams: "The consumption function in particular has given the mathematicians . . . an ideal concept for building models of national income and making forecasts. Thus far, the forecasts have been almost uniformly bad." [3]

[2] *Science,* Nov. 21, 1958, pp. 1261-1262.
[3] *American Economic Review,* May, 1948, p. 284.

Chapter XXVIII

THE KEYNESIAN POLICIES

1. *Do Deficits Cure Unemployment?*

In our chapter-by-chapter analysis of Keynesian theory we have had occasion to examine in passing the implied Keynesian policies and their probable consequences. But it may now be useful to discuss some of these main policies more explicitly.

In Keynesian policy, unemployment is never to be corrected by any reduction of money-wage-rates. Keynes recommends two main remedies. One is deficit spending (sometimes euphemistically called government "investment"). How good is this remedy? It was tried in the United States (partly because of Keynes's recommendations) for a full decade. What were the results? Here are the deficit in the Federal budget, the number of unemployed, and the percentage of unemployed to the total labor force, year by year in that decade. All the figures are from official sources:

	Deficit (billions)	*Unemployed (millions)*	*Percentage of Unemployment*
1931	$ .5	8.0	15.9
1932	2.7	12.1	23.6
1933	2.6	12.8	24.9
1934	3.6	11.3	21.7
1935	2.8	10.6	20.1
1936	4.4	9.0	16.9
1937	2.8	7.7	14.3
1938	1.2	10.4	19.0
1939	3.9	9.5	17.2
1940	3.9	8.1	14.6

In the foregoing table the deficits are for fiscal years ending on June 30; the unemployment is an average for the full calendar year. (The deficit figures therefore lead the unemployment figures by six months.) Advocates of deficit spending, no doubt, will try to find a partial negative correlation between the size of the deficit and the subsequent number of unemployed. But the central and decisive fact is that heavy deficits were accompanied by mass unemployment. The average unemployment of the ten-year period was 9.9 millions, which was 18.6 per cent of the total working force.

The average deficit in this ten-year period was $2.8 billion, which was 3.6 per cent of the gross national product of the period. The same percentage of the gross national product of 1957 would mean an annual deficit of $15.6 billion.

2. *Does Cheap Money Cure Unemployment?*

The other main Keynesian remedy for unemployment is low interest rates, artificially produced by "the Monetary Authority." Keynes incidentally admits (e.g., p. 205) that such artificially low interest rates can only be produced by printing more money, *i.e.*, by deliberate inflation. But we may let this pass for the moment. The question immediately before us is: Do low interest rates prevent mass unemployment?

The policy of cheap money has had an even longer trial than the policy of planned deficits. Let us look at the record of interest rates and unemployment for the same period that we have just reviewed, adding, however, 1929 and 1930. In the table below, the first column after that of the years represents the average rate in each year (the average of daily prevailing rates) of prime commercial paper with a maturity of four to six months. I have chosen this rate rather than that on three-month Treasury bills because it is the most available statistical series reflecting the short-term interest rates at which business actually borrows. (Actually, the greatest volume of business borrowing from banks in the U.S. consists of "line-of-credit" loans; but these vary with the more sensitive commercial-paper rate.) The final column once again gives the percentage of unemployed to the total labor force. Both sets of figures are from official sources:

Year	*Commercial Paper Rate (%)*	*Percentage of Unemployment*
1929	5.85	3.2
1930	3.59	8.7
1931	2.64	15.9
1932	2.73	23.6
1933	1.73	24.9
1934	1.02	21.7
1935	.75	20.1
1936	.75	16.9
1937	.94	14.3
1938	.81	19.0
1939	.59	17.2
1940	.56	14.6

In sum, over this period of a dozen years low interest rates did *not* eliminate unemployment. On the contrary, unemployment actually *increased* as interest rates went down. In the seven-year period from 1934 through 1940, when the cheap money policy was pushed to an average infra-low rate below 1 per cent (.77 of 1 per cent) an average of more than 17 in every 100 persons in the labor force were unemployed.

Let us skip over the war years when war demands, massive deficits, and massive inflation combined to bring over-employment, and take up the record again for the last ten years:

Year	*Commercial Paper Rate (%)*	*Percentage of Unemployment*
1949	1.49	5.5
1950	1.45	5.0
1951	2.16	3.0

Year	*Commercial Paper Rate (%)*	*Percentage of Unemployment*
1952	2.33	2.7
1953	2.52	2.5
1954	1.58	5.0
1955	2.18	4.0
1956	3.31	3.8
1957	3.81	4.3*
1958 (June)	1.54	6.8*

* (Unemployment percentages before 1957 are based on Department of Commerce "old definitions" of unemployment; for 1957 and 1958 they are based on the "new definitions," which make unemployment slightly higher—4.2 per cent of the labor force in 1956, for example, instead of the 3.8 per cent in the table.)

It will be noticed in this table that though the commercial-paper interest rate in this period averaged 2.24 per cent, or three times as high as that in the seven years from 1934 through 1940, the rate of unemployment was not higher, but much lower, averaging only 4.2 per cent compared with 17.7 per cent in the 1934-40 period.

And within this second period itself the relationship of unemployment to interest rates is almost the exact opposite of that suggested by Keynesian theory. In 1949, 1950, 1954, and June of 1958, when the commercial-paper interest rate averaged about 1.5 per cent, unemployment averaged 5 per cent and over. In 1956 and 1957, when commercial-paper rates were at their highest average level of the period at 3.56 per cent, unemployment averaged only 4 per cent of the working force.

It is very difficult, if not impossible, to prove a positive proposition in economic theory by the use of statistics; but it is not difficult to *disprove* such a proposition (unless it is elaborately qualified) by statistics. We must conclude at least that *neither deficit spending nor cheap money policies are enough by themselves to eliminate even prolonged mass unemployment, let alone to prevent unemployment altogether.*

3. *Race with the Printing Press*

But these are the chief Keynesian remedies for unemployment. In 1936, reviewing the *General Theory,* which had appeared in the same year, Professor Jacob Viner ventured a prediction:

> Keynes's reasoning points obviously to the superiority of inflationary remedies for unemployment over money-wage reductions. In a world organized in accordance with Keynes's specifications there would be a constant race between the printing press and the business agents of the trade unions, with the problem of unemployment largely solved if the printing press could maintain a constant lead and if only volume of employment, irrespective of quality, is considered important.[1]

This characterization has proved, in part, remarkably prophetic. There may be some doubt whether the problem of unemployment has been "largely solved." But we have certainly been *trying* to solve it since 1936 in accordance with Keynes's specifications, and we have certainly embarked upon a race between the printing press and the trade unions.

And our failure to solve the problem of unemployment even by this method is partly the result of a development Professor Viner could hardly have been expected to foresee: the spread of "escalator" clauses in labor contracts which provide not only for automatic increases with every increase in the cost of living, but for so-called "productivity" increases which come into effect whether marginal labor productivity actually increases or not.

The truth is that the only real cure for unemployment is precisely the one that Keynes's whole "general theory" was designed to reject: the adjustment of wage-rates to the marginal labor productivity or "equilibrium" level. This does not mean a uniform *en bloc* adjustment of "the wage level"

[1] *Quarterly Journal of Economics,* LI (1936-1937), 149.

to "the price level." It means the mutual adjustment of specific wage-rates and of prices of the specific products various groups of workers help to produce. It means also the adjustment of various wage-rates to each other and of various prices to each other. It means the *coördination* of the complex wage-price structure. It means the maintenance of a free, fluid, dynamic equilibrium, or a constant tendency toward such an equilibrium, through the economic system.

In sum, neither government spending, nor low interest rates, nor an increase in the money supply is either a necessary or a sufficient condition for the existence of full employment. What is necessary for full employment (using the word in a working, practical sense) is a proper relation among the prices of different kinds of goods and a proper balance between costs and prices, particularly between wages and prices. This functional balance will tend to exist when wage-rates are free and fluid and competitive, and not dictated by arbitrary union coercion. When this balance exists, full employment and maximized production and prosperity will tend to follow. When this balance does not exist, when wage-rates are pushed above the marginal product of labor, and profit margins are doubtful or disappear, there will be unemployment.

The presence or absence of monetary inflation, in brief, is by itself irrelevant to full employment. All that government policy needs to do, besides keeping the currency sound, is to enforce the laws against violence and intimidation, and to repeal the laws which confer exclusive legal privileges and immunities on union leaders, or abridge the freedom of employers and individual workers to bargain. As Professor Sylvester Petro has put it, the legal reforms needed "may all be subsumed under a single heading: Unqualified supremacy of the principle of free employe choice." [2]

[2] "Personal Freedom and Labor Policy," (Institute of Public Affairs at New York University, 1958).

Chapter XXIX

SUMMARY

In the present book we have followed the exposition and argument of the *General Theory* as Keynes presents it. This means that the argument has taken a winding course, often involving repetition. The reader may find it helpful, therefore, if we now briefly summarize some of the main negative or positive propositions in each chapter.

Chapter I. Though Keynes has been praised as the peer of Adam Smith, Ricardo, and even Darwin, not a single important doctrine in his work is both true and original.

II. Keynes's effort to overthrow the "orthodox" contention that the most frequent cause of unemployment is excessive wage-rates is unsuccessful. His arguments characteristically rest on *en bloc* thinking that assumes away the individual differences that make up reality. Prices and wage-rates never change uniformly or as a unit but always relatively and individually. "Aggregative" and "macro-economics" conceal real interrelationships and real causes.

III. Keynes did not succeed in refuting Say's Law of Markets. His attempted refutation consisted merely in ignoring the qualifications that the classical economists themselves insisted on as an integral part of the doctrine.

IV. Keynes's thought is honeycombed with contradictions. His central idea of an equilibrium with unemployment is self-contradictory by the very concept and definition of equilibrium.

V. Keynes's "choice of units" for economic measurement was hopelessly confused. What he calls a "quantity of employment," and puts into algebraic equations as such, turns out, on his own definition, to be not a quantity of employment but a quantity of money received by laborers who are employed.

VI. There is nothing particularly original in Keynes's treatment of the role that "expectations" play in economic life. He does not, in fact, sufficiently recognize that role. He sees that expectations affect current output and employment but seems to forget that they are also embodied in every current price, interest rate, and wage-rate.

VII. The current disparagement of "static" theory is mainly the result of confusion of thought. "Static" theory is necessary not only for the solution of many basic problems but as a preliminary to "dynamic" theory. There is no difference in kind between the methods of "static analysis" and the methods of "dynamic analysis." There is merely a difference in the specific hypotheses made. The appropriateness or utility of any hypothesis depends mainly on the particular problem we are trying to solve.

VIII. Keynes's definitions of his key terms—Income, Saving, and Investment—are merely circular; they are all defined in terms of each other. He so defines Saving and Investment that they are not only necessarily equal, but identical. He repudiates and apologizes for his "confusing" definitions of these same terms as given in his *Treatise on Money,* but absent-mindedly returns to these old definitions in his subsequent discussion, particularly when he tries to prove that investment *increases* employment and that saving *reduces* it.

Keynes treated saving with contempt as far back as *The Economic Consequences of the Peace,* in 1919. His *General Theory* was merely his last rationalization of that contempt.

IX. "Mathematical economics," as Keynes and others use it, can at best give precision to purely hypothetical assumptions. To mistake these hypotheses for known or determinable realities leads to a merely spurious precision and compounds error.

Keynes's alleged consumption "function," his "fundamental psychological law" governing "the propensity to consume," is an unsuccessful attempt to turn a loose truism, known from time immemorial, into a precise and predictable relationship. Even if this relationship existed, it would not have the economic consequences that Keynes attributes to it.

X. Keynes's list of eight motives for saving is arbitrary. It could either be expanded to a much larger number, or reduced to one—to build up a reserve against future needs or contingencies. In addition to this motive for "plain" saving, however, we must set down the motive to *capitalistic* saving (to make roundabout methods of production possible), which is quite overlooked in Keynes's eight.

His argument that a rise in the rate of interest will diminish investment rests on the fallacy of assuming an arbitrary or *uncaused* rise in the rate of interest, rather than a rise that may be itself caused by an increase in the "demand schedule for investment."

XI. Keynes's investment "multiplier" is a myth. There is never any fixed, predictable "multiplier"; there is never any precise, predeterminable, or mechanical relationship between social income, consumption, investment, and extent of employment. An "equilibrium with unemployment" (to repeat) is a contradiction in terms. No investment "multiplier" can be calculated or even discussed except in relation to the extent of maladjustment or discoördination among prices and wage-rates, or to the state of business sentiment.

Keynes's implied definitions of "saving" and "investment" constantly shift. He tacitly assumes that what is not spent on consumption goods is not spent on anything at all. By "investment" he most frequently means government deficit spending financed by inflation.

His "multiplier" easily lends itself to a reductio ad absurdum.

His belief that gold or money is "sterile" is a relic of medieval prejudice.

XII. Keynes uses one of his key phrases, "the marginal efficiency of capital," in so many different senses that it is difficult, if not impossible, to keep track of them. He fails to recognize that interest rates are as much governed by expectations as is "the marginal efficiency of capital." Instead of using this latter term to cover at least six different possible meanings, he should have been careful at all times to distinguish between these meanings. But if he had, he might not have written the *General Theory* at all.

XIII. Keynes's arguments against "liquidity" and against "speculation" are untenable. Speculative anticipations and risks are necessarily involved in all economic activity. Somebody must bear them. What Keynes is saying is that people cannot be trusted to invest the money they have themselves earned, and that this money should be seized from them by government officials and spent or "invested" in the directions in which those officials (seeking to hold on to political power) deem best.

XIV. It is not helpful to explain interest rates as "the reward for parting with liquidity," any more than it would be to explain the price of tomatoes or a house as the "reward" to the buyer for parting with cash for them. Without previous saving, moreover, there can be no "liquidity" to part with. If Keynes's theory of interest were right, interest rates would be highest at the bottom of a depression and lowest at the peak of a boom, which is almost precisely the opposite of their actual tendency.

Keynes is wrong in regarding money as "barren"; it is a productive asset, and productive in the same sense as other assets.

Keynes is also wrong in regarding interest as a "purely monetary" phenomenon. His fallacy consists in assuming that because monetary factors can be shown to affect the rate of interest, "real" factors can safely be ignored or even denied.

Whatever is true in Keynes's theory of interest was already recognized by Knut Wicksell and is fully taken account of in the work of the best contemporary economists.

XV. Though Keynes attacks "the classical theory" of the rate of interest, there is no uniform classical theory of interest. Current theories of interest might be divided into three broad categories: (1) productivity theories, (2) time-preference or time-discount theories, and (3) theories which combine productivity and time-preference.

As a borrower of funds in effect buys or borrows *time,* or the use or enjoyment of goods before he could otherwise use or enjoy them, time-preference or "time-usance" must be recognized as the chief factor in explaining interest and the rate of interest. But "investment opportunity," the prospective "rate of return over cost" (or the expected net value productivity of specific new capital goods), also plays a role, because of its influence on the demand for loans and the rate that borrowers are willing to pay.

Any complete theory of interest must deal not only with "real" but with monetary factors. At any given moment the rate of interest is determined by the point of intersection of the supply curve of savings with the demand curve of investment (or the supply of loanable funds with the demand for loanable funds).

But the chief "long-run" determinant of the interest rate is the community's composite rate of time-discount.

XVI. While Keynes formally defines saving and investment as "necessarily equal in amount" and "merely different aspects of the same thing," his theory repeatedly depends on the tacit assumption that saving and investment are separate and independent.

Under the assumption of a constant money supply, saving and investment are necessarily at all times equal. When investment exceeds *prior* genuine saving, it is because new money and bank credit are being created; when ordinary saving exceeds *subsequent* investment, it is because the money supply is contracting. An excess of saving over (subsequent) investment is but another way of describing deflation, and an excess of investment over (prior) saving is but another way of describing inflation.

Keynes's assumption that it would be "comparatively easy to make capital-goods so abundant that the marginal efficiency of capital is zero" is fantastic, and has absurd implications.

XVII. Keynes's theories of "own rates of interest" are completely untenable. What he is talking about is not interest rates at all, but merely speculative anticipations of price changes.

Keynes's belief that the world is "so poor in accumulated capital-assets" overlooks the fact that at least two out of every three persons in the world today owe their very existence to accumulated capital since the Industrial Revolution.

XVIII. Keynes had confused ideas about economic interrelationships. Particularly absurd was his idea that flexible money wages (adjusting to *prior* changes in prices and demand) would cause violent oscillations in prices, and that we could stabilize the economy by trying to hold up wage-rates regardless of what happened to prices. His remedy would unstabilize the economy, and create or prolong the very mass unemployment he professed to be trying to cure.

XIX. Keynes is unsuccessful in his attempt to deny the most strongly established principle in economics—that if the price of any commodity or service is kept too high (*i.e.*, above the point of equilibrium) some of that commodity or service will remain unused or unsold. When wage-rates are too high there will be unemployment.

Adjusting the myriad wage-rates to their respective equilibrium points may not always be in itself a *sufficient* step to the restoration of full employment, but it is an absolutely *necessary* step. Keynes tried to substitute general monetary inflation for piecemeal wage-and-price adjustment. But without proper wage-price coördination, inflation cannot bring full employment.

XX. There is no reason to suppose that there is a genuine and determinable "functional" relationship between "effective demand" and the volume of employment. There will be full employment with all sorts of changes in "effective demand" if a fluid and dynamic equilibrium exists among prices, wage-rates, etc. There will be unemployment with no matter what "effective demand" if this equilibrium does not exist.

Keynes was unjustified in declaring that previous economists had failed to reconcile "value" theory and monetary theory.

XXI. Inflation is at once an *uncertain* remedy for unemployment, an *unnecessary* remedy for unemployment, and a *dangerous* remedy for unemployment.

"Elasticity" of demand is not measurable. The mathematical method is misapplied to it.

To try to cure unemployment by inflation rather than by

adjustment of specific wage-rates is like trying to adjust the piano to the stool rather than the stool to the piano.

The rate of interest is a market price like any other market price, and determined as much by the demands of borrowers as by the offers of lenders.

XXII. The explanation of an economic crisis as a "sudden collapse of the marginal efficiency of capital" is either a useless truism or an obvious error, according to the interpretation we give the phrase "the marginal efficiency of capital." If this means simply a collapse of *confidence,* the explanation is a truism. If it means a collapse in *physical productivity,* it is nonsense. If it means a collapse in *value productivity,* it reverses cause and effect.

The Keynesian cure for crises is perpetual low interest rates. The attempt to attain these would lead to a policy of perpetual inflation.

The Jevonian theory that business conditions vary directly with the size of crops is untenable, and particularly implausible in the form maintained by Keynes.

XXIII. Keynes's "system," as he came to recognize at the end of the *General Theory,* was actually a reversion to the naive and discredited theories of the mercantilists and underconsumption theorists, from Mandeville and Malthus to Hobson. It was also a reversion to all the inflationist theories of the currency cranks, from John Law to Silvio Gesell.

XXIV. Keynes's proposals for "the euthanasia of the rentier, of the functionless investor," were proposals to rob the productive and expropriate their savings.

Keynes's plan for "the socialization of investment" would inevitably entail socialism and state planning. Seriously carried out, it would remove any significant field for the exercise of private initiative and responsibility. Keynes, in brief, recommended *de facto* socialism under the guise of "reforming" and "preserving" capitalism.

"Domestic *laissez faire* and an international gold standard," blamed by Keynes as among the "economic causes of war," were, in fact, powerful forces for peace and international coöperation. It is the national planning policies recommended by Keynes that would tend to provoke wars.

XXV. Because Keynes was continually contradicting himself, we may not be justified in calling his 1946 article in *The Economic Journal* a "recantation" of the *General Theory*. But his praise of "the classical medicine," plus his reference to "much modernist stuff, gone wrong and turned sour and silly," may have indicated that he was on the verge of recantation.

XXVI. If we try to use the term with "scientific" or objective precision, "full employment" is not even definable. "Full employment at whatever cost" is not even desirable. It is best either to use the term in a loose common-sense way to mean the absence of abnormal involuntary unemployment, or to replace it by the term *optimum* employment. It is not an end in itself, but a means to, or an accompaniment of, much broader ends, including mainly the maximization of consumer satisfactions. The economic objective of mankind, after all, is not more work but less.

XXVII. Efforts to determine the national income in monetary terms have merely a limited usefulness for special purposes. Actually, all estimates of national income rest on certain arbitrary (and sometimes false) assumptions. They are not purely objective or strictly determinate. The present fetish made of such estimates leads not only to confusion of economic cause and effect, but to inflationist and totalitarian policies.

Economic forecasting based on "aggregative economics" or "the national income approach" has been almost uniformly bad.

XXVIII. It is not true that deficits in the government budget cure unemployment. It is not true that low interest rates cure unemployment. The Keynesian prescription leads to a constant race between the money supply and the demands of the trade unions—but it does not lead to long-run full employment.

A NOTE ON BOOKS

There must be hundreds of economic books that may be variously described as Keynesian, pro-Keynesian, quasi-Keynesian, semi-Keynesian, or "post-Keynesian," and there must be thousands of such pamphlets and articles; but there is a great dearth when we come to any literature since 1936 that may be described as definitely anti-Keynesian—in the sense that it is explicitly and consistently critical of the major Keynesian doctrines. In the works of such writers as Ludwig von Mises, F. A. Hayek, Wilhelm Röpke, Frank H. Knight, Jacques Rueff, and others, we do indeed have an impressive *non*-Keynesian literature, based on "neo-classical" premises, with occasional explicit criticism of Keynesian tenets. But full-length books exclusively devoted to a critical analysis of Keynesism may be counted on the fingers of one hand.

First among these I should like to mention L. Albert Hahn's *The Economics of Illusion,* a collection of essays, originally published separately, on various Keynesian themes. The same author's *Common Sense Economics* is mainly devoted to developing a unified constructive doctrine, but involves explicit as well as implied criticism of Keynesian doctrine. A small volume by V. Orval Watts, *Away from Freedom,* especially emphasizes the moral and political weaknesses of Keynesism. And not even the shortest "anti-Keynesian" bibliography should omit Arthur W. Marget's monumental study, *The Theory of Prices* (two volumes, 1,426 pages). This work is distinguished both for its penetrating comment and for the immense range of its scholarship, but its relentless prolixity and disheartening length have caused it to miss the influence it might otherwise have had.

Not until I had finished the present book did I have the good fortune, through his generosity, to spend an hour over the manuscript of a work in preparation by W. H. Hutt, now dean of the faculty of commerce at the University of Capetown, South Africa. This will be both a thorough and a thoroughly admirable work, which I am convinced will make a deep impression when it appears. Meanwhile I feel encouraged and corroborated in my own analysis by the numerous points of similarity to the analysis by Professor Hutt made from so distant a geographical perspective.

David McCord Wright, Dow professor of economics and political science at McGill University, Montreal, is now also engaged, I am informed, on a book on *The Keynesian System.* Judging from his article, "Mr. Keynes and the 'Day of Judgment,' " which appeared in *Science* of Nov. 21, 1958, this book will throw much added light on the problems with which it deals.

Individual volumes have appeared devoted to criticism of single aspects of Keynesian doctrine. Among these W. H. Hutt's *The Theory of Idle Resources,* and George Terborgh's *The Bogey of Economic Maturity,* are outstanding. Milton Friedman has devoted a critical and careful study to *The Theory of the Consumption Function,* and Ernst W. Swanson and Emerson P. Schmidt, in *Economic Stagnation or Progress,* have written a critique of doctrines on the mature economy, oversavings, and deficit spending.

But much of the best critical analysis of Keynesian doctrines has appeared merely in individual chapters in a few pages of works by such writers as Benjamin M. Anderson, Arthur F. Burns, Philip Cortney, Gottfried Haberler, F. A. Hayek, Frank H. Knight, Ludwig von Mises, Melchior Palyi, Charles Rist, Wilhelm Röpke, and others, and in widely scattered articles, mainly in learned journals, by Harry Gunnison Brown, W. H. Hutt, Frank H. Knight, L. M. Lachmann, Joseph Stagg Lawrence, Etienne Mantoux (only in French), Franco Modigliani, Edwin G. Nourse, Melchior Palyi, Jacques Rueff, Jacob Viner, R. Gordon

Wasson, John H. Williams, David McCord Wright, and others. These articles would have a far greater impact on current thought than they have had if they could be collected and made readily available between the covers of a single book.

I have not mentioned any pro-Keynesian literature because it is so vast and so easily available. But Seymour Harris appends a bibliographic note to his laudatory book on *John Maynard Keynes: Economist and Policy Maker* in which he lists seventeen volumes, mainly sympathetic, of which I should especially like to mention Dudley Dillard's *The Economics of John Maynard Keynes* and Alvin H. Hansen's *A Guide to Keynes* because they are so much better organized and so much more lucid than the *General Theory* itself.

APPENDIX A

THE 1919 PROPHECIES [1]

A few months ago The London Economist remarked that "Many people will be turning to read or reread Lord Keynes's 'The Economic Consequences of the Peace.' They will find the task rewarding, not so much for the brilliant analysis of the 'economic consequences' as for the inspired account of the 'peace' itself and the process of its making. There are passages in it which, in the setting of today, have an almost frightening urgency."

The passages to which The Economist referred include the picture of Europe at the end of World War I, almost completely lost from sight in piecemeal settlement and in "empty and arid intrigue." Here was "a matter of life and death, of starvation and existence, and of the fearful convulsions of a dying civilization"; here was Europe forgotten, yet, "deeply and inextricably intertwined [victors and defeated alike] by hidden psychic and economic bonds." The Economist referred also to the picture of the World War I peacemakers themselves: the portrayal of "the complex struggle of human will and purpose * * * concentrated in the persons of four individuals in a manner never paralleled"; the portrait of the righteous President Wilson, refusing to discuss the final decisions lest he should thereby be shaken in his faith that "in the sweat of solitary contemplation and with prayers to God he had done *nothing* that was not just and right."

"It was the task of the Peace Conference," wrote Keynes, "to honor engagements and to satisfy justice; but not less to re-establish life and to heal wounds." And neither part of the task, he concluded, had been performed.

When we turn back to *The Economic Consequences of the Peace,* and look at it again in the light of twenty-five years' ex-

[1] This was first published in *The New York Times* Sunday Magazine of March 11, 1945.

perience and perspective—with the added illumination brought by the striking parallel in some respects between conditions at the time it was written and conditions today—we still find it undeniably a brilliant piece of writing. The most fascinating section is still Chapter III, in which the personalities of the "Big Three" of that time—Clemenceau, Lloyd George, and Wilson—are described in unforgettable terms:

Clemenceau, with his weary cynicism, sitting with closed eyes and an impassive face of parchment, his gray-gloved hands clasped in front of him, awaking to sudden outbursts only when the interests of France were directly concerned; Lloyd George, with his "unerring, almost medium-like, sensibility to every one immediately around him * * * with six or seven senses not available to ordinary men, judging character, motive, and subconscious impulse, perceiving what each was thinking and even what each was going to say next, and compounding with telepathic instinct the argument or appeal best suited to the vanity, weakness, or self-interest of his immediate auditor"; and finally "the poor President" Wilson himself, "playing blind man's buff in that party," a "blind and deaf Don Quixote," like "a Nonconformist minister, perhaps a Presbyterian," rigid, with a temperament theological rather than intellectual, appallingly incompetent in the agilities of the council chamber, and Lloyd George, "desiring at the last moment all the moderation he dared," finding to his horror that "it was harder to de-bamboozle this old Presbyterian than it had been to bamboozle him."

These portraits are as vivid as those of Lytton Strachey. (It is interesting to recall that Strachey dedicated one of his early volumes to Keynes.) But, like Strachey's, there is also a little trace of the smart-aleck in them. This trace is even more pronounced in a well-known passage in the book in which Keynes contemptuously compares modern railroads to the pyramids of Egypt, and ridicules the capitalistic cake which must always grow and never be enjoyed—a passage calculated to delight gourmets of paradox, but easily demolished by serious argument.

This brings us to the economic sections of the book. For a quarter of a century now, Lord Keynes, on the basis of this work, has ranked in some circles as a major prophet. On the surface, indeed, his prophecies seemed to be uncannily accurate.

At a time when Allied statesmen were talking of reparations claims that would have reached something in the neighborhood of $40 billion, he contended that "a safe maximum figure of Germany's capacity to pay" was $10 billion. The most that Germany could pay annually, he thought, was $500 million. He also urged the total cancellation of inter-Allied war debts, and added: "I do not believe that any of these tributes will continue to be paid, at the best, for more than a very few years."

What actually happened was that after endless conferences, the reparations claims were steadily scaled down until under the Young plan in 1929 they reached almost exactly the $500 million annually that Keynes had seen in 1919 as the maximum collectible. In the end even these were not paid, nor were the inter-Allied loans either: the whole process was brought to an abrupt end by President Hoover's moratorium in 1931 and never revived. Could a prophet ever have had clearer vindication?

But a few questions obtrude themselves. Does the fact that Germany did not pay on net balance practically any reparations at all, prove that she could not have paid them? (The German reparations were unintentionally paid, in fact, chiefly by trusting American investors.) And were the reasons why German reparations and inter-Allied war debts bogged down the same as the reasons why Mr. Keynes thought they would? The evidence does not show it.

Let us look at the size of the reparations ultimately asked for under the Young plan. At an annual level of around $500 million (or 2 billion gold marks) they were less than 4 per cent of the total German national income, and less than a fifth even of the pre-Hitler (and post-inflation) annual governmental expenditures. It would be absurd to call such a burden crushing.

Where did Keynes's arguments go astray? He was right in seeing that all reparations would have to be paid—ultimately—not in cash but in goods and services—that is to say, in a German export excess. He was right in contending that a world that insisted on reparations would have to open its doors to imports from Germany. But he was wrong in arguing that Germany's ability to produce this export excess was to be measured by her pre-war trade balance. He was wrong in his effort to give an itemized demonstration of Germany's inability to reach a high export surplus. He was wrong in assuming that the effects of this export surplus would be just like those of any other export surplus. For his whole discussion overlooks the obvious fact that Germany, in sending this export surplus, would also be sending to the Allied countries *the purchasing power with which to buy it.* The transfer of goods, in the absence of barriers to imports on the part of the Allied Governments, would have followed as a natural consequence of the transfer of cash to pay for them.

Finally, he too often forgot that the war damage had actually been done: insofar as Germany failed to pay for reparations, her victims would have to do so. The blunt fact is that when the Allies permitted the reparations payments to stop, they enabled Germany to use the money thus saved for an immense armament program to launch against them the most destructive war in history.

But it was partly because the world suffered from importphobia, and was influenced by Keynes's neo-mercantilist arguments, that it was willing to grant that Germany could not pay the reparations. This gave Germany the excuse for default. The influence of Keynes's own arguments, in short, was partly responsible for the success of his predictions. That influence remains to this day, so that the Yalta announcement, for example, talks only of reparations "in kind." Actually, if there is a willingness on the part of the victors to receive goods there is no essential economic difference between reparations in "kind" or in "cash," except that the latter are more flexible. In each case there must be a transfer both of actual goods and of the cash values that they represent.

Keynes's own proposals for reparations settlement are not entirely free from disingenuousness. He proposed, for example, a total indemnity for Germany of $10 billion. He then suggested that Germany be given a credit against this of $2.5 billion for the surrender of merchant ships, cables, war materials, and other items. The balance of $7.5 billion, he adds, "should not carry interest pending its repayment, and should be paid by Germany in thirty annual installments of $250 million, beginning in 1923." This is not only half the annual sum that Keynes had conceded earlier in his book that Germany might pay, but it is not $7.5 billion. The present value of thirty annual installments of $250 million beginning three years hence (*The Economic Consequences* appeared late in 1919), on an assumed interest rate of 5 per cent, is less than $3.5 billion. In other words, on the usual interest rate assumptions, Mr. Keynes was actually suggesting a capital payment from Germany of approximately half of $7.5 billion.

A fresh reading of Lord Keynes's old book reminds us of one thing more. It is oversimplification, if not naive melodrama, to assume that America failed to enter the League of Nations, and turned isolationist after 1920, because a few wicked old reactionaries, like Senator Lodge and President Harding, prevented us. On the contrary, the drive against the Treaty of Versailles, which embodied the League of Nations, was led by the then left-wing liberals under the leadership of Keynes and his *Economic Consequences of the Peace.* "This is a very great book," exclaimed Harold Laski in his review in The Nation. "If any answer can be made to the overwhelming indictment of the treaty that it contains, that answer has yet to be published." The New Republic took up the cry. Its reviewer found the book like "a fresh breeze coming into a plain where poisonous gases are yet hanging." The League was rejected as the mere instrument of a vicious treaty.

The lesson is twofold. The liberals of today would do well to be something less than perfectionists in their demands. But the framers of the new treaties, in their turn, should try to establish a peace that recognizes the economic interdependence of Europe and of the world; a peace that, while it meets the demands of justice and prevents another aggression, will be of such a nature that humane and liberal public opinion in the democracies, when the passions of war have cooled, will still be willing to support it.

APPENDIX B[1]

AMERICAN ICE CO.

Year	January-February High	Low	Avg.	July-August High	Low	Avg.	July-Aug. Avg. Related to Jan.-Feb. Avg. (per cent)
	(dollars)			(dollars)			
1932	17½	12	14¾	11¼	7⅝	9⅜	63.6
1933	6½	3¾	5⅛	17	8½	12¾	226.7
1934	10	6⅛	8	6⅜	3½	4⅞	60.9
1935	4⅞	3½	4⅛	3⅝	2⅜	3	72.7
1936	5⅝	3	4¼	3¾	2½	3⅛	73.5
1937	4¼	2½	3⅜	3⅝	2⅞	3¼	96.3
1938	2⅛	1⅝	1⅞	2¼	1¾	2	106.7
1939	1⅞	1⅜	1⅝	3⅛	2	2½	153.8
1940	3¼	2⅜	2¾	2¼	1⅝	1⅞	68.2
1941	1¾	1½	1⅝	1⅞	1½	1⅝	100.0
1942	1½	1⅛	1¼	2	1⅝	1¾	140.0
1943	3½	2	2¾	4⅞	3⅝	4¼	154.5
1944	6⅛	4	5	7⅞	6¼	7	140.0
1945	10⅛	6⅜	8⅛	9¾	7⅝	8⅝	106.2
1946	17⅜	11⅞	14⅝	15⅞	12	13⅞	94.9
1947	10¼	8½	9⅜	8	7	7½	80.0
1948	7½	6⅛	6¾	7¾	6⅝	7⅛	105.6
1949	6	5¼	5⅝	9¾	7⅞	8¾	155.6
1950	8¼	7⅝	7⅞	8½	7⅛	7¾	98.4
1951	8¼	6¾	7½	8	7	7½	100.0
1952	7	6	6½	8	6⅝	7¼	111.5
1953	7⅜	6⅞	7⅛	8⅜	7½	7⅞	110.5
1954	9⅛	8⅞	9	12	10	11	122.2
1955	12⅛	11	11½	12⅞	11½	12⅛	105.4
1956	11¾	11⅛	11⅜	13	11⅞	12⅜	108.8

[1] See discussion pp. 175-176, Chap. XIII.

CITY PRODUCTS COMPANY
(FORMERLY CITY ICE & FUEL CO.)

	January-February			*July-August*			*July-Aug. Avg. Related to Jan.-Feb. Avg.*
	High	*Low*	*Avg.*	*High*	*Low*	*Avg.*	
	(dollars)			*(dollars)*			*(per cent)*
1932	28 1/2	25 7/8	27 1/8	15 3/4	11 1/8	13 3/8	49.3
1933	12 1/2	10 1/8	11 1/4	25	15	20	177.8
1934	24 3/8	17 1/4	20 3/4	20 3/4	18	19 3/8	93.4
1935	21 1/2	20	20 3/4	21 1/2	16	18 3/4	90.4
1936	19 7/8	15 1/4	17 1/2	18 1/4	16 7/8	17 1/2	100.0
1937	21 3/8	18 3/4	20	18 3/8	17 5/8	18	90.0
1938	13 1/2	11 1/8	12 1/4	11 3/4	8 1/4	10	81.6
1939	10 7/8	9 5/8	10 1/4	14 1/4	11 1/4	12 3/4	124.4
1940	14 1/4	12 3/8	13 1/4	10 3/8	9 1/2	9 7/8	74.5
1941	10 3/4	9 1/4	10	10 3/4	10 1/8	10 3/8	103.8
1942	10 1/4	9	9 5/8	10 3/4	9 7/8	10 1/4	106.5
1943	13 1/4	10 1/4	11 3/4	15 3/4	14 1/4	15	127.7
1944	16 3/8	14 3/4	15 1/2	25 1/8	20 1/8	22 5/8	146.0
1945	23 1/4	20 5/8	21 7/8	23	21 1/8	22	101.0
1946	35 1/4	28 1/2	31 7/8	37 1/2	31 1/4	34 3/8	107.8
1947	32 1/2	30 1/8	31 1/4	32 3/4	30	31 3/8	100.0
1948	32	29 3/8	30 5/8	31 1/8	29 3/4	30 3/8	99.2
1949	29 1/2	25	27 1/4	29	26	27 1/2	101.0
1950	33 3/4	31 1/2	32 5/8	31 1/2	28 7/8	30 1/8	92.3
1951	32 1/4	29 1/2	30 7/8	30 3/8	27 1/2	28 7/8	93.5
1952	30 3/8	28 7/8	29 5/8	33 3/8	31 1/8	32 1/4	108.9
1953	33 1/8	30 1/2	31 5/8	32	31 1/8	31 1/2	99.6
1954	33 1/2	27 1/4	30 3/8	35 3/8	33 3/4	34 1/2	113.6
1955	40 1/2	35 7/8	38 1/8	32 1/2	31 1/8	31 3/4	81.7
1956	31 3/8	30	30 5/8	42 7/8	38 5/8	40 3/4	133.1

APPENDIX C[1]

COMPARISONS OF MARKET PRICES OF
SOUTHERN RAILWAY CO. DEFERRED ORDINARY SHARES

Year	*Day in February*	*Price*	*Day in August*	*Price*
1923	28	36½-37½	7	36 -37
1924	29	42½-43½	5	41 -43
1925	27	43 -44	4	39½-40½
1926	26	44½-45½	3	43 -44
1927	28	42½-43½	2	37½-38½
1928	29	33½-34½	7	32½-33½
1929	28	31½-32½	6	27 -28
1930	28	30½-31½	5	25 -26
1931	27	18½-19½	4	10 -11
1932	29	8½- 9½	2	6 - 7
1933	28	10 -11	8	19½-20½
1934	28	25½-26½	7	21½-22½
1935	28	19½-20½	6	21 -22
1936	28	21½-22½	4	22 -23
1937	26	23½-24½	3	22¼-23¼
1938	28	19½-20½	2	14 -15
1939	28	13½-14½	8	12½-13½
1940	29	19¼-20¼	6	9½-10½
1941	28	10 -11	5	12½-13½
1942	27	14½-15½	4	16 -17
1943	26	21½-22½	3	23½-24½
1944	29	22¾-23¾	8	25¼-26¼
1945	28	25 -26	7	21 -22
1946	28	21½-22½	6	19½-20½
1947	28	21¾-22¾	5	21¼-22¼

1 See discussion on pp. 176-177, Chap. XIII.

APPENDIX D

INTEREST RATES AND BUSINESS CYCLES

It was the contention of John Maynard Keynes, still accepted by many academic economists, that interest rates are a purely monetary phenomenon. In his own words: "The rate of interest is the *reward for parting with liquidity* for a specified period . . . a measure of the unwillingness of those who possess money to part with their liquid control over it."

This theory not only ignores or contradicts most of what has been written by economists for the last two centuries, but is clearly contrary to the facts it presumes to explain. If Keynes's theory were right, short-term interest rates would be highest precisely at the bottom of a depression, to overcome the individual's reluctance to part with cash then. But it is in a depression that short-term interest rates tend to be *lowest.* If the "liquidity-preference" theory were right, short-term interest rates would be lowest at the peak of a boom, because confidence would be highest then, and everybody would be wishing to invest in projects and "things" rather than in money. But it is at the peak of a boom that short-term interest rates tend to be *highest.*

It is not easy to "prove" this relationship statistically, partly because so many influences govern interest rates, and partly because there is no "pure" index of "depression" and "prosperity." But Geoffrey H. Moore, associate director of research of the National Bureau of Economic Research, who has done much work along this line, has at my request kindly furnished the data, and H. Irving Forman of the same organization has prepared the accompanying chart,* comparing the Federal Reserve index of industrial production with bank rates on short-

* I hasten to add that neither is responsible for the conclusions I have drawn from it. The chart accompanied an article of mine in *Newsweek* of Oct. 13, 1958.

term business loans in the ten-year period running from 1948 through part of 1958.

The industrial production scale on the left and the interest-rate scale on the right are ratio scales, in order to bring out more clearly the *proportional* changes in the two indexes. The dots indicate comparative high and low points.

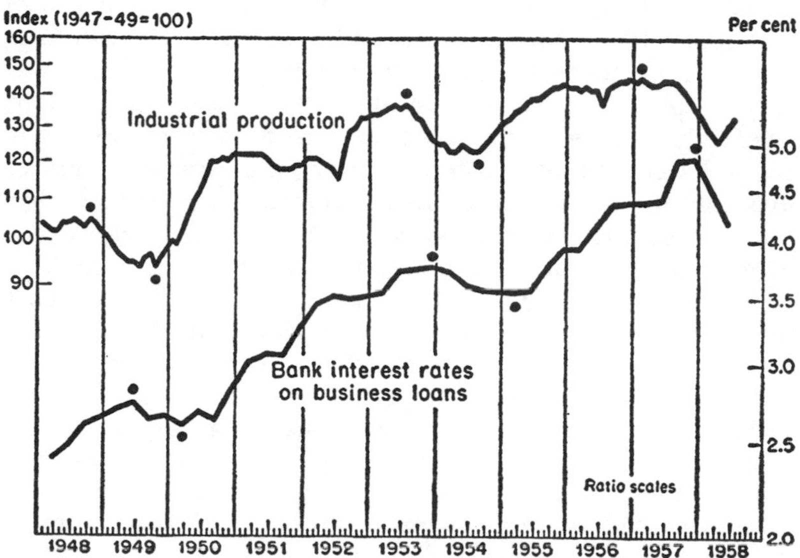

The results show that the two indexes tend to go up or down together. Or, more strictly speaking, the industrial production index leads, and the interest-rate index lags. This is what we might expect. When production has been low, demand for loans is low and interest rates are low. As production increases, the demand for loans to expand production increases, and if the money and credit supply is not too "elastic," interest rates tend to rise, but with a time lag.

There is also, no doubt, a reciprocal and inverse influence of interest rates on production. Low interest rates (other things being equal) tend to encourage borrowing for subsequent production, and high interest rates to discourage borrowing for subsequent production.

The chart gives only short-term interest rates. For completeness long-term interest rates should be considered also. But the historical record does not lead to any substantial modification of the conclusions just reached. Those interested will find the relevant charts both in the monthly *Federal Reserve Chart Book* and in the *Historical Supplement* to it (both published by the Board of Governors of the Federal Reserve System). There they will find (e.g., on p. 21 of the monthly issue of October, 1958 and on p. 37 of the *Historical Supplement* of September, 1958) that short-term and long-term rates tend to go up and down together. From the monthly chart which covers only the period from the beginning of 1950 to the end of 1958 one might get the impression that short-term rates are almost always lower than long-term rates. From the historical comparisons running from 1865 to 1958, however, one may see that, until about 1929, short-term rates oscillated both above and below long-term rates and were as often higher as lower.

This is what theory would lead us to expect. The long-term interest rate for a given period is, at any moment, the composite speculative anticipation of what the average of future short-term rates will be over that period (corrected, in periods of deflation or inflation, for anticipations regarding the future real purchasing power of the currency unit). These speculative anticipations will of course often prove wrong. But long-term rates will tend to vary less erratically, and through a much narrower range, than short-term rates.

INDEX